MW01015548

A STUDY GUIDE TO HAUNTINGS

PARANORMAL

BY
THOMAS COONEY

Bloomington, IN

Milton Keynes, UK

AuthorHouse™
1663 Liberty Drive, Suite 200
Bloomington, IN 47403
www.authorhouse.com
Phone: 1-800-839-8640

AuthorHouse™ UK Ltd.
500 Avebury Boulevard
Central Milton Keynes, MK9 2BE
www.authorhouse.co.uk
Phone: 08001974150

First published by AuthorHouse 5/10/2006

ISBN: 1-4259-3019-0 (e)
ISBN: 1-4259-3018-2 (sc)

Library of Congress Control Number: 2006904358

Printed in the United States of America
Bloomington, Indiana

This book is printed on acid-free paper.

To my loving wife Patricia whose constant support and occasional kick in the butt made this dream possible. Also, my thanks go to Alan Knofla for his patience and time in editing most of this book.

TABLE OF CONTENTS

SECTION 1: General Information

SECTION 2: Basics Of An Investigation

SECTION 3: Anatomy Of An Investigation

SECTION 1:

General Information

PREFACE

As a child, far too many years ago, I lived in what can only be described as a haunted house. Many unusual, bizarre and frightening things took place in that house to the point where the supernatural seemed natural. Needless to say, many of the things that happened there still have a profound affect on me to this day. Some of those effects are bad, such as nightmares that seem to recur anytime I am under periods of heavy stress. Some of the effects are good, such as having the ability to help others facing hauntings of their own. Since leaving that building, I have had a tremendous desire to learn everything I possibly can on the subject of ghosts, demons, and the like. I felt I had to find a way to understand and even make sense of what happened to my family and me. That quest will last a lifetime, I am sure. Towards that end, I have traveled many a road. I have poured over every book I could find on the subject and there have been tons of them. Some of them made a great deal of sense; others dismissed the supernatural as being little more than fantasy or the product of overactive imaginations. I also combed through countless magazines looking for articles that dealt with hauntings. There were and are, precious few to be found. That needs to be corrected.

I also found myself constantly checking television listings for shows such as "Sightings" or the now defunct "The Other Side." If there was a paranormal segment on the talk show circuit, I caught it. I took classes on the subject, be it demonology or parapsychology, when I could find them and I attended lectures and conferences, as long as they were in places that were in the same time zone as mine and did not require a home equity loan to pay for them. Some were good, some were informative and some were out and out silly. For the record, all were fun. Is there a point to this? Yes, there is, trust me. What I began to realize is that there is a need for a book that deals with haunting phenomenon in all of its various forms and how to investigate it when you come across it. Yes, there are a few out there, written by many renown authors such as J.B. Rhine, William Roll, Hans Holzer, Colin Wilson, Tony Cornell and Loyd Auerbach just to mention a few. Everyone knows about the Warrens, Ed and Lorraine. The problem is that in most cases, these books would discuss particular cases or just one type of phenomena, such as poltergeists. Other books touch on ghosts but are slanted more towards the world of *parapsychology;* that being the scientific study of a field that cannot be studied scientifically. That would include ESP, out of body experiences and the like. I found none that explained what happens in a haunting, why it happened and most importantly, how to deal with it and make it stop. The point is that there is a need for a book that covers all areas of haunting phenomena, or so I hope.

That is what I am trying to do here. You will learn all about investigating haunting phenomena. You will learn how to set up investigations and how to determine just what you are dealing with, if anything is there. If there *is* a spirit, or entity involved, I will show you how you can tell what type of spirit is causing the problem and how best to stop it from doing any more damage, either physical or mental. I will discuss which spirits are friendly and which ones are not. There are some to be feared and there are some to be enjoyed.

Many of you have a desire to do case work; that is help people who are being haunted. Others are interested in studying ghostly phenomena for fun. Those are the "ghost hunters." It certainly is a fun area of interest. There is a lot here for you. I never had to hunt ghosts myself; they seemed to hunt me. Whether you are reading this as someone who wants to be a paranormal investigator or you are a person under siege from unseen forces, I will teach you coping skills that are designed to make it easier to deal with whatever forces you are up against. The first step is to realize that hauntings *do* happen and that they are a part of life. They are rare but they happen more than most people imagine. Once we realize that, we are on our way towards a greater understand of what these entities are and how they work. You will learn that there is a strategy involved in a haunting and you will learn how you must foil the spirit's strategy while creating a defensive one for yourself. Most of all, I think you will finish this book with a greater understanding of our present physical plane and more importantly, how our souls survive physical death and move on.

I think you will find this book is easy to read. While I will be using many technical terms, I will try to explain them in such a way that they will be understandable. Where applicable, I will use examples from my own experiences of living in a haunted house and in the many, many cases I have worked over the years. Some of those examples are embarrassing but what the hell. Perhaps that is a poor choice of words. We will talk about the bad spirits and the abominations but we will also look at the good ones. Fortunately, the good way outnumber the bad. This book will explain how and why some people become haunted and who are the most vulnerable. It will also show the best ways to avoid bringing something unwanted into your life. Yes, we sometimes cause our own hauntings, albeit unintentionally. We will explore some of the mysteries of life. Most will remain mysteries. I will discuss that which is terribly confusing and I will probably add to that confusion. If I sound like I know it all, believe me, I do not. For that matter, neither does anyone else, despite what they say on TV shows or in their books. Sadly, some do not even have a clue. What they do have are good marketing skills and excellent website designers.

There are some frightening things in this book to be sure. Things happen that defy the laws of physics and things happen that are patently unnatural. Unfortunately, some people are singled out for the terror. People are sometimes victimized for reasons that escape logic and reason. It is not fair but that is the way it is. However, there are some very positive things to be found in here as well. Lastly, you will find some humor every now and then, usually in spite of me. While investigating the paranormal is a serious profession, there is a danger in taking yourself too seriously. And oh how some do! Pomposity reigns! Arrogance abounds! Save me, please. Sorry, sometimes I get carried away, or should be. In truth, this can also be a very humbling profession, as I well know but it is also a rewarding one. I am fortunate to know that too. The good usually outweighs the bad.

At the end of this text, you will have a greater understanding of the world of the paranormal. It is not as complicated as it seems. There are, believe it or not, some "laws" for the lack of a better term that governs the spirit world. In some ways, it is less complicated than the physical world. There appears to be less gray area on the other side. However, that creates more gray area for *our* side of the plane. More importantly, you will have a greater respect for the people who suffer from the siege of a haunting and those who do their best to end that suffering.

INTRODUCTION

Psychic phenomena, ghosts, haunting, demons ... these are words that crop up from time to time. You often find television programs dealing with the subject. They are sometimes discussed in a serious vane, sometimes in a joking manner. Most offer entertainment if not answers. Those who believe in their existence are often ridiculed for their belief. They are told such things as: "You don't really believe in that stuff, do you?" or "you should grow up" or "get grounded" or a host of other things, some of them clean. Of course, they have never walked in my shoes or the shoes of countless others who *know* what the paranormal is because they live their lives surrounded by it.

The media often treats paranormal reports in a flippant way when they report it at all. They will sometimes run an article on some unusual happening but they rarely follow up on it. Perhaps that is due to lack of interest. Of course, it could be due to lack of knowledge too. Television shows and movies about the paranormal usually are about blood, gore and precious little else. There are very few movies about real hauntings and they are sometimes sensationalized to the point of borderline fiction. How much fiction constitutes fiction is a question that haunts those seeking the truth and those who try to teach it.

The purpose of this book is not to try to convince you of the existence of spirits or other forms of beings. If you are reading this, it is reasonable to assume that you already do believe in spirits to some degree or you at least have an open mind on the subject. That is all anyone has the right to ask for. My purpose here is to try to help you understand how to go about determining whether there is something natural or paranormal going on. If the problem is paranormal, this guide can help you determine what these entities are and how best to study them safely. There are indeed forces out there that defy logic but not explanation. More importantly, you will learn how to help those who are being bothered by them, should you choose to go that far. You might be surprised at how many do. Even if you only want to investigate for fun, you will learn much in this text.

There is a great deal of debate about the existence of ghosts and hauntings. You will find two schools of thought on the subject. On one hand, you have your scientists who pretty much doubt the existence of these entities altogether. On the other hand, you have psychic investigators, demonologists and even some parapsychologists who study the phenomena and are quite convinced that spirits *do* exist and even offer some proof to support it. The problem is that all the proof in the world will not convince the scientists unless they can duplicate the phenomena in a controlled laboratory setting. Ghosts just do not do this.

There are many devices that you can use to help prove the existence of spirits. There are cameras, (video and stills, standard film, infrared and digital) electromagnetic field testers, thermometers, Geiger counters, computers, tri-field meters and on and on. You can spend a small fortune on this equipment and I have. Still, none of the data or evidence obtained from these devices can be duplicated in a controlled, laboratory setting. Even if they could, you will see that there are at least two theories for each type of phenomenon that the equipment picks up. You will soon learn about these "toys" and their value to an investigation. They can be very helpful although one would do well to avoid becoming too dependent on them. There are those who will look at a meter and swear there is nothing present while a spirit is in the process of pulling their socks down or doing something more mischievous or in some cases, heinous. Looking at their meter, they will say something like: I'm getting no readings so there can't be anything here," all the while screaming because some unseen (and obviously unrecorded) force is tearing their hair out.

If you work in this field, the bottom line is you can expect to be criticized and in some instances, ridiculed. To make matters even worse, many parapsychologists themselves do not believe in ghosts as actual entities. Rather, they try to prove other causes for ghostly sightings. That is fine. Skepticism is a good thing. Many times they are right;

there are natural, scientific causes for certain types of phenomena and you need to know that. But, and it is a big but, there are times when things happen that cannot be explained by even the most skeptical of parapsychologists. Fortunately, the vast majority of them are sincere, open-minded individuals who seek the answers to the many mysteries of the paranormal world. I will try to show how both disciplines, the parapsychologists and demonologists, are far more related than they realize. You will see that there is a lot of gray area to deal with. Very often "poltergeist activity" is very similar to a phenomenon known as "Recurrent Spontaneous Psychokineses," or RSPK, as it is usually referred to. I will attempt to distinguish the difference between the two. I will try to do that in all areas where there are multiple possibilities. (Which is just about everything.)

Most importantly, I will help you learn how to set up an investigation from start to finish and how to determine what you are dealing with (whether natural, preternatural or supernatural.) They are all similar yet different and sometimes quite ambiguous to boot. For those who choose to work with victims, you will get an eyeful about what it is like and that can help you decide whether you truly want to go that route. No one would blame you if you did not. Those who would call you a coward have never stepped into a haunting involving negative forces. Should you choose to go that route, you will find that your major objective should be to learn how to help those people who really need it. That becomes goal number one. There is so much that can be done to ease their suffering and much of that is easy to do. There is a lot to learn but it will be an exciting and occasionally frightening journey, especially when we reach the area of evil spirits and demons, the "supernatural" area.

So buckle your seatbelts and let us take a ride into the world of the paranormal. It is a world we will enter carefully. We will look at the light and the dark and the frightening and the funny and at all points in between. It will be quite a ride, I assure you. Some of it you will believe; at other areas you will consider the possibility that I need to be committed to the nearest psychiatric ward. You may be right. However, all of it is true. I hope you enjoy the journey.

IN THE BEGINNING

(Experiencing The Paranormal)

The squeaking sound had been going on for some time. I heard it almost every night for months ... "squeak, squeak, squeak." All night long, night after night, the squeaking continued. I had mentioned it to my mother on a few occasions but she told me it was just my sister's bed making the ominous noise. I believed her. After all, I had no reason not to. Some things bothered me though. To me, the sound seemed to be coming from the corner of the room beyond my sister's bed. In addition, I wondered how the bed could squeak even while my sister was lying still. There was another thought too; I always had a weird feeling whenever I heard that noise. I sometimes felt as though I was not alone, or that I was being watched. Still, what does a ten-year-old know?

It was another sleepless night; the noises were becoming common, though no less frightening. My mother always said it was because I thought too much when I went to bed. She told me that the best thing to do was to keep my mind blank when it was time to go to sleep. (I still cannot do that.) She also pointed out that I could not "will" or "force" sleep to come; it had to happen naturally. She would tell me that the harder I tried to sleep, the longer I would find myself awake. Of course, she was right. I really did try to do what she said; it just did not seem to work. I was thinking about that when I heard the old, familiar: "squeak, squeak, squeak." That annoying sound heard, again and again and again. I had finally reached the point where I could not stand it anymore A few weeks earlier I had started keeping a flashlight on the floor next to my bed. That uneasy sense I felt at night was getting stronger. I began to feel the need to keep a light on at night, although I had never been afraid of the dark before. Since I shared a room with my older brother, keeping a light on was not possible. He hated lights on at night; he said that he could not sleep that way. My father, in order to keep us both happy went out and bought me a flashlight to keep by my bed. I have to admit it did make me feel better.

I got out of bed, trusty flashlight in hand and walked into my sister's room. We lived in a railroad apartment, meaning that to get to any room in the house; you had to walk through another one. Well, I walked into her room and shone my light around. "Squeak, squeak, squeak;" the sound seemed to be coming from the far corner of the room where my sister kept her baby stroller, not from her bed. For some reason I could not understand this. The hair on the back of my neck stood up. Frightened, I pointed the light to that corner of the room and froze. The squeaking noise was coming from the stroller, which was rocking back and forth! "Squeak, squeak, squeak."

That experience and other similarly unusual experiences in my life and those of others spurred my interest in learning more about the unseen world of the paranormal. It is not always unseen.

Investigating The Paranormal

I have spent just about all of my life studying the "paranormal," which means, literally, that which is beyond normal. I say that because as a child, I heard many stories about ghosts, seances, and Ouija boards. Seances and Ouija boards are both vehicles for contacting ghosts, or spirits, as they are called. During a seance, you try to contact the spirits directly. The Ouija board has letters and numbers printed on it. Those present place one or two fingers on a pointer, or planchette as it is called, and in theory, the spirit guides the pointer to spell out words. Some of those stories were funny; others were scary. My mother and grandmother believed in those things so I believed at an early age that such things existed. My father said that he did not believe in "all that nonsense." I am not sure if he said that because he really did not believe in it or if that was his way of dealing with something he did not understand. I know that some people say they do not believe in spirits because they are actually afraid of them. I cannot say this was true of my father because, frankly, I do not think he was afraid of anything. As I grew older, I wondered more and more about the invisible world.

Around the time I was thirteen, I began to study the supernatural. By definition, the supernatural is anything that happens outside the *known* laws of nature. Now, too many years later, I am still studying it. Believe me, you never know it all. My formal training is in parapsychology. Parapsychology is the study of paranormal phenomena from a scientific view. Let me explain what I mean by that. Parapsychologists study things like extra sensory perception, or ESP as it is often called. This is the study of people with abilities that go beyond the five, natural senses. It is often referred to as the sixth sense. This is actually incorrect because this sixth sense is actually the first sense to develop. While still in the womb, a baby develops ESP. Once the child is born, it uses that sixth sense exclusively until the other five senses begin to develop. As those senses develop, this sixth sense starts to diminish. This sense does not go away completely. Children remain psychic, that is, they have ESP to some degree, until sometime between the ages of seven and twelve. Usually, they lose most of that ability. Some keep it longer than others do as some have stronger abilities than others. However, it never goes away completely.

Some of the topics, which fall into the category of ESP, are "clairvoyance," which is the ability to see people or events, which are distant. In other words, someone who is clairvoyant can see into the future, although for some reason they never see lottery numbers. They can also see ghosts. Two other forms of ESP, which are similar, are "clairaudience" and "clairsentience." The former is the ability to hear sounds or voices not audible to the normal ear. The latter, clairsentience, has to do with feeling things through means other than that which is considered natural and are not felt by most people. Also falling under the umbrella of ESP would be "telekinesis" or "psychokinesis." Briefly, both mean the ability to move objects using only the power of the mind. Simply stated, it is mind over matter. "Remote viewing" and out of body travel, or "astral projection" as it is also called, are very similar. The idea is that the spirit of a person may leave his body and travel throughout our physical plane. The spirit may also travel to the astral plane, which is the plane through which spirits must pass on their way to the next level. Remote viewing is where the spirit leaves the body and goes somewhere on our plane for the purposes of seeing something at that location. Remote viewing is quite popular with many governments including our own, since it has serious spying implications. The preceding topics represent some of the ESP areas of investigation by the parapsychologist.

A parapsychologist will not necessarily believe in ghosts in the sense of them being spirits of the dead. They will say that apparitions are the result of psychic imprints or recordings. This concept is explained later in more detail but it means that what you are viewing is a form of projection, a residue from a past life. There is no ghost, or spirit, actually present. You are watching a movie from the past. Thus, what you are seeing will not react to you. In addition, it will do the same things repeatedly. By now, you are no doubt in jeopardy of succumbing to the weight of all of these terms that are being presented. Bear with me, if you can. Let us get as many of them out of the way as we can. This will help you later.

One of the most interesting forms of paranormal phenomena is the "poltergeist." To those who study demons, "demonologists," as they are known, the poltergeist is a spirit capable of manipulating the environment in such a way as to bring about the movement of objects. This would have to be an inhuman spirit, one that has never lived on the physical plane. A human spirit, one who did live on this plane, would not have the ability to do all the things a poltergeist can. For example, a poltergeist could move a heavy sofa with ease. A human spirit could move something that weighs about two pounds. To the parapsychologist, poltergeist phenomena is something known as "recurrent spontaneous psychokinesis." (RSPK.) This basically means mind over matter. They believe that when kinetic events take place, such as chairs moving, that is actually happening through the unconscious mind of someone present. They do not believe it is a spirit causing the activity. Someone, usually a girl entering puberty, is expelling bursts of energy, which causes objects to move. We can go into more examples but I think you get the idea. I will make an in-depth presentation of the poltergeist/ RSPK phenomenon later in this book. For the most part, parapsychologists believe there are always natural causes for all unusual happenings. This is what I studied. I do believe in psychic recordings and I do believe in RSPK. There is so much evidence to support these theories. Therefore, I must not believe in ghosts, right? Wrong.

(Living In A Haunted House)

From an early age, I experienced unusual phenomena. Everyone does, to some extent, whether one admits it or not. In some cases, they simply fail to notice it or see it for what it is. At the age of ten, my family moved into another tenement building. Our third floor, railroad apartment was much bigger than the one we had been living in and it actually had a bathroom in the apartment ... amazing! Where we had been living, the bathroom, a water closet as it used to be called, was in the hallway. This was definitely a step up for us. Almost from the first day in the apartment, weird things began happening. Items were not where you were sure you left them. Odd noises would wake us up in the middle of the night. Sometimes, the bed I was laying on would vibrate. The vibrating bed was not like a magic motion bed, rather, I felt just a little vibration, much like an electrical current. Sometimes the pets would act spooked or they would look up and follow something. I always found that particularly disturbing. Ditto when they growled at something, only they could see.

As time passed, those weird happenings became more pronounced. Falling asleep was difficult and nightmares were common, when I did sleep, that is. Every once in a while, I would see something dart across the room. I always saw this peripherally, never directly. It was usually from the left side of my peripheral vision. Sometimes I would walk into a room and be greeted with a foul smell. Not all the cleaning in the world would get rid of it. Lights and other electrical appliances would turn themselves on and off. (This is something my computer still does every now and again.) Family arguments would erupt from seemingly minor things. Stress levels rose and patience ebbed. Odd noises became the norm. Sometimes I heard heart wrenching crying, sometimes sinister laughter. Furniture would begin to move on its own accord.

These problems continued to escalate. It did not take long for the spirits to manifest, or in other words, to show themselves. Objects would start flying around the room. Glass items would be smashed into the walls and shatter into a million pieces. The foul odors became more prominent. Often I would hear the sound of glass breaking but I would never find anything broken. Sometimes I would be sitting on the sofa watching TV only to be touched by something or to feel a breeze, as if something moved quickly past me. After awhile, I started questioning my own sanity. I asked myself many questions such as: "Did that really happen" or "I must be seeing things." I would talk to my parents about these strange manifestations but all I was ever told was that I was "imagining them" or "my imagination was running away with me." Soon though, there was just too much evidence to deny. That is when things get bad, once you can no longer lie to yourself.

There is a strategy here and it is a good one. Progressively, things escalate. It gets a little harder with each passing day. Poundings in the walls begin, and mysterious illnesses occur. The sightings become more frequent and more terrifying. You find yourself in a full-blown haunting. What compounds the problem is that it seems that no one believes you. This can be the most frustrating part of it all. This is when the haunting starts to wear you down. Moreover, it wears you down quickly. Part of the spirit's strategy in a negative haunting is to play "divide and conquer." In other words, an evil entity wants to cause as much friction between members of the household as it possibly can.

It affects your relationships in many different ways. Now, it stands to reason that when you are under stress, you tend to be short tempered. A haunting produces a great amount of stress. Thus, your nerves are on end. The evil spirit plays on this. Again, it wants to divide and conquer. The unnatural stress leads to many fights. So often, the causes of these fights are so silly that afterwards, you find yourself amazed and feeling guilty because of how trivial the incident was that led to the argument. On the positive side, family unity is a very powerful defense. The more a victimized family pulls together, the harder it is for the spirit to harm you, emotionally or physically.

(Help When Your House Is Haunted)

Most people do not know where to look for help. Think about it, you think your house is haunted. Where do you go? Whom should you call? Today there are many options, especially if you have access to the Internet. Unfortunately, back in the late 60's and early 70's, there was no such form of communication. So, about the only thing you could do was buy books and try to solve the problem yourself. More times than not, you made the problem worse. That is the danger here. For example, it is easy enough to provoke a demon by blessing the home, unless you know what you are doing. It can be very dangerous if you do not know what you are doing. Probably the biggest mistake you can make is trying to contact whatever force is causing the problem. People will conduct seances or use a Ouija board in an attempt to see what the spirit wants. This is a serious mistake. By doing this, you are opening yourself up to the influence of the invading spirit or demon and maybe letting something else in.

(Demonologist Vs The Parapsychologist)

As I mentioned earlier, there are two schools of thought on almost any paranormal phenomenon. The big question here is who is right, the demonologist or the parapsychologist? They each explain the phenomena, although they are often on opposite poles on this subject. My feeling is that the two disciplines are quite similar. Furthermore, I think there is a common ground where they can meet, providing they are open-minded enough to try. They should listen to each other and see where they differ and where their findings are similar. Yes, I am technically a parapsychologist based on my education but I am one who lived through a haunting. By the way, when I am asked for the definition of parapsychology, I always answer that: "Parapsychology is the scientific study of a field that cannot be studied scientifically." Having said that, I feel that there have just been too many unusual occurrences in my life to say that ghosts do not exist.

On the other hand, there is strong evidence in regards to psychokinesis. There is no doubt that people can manipulate the environment to some degree. However, the thing is that even the strongest of those with ESP cannot move large objects. In controlled studies, people have been able to move small objects using just the power of their minds. They have not been able to move refrigerators. For the record, I have seen this happen. Whatever it was, it was not ESP. The same holds true for levitation. For those who may not know, levitation is the rising of an object without any visible, physical means. I have seen this happen on a few occasions and I have seen some heavy objects levitate. This has never been duplicated in a controlled laboratory setting. You would have to think that somewhere along the line, someone would emerge who has the ability to do this but it has not happened and I do not think it ever will. Time may prove me wrong but I just do not think our minds are powerful enough to do this. Of course, if we ever learn to use a larger percentage of our brains, my theories may well change since theory is often a product of experience.

This is one of the arguments that always comes up when people discuss poltergeist activity. The parapsychologists say it is always RSPK, (recurrent spontaneous psychokinesis) while the demonologists point to a spirit. Since it is believed that a prepubescent female is often the "trigger" or "agent" behind the phenomena, it is hard to imagine that a child entering puberty could cause great havoc in a home. If that were possible, surely by now we would have some impressive documentation on the subject. The fact of the matter is that there is none and there probably never will be.

What is needed is for the two disciplines to get together and have open-minded discussions on the subject. There is indeed a phenomenon called RSPK. There is also a phenomenon known as a poltergeist. There certainly are instances of psychic projections. There are also ghosts. At some point in time, members of both disciplines must get together, check their egos at the door, and listen to each other. They could go out in the field and investigate together. Should that happen, great strides can be made and we can come that much closer to understanding the phenomena that has remained a mystery for so long. We must learn to work together to unravel the secrets that have existed for centuries. When you think about it, isn't that what we all want?

Another point to bring up is the large amount of photographs that show anomalies, or unusual things in the pictures. With today's technology, getting psychic pictures is easier than ever. The advent of digital cameras has turned finding ghosts into an art form. Digital cameras let you see what the camera is picking up immediately. In the past, infrared cameras were the things to have. Infrared cameras photograph heat. "Kirlian photography," which requires the use of a special camera used to photograph human auras, was once the state of the art tool of the parapsychologist. Auras are the energy fields that surround all living beings. Much information was learned as a result of these cameras and there is no questioning their usefulness today. The thing is that there is so much evidence of globules, little round orbs of energy, believed to be the result of spirit and energy fields available today. One simply cannot write off anomalies so easily. As our technology improves, so will our ability to prove or disprove paranormal happenings.

It is an exciting time in the history of paranormal research. For the open minded on both sides of the coin, there are truly great advances waiting to be discovered. All we have to do is work together on this. The evidence is there. So is the technology and the technology improves every day, even if we do not. We have devices today that can measure things like electromagnetic energy. It is believed that spirits create or manipulate electromagnetic energy fields when they manifest. We can record these phenomena with a device called an EMF detector. It is also called a Gauss meter or magnetometer. We have better equipment than what was used in the past. We have easy access to the wonderful world of the computer. In short, we have a lot going for ourselves.

In the future, I think you will see more and more cooperation between the opposing camps, or so I hope. That is all anyone can ask for. When you really think about it, the two fields are interconnected. We are all searching for answers. Skepticism can be a good thing. It can be a healthy thing. We need skeptics in this field, pushing us further and further towards our goal of understanding ESP *and* haunting phenomena. I sincerely believe that we will get there. As you read this material, you will see things from the viewpoint of both the demonologist and the parapsychologist. We are all paranormal investigators. We are a lot closer to each other than we think. All that is needed is for everyone to check their egos at the door, throw out all of the initials after their names and work together and *share* their information, rather than hiding it, as is so often the case these days. Each group must stop dismissing the other out of hand. There is so much to be learned but with humans being the way they are, gains are slow.

At times, there are too many experts running around out there although what qualifies them as experts is beyond me. Plus, everyone wants to be the first to prove a theory. All of this falls into the category of "human nature," which in my estimation is a self-imposed handicap if ever there was one. If you cannot change an unwanted or undesirable trait, call it human nature. We seem to enjoy living with our "created" handicaps because it puts us in a position where we do not have to think or take much responsibility for our failures or our inability to grow. That is probably more evident in this field than in any other since this one is the hardest to pin down.

WHY DO WE DO THIS?

(The Motives of Investigators)

There are many different reasons why people go into the field of paranormal investigating. Some do it for thrills, the adrenaline rush, I guess; some do it simply because it is fun. Still others do it out of a burning desire to learn some of the mysteries of the universe. Still others do it for spiritual growth. For many, it is just a fascination. Sometimes they do it for a need that they themselves do not understand. Many investigators, I have found do it because they themselves lived in a haunted house or experienced phenomena which, on the surface, appeared to be outside of what they were taught was "normal," whatever that is. They may spend years trying to make sense out of their past. Occasionally, you will find people who get into it for sinister motives. Those few believe they can somehow harness supernatural powers and make them work for them. They are dead wrong.

Most, however, do it because they want to help others who are experiencing unusual phenomena in their lives and do not know where to turn for help. Regardless of their motives, more people than ever are getting into this field. When you discount the ones who have sinister motives, those seeking power or access to darker forces, this is a favorable happening. There is an ever-growing need for dedicated investigators, those who take the time to learn the field and who do it for the benefit of others. The thrill seekers do not last too long in this business. They usually end up being scared off when they experience what they were looking for in the first place. That is the old "be careful what you ask for..." syndrome. Hopefully, they avoid being hurt physically or mentally. If you are interested in this as something more than just fun, you must have a sincere desire to use your knowledge to help others. If you do not, you run the risk of hurting yourself and the person or persons who you are trying to help. This field is very humbling and can easily scar the strongest investigators. Your motives have to be pure if you want to avoid being "eaten alive," so to speak. You certainly can bite off more than you can chew.

Combating What You Cannot See

If any of you reading this have experienced a true haunting yourself, you know the abject terror that results. You know the damage that comes with living in a situation that defies reason and logic. You know the effect it has on your head. There are cumulative effects of living with unnatural stress, broken sleep patterns, and the constant fear for the safety of yourself and your family. It affects the way you think, how you eat, and kills your spirit. Depression is common in hauntings, as are anxiety disorders. So is a sense of isolation. It is difficult to imagine living in a situation where at night, before going to bed, your children say their prayers and ask God to not let them be pulled out of their beds by some unseen force. Imagine, if you can, the terror that child feels. Then think how a parent feels when their child says those prayers. It is, no doubt, frustrating and heartbreaking. With it comes a terrible sense of impotence.

If you have experienced it, you know the terrible fear that comes from trying to combat something you cannot see. The enemy has the advantage and is capable of striking at will, picking the target or targets it chooses. It usually picks on the weaker ones, or at least the ones it *perceives* as being the weaker ones, those closer to breaking from the massive weight of the haunting. Negative spirits *love* to kick you when you are down. Are you teetering on the edge? If so, prepare for a solid push. Victims quickly learn all about paranoia. There is an incredible sense of frustration and impotence when you live under these circumstances. Your emotions run the gamut. First, there is fear, followed closely by anger, if not rage. Then you hit the frustration factor. Sadly, the next step is apathy. With that comes a pervasive sense of hopelessness and helplessness. This is where the victim is in serious danger. This is where their will is being broken down.

Hauntings can also be subtle. It is not necessarily a war being fought each night. There are periods of intense activity and periods of relative calm. There are also periods that fall somewhere in between. However, imagine the roller coaster ride of emotions that takes place every time you think the problem is over only to have the activity start up again. Each time, the feeling is worse and it builds up. Supernatural forces, for the most part, are not subject to the laws of time and space. Whether they attack the next day or three months later, it is the same to them. They could not care less. However, for the family, they are very well aware of time. Each day without activity is a Godsend to them. Still, the fear is always there, that terrible fear that it will start up again. That does not go away easily, if ever. Time affects them in another way too. The longer the period of inactivity, the more optimistic they begin to feel. They start to believe that maybe, just maybe their lives are turning normal. If that is the case, now all they have to worry about are their children growing up and the financial pressures we all face. They can concentrate on matters of health and all the other things normal families have to deal with. At least they are not being haunted anymore.

Then, one day, the activity starts up again, this time with a vengeance. The better and more optimistic they began to feel, the harder their fall when it all comes rushing back. That is part of the strategy of the spirit. Again, the spirit world, be it good or evil, is not bound by time. It can wait as long as it wants. The goal is to hurt the victim and it knows well how to accomplish its task. This is where the cumulative effects become a factor. Each time this happens, the burden on the victim becomes heavier and heavier. In addition, part of the strategy is in timing. You can bet that whenever there is some sadness or tragedy in the victim's life, such as a death in the family, the evil forces at work will choose that particular time to strike. Like I said, they love to beat the victim's when they are down. After all of that, those suffering individuals know all about the terrible feeling of helplessness and hopelessness that comes with not knowing how to combat an unseen enemy or where to turn for help.

Seeking Help To Solve A Haunting

In many cases, people have turned to their religious leaders only to come away feeling defeated by their lack of support and insight in these matters. Sadly, those religious leaders often cause more problems for the family. They are sometimes made to feel that they are delusional, that the problem is really all in their heads. Friends and family can also add to this problem. At the very mention of invisible phenomena, they are often ridiculed and told to "stop doing this to themselves," as if they somehow chose their suffering and embrace it. Trust me, I have never found anyone who *wanted* to be the victim of a haunting.

If you have never experienced a haunting yourself, you now have an idea what it is like. What often happens in these cases is that the family being haunted tries to find a way to solve the problem on their own. Here is an area where they can get themselves in big trouble. They may buy a few books that deal with hauntings but they will find it hard to find one that will tell them how to stop it. Worse still, they may try something they read about not knowing what forces they are dealing with. A sad fact is there are many books out there that trivialize the supernatural and the realm of the demonic. These books often make exorcism, a major religious ritual designed to cast demons out of either a person or place, sound like something everyone can do before breakfast. You get the feeling from reading some of these books that your morning should start off something like this: brush your teeth, take out the garbage, perform an exorcism, walk the dog, and eat breakfast. They trivialize a dangerous ritual. You will see many books on "deliverance," which is a form of exorcism although it differs greatly from the solemn ritual. There are many books on the market that contains information that is dangerous when applied by the reader. They should be used only by those who are experienced in dealing with evil, not some poor bastard under siege by God knows what and for reasons maybe even God Himself does not know.

(Communicating With Spirits)

Sometimes, those being oppressed will try things such as a seance, a method by which you sit in a darkened room and attempt to make contact with a spirit. They do this in the hopes of communicating with their unwanted visitor. The results can range from absolutely nothing to flat out disaster. They can attract something else into their home, possibly something worse than they were dealing with in the first place. Many people try using a Ouija board for the same reason. They try to communicate with the spirit that they think is haunting them. On the surface, this may not seem like a bad idea. However, you have no way of knowing who or what your are in contact with.

The way this works is the people trying to communicate with the spirit will each place one or two fingers on the planchette. They will then ask the spirit questions, such as "who are you?" and "what do you want?" The pointer then moves to letters and, in theory, spells out words. There is great debate as to whether you are contacting spirits in this manner. There are those who believe that the movement is a result of "automatism," a process by which the movement of the pointer is controlled by the subconscious mind of one or more of the participants. Whatever the cause of the movement, the process can be is dangerous, especially if you are already under siege by some foreign entity. The solutions garnered from the board can be extremely dangerous and usually only serve to exacerbate a problem that was serious to begin with. Assuming it is contact with a spirit that is guiding the planchette, or pointer, it seems highly unlikely that a spirit that means you harm (if it is a negative spirit) will sit down and discuss the situation. If anything, as with the seance, you may end up attracting something else. It is doubtful that any good can come out of an attempt to contact the spirit that is causing the problem. Think of it this way, if it was reasonable, it would not be haunting you in the first place.

Others will try using a cross and holy water and ordering the entity to leave. Depending on what they are dealing with, this may help. Certainly we all know the power of these objects and they are a necessity in surviving a haunting. However, if you do not know what you are dealing with and if you do not know what you are doing, you may very well provoke the entity into retaliating. That happens often, I am afraid to say. Another thing that many desperate people do is contact a local psychic. The problem here is that there are a lot of people out there who claim to be psychics but are nothing more than frauds looking to capitalize on someone's misfortune. They will tell you that they can solve your problem by doing some ritual or by contacting the entity "through their spirit guide" and asking it to leave. Of course, they will gladly do this for a small fee. When the first attempt fails, they will tell you that the entity, that is the invading spirit, is much stronger than they originally thought but they will cleanse the premises for you for a slightly higher fee. By cleansing the premises, they are talking about ridding the location through some form of ritual. Some of these rituals, were it not so serious a matter, would be laughable. Both of those words describe the religious ritual of casting out a demon, or devil. However, what they do is far from a religious ritual. When all is said and done, your haunting is worse than ever and you are out a considerable amount of money. Add to that, you most likely feel like a "Grade A" fool. This is not a blanket condemnation of all psychics but the truth is that there are many frauds out there and they are looking to make a buck. Profiting from someone's suffering is hardly a new concept. Humans do that well and what we also do is find new and improves ways of doing it.

So whom can these people turn to for help? Many psychic research organizations can help them. With the advent of the Internet, many doors are now open to these misfortunate people. The only problem here is that in many instances, these psychic research organizations consist of well-intentioned but poorly trained investigators. While the Internet can be so helpful, it is can also create a problem. Anyone can create a psychic research organization, complete with a great web page. They can add a catchy name, something that makes for nice initials. It does not make them reputable. Therefore, the bottom line here is that they have to be careful whom they call. My advice to everyone is to call around different places and ask as many questions as possible. If the answers are not acceptable, move on to another one. If there is a fee for service, skip that organization altogether.

We, as investigators, need to do our part. We must make sure that we are professional through and through. You have to do your homework and try to find out of their members are well trained. Their goal should be to help people on many different levels. They should not just investigate; they should work with the family from the beginning to the end, however long that might be. If they tell you that they can only commit so much time to the case, look elsewhere. A good organization should also work on teaching valuable coping skills to make things easier on the family until the problem can be corrected. Many organizations investigate and recommend advice but do not stay with the family through completion.

There is a great need for good people to work in this field. The sad fact of the matter is there are people out there who really need help. However, in order to do this, you must be properly trained. There is a danger in doing this work if you do not know what you are doing. However, you can learn to do this safely. That is very important. Read everything you can; especially material that deals with actual cases. Imagine yourself working those cases. Get a feel for what it is like to do the case. Put yourself in the victim's shoes. Get a sense about whether you really want to go into it. Look for conferences being given by experienced investigators. Every so often, you will come across one. The Internet can help you there. Watch TV programs that feature investigators. Learn, learn, and learn.

You do not get a lot of recognition doing this type of work. However, people are suffering at the hands of evil forces. They may be preternatural, that is "human" spirits. The word "preter" meaning literally "beyond." They may be supernatural or "inhuman" spirits. This type goes way beyond natural. They have the ability to do things that no human could do. An example would be teleportation, where they take an object, make it disappear and later reappear in some other location. Before we go further, realize this: when dealing with inhuman spirits, they can be good as well. We know them to be Angels.

Investigator Profile

Those who choose to do this have the ability to help people in the most profound way. They have the ability to help save people from the worst forms of evil, from demons themselves, if necessary. Not many people can lay claim to that. I believe those who do this are chosen. You are not going to be the one fighting the actual battle but your work will lead to bringing in the ones who will. Those who do this work may come from different backgrounds, have different jobs, different belief systems. However, they all share some things, the desire to help others being tantamount. I do not think that those of us who do this are special people but we are different. Those who think they are special do not last long in this business. We have been given a precious gift, the ability to study and if necessary, fight the unknown, the evil. We must make the most of our gift. If we do not man the battle lines between good and evil, who will?

The Rewards of Investigating

It was mentioned earlier that the work we do is dangerous in the extreme but rare cases. It is also very rewarding. It is almost impossible for people to imagine the horrors of a haunting unless they have had the misfortune of experiencing one. Those of us in this business know that horror. After all, we subject ourselves to that horror every time we go on a bad investigation. However, and never forget this, we get to see the hope on the faces of the victims when we meet them. Hope is a biggie and they need that. We represent that hope. We get to see the joy on their faces when our efforts lead to the end of their personal nightmare. We may not be the ones actually doing the fighting, but we are the ones who identify the problem and help them to obtain the help they need. Our investigation, if thorough enough, can determine the problem. If our documentation is done properly, it may serve as the proof needed to get that help. When we do our jobs well, the benefits are obvious and so are the rewards.

On top of that, we get to see a whole different world. It is a world that most people do not realize is all around them. We see things that few people ever see. We are fortunate enough to see things that make us challenge our beliefs in a positive way; our belief systems are so different from the average person. It can be very exciting. Those who do paranormal investigations get a glimpse into what may lie ahead for all of us. Thus, it gives us a unique perspective on life. Yet, as with anything, there is a downside. On the other hand, experiencing the rewards of seeing into another dimension can make it difficult for us to live in our "real" dimension. The day-to-day grind can prove to be very boring and unfulfilling, if we let it. That is something we must guard against lest we fall prey to that trap. When you see all the wonders of the spirit world, even the bad, it can make the physical world seem very mundane.

Still, it is something I am glad I do and I cannot imagine doing anything else. Though investigations do not pop up too often, there is still so much to do. There are always cases to study. There are always new experiments taking place that are worth studying. There are always plans to make, techniques to refine. There is knowledge out there to be learned if you know where to look and are willing to keep an open mind. There are different worlds to uncover and secrets to search for. If I learn just a few, I will be the better for it.

KNOW WHAT YOU ARE GETTING INTO

This chapter was not in the first printing of this book. It is one that I felt compelled to add. I have been involved in many investigations in the few years since this book was originally published. In many cases, my organization and I were the first people called into a case. However, there were several cases where we were the second or third group called in. Sadly, in many of those cases, we found ourselves dealing with people who had had terrible experiences with other investigators. These experiences were sometimes the result of well-meaning but unqualified investigators. They discovered too late that they were in over their heads. Others thought they knew it all and were terribly surprised to learn they didn't. Some were just naïve. A few were just stupid. The members of one of the groups would spend plenty of time talking about the supernatural and going to haunted locations. Between them, they read many books on the subject. They kicked around ideas. On several occasions, they sat in a friend's basement because occasionally, odd things happened there. They felt that made them qualified to do case work. They were wrong.

Then there were the others, those that mistook themselves for the case. Their concern was either profit or reputation. These people put their needs on the forefront and their clients were an afterthought. They were not doing a case out of the desire to help people; they were doing it out of their own self-serving needs. Some people have no business being in this business. Period. I am not going to get into names here but there are many of them out there. God help those who come across them. The potential for doing harm to people is incredible and sometimes immeasurable. Unless you have been haunted, you have no idea what it is like. If you are a sensitive enough individual and have good empathic powers, you might have a fair idea. I have known a few special people who have been able to put themselves in that position. They are even more rare than demons. Those who are haunted suffer greatly mentally. They do not understand what is going on and they have no idea how to stop it so they reach out for help. That is not an easy step to take. More times than not, they have had little if any support. They are used to hearing how it is "all in their heads." That is where the isolation comes in. Unfortunately, criticism is always flung their way.

When they finally do reach out for help, they have taken a big step. Knowing full well that they face further criticism, they put all of their faith in the hands of the investigator. After all, the investigators are experts, right? I will let the answer to that question go in the wind. Those poor people put their faith and trust in the investigators and will often do whatever they are told to do. I have seen people put their houses up for sale because they were told by an "expert" that they needed to get out of the house since that house was a "portal to hell." I guess they forgot the part where it says that spirits will often follow people from location to location. Of course, maybe the thinking was that portals cannot follow people. Of course, that is assuming there was some thinking in the first place. That marriages can be ruined and money lost seems to be of little consequence to some of these "experts." In some cases every penny the victims had was lost and many people have gone through other forms of misery and suffering at the hands of these "experts." Instead of feeling liberated by the investigators, they found themselves even more afraid than when they started. (I'll mention why shortly.) For many, they find themselves facing more criticism. "You see, I told you that you were nuts to bring strangers in your house. Like I've said a thousand times, it's all in your head. There are no such things as ghosts. Maybe you'll listen to me next time." I do not want to sound like an arrogant prick here but like I said before, some people have no business being in this business. I have had to do a lot of damage control and I have had to undo a lot of serious mistakes. I am not talking about honest mistakes here; God, no. I am talking about "who gives a damn about the victims" mistakes that are done for the sake of profit or self-promotion. In all of the years I have done this work, I have come across three or possibly four cases of a demonic presence. I have been called into many cases where my job was to prove there were no demonic entities at work. I have said many times, if you *think* you are being haunted by a demonic force, you are not. Believe me, if you are, you will *know* it.

In coming chapters, you will see basically how to set up an investigation and details regarding what you might expect to see and experience. However, what I want to do now is help you to realize what you might be getting yourself into. Hopefully after this chapter, you will be able to decide where you are going in this line of work. I am going to discuss exactly what it is like being in a haunted house. In some cases, I will give worst-case scenarios. Chances are you will never come across the worst-case haunting but before you do, we need to find out if you believe you can and want to do it. I will now take you into a haunted house. After this, you will have a better idea of what you might be up against.

Okay, the call comes in and you find out a few details and you say all the right things and give the person hope and the victim asks for your help. So now you and a couple of friends decide that you want to try the case. You load up your car that night, making sure that you have your camera, your Gauss meter, a thermometer and your camcorder. You and your friends are all excited because this case really sounds like it will be a good one. After all, there have been lots of noticeable outward manifestations. Excitedly, you reach the destination. Hopefully you will find the location easier than I would; I am notorious for getting lost. Almost immediately upon entering, you can just sense that something is there and that something cool is going to happen. Right off the bat, if you are waiting for something "cool" to happen, you are already at a disadvantage. "Cool" stuff can mean trouble and "cool" can quickly turn into harrowing. A famous demonologist once asked me what one thing I would like to see again. My answer, and it was honest, was that there was nothing else I wanted to see. I have seen plenty although not everything by a long shot and while some things are mind-boggling and therefore exciting, seeing that stuff means someone is in trouble. In an ideal world, no one would be in trouble. Unfortunately, it is not an ideal world; quite the contrary, it is not even a good world. Since that is the case, I will probably see plenty more. Seeing it now means documenting it and that is critical to solving a case. I just do not need to see it because it is "cool." I have had a lifetime of "cool."

At a job I used to work eons age, we had a sign written over a chalkboard that read: "All Good Ideas Ultimately Degenerate Into Work." That is the stage you are at now. After you talk to the client, you decide to split up. One of you will take the second floor; another will take the main floor and the remaining one will sit in the basement. Let us take a look at the investigator in the basement. After 20 minutes down there, you go back up and talk to the lead investigator. He or she tells you to go back down there and also tells you that it would be a good idea to sit in the dark in the hopes that whatever is down there might be more comfortable moving around. Slowly, your heart starts to pump a bit faster. "Sit in the dark?" you think to yourself. In many cases, you begin to feel a little frightened. That is normal enough. However, once the light is turned off, you anxiety level begins to build. Suddenly, you begin to feel that you are not alone. In fact, you are sure you are being watched. The hair on your neck starts to stand up a bit and you can feel goose bumps on your arm. You listen intently for the slightest sound. However, the only sound you hear is your own breathing and what sounds like the pounding in your own chest. Or is that all you hear? Now your mind begins to wander to the last case you worked. You remember how frightened you were when the knocking in the walls started. After a couple of minutes, you hear an odd noise coming from the corner to your left. You are startled now. Next, you hear what sounds like something small dropping a few feet away. Your mind now starts to race. "Maybe this isn't such a good idea," you say to yourself. You tell yourself to calm down. After all, nothing is going to hurt you. Just the same you wish you had kept the light on.

Once again, you get the strong impression that you are not alone. Furthermore, you *know* you are being watched and probably sized up. Whatever is haunting this house is down there, you fear. To keep yourself calm, you try thinking about the football game coming up on Sunday. You tell yourself that it is an important one and you are hoping that your team will play a decent game. While you are thinking that, you hear a fairly loud bang not far from where you are sitting. That makes you jump up. You are not quite sure where the noise came from but you know that it was close by. You start fumbling in the dark looking for the light switch but you cannot seem to find it. Once again, you try telling yourself that nothing bad is going to happen. Then your mind starts to race a bit more and you remember the client telling you that sometimes when things start getting noisy, the lights will not go on at all. Now you really want to kick yourself for not bringing your flashlight with you. However, before you beat yourself up too badly, you hear a loud growl. The hell with the flashlight, you race for the stairs and try going up them three at a time.

Needless to say, you stumble on the stairs making all kinds of racket and hopefully, avoiding injury. Mercifully, the door opens and your friend is waiting at the top of the stairs for you. Once you are safely in the kitchen, you start to relax. Slowly, your blood pressure begins to lower back somewhere near normal. You have a newfound conviction: you will not go down in that basement alone again. Excitedly, you tell your friend what you just experienced. You are talking a mile a minute and your friend is trying to get you to slow down. By now the client is there as well. "There is something bad down there," you gush out. "There is no way I am going down there again, at least not alone." This really frightens the client. If the experts are afraid to go down there, how is the client supposed to feel? As an investigator, you believe that there is a spirit down there. Furthermore, you have every reason to believe that it is malevolent by nature. You could just *sense* that. You may well be right too. Then again, it may just be Fluffy, the client's cat, chasing a mouse. That is just one example and certainly not a worst-case one by any means.

In one case I worked, a scenario similar to that actually took place. In that case, two investigators were in the basement together. In less than 15 minutes, they came flying up from the basement and told their team leader and the clients that the "demon" touched them (I would love to know how they derived it was a demon) and that there was "no way they would go down there again." Can you imagine what that did to the poor woman who lived there? Her washer and dryer were down there. How was she supposed to go down there again when the two men, investigators no less, refused to go down there? For months, that poor lady drove fifteen miles to wash and dry her clothing every week even though she had a washer and dryer. That is the kind of damage you can do. It can be severe and very difficult to overcome, if it can be overcome at all.

That brings us to the next item. It is a rare case when you encounter a demon, very rare. It is even more rare when a demon shows itself quickly. You can spend months on a case and still not be sure whether there really is one operating there. These two knuckleheads from the previous example decided that it was a demon, not based on any evidence, not based on anecdotal information; they decided it was a demon because of the way they *felt* when they walked into the house. After they terrified the family by telling them that there was a demon loose, they did their basement thing and after that, they proceeded to fall asleep. One slept on the couch; the other in a recliner. This happened around 10 pm that night. Pretty early to be catching a snooze, wouldn't you say? I, for one, would not fall asleep in a house where I suspected there was a demonic force at work. I would not put myself into a dangerous position like that. However, they did say upon awakening that the demon touched them while they slept. Fortunately, that was their only night on that case. Only a fool announces the presence of a demon without a shred of evidence to back it up. Sure, it is great to tell you friends how you worked on a demonic case. If you really feel the need to do that, find another hobby. Don't hurt people needlessly. Please do not make that mistake.

Let us go back into the haunted house. You are now sitting in the living room with the clients. You have asked them a bunch of questions and they have done the same. Since nothing much is happening, you start to tell them amusing ghost stories. (A wonderful idea; it helps build up a solid rapport with the client and makes them see scary phenomena in a lighter way. That can be priceless.) While telling them a story, a door suddenly slams shut. Loud! You jump up from the couch and look towards the kitchen where the sound appeared to have come from. Seeing nothing, you walk back into the living room. Just as you go to sit down, you (and everyone else there) hear three loud bangs. This makes everyone jump. Before you can determine where the sound came from, the front door flies open and slams shut. Your heart is racing and to top it off, the lights in the room go off. Before you have time to move, pounding starts in the walls. The pounding is so loud that you cannot hear yourself think and the speed of the pounding increases to the point where it sounds like someone is firing off a machine gun in there. This pounding lasts for close to a minute before it mercifully stops.

For several minutes, no one says a word. The only sound you hear is that of your heart, pounding in your chest. You look across the room. First you notice your partner. He has a blank look on his face and it looks as if he is zonked out. Near him is the father of the family. He too looks stunned but he is doing his best to comfort his wife who now becomes hysterical. The next thing you are aware of is your friend who just came racing up from the basement. He is quickly packing his bag. The camera goes away as does the gauss meter. The youngest child, a 10-year-old girl is sobbing. You cannot believe how pale she looks. You know that you need to say something but you cannot think of any words. Just as the pounding in your chest begins to slow down, you hear a crash behind you. As you turn to look, something bangs into your head, something hard. That something was a figurine that had been on a shelf across the room. Suddenly another object shoots towards your head. You manage to duck from that one. A picture flies off the wall, hitting one of your investigators. Then everything stops.

How you react at that point is critical. It is quite normal to be excited, even frightened. However, you have to remember that the clients are looking up to you. If you decide to bolt from the room, you are sending a very damaging message. If you decide to leave at that point, the damage done may be irreparable. The client has to live there; if you are too frightened to stick around, the show is over. This may sound hard to believe but I have seen this happen. I know of one organization that had several investigators leave after a similar event. They left so fast that they left behind most of their equipment. The following day, they would not go back into the house to get it. They sent a friend instead. Even a whispered conversation between investigators can cause some harm. No matter how frightened you might be, you have to be there and be strong for the client because they sure as hell are scared. You may rightfully be scared too but you do not have the luxury of showing that. You have to make it a point to help calm them down. Think of the task at hand. What I like to do in events such as those is time them. Note when it starts, note when it stops. Record the duration. On top of that, it is good information to know. You can test the strength of the spirit. If the pounding lasts two minutes one time and only a minute and a half the next time, it may be a sign that the spirit is weakening. That alone cuts down on your fear and it shows the client that you know what you are doing and that you are not letting a frightening occurrence affect you. They will start to build off of that. Remember, a huge part of your function there is to teach the clients how to deal with their haunting. In this field, you must lead by example.

My point here is that investigations can be quite frightening. Granted, many aren't but going in, you do not know that for sure. Even the seemingly easy ones can go bad in a hurry. Also, what may seem mild to one investigator might be frightening to another. Before you go into an investigation, you have to make sure that you are ready for it. To those of you out there who have experience with frightening hauntings and know how you will react, you still have to think about those investigators that you are planning to bring with you. There are some questions that you should ask yourself. For example, how much experience does that person have? Do they believe that they know everything that there is to know? Stay away from those types. Have you seen them in a frightening situation before? Are they easily spooked and do they have a tendency to spook themselves? That is more common than you think. You might want to try a few tests with them. Ask them a lot of questions. Run scenarios by them and ask them how they would handle them. Make some simple, others frightening.

Play a fantasy or role-playing type of game. Have that person mentally put him/herself in a situation such as a serious haunting. Have them visualize different scenarios. For example have them imagine themselves alone in a dark basement and hearing different sounds, growls or the like. You can even have him try sitting in a dark basement and create those scenarios. It might tell you a lot. Think back to other cases they have been on and think about how they acted and reacted. Most importantly, when you bring someone new in, keep him or her close to you. Do not send them off by themselves. Also, instruct them to discuss activity and theories only with you.

If someone that you know has expressed fear regarding investigations, do not bring them along with you if you think you might be looking at a bad case. You can get a good idea from what the client has told you. Do not make it a testosterone thing. If a person tells you that they are afraid, do not try to convince him to go along with you.

There is a huge difference between investigating haunted landmarks and helping someone with a serious problem. When you agree to investigate someone's haunting, they will look to you as an expert. You can do a great deal of harm to the victim of a haunting. Always envision a worse case scenario. How will everyone react if they hear terrifying sounds? How will they react if they see a ghost? How will they react if that spirit starts moving toward them? What will happen if something touches them? Ask yourself whether *you* can handle that. Ask yourself whether your people can handle that. If there are any doubts, stay away. There is nothing wrong with saying "no" to an investigation. Furthermore, if you find yourself in over your head, don't be afraid to look for help or end the investigation. In the long run, it is better to say no to an investigation that to run into big problems once you are in there.

Be careful what advice you give to the victim of a haunting. I did a case where an investigator involved in a human haunting suggested to the victim that they watch a movie called: "The Haunted," based on the book by Jack and Janet Smurl, Ed and Lorraine Warren and Jack Curran. It is a great book and movie. However, it does not help a person being victimized by a haunting to read about someone else's frightening haunting. Furthermore, you probably could not pick a worse story to have them see. In the book, a powerful demon terrified the Smurl family. The bad part of it was that in the book, three exorcisms were performed and all failed. In the movie, the Smurl family moved to another house and it ended with the demon calling Janet's name in the new house. Not only had the exorcisms failed, the demon followed the family to the new house. That would surely cheer the frightened victims up and give them unending hope to boot. I do not know what he was thinking when he made that suggestion, or was he thinking at all? Everything you do must be weighed carefully. You have to think ahead of the impact your moves make. All actions have consequences. I cannot possibly stress enough that you have to know what you are getting into. As I said earlier, while a case may seem benign, you can never really be sure what it actually going on there. Never make the mistake of assuming that a case will be a cakewalk. Even human hauntings can be difficult to work. In some ways they are more frustrating that the bad ones.

Here is another point. Cases can sometimes last a long time. Once you agree to take one on, you have to honor that commitment. You cannot agree to take a case then decide later on that you are tired of working it. If you find yourself with time constraints, do not take on a case. To leave a frightened family in the lurch is flat out cruel. It is also damaging. I have worked cases that have dragged on for months. They were not of the variety where I had to be in the house every week but as the activity picked up, so did the amount of time that was needed to work the case. That meant making some sacrifices. I know a well-meaning investigator who often ran into problems with his wife because of the amount of time he spent working on a case. This led to a severe conflict of interest. It led to a lot of arguing and it made it difficult to work the case when he was there. If you have a spouse, you have to make sure that he or she understands the commitment you are making. If it is going to create problems, do not take the case.

Probably the best thing I can say at this point is to learn to put yourself in the place of the victims. Imagine what it is like to live in fear. Imagine what it is like to fear for the safety of your children. Try to imagine, if you can, the impotence a parent feels when he or she knows that they cannot protect their children. Then try to imagine functioning at your daily tasks with that kind of pressure on you. They have jobs or school to be concerned with. They have responsibilities that they must take care of. They are trying to deal with those responsibilities while under the enormous pressure of the haunting and doing it on virtually no sleep at all, in most cases. Certainly not good sleep. Now imagine that you are there to help them. Just think about how much they will depend on you. It can be tough because you have your own life and responsibilities too. When your phone rings at three in the morning because something terrifying has just occurred, you have to be there for them. You may be the only thing keeping them together. That is an awesome responsibility, I know. However, it is all part of it. I remember one Saturday night where my wife and I were watching TV when the phone rang. It had been a brutal day for me and I was beat. When I answered the phone, the party in question simply asked: "How soon can you get here?" It was a rare demonic case and at that moment, things were flying around her living room. She was alone except for her three-year-old daughter. (Her husband was away on a business trip and he would not be back until late Sunday night.) She was new to her area and really had no place else to go. Well, it was a ninety-minute ride for me and I made it in just over seventy minutes. My wife stayed on the phone with her until I got there. Things were still flying around when I arrived. After stopping it with some prayers and holy water, I spent the entire night sitting on her couch while she and her daughter slept in the next room. That is the type of thing that occasionally happens and I was glad that she called and I was glad that I was able to help.

YOU NEED PASSION

I worked with an investigator who talked a lot about his passion for the work but he only seemed to want to work cases from about 9 to 11 pm on Friday nights and only if they were located around the corner, and it had to be a "good" case, whatever that is. It is not like you can tell in advance what is going to happen or whether it will be a "good" case or not. That is a bit of an exaggeration but not by much. Whenever I mentioned that we had a case to work, his first reply was always: "We don't have to stay over all night, right? There is no need to, right?" We worked very few cases together. An attitude like that is devoid of real passion. You cannot look at working a case that way and be any good at it. Also, if you do not want to take late night calls, if you do not want to have to run over to their house on a freezing night, you should not take the case. That stuff does happen sometimes. It is not to say that you have to be there 24/7, but there will be times when you are needed. It can ruin many a plan I can assure you. You have to make sacrifices in this work. This is why I feel that with some exceptions, the best investigators are the ones who have been haunted themselves. It is not that we are an exclusive club. People who have been haunted can relate to the victims and their commitment runs deeper. I have met a few investigators who had never experienced a haunting themselves but were still committed to the victims because they were able to understand what that family was going through.

I was at a conference one time and I was talking to a few investigators from different organizations. At one point, one in particular, a blowhard of the highest order starting complaining to me that this one family were being "pain in the asses." When I ask him why, he told me that they wanted him and his group at their house "all the time." (He had only been over there once.) He could not begin to understand why they were so frightened by "such little crap" as doors opening and closing and lights flickering on and off. "They need to grow some balls," he told me. I told him to find another hobby. Unless you walked a mile in their moccasins, don't judge them. In short, before you elect to take on a case, make sure you know what you are getting into and make sure you have the commitment and the ability to work it before you accept it.

If you are just looking for fun or you are hoping to find fame and fortune, stay away from casework. Fun is going to haunted landmarks or hotels and allegedly haunted cemeteries. That is safe and entertaining. Fame is fleeting even if you find it. Forget fortune altogether. There is virtually no money to be made working cases. You can make some money doing lectures and the like but working cases will not do it. All it will do is give you some material. If you are looking to have a few good "war" stories to tell, stay away from casework. You can find "war stories" anywhere.

Okay, that is more than enough pontificating from me. By now you are muttering something like: "What an asshole!" Sorry. I have to say this stuff because I have seen the damage some investigators have done. Just remember that working cases is far different from ghost hunting. The responsibility is awesome and you have to have a selfless attitude.

OVERVIEW OF AN INVESTIGATION

Investigators Play Many Roles

When you begin an investigation you will find that you have to play several different roles. You will be an interviewer, counselor, and teacher as well as an investigator. You also need to be a friend to the family. They are going through some rough times dealing with phenomena most people do not realize even exists. This makes them feel detached, isolated, and disassociated. They need all the help and support you can give them. Education is one way in which you can help them. You can also help them develop coping skills. We will talk about that in detail in the pages that follow. The good part is that this is something you can do on your first night with the family. Since investigations can take a long time, this is sometimes the only way you can really help them in the beginning.

The Initial Interview

You always begin the investigation by interviewing all of the people involved. The purpose of the initial interview is to find out what type of things are happening and whether or not an investigation is warranted.

There may be natural explanations for the occurrences they describe. Most of the time, however, you will feel the need to investigate based on what they tell you. It does not necessarily mean there is something paranormal going on. That can only be determined after a thorough investigation. It simply means that it is worthwhile to look a little further.

(Seeking Solutions)

Finally, you have to become the investigator. You need to determine 1) *Is something there?* 2) *What is it?* 3) *Why is it there? 4) If the spirit is human, who is it?* Once those questions are answered, you can then begin to look for ways of resolving the problem. Usually it is easy finding out whether something is there. You will have an idea based on the initial interview. The client may tell you the reason they believe they are haunted is because they heard a strange noise in the basement and they once saw a door close by itself. After a little questioning, you may find out that this only happened once and that was right after the client had watched *The Exorcist*. Most likely, the client spooked himself. In other words, his imagination got the better of him. However, if the client reports the manifestation or materialization of a spirit, or describes loud poundings coming from the walls, it is a good bet that something is indeed there. Also, at some point, activity may take place while you are there. That makes things easy.

(Human and Inhuman Spirits)

Trying to determine what is there can be little harder. There are certain types of phenomena that would point to a human spirit, that is, a spirit who once walked the earth in human form. These spirits can be evil or they can be good. This all depends on how they were when they were living. Good people do not become bad spirits although the reverse sometimes happens. Human spirits may appear as they were when they lived, although they would probably seem to be transparent. In some cases, they may be able to move light objects. They are also capable of generating sound although conversations with human spirits are usually rare although some good voices have been caught on tape. In one investigation, we were taping while I spoke to the spirits in that particular house. I would say something and then wait about 30 seconds before saying anything else. We played the tape back and after I announced that the spirits would have to leave, the tape clearly says: "You bastard!" However, you are most likely to hear moaning, crying, laughing and an occasional word.

Other types of phenomena point to an inhuman, or demonic spirit, which is a spirit that never existed in human form These spirits are capable of doing just about anything they like. They can move large, heavy objects and do so at amazing speeds. They can make objects disappear and reappear ... this is called teleportation. In addition, they can manipulate things, although they are not able to create things. For example, they can make a rock fall in your living room but they cannot create that rock. They can appear as a human, an animal, or as a combination of both.

They can also make any sound they like. Let us look at a couple of examples. Crying, manifestations of a spirit and the movement of small objects would point to the human spirit. The movement of heavy objects, such as a sofa or a person, and the desecration of holy objects would be demonic in origin. Activity may not be that easy to determine. There are instances where a demonic spirit is present but the phenomena taking place may be pointing to the human spirit. That is why you always have to be sure what you are dealing with before you give the client a diagnosis. In later chapters, I will present a scale of symptoms designed to help you determine what it is you are dealing with.

In some cases, an invading entity will make itself known to you immediately. This is rare and not necessarily a good sign. It usually means that the haunting is bad. When an entity makes itself known from the start, it can mean that it is not particularly scared of you. Sometimes though, there is just so much activity that anyone at anytime can witness it. If on the other hand, a spirit hides from you, it may mean the entity views you as someone who could hurt it. This would most likely be true when dealing with a human spirit. Demonic spirits are usually not afraid of investigators. It is also a matter of how you view it. You could say that when then negative spirit tries to scare off the investigators right away, is doing so because it views the investigator as a threat. If that is the case, it knows that it can be beaten. In benign cases, the good spirits may show themselves right away. It depends on why they are there and what they want. If they have a message for a loved one, they may try to convey it quickly. After they have completed their goal, they will usually leave. In bad hauntings, they tend to stay around.

Why Is The Spirit Present?

In some cases, finding out why it is there can be very difficult. In fact, there are times when you never really determine why a haunting occurred. In many cases, there can be obvious reasons for the haunting, if that is what you are dealing with. For example, you may have learned during the interview process that the shy young boy went out and bought a book on how to cast spells hoping to increase his popularity with his peers. When you review the book, you discover that satanic forces direct the particular spell he was using. At that point, you know you are dealing with a spirit of the occult. The word occult means hidden, or secret. Therefore, a spirit of the occult would be one that has been conjured or summoned, from hidden or secret knowledge. (The spell.) It is, therefore, a negative or evil spirit. You now know why the spirit is there; the boy invited it in. This is known as "the law of invitation" and that is why dabbling in the occult is so dangerous. When you combine that knowledge with the information the parents told you about the activity going on in the home, you may determine that you are dealing with an inhuman spirit, the demonic. Now you know what you are up against and you know what direction to take to end the haunting. Being demonic, you are going to need religious help. Although, in some cases, simply stopping the precipitating activity will end the siege. This is usually true when the problem is with a human spirit, rarely with a demonic one.

After investigating for a while and winning the trust of some members of the family, you may find out that there is some form of abuse going on in the home. Here you are dealing with "the law of attraction." In short, this means that there is something going on that has attracted an evil spirit. It is the theory of "like attracts like." If the spirit causing the commotion is of the human variety, eliminating the attracting element may stop the problem. Again, if the spirit is evil or demonic, you most likely will have to get religious intervention to correct the problem. Sometimes, you will find that the house you are investigating has been the scene of a murder or some other tragedy. It may also be a case where the spirit was there before the family moved in. Sadly, in other cases, a person is haunted, for any number of reasons. Wherever the person goes, he will be haunted. Only an exorcism, the religious ritual designed to cast out spirits, will free the person. It may be happening to a loving, nurturing, and religious family. They may have been targeted because they are good people. What better way for the devil to score points than to pick on a family that represents goodness? Sadly, this is the worst haunting in terms of the severity of the haunting and the difficulty in expelling the evil spirit. However, there are cases where you never find out why a haunting is taking place. What caused the problem may have taken place many years earlier. For example, a satanic ritual may have taken place long before a house was put on the land.

Solving the Problem

Lastly, you want to make the problem end. This is by far the hardest part. The solution depends upon the answers to the questions: 1) *Is something there?* 2) *What is it?* 3) *Why is it there? 4) If it is human, who is it?*

Again, if the spirit is demonic, religious intervention will be necessary. If the spirit is human, you have several options available. Ceasing the cause of the problem may do the trick. Praying and blessing the home may do it also. Certainly, having a Mass said will usually eliminate the nasty human spirit. You have to be sure what you are dealing with. Blessing the house will help in the case of a human spirit but if it is demonic, you may very well provoke it into retaliating against the family. This is known as "religious provocation" and it is a dangerous situation.

There are some things to bear in mind though. You should never rule out natural causes. Do not go into an investigation assuming that you will find a paranormal cause. Often, there are natural explanations for seemingly paranormal phenomena. The worst thing you can do is go into an investigation with any preconceived notions. Go in there with an open mind. You have to be objective and thorough in your investigation by considering all possibilities. We will discuss this in much more detail in later chapters. So again, do not assume that there are paranormal causes and if there are, do not assume that they are demonic.

In order to get outside help, should you need it, you need to have as much evidence as possible to offer. There is no scientific way to prove the existence of a ghost or a demon. It cannot be done. In order for something to be proven scientifically, it must happen under controlled, laboratory conditions and it must be duplicable. Spirits do not cooperate in this manner. Enough said. However, you can and must, amass as much evidence as possible. You need pictures, equipment readings, and eyewitness statements. If there has been some level of involvement by a clergyman or the police, get their statements. In case of police involvement, obtain a copy of their report. It is a public record. Get every bit of evidence you possibly can. If you end up needing the assistance of the church, depending where you live, you may be in for a rough time, even with favorable documentation. You will, most likely get nowhere without it.

One thing that cannot be stressed enough is that you must always know your role. We are trying to determine what it is with the thought in mind of how to end the problem. However, remember this, we are not likely to be the ones who are going to end it. Depending on what you are dealing with, that will be left up to the demonologists or the clergy or, in some cases, a medium. A medium is a person who has the ability to communicate with spirits. They may be able to help a human entity. In some cases, a medium can attempt to send an evil entity away but that is rare and it does not always work. Also, more experienced investigators will make an occasional attempt to do certain things such as religious provocation and cleansing prayers but for now, you need not worry about that. In time, you may want to graduate to that point. Always remember your role. You are investigators; your role is to gather information, and evidence, which can then be used to determine what, if anything is going on. Ultimately the evidence will show you where to look for the help necessary to solve the problem.

(PROTECTING YOURSELF AND OTHERS)

Are there going to be risks involved? Yes, there are, depending on what is operating and how you respond to it. Although later chapters will discuss the risks and the ways to protect yourself in detail, it will not hurt to mention some concepts now. We have to keep in mind that we are exposed to entities, benign and malevolent at times. They are out there. They live on a different plane of existence but they can sometimes jump from plane to plane under proper conditions. Anyone who goes into an investigation is going to attract a lot of attention. After all, that comes with the turf. Of course, I need to point out that human spirits cannot do too much to hurt you. They are limited in the abilities. Most human spirit related injuries result from trying to get away from them. Just the same you have to protect yourself at all times. How? Before going on an investigation, say a prayer. It does not matter what your religion is, there is only one God. It is the same God for all of us. He just goes under different names. Let us leave the labels to the theologians. We need to be concerned about our safety. Being a Catholic, I know full well the power of the Rosary. For that reason, I always say one before going on an investigation. I will also go to my favorite Church and pray that I will be safe and also helpful to the person who needs it.

Bless your home, your pets, and your vehicles before you leave for an investigation. It may sound silly but there have been a number of instances where investigators would develop car trouble in route to a case. It is amazing how often that happens. Use holy water for the blessing. No matter what religion you believe in, holy water has been proven to work. Always keep it with you on an investigation, whether it is a possible haunted house or a photo shoot in a cemetery. Once you have reached your destination, say a prayer for protection. It does not have to be a formalized or ritualized prayer. Just ask God for His help and protection. The next thing to do is to put yourself in a God light or a white light. Picture yourself enveloped in this light. Christians call this a Christ light but again, it is not so much what you believe in as much as it is that you do believe. When you leave an investigation, again bless your car and say a prayer of protection. Ask God to prevent any entities from following you and to give you a safe journey home. Once you are home, say a prayer and again bless your home always asking for protection. You are probably thinking that you will be walking around all day mumbling like a monk in a monastery. That is not true. Prayers for help and protection do not have to be long. In fact, they can be very simple. They just need to be heartfelt. A common mistake that many investigators make is they sometimes get complacent. They have done so many investigations, some with terrifying results, others where nothing happened. They often forget to say a prayer of protection, especially in an investigation where it appears nothing was there. As photographs show, there may well have been something there all along. I am the biggest abuser of this. Most likely, the worst that would happen would be something might follow you home but it is best to protect yourself. It does not hurt.

Now, nothing is fool proof. At some point in time in your career, something may well reach you. You may feel something around you, or you may be touched, or you may have activity in your home, such as furniture moving, or horrid smells, or any of the things you have experienced while on other investigations. Do not panic. There is only a minute chance of being hurt by a spirit and you know how to protect yourself. Picture yourself in a light. In addition, do not be afraid to tell this entity where to go. Do that and do it with as commanding a voice as you can muster. Remember though; whenever you command something to leave do so in the Name of God. *We* are not commanding it to leave. God is commanding it through us. Never forget that. Ever! No spirit, human or inhuman can defeat God. The devil himself cannot although he tries hard to defeat God. We must always keep that in mind. I always remember a story I heard about my Grandma Scully, as feisty a woman as you could ever meet. As the story goes, Grandma walked into her dark bedroom one night and as she was reaching for the light, (the old kind with the pull chain) something grabbed her wrist. Well, she yelled to this entity "Let go of my hand right now, you son of a bitch." It did. Do not be afraid to tell these things where to go. Believe it or not, a little defiance will go a long way. This is an example where you can literally tell the evil spirit to go to hell. Believe it or not, it has to listen. The generation or so before us were raised to believe in spirits and they were not awed by them. They accepted spirits as a fact of life. We must too.

One last thought. I am by no means trying to minimize the dangers of dealing with evil spirits or demons but you need to put them in perspective. Whether they like it or not, they are bound by certain laws too. They must answer to God for their actions and they will. These entities are bullies and like all bullies, they try to scare you. That is their biggest weapon. They will move furniture, subject you to the foulest smells imaginable, pound on the walls, growl at you, turn off the lights, and all sorts of other things. They will touch you lightly or heavily. They will whisper around you. If you can think of something that causes you terror, they know it too. They do this to scare you. The more scared you are, the more energy they are able to take from you. They are vampires, psychic vampires. They suck the energy out of you the way mythical vampires sucked blood from their victims. It is quite natural and human to be afraid. It is just that you should not make the mistake of giving them too much power. With God on your side, you can beat them. Bullies tend to back of when you fight back. The only thing you must remember is never personally challenge them. Do so only in the name of God. I am not saying it will be easy. Trust me, it will not. You must fight and you must persevere. Most of all, you cannot give up. Good does triumph over evil but it can take some time.

You are going to see many things repeated in this manual. You may find it annoying but it is also necessary. Certain concepts must be remembered. These ideas can make or break a case and in the rarest of cases, they can save your life, or at least your sanity, so bear with me when you see something repeated for the umpteenth time. There is a method to my madness. You may also note that there is also a lot of madness to my methods. You will see that for yourself soon enough.

RISKS TO AN INVESTIGATOR

Every so often in this textbook, you will read about the need to protect yourself and the different ways to do so. However, it is very important that you realize the risks associated with being a paranormal investigator. You must be very careful not let the hunters become the hunted. You need to know this. Then and only then can you make the decision whether or not to go on in this field. For this reason, I feel it is very important to devote a section to the risks involved in paranormal investigating. Bear in mind though that these risks are proportionate to the entity or entities causing the phenomena. A simple haunting where you have an earth bound spirit poses no threat to you whatsoever. That spirit may be trapped on this plane because it does not know either that it is dead or it does not know how to move on. This is far and away the type of spirit that you are likely to encounter.

For those of you who are not interested in case work but want to explore the paranormal for fun, there really are no risks involved, save for maybe bringing something mischievous home with you for a short visit. The only time you might have to be careful is if you decide to go to someplace where there was some form of evil activity such as a murder or the like. This should be common sense but avoid areas where you know satanic practices take place. You do not know what might be hanging around there although you probably have to worry more about the living than the dead. However, I know one thrill seeker who goes to places like that and he often brings a Ouija board with him to boot. He will most likely end up as a case for someone.

An evil, human spirit can cause problems but they are limited in their ability to hurt you. I tend to talk about worst-case scenarios because those are the ones you need to protect yourself from. However, while I talk about risks associated with demonic entities, I have to point out that those cases, thank God, are extremely rare. My point here is that we have to prepare for the worst but it does not happen often. Most investigators go through long careers and never come across a demonic haunting. Again, thank God.

The risk factors are greater or lesser depending on your role and involvement in a particular case. One of the most important things is to remember your role. Just the fact that you are investigating a possible haunting puts you at some risk to begin with, depending on what, if anything, is involved. Should you make the mistake of overstepping your boundaries, you can be putting yourself at a greater risk than is necessary. It is one thing if an entity knows you are investigating it. It is not going to be too thrilled with you to begin with. If it thinks you are going to try to remove it completely, it may attack you ferociously. Never forget that. Never cross the line. Also, follow your instincts. If you are about to do something but that little voice inside tells you it is a bad idea, follow your instincts and do not do it.

Investigator's Home And Property

Let us start to discuss the types of things that commonly happen to investigators. Depending on the type of case you are working on and what is causing the problem, it is not unusual to experience activity in your own home. This can serve as an early warning sign. The activity is not usually pronounced, that is, it is not of the horrific variety. It may be caused by whatever force is operating in a future client's home. The other possibility is that it is energy created by you. This could be a situation where your own senses are awakening as a case draws closer. This does not happen in all cases but it is a common enough phenomenon.

Sometimes the activity in your home will become noticeable. It may become severe. This can happen before cases are started involving inhuman spirits. As I said, it can be interpreted as a warning to stay away from a case. For many investigators, it only makes them even more determined to get involved. In these cases, poltergeist activity may start up, resulting in objects flying around your home. It is common to hear footsteps and have doors open and close. This can be very troubling to you and your family, especially if you have children at home. Blessing the home using holy water is very effective in these situations. It will usually stop the occurrences immediately. It serves as a warning to whatever was behind the problem that you know how to protect yourself and your family. Further, it lets the spirit know that you will not be intimidated. Bless every member of your household with holy water. This definitely includes any pets you have. In addition, it is a good idea to bless your cars as well since you spend so much time in them and an accident can have catastrophic results. This is not to say that a spirit is going to cause the accident by jerking the wheel or anything like that; rather what may happen is you may see something in your rear view mirror that may frighten you enough where you may cause the accident. That has happened more than once.

Forms of Demonic Attack

The most common form of attack that an investigator has to be on the lookout for is the mental attack. The demonic knows what you fear and it knows your weaknesses. If you have low self-esteem, it may attack you in that area. It may try to make you feel worse about yourself because you will question your ability to help in an investigation, causing you to drop out. The same is true if you suffer from depression. Again, it knows your weaknesses. You have to be on your guard against this. Do not let yourself be bullied. Another preferred method of mental attack is self-doubt. Before an investigation, many investigators begin to question whether they really know enough to be helpful, although they may have done many investigations. Should you find yourself suffering from any form of mental attack, simply say a prayer to God asking that He relieve your problems. Surround yourself with the white light of God. Also, remember that this is a strategy of the demonic. See it for what it is and take it easy on yourself.

When going to or from an investigation, your car may suddenly die on you for no apparent reason. For that reason, it is a good idea to carry a cellular telephone with you, if you have one. You really should have one if you do case work, if for no other reason than to be able to call the client's house when you are hopelessly lost trying to find them. However, if you bless you car or sprinkle holy water on it, this usually prevents any problems. In cases of severe demonic infestation, investigators have reported seeing apparitions in their cars. In some cases, a presence is felt. There have also been reports of being touched or pinched while driving. This is an attempt to scare you and it works! It is an attempt to try to get you to injure yourself by causing an accident. The most important thing to remember is that this is a scare tactic. The only threat of real danger lies in how you respond to the situation. Put yourself in the white light and do not be afraid to tell your unwanted guess go to hell… literally. Do not forget though, do so in God's name.

The above example is an extreme and it is very rare. These are some common forms of attack. A severe situation only arises in cases where there is a strong demonic presence and where that presence feels that you are its main threat. Another from of the extreme would consist of being pushed down stairs or otherwise tripped. Again, physical attacks are rare and are usually reserved for the one who will be attempting to banish the entity.

One of the more common and nerve wracking problems you may face are lights that will not come on when you need them or they go off at a critical time. This usually happens on the site of the investigation but it does sometimes happen in the investigators home. You will find yourself facing a barrage of annoyances. Things have a tendency to break around your home causing any number of problems. Bulbs will break, faucets will leak, and telephones will not operate. The pizza you put in the oven 12 seconds ago will burn to a crisp. The TV is going to act up in the bottom of the ninth when you favorite pitcher is pitching a perfect game. Hot water heaters will break and other major appliances will act bizarre. Get the picture? These things happen under very natural circumstances so do not race for the holy water whenever a light bulb burns out. You can go through a lot of holy water that way, not to mention being locked in your nearest mental hospital for telling all of your friends and relatives that the devil is the reason why your hot dogs keep burning. All I am saying here is that you will experience situations where many things may go wrong at once. This could be bad luck but it could also be a warning. Just try not to read anything into a single event.

You may find that you are followed after an investigation. We sometimes bring things back with us after working a case. That too comes with the turf. It is a job where you can most definitely take your work home with you. We know enough to protect ourselves in obvious haunting situations. We have to remember to do that even on those investigations where nothing seems to be happening. Because we do not see it does not mean it is not there. It is the "better to be safe than sorry" theory.

This is hardest on our families, especially those living with you. However, it can, affect other family members, even if they do not live with you, especially the ones closest to you. You may find yourself accident-prone. You may suddenly get sick on the day of an investigation. Flu like symptoms, complete with high temperatures has been known to happen. More than one investigator has had a bad case of the runs while driving to a case. Again, do not become paranoid and blame a demon for your heartburn after you just ate 5-alarm chili but realize that illnesses do occur.

The purpose of this is not to scare you away. I have mentioned these things because they *can* happen to you but that is not to say they *will.* There may be many things that I failed to mention. The point is that there are some risks involved when you deal with the paranormal and you have to be aware of them. It would be wrong to let anyone get involved in an investigation without knowing what can happen. But remember, can does not will. Take this seriously because this is a serious business. However, have fun with it too.

Investigators Are Unique

These types of problems do not happen before every investigation. When you see the phrase "these are the things that commonly happen," it does not mean that activity happens often, it just means that when things *do* happen, these are the most common things that do. Surely, if phenomena occurred in the homes of investigators before every case, there would not be too many investigators left. It is safe to say that in the vast majority of cases, nothing seriously bad happens. You may go throughout your entire career in this field without ever experiencing major unusual phenomena. Also, just as hauntings themselves can happen to one family and not another, some investigators will report problems from time to time while others never do. To be honest though, minor stuff happens to most of us.

We do not know why this happens although the theory is that some people are just more susceptible than others. This may have to do with the psychic abilities of a given individual. The strength of their discernment abilities play a major role too. Those with the strongest abilities to discern will likely be more susceptible than someone who has very little discernment ability. Personal belief systems probably play a role too. There are sometimes what we call "victim souls." Another factor is fear. Someone who is easily scared will often be targeted more often than one who is not. Remember that demons are bullies. They will pick on the most vulnerable target first. Experience plays a major role too. More experienced investigators know what to expect, have experience in dealing with it when it occurs, and are better at protecting themselves. Newer investigators may find themselves tested from time to time. Remember that these are not things that will happen often. It is just that when they do happen, this is the type of thing that happens most commonly.

New Investigators Need Supervision

Every new investigator should always talk to a more experienced one before making the decision to go into a home. In the beginning, you should never be given an assignment by yourself. You would always be teamed with an experienced investigator. It is best to discuss a few cases with an experienced investigator before going on one. You will find that experienced investigators love talking about past cases and will gladly share their knowledge, almost to the point where your eyes glaze over or you want to strangle them. They may also tell you things that are not included here. We each see events differently and have different ways of handling them. We always share our experiences with other investigators and vice versa.

To sum this up, there are risks involved and you need to know them. However, there are many rewards too. What it all boils down to is that you have all of the information you can possibly get in order to make the final decision on whether to stay in this field and in what capacity. I will now include a general list of do's and don'ts that pertain to the investigators.

Investigator Do's & Don'ts

1) Whenever possible, work in pairs. In many cases, this is difficult, depending on the number of investigators and the size of the site being investigated. If you can do it though, it is a good idea. Finding yourself in a dark basement and hearing growling is a lot easier to take when you have someone with you. It is the old strength in numbers routine.

2) Always carry a flashlight that works. This is one of my main foibles but it is very important. Since much of the investigation is done in the dark, a working flashlight is necessary if you are going to avoid banging into things when you are on the move. In addition, it can be quite frightening to have all the lights go out while you are up in someone's attic and you are not expecting it. In one case I worked, I had a tape recorder set up in the basement of the house. When it was time to change the tape, I started going down the stairs when I realized that I had not taken my flashlight. I figured it was no big deal since I would only be down there for a second. I did think to myself that I hoped the spirit would not turn the light off. Sure enough, as soon as that thought registered in my head, the lights went out. Needless to say, I banged my shin on something and tripped as well. With that thought in mind, do not just grab the old flashlight that has been sitting in your car since the Eisenhower administration and expect it to work. Always test your light before going on an investigation and always carry spare batteries and an extra bulb or two. Batteries are easily drained when a spirit uses their energy to manifest.

3) Always protect yourself. Even seasoned investigators sometimes forget to do this. (Me!) Always remember to say protection prayers and put yourself in the white light. Also, use common sense. Should you suddenly feel threatened, get out of the area. I am not referring to the natural fear that everyone experiences; I am talking about the sense that you are suddenly in danger. Always follow your senses. Do not expose yourself to increased danger just to get that one last picture. Be sure to locate a convenient exit and use it.

4) Carry religious objects with you. Holy water should always be with you whenever you go on an investigation. The types of objects you bring are determined by your particular religious beliefs. For Christians, crosses are common. Relics are also a great thing to have. Again, follow your religious beliefs. I would like to make one suggestion though. If you are wearing something like a cross or medal around your neck, wear it under your clothing. Chains have a way of being broken and if that happens, you do not want to lose something precious. By wearing it under your shirt, it will likely stay in your clothes. My wife Pat and I went to a cemetery one night where we had gotten many good photos. On that particular night, there seemed to be something different about the place. Normally it felt peaceful there but that night, I sensed that we were not welcome. After shooting a roll of film, I got the feeling that we would be wise to leave. It was not fear that I felt, just a sense of dread. I long ago learned to trust my feelings. To make a long story short, when we got back to the car, Pat realized that her cross and a relic she was wearing were missing. This ticked me off big time because both of those items were very old. I wanted to go back and look for them but Pat felt that we should just leave. I went back the next day hoping to find them. Of course, that was like looking for a needle in a haystack. Amazingly enough, I did find them. They were together on a path we had not been near the night before. Oddly enough, in order to put them back on the chain, I had to open the clasp; there was no way they could have simply fallen off.

5) Never, ever challenge an entity. It is impossible to stress this enough. There is nothing to gain and everything to lose if you challenge it. You may be dealing with a demon and it has all of the advantages. Space, time, or the laws of physics do not bind it. Moreover, it will usually take you up on the challenge. In some cases, you might issue a challenge and the entity might respond by doing something to your spouse or a team member. That is done to cause you the most grief. Only through the power of God can a demon be defeated, not through man. Even if the spirit is not demonic, I still would not issue a challenge. It is invisible; you are not. There is nothing to be gained by it.

6) Do not respond to voices or commands. If you are in a house with a lot of activity and you hear a voice tell you to go down to the basement, do not do it. You have no idea what may be waiting for you or what you might find. I am not saying that the spirit will attack you but it may have set a trap like putting something on the stairs that will cause you to fall. The exception to this rule would be if something told you to go into a room where you know someone else is in it. They may be in danger and need your help.

7) Try to avoid panic. You will be scared; if you are not it may be a good idea to check your pulse. Mark Twain once remarked, "Courage is resistance to fear, mastery of fear, not absence of fear." However, panic can be avoided by falling back on your training. Doctors, nurses, and paramedics all find themselves in situations where panic is just beneath the surface and that is how they are able to do their job. In addition, if you panic in front of the people you are trying to help, the results for the family can be devastating. They are looking to you for support and you need to be able to provide that for them. After particularly frightening activity, many an investigator has calmly walked outside, ostensibly to have a cigarette and discovered their hands beginning to shake. It happens so don't fret it. Just do you best to keep yourself "together" as much as possible. I tend to use humor when something serious happens.

8) Never diagnose the problem until you are 100% sure of the problem. Always keep in mind the scientific equation: what do we think, what do we know, what can we prove? We may think we know what the problem is. We may even know in our heart and soul what the problem is. However, we can only tell the client what we can prove. Can you imagine the terror you can inflict on someone if you tell them that there are demons from hell running loose in their home when in fact, that is not the case. In the past year, I have worked on 2 cases that were "diagnosed" as being demonic in origin by "leading experts in the field." (That may be true if you count marketing as their field of expertise. God knows they have gone a long way with little to sell.) In both instances, there were human, benign spirits at work. For that matter, there was evidence that they were benevolent. In one house, the "demon" covered a child when it was cold. That sounds real demonic to me. In the other case, the "demon" played Christmas music. I cannot imagine that there are too many demons around that pay homage to Christ. In both cases, the results of the mistaken diagnosis were terrible. One immediately put up a "For Sale" sign in front of the house. Once they victims realized that what was in their home was not demonic or evil, much of the activity settled down. When things did occur, the family was not nearly as frightened as they were before. In some senses, they were even grateful.

9) Make sure you always record and document activity. You should record anything that seems to be paranormal. It is always better to have many items that are not paranormal recorded than to miss one thing that is. During your skull sessions, or gatherings with other investigators, you can throw out what is most likely to be a natural occurrence. You can use the weighing system that you will see soon to help with this. In addition, it is important that you keep your records up to date. Should you need to look for outside help, your records will be very important. It is amazing how much information there is to document even on those nights when nothing seemed to have happened. It can add up in a hurry if you are not careful. However, all of your documentation must be in order should you have to make a case for someone else. Besides, it is very easy to forget things when you are tired. The one thing you forget may turn out to be important.

10) Never lose sight of how much pressure the family is under. They are going through something that is terrible beyond imagination. Not only are they experiencing bizarre phenomena, their entire model of their world has probably crumbled. At times, this will show up in their demeanor. Do not take harsh statements made by them to heart. You are the one they have turned to for help, so it is only natural for them to lash out at you. "Why can't you stop this?" and the like. Be tolerant and understanding of their situation. It can be difficult when you are giving so much of your time and energy into helping them but what they are experiencing must be taken into account. Yes, you will occasionally come across a client that is harsh to the point of being abusive. Try as best you can to understand what they are feeling but don't become a doormat either.

11) Remember your own family. This is something that affects all investigators at some point in their career. When you are working on a case, especially an active one, it is very easy to forget your own family. If you are going to keep your marriage together and your career going, you must find a balance. When you are working a case, it is easy to become obsessed with it. You may spend weekend after weekend working it. However, if you do that, you are neglecting your family. In the beginning you may find that your family is very supportive. However, as the case wears on, it will begin to take a toll on your family. They may feel neglected. They may be frightened about the case itself.

You have to find a balance and that is not always easy. If you and your family have been looking forward to an upcoming wedding, don't cancel out at the last minute. That can result in resentment and lead your family to believe that they are playing second fiddle. That you do not want. Let me tell you a quick story. The organization I was working with at the time had set up an investigation at the famous Ledge Lighthouse in New London. We had a date scheduled and it was all I thought about for weeks. The night before we were supposed to go, one member said they could not make it, so they rescheduled it for the next weekend. The only problem for me was that I was going to a wedding with my wife on the day they set up the new investigation. I thought about it quite a bit. However, as badly as I wanted to go on the investigation, I knew my wife would be either sad or hurt. It did not take me long to decide. I opted for the wedding. Besides, no matter how interesting the case may be, there is always the risk of burnout. You need a break every once in a while too.

INVESTIGATOR BYLAWS

1) Always protect yourself.

2) Always be professional.

3) Never be judgmental.

4) Primary goal is to help the client.

5) What the client says goes. (To a point)

6) Respect the client's privacy.

7) Be sensitive to the client's needs.

8) Never put yourself at risk.

9) Always respect each other.

10) Never lose sight of your role.

11) Always be thorough.

12) Any one can leave at any time.

13) Always remain positive.

The above bylaws are for the most part common sense but they are very important and therefore we will go over them. They cover how we investigate from our standpoint and the standpoint of our clients. How well an investigation turns out often depends on how closely we follow these guidelines. We have to keep in mind that our main goal is to help the client. Part of that has to do with creating an atmosphere where the client feels comfortable *with* us and has confidence *in* us. We can create that atmosphere by acting in a professional and friendly manner. We also have to be as human as possible and that means to be as kind, courteous, and understanding as possible. However, we also have to make sure that we are doing everything possible to ensure our safety as well as the client's safety. Let us take a closer look at these bylaws.

Item # 1 Always protect yourself is the most obvious and most important. We can do that in a number of ways. Prayer is the best way. The most important thing is that you do believe in God. It is by far your best defense before, during and after an investigation. Before starting an investigation, it is always a wise idea to say a prayer before leaving your home. This leaves nothing to chance and it helps you to prepare for your investigation. It is also a good idea to bless the house and your pets. It is not uncommon for activity to break out in your own home before and during an investigation. After spending a long night with your client, the last thing you want to find when you get home is a mess in your own home. It does happen. Also, bless you car. You want to insure that you will get to your destination safely and in as timely a manner as possible. More than one investigator has found that their car will not start prior to going on an investigation or they get stuck in some desolate location. These do not have to be longwinded prayers, just ask God to protect you and yours. In addition, you should always keep holy water around the house and with you during an investigation. It works no matter what religion you believe in. If it turns out that the phenomena are of natural origin, you certainly do no harm by praying for yourself. Also, always keep holy water in your car. This is a "just in case" item. Should you find yourself sharing a ride with something you cannot see, the holy water will come in handy. This is especially true if you are driving alone. The last thing you need is to be driving in horrible weather conditions and when you look in your rear view mirror and see someone's smiling face looking at you from the back seat. That will get the blood pumping fast. There seems to be some safety in numbers so if you can, go with someone when you are heading out on a case.

Item # 2 Always be professional. This is one rule that cannot be stressed enough. How you present yourself and how you behave affects both your reputation as well as your organizations reputation. It also has a strong effect on the family you are trying to help. Behaving in an unprofessional manner makes everyone look bad and as I said, acting unprofessionally can also ruin your reputation. It takes a lot of time and hard work to build a good reputation, especially in a field as open to criticism as this one is. However, that can be destroyed in one night. Such is the nature of this business. In addition to that, the family is looking to you for help. You must act in a manner that gives them the utmost confidence in you. That in itself will make them stronger, which in turn makes them a little less susceptible to the paranormal influences in the home. Does this mean that you should be rigid and stuffy? Absolutely not. You want your personality to show. You want to appear "human." It is good to display a sense of humor. I cannot stress enough that humor is a tremendous weapon in a haunting situation. However, acting like the class clown will hurt your reputation. Being too formal is no good either. You need to establish a rapport with the client if you are to have a good chance of helping them. You just have to avoid going overboard. It is best to relax and just be yourself. Always avoid extremes. Also, work with your team. If you have trouble getting along with another investigator, keep that from the client. Never let them see an internal dispute. That can screw up a case in a heartbeat. If there is a major disagreement, take it outside or wait until you sit down for a post investigation skull session. Never argue in front of a client.

Item #3 Never be judgmental is very important. As we know, finding out why something is there can be critical in an investigation. In order for us to determine that, we need the help of the family. If they sense that we may be critical of them, they may not tell us all the information we need to know. Here is an example. Let us say that the family has used a Ouija board a number of times. That can be a critical piece of information to us as it tells us that we may be dealing with a spirit of the occult. This is the worst kind of spirit to deal with. If the family thinks that they will be criticized for using the Ouija board, they may feel it is better to keep that information to themselves. That can cost all of us considerable time and effort. Right from the start, we must make the family feel comfortable about telling us everything. I have used Ouija boards so when I ask a client about their possible usage, I always tell them how I have used one in the past. I will also tell them why they should be avoided and I will do that using example from my own usage. They must see that we are supportive of them and not judgmental. They must realize that we need that information only to better help them, not to pass judgment on them. The last thing you want to do in a haunting situation is create an atmosphere of guilt. That alone can add strength to the haunting.

Item # 4 The Primary goal is to help the client. This item is the easiest one on the list to forget. During an investigation, we are trying to gather evidence. We want to get as much as we possibly can so that we can make an accurate assessment regarding what is transpiring there and who or what is behind it. That helps us to determine how best to deal with whatever is there. However, the major goal is to help the client. While gathering evidence can be crucial to that goal, there often comes a time when we have the opportunity to get more evidence but also have the ability to end the paranormal happenings. When this happens, we have to remember that ending the phenomena or in some cases, understanding it, is the ultimate goal. Once we have enough evidence to make a conclusion, it needs to be presented to whatever authority is going to actually attempt to stop it, assuming that is that it is a negative spirit at work. That can be a clergyman, a demonologist, or even a psychologist, depending on the results of our investigation. If we can end a situation without even taking one picture, then we have to do that. I realize that this can be extremely hard to do sometimes. We rarely get the opportunity to record great evidence but there may come a time when you have to pass up that chance if it will help the person you are working with. For example, seeing poltergeist-like phenomena can be awesome and it is great to catch that on film. However, in thirty seconds time, everything precious to the client may be destroyed. That is not worth the pictures. Besides, the victims are already under incredible stress so the quicker it ends, the better off they will be.

Item # 5 Whatever the client says goes (to a point) can be the toughest of these rules to follow. If a client decides that a certain part of the house is off limits, then it is off limits. It is certainly appropriate to explain why you may need access to that area but we have to respect the client's wishes, even if it makes our job more difficult. The same is true if the client only wants a certain number of investigators involved. Again, you should try to accommodate their request. However, if their requests create a situation where it makes it all but impossible for you to do your job properly or safely, then you can turn down their request for an investigation or cancel it at the point where the problem arises. We always have that option available to us. We will not work any investigation where our safety is needlessly compromised by a client's request. That is where you have to draw the line. Also, if their request means that the investigation will end up lasting forever, drop it by all means. However, rare is the case where a client will insist on something that will hurt the case. You will almost always find that the client will do anything you ask. When they appear not to be, a red flag should go up. If there is just one room that is off limits, you have to ask yourself what they are hiding in there. It could be Hoffa's body or Kennedy's brain. It could also be an altar where satanic rituals have taken place. However, if they ask you not to smoke or something like that, then don't. If they want everybody to take off their shoes, then do so. Again, it is really just common sense. I did a case where everyone in the household tried to be as cooperative as possible with the exception of one member of the family. She refused to talk to me and would not allow me to enter her bedroom. I explained to the rest of the family that it would be difficult to help them without at least being able to see what was in the room. One person admitted that she allowed no one to enter her room under any circumstances. They suspected that she was doing some form of ritual in there. That was probably the case. In any event, it was a single night investigation. I would not put my team or myself in a potentially dangerous situation under those circumstances.

Item # 6 Respecting the privacy of the client is crucial. Never give out the client's name to anyone not associated with the investigation without the permission of the client as well as the group leader. Publicity seldom, if ever helps an investigation. It will only turn the situation into a circus and make it all but impossible to continue with the investigation. More importantly, it will make the client's life far more miserable. Often the effect of the publicity becomes even worse than the problem that brought the publicity in the first place. It is sad to think that humans can sometimes prove to be more of a problem that a demon from hell but it has happened a frightening number of times. In addition, when word of a haunting leaks out, it can be very rough on the children, who will almost invariably get teased cruelly at school. It may also cause grief in the adult's workplace as well. Once word of a haunting gets out, every whack job in the neighborhood comes out and camps out in front of the house.

Item # 7 Be sensitive to the clients needs. There comes a time when you have to back off from the investigation in order to give the client some space. Sometimes that is a blessing. If a case is severe, the victims may want you to do everything short of moving in with them. Needless to say, that can cause some problems. Should that be the case, you have to do a balancing act. You cannot afford to spend all of your spare time with them but you do want to help them as much as possible. You do not do them any good if you allow yourself to burn out. Tired minds make mistakes at an alarming rate. There is no easy solution. On the other hand, you might have a situation where activity is taking place in front of you right from the get go. That too can be a problem. While you may be collecting lots of evidence, they may need to have some sense of normalcy again. That is when you have to back off for a time. That does not mean that you should abandon them, it just means that there may come a time where you need to back off for a week or so. In other cases, you may find that you have to play the role of counselor. This can be a tough one because you have to limit yourself to only giving advice related to the haunting. Certainly there will be times when you just cannot give them what they want. There are not always answers to every problem. When you are stumped, you have to be honest about that. Do the best that you can walking that tightrope. Remember that our number one goal is to help the client. We have to be as sensitive as possible to their needs, whatever they may be.

Item # 8 Never put yourself at risk. This cannot be emphasized enough. Staying in a dangerous situation to try to get that last picture can get you injured. If objects start flying around, you have to be careful. However, whenever you feel threatened, get out. There is no need to be a hero. If there is that much activity going on, you will get your pictures and all of the other evidence you want. Always follow your instincts; they are usually right. If that little voice in your head tells you to leave an area, do so. That is not to say that the minute you feel frightened you should leave. You would not be of much help in that case. However, there will be times when something is telling you to leave, some inner voice. It may be on a haunting where you are helping someone or it may be in a haunted house that you are visiting for fun. These feelings are very different from fear. You only have to experience it once to know what I am talking about. Another point has to be made again. Never challenge an entity. That can be disastrous! If you happen to find yourself in a demonic case, you have to remember that demons will accept your challenge. Do not confront them. Keep in control of your emotions as much as possible. Anger especially can get you in trouble. Drill that into your client's heads too. Also, never respond to a voice that you cannot verify. If something calls your name from a room where you know no one is in, do not go in there! That is very important. You have no idea what might be waiting there or what it wants. In all likelihood the worst that will happen is that something will be done to frighten you. However, that is not a chance for you to take.

Item # 9 Always respect each other. You would think that this item goes without saying but surprisingly, it does not. There are many egos out there and many who are "experts" out there and more still that mistake themselves for the case. Unfortunately, you may find yourself working with someone who thinks he is the ultimate authority. (Of all things!) Try to ignore that person as best you can. There are jerks in every field, this one included. Make sure you show respect to your comrades, especially the veteran ones. Respect their knowledge. I have come across a few cases where people who had miniscule experience act as if they are the great and powerful Oz. They may laugh at the older guys because they are the *real* experts. Also, there are many different types of paranormal investigators. There are demonologists, psychic photographers, light trance mediums, and parapsychologists, to mention some. Beware of labels or titles. Titles mean nothing in this business and they can come back to bite you. Everyone involved in an investigation plays an important role. This applies to everyone involved, whether their contribution is on-site or off. The people that help out with the paperwork, the note taking, the filing, reports, activity sheets, cataloging of pictures, all play an important role. If you do not believe me, try going through 200 pictures looking for the one shot that you got on your last investigation. Or was that two investigations ago? Do you see my point? Investigations often result in mountains of paper work. If someone did not do the clerical work, we would have less time to do the on site work.

Item # 10 Never lose sight of your role. We are paranormal investigators, not exorcists. Our safety in an investigation may very well depend on how clear we are in our role. In a situation where an inhuman spirit may be involved, we are at risk enough just by being the investigators. We are a threat to the entity or so it may believe. That puts you in the forefront and more accurately, in the crosshairs. If you go into a case thinking that you are going to fight this thing, then you are putting your clients and yourself in unnecessary danger. Make sure you know exactly what you are dealing with and plan you strategy accordingly. If you have the misfortune of finding yourself in a negative haunting, the last thing you want to do is overstep your training and ability. Also, while the victim may come to depend on you for advice, you have to make sure that you stick only to the haunting. You cannot try to solve family problems. Believe me, they sometimes come up. You may ask in your interview if they can think of anything really negative happening in the house that might be feeding a negative spirit and they may tell you there are marriage problems. Fine, stop there because the next thing you know, they think you are Dr. Ruth. Tread carefully in that area. You are not a marriage counselor nor are you a psychotherapist.

Item # 11 Be as thorough as possible. No matter how many investigations you have been on, never assume anything. Just because you think you have dealt with a particular type of paranormal happening twenty times, always investigate it as if you have never seen it before. This is a very humbling profession as I have found out the hard way on more than one occasion. Often an investigation starts one way and it turns out to be something completely different. Assuming anything can only get you in trouble. Do not take shortcuts just because that is what you did at the "so and so" haunting. Miscalculating a case can lead to nasty results. You can end up looking like a fool and the last thing you need to do is develop a bad reputation. It is hard to gain respect in this field so it does not take much to ruin a good reputation. You can also prolong a case by misreading it. You might miss a simple solution because you have interpreted the evidence incorrectly. As in life, there are sometimes strange twists in a haunting. Do not take anything for granted. Also, avoid sloppy reports and notes. It is very easy to miss clues if you note taking is poor are your work habits are sloppy. You should always be as neat as possible. This is especially true where you are going to share your notes and it is critical if you need outside help to end a haunting.

Item # 12 Anyone can leave at any time is so important to remember. There is no way to prepare yourself fully for what you may face. I can tell you 2000 times how loud rapping can be but until you hear it for yourself, you are never prepared. We can talk all we want about the various types of phenomena we will face. The fact is that no one knows how they will react until they are actually facing the situation. (I will offer suggestions about this topic in a later chapter.) Many people get into this field with the best of intentions only to find that they cannot do it. There is no shame in this. Not everyone can do this. It does not make the ones who can any better than the ones who cannot. We each have our own abilities, those things we *can* do. I could never be a paramedic. Sure, I can learn all about the job. I just do not have the makeup to do that. I really do not think I could deal with the pressure of saving someone's life on a daily basis. The same is true with any profession. Not everyone can do everything. If at any time you decide that you cannot do this, remember that you can withdraw at any time with no questions asked. This is true if you want to leave an investigation or if you do not feel comfortable doing a particular assignment within an investigation. Make a fair assessment. If you do not think you can sit alone in a darkened room waiting for something to appear, be honest about that. There is no shame in that but it is best if you know that before hand. It is not a good thing to lose your cool in front of a client.

Item # 13 Always remain positive is very important for the sake of the client. If we appear negative, this is going to rub off on them. If we act positively, that may rub off as well. Dealing with a frightened client is similar to dealing with a spirit in the sense that both feed off of your emotions, although they do so in a different way. The client will often pick up on your mood and change theirs to match yours. That is not a good thing. You always have to keep in mind that we are only going to be in the home for a limited amount of time. They have to live in it all of the time. If they stay in a negative mood, the haunting will likely grow worse. Investigations can be incredibly stressful and therefore, the time may come when you need to skip an investigation or two, especially when they are coming on the heels of another case. You might go months without a case and then, bang, you get three in a row. It happens to everyone at some point. It is far better to skip one than to let yourself become negative because you won't be doing anyone any good. You won't be doing yourself much of a favor either. Living with a negative mindset is horrible, plain and simple. However, it can happen to anyone. Walk away from the field before you let that happen to you.

Conclusion

The above rules should give you an idea about how to handle an investigation, big and small. Never minimize their importance. They are just as important in a small case where you are visiting a haunted hotel as they are in a demon-infested house. They are not all inclusive by any means and you should therefore always exercise common sense. It is all about making things as easy as possible. When you have parameters around which to work, it can take away a substantial amount of guesswork. If you have basic rules to follow, you will avoid falling into any of the myriad problems you may face in a haunting. Always keep things as simple and straightforward as possible. In the long run, it will save you a considerable amount of grief.

SKULL SESSIONS

Skull sessions are referred to by different names such as briefing or debriefing sessions. (Debriefing sessions being post investigation skull sessions.) If you think about and I am going to be corny here, (You have been forewarned) skull means head so if you want to put your heads together, as you should before an investigation, it would be a skull session. Okay, so I am not a great humorist. Sorry. The purpose of these sessions is to discuss the case before going on site and again after leaving the site, if possible. Both of these sessions are important. When you are going on an investigation, especially for the first time, there are many things you need to know. Chances are that some form of interview will have taken place before going on site. It probably was not a formal interview but the fact that you have decided to investigate means you do know something about the case. You should have enough information for you to make an assumption of what might be happening with the client. For example, if you were told that objects routinely fly around the house, you know a little of what to expect and everyone can be warned. At that point, someone might decide that it is not a case they feel comfortable working. Every investigator should know every bit of information available before going in. Ideally, you want as few surprises as possible on the night the investigation begins, especially the type will hamper your efforts. An example would be arriving at the house in question and seeing twelve cars parked in the driveway. However, that is another issue altogether. For the sake of thus chapter, we are interested in what you might expect in terms of the actual haunting.

ROLE OF THE LIGHT TRANCE MEDIUM

No one should ever walk into a potentially haunted house without an adequate idea of what might be encountered. The only exception to this rule is with a light trance medium. LTM's, as I will call them from now on, are individuals who have the ability to discern or sense the presence of spirits. There are different forms of discernment, as you will see later. However, in short, a LTM can sometimes make contact with any spirits that may be involved in a haunting. Well-developed mediums can actually tell you not only whether there is a spirit present but may be able to tell you how many are operating there at any given time. We will talk more about mediums later. I should point out that over time, you might reach the point where you will also be able to do this, as well. The LTM may also be able to tell whether the spirit is human or inhuman. Although you must still investigate the phenomena fully in order to be sure about what is going on, the LTM can save you considerable time by giving the investigation direction.

As a rule, the LTM is not involved in the skull session that takes place before the investigation. The reason for this is simple. The information the LTM is going to gather is based on their "feelings." For that reason, you do not want them going in with any preconceived notions. If all goes well, the findings of the LTM will coincide with the information obtained from the client. This confirmation can be very important. In a haunting situation, images are routinely projected into the minds of the investigators. This tends to happen more with the LTM's. What they pick up and where they pick it up can make or break a case. We need to have independent assessments to come up with a complete picture. Let us say that one particular bedroom has a lot of activity. By having the LTM pick out that one room confirms the gathered information. If the medium knows from prior client information that certain types of phenomena occur in that room, it can cloud his or her ability to be objective. The LTM will be involved in the skull session at the end of the day's investigation.

Formulating An Investigation Plan

Another reason to have a skull session before entering the site is to formulate a plan of action. Things do not always go according to plan but investigations, if they are to be successful, need to be organized. The last thing you want is confusion once everyone is on site. It does not look good and it also slows things down a lot. Another point is that during the pre-investigation meeting, many ideas can be shared. We all see things from our own vantage point and sometimes that results in a form of tunnel vision. Everyone thinks differently and every opinion is important. You would be surprised at how many times someone has come up with a suggestion that can make a big difference. There have been numerous situations where someone with very little training and experience has come up with a valid point. In many cases, it turns out that all of the experienced investigators missed that point. For that reason, never be too proud to ask questions of newcomers. You will often find a wealth of information that way. In a serious haunting, pride, arrogance and egotism can be a big problem. Let me give you an example. When you are discussing a case, it may have similarities to a case one of the other investigators worked on. If that is the case, you can discuss what was done on that case, what worked and what didn't. That might save you a little time when you work your case. It may also help you determine who you want working the case or who you definitely do not want working it. You may be able to avoid any number of pitfalls that took place on the other case. Either way, it may be a valuable bit of information to have. Use everything you can to help you work a case.

These pre-investigation meetings are not designed to be rah-rah types of motivation. Everyone knows why he or she is there so there is no need for a motivational speech. These sessions are to create a game plan and to prepare for those things that somehow always manage to go wrong. Therefore, the meeting is designed to prepare for any contingency. In many cases, no matter how much planning was done, something always seems to happen to destroy the plan. On more than one occasion, I have thrown up my hands and started an investigation from scratch. Therefore, you need to have alternate plans. It also gives you the opportunity to discuss specific assignments and help you determine where to put investigators. We each bring a different skill to an investigation and no one role is more important than another. It truly must be a team effort if the investigation is to be successful. However, there are instances where some people are more suited to a particular function. You have to play from your strengths. When you work with the same investigators enough, you get a feel for how they work and this makes the association more workable. Some investigators have more discernment ability than others while some are better photographers. Planning cuts down on a lot of the confusion that usually is present at the start of any investigation. Remember that organization is very important to the success of the investigation. It also gives the client the right impression.

Now, it is not always possible to set up the pre-investigation meetings for a variety of reasons. Time and distance traveled by investigators can create havoc. Availability is also a factor. You might be able to get your investigators together for the case itself but it may be difficult to get everyone together for the meetings prior to going in. Let's face it, we all have to work and that can make planning difficult. In some instances, you are forced to go in without a plan. Still, once you have done a few with the same crew, you already have a solid framework in place and everyone starts off with a good idea of what is expected and needed. This is one reason why it is good to have a small group of individuals work with you all of the time. It makes things much easier.

The Post Investigation Session

The post investigation discussion is very important. However, after you have been up all night doing the investigation, the last thing you want to do is have a meeting. The meeting does not have to be conducted that day. However, you should plan to have one as soon as possible while everything is still fresh in everyone's mind. There is much to learn from these meetings. No two people are alike and no two people see the same thing the same way. Everyone has a different understanding of the investigation. The wise team leader listens to everyone's opinion. We all miss things. Take anyone who writes for a living. You may think you have gotten all the typos out but chances are you did not. In fact, I can almost guarantee it. We tend to see things from our own vantage point. We are influenced by our own feelings. That is why you should listen to even the most inexperienced investigator. What they have to say could be vitally important. The post site session should be done before going back into the site. You are not necessarily going to have a skull session every time you go into the site. You will have the initial one, after that, you will discuss your findings, and set up a new strategy during the post site session. An exception to that would be if you experienced a particularly active or harrowing night or if you are planning to try an experiment of some sort. In that case, you may set up a meeting before going back onto the site.

These post investigation sessions give everyone the opportunity to compare notes. You can also assess how many people you might need for future sessions. You may determine that you need one or two more due to the activity witnessed. You may decide you need less. This is also the time to determine if someone wants out of that particular case. This can only help the big picture. Whenever you have an open forum discussion, people tend to feed off each other's experiences. For example, I may have been up in the attic of the home while another investigator was in the basement. I may have felt that nothing much was going on but that other investigator may state that he heard three loud knocks in the basement and some doors began slamming downstairs right after the knocking. Then, although I did not notice it before, I may have realized that at one point I did hear three faint knocks followed by a soft bang. At the time, I may have written this off as the door closing from a draft. Now, we have discovered a pattern. Three knocks occur just before doors start slamming shut. We can then set up a strategy. When we hear three knocks, we will point the camcorders towards the nearest door. This is an example of making something out of seemingly nothing. It also serves as a reminder to me to pay more attention when I hear something.

At post sessions, investigators should review activity logs and reports, if they have been done. (And they should have.) It also gives each investigator an opportunity to state their feelings. An investigator may have sensed something around two thirty a.m. That is important to know. As a result of that information, you may decide to stake out that particular area at around the same time. You may want to set up some equipment there as well. Granted, nothing may happen but still, it is worth taking the chance, especially if you are finding little usable evidence. It is also important to know how the investigator felt and reacted to the phenomena. It is a way of relieving some of the stress brought on by the investigation. Stress and terror can be a major part of the job although boredom and frustration are by far more common. Discussing harrowing experiences with other investigators can diffuse much of the tension. It also gives you the chance to suggest better ways of dealing with things. It can help the team leader decide whether or not to continue using that particular investigator. Sometimes an investigator will be frightened badly but they will not say anything because they do not want to appear weak. The team leader must be aware of this. Should he sense that one team member is having a particularly difficult time, he (or she) should wait until the session is over and then talk to that investigator. He may find that the investigator no longer feels able to contribute anything to the case. That does happen, especially on a harrowing case. This allows that person to make their decision without fear of being embarrassed in front of the group. Plus, you have a better idea of the mental makeup of the victims and to see first hand the affect the haunting is having on the family. You also have a better idea of the family dynamics and that may help you down the road. This is where you can assign weights to the phenomena you have witnessed or what has been reported to you from the victims. You may have done this before you went in but now you may have a different perspective on which to rate the phenomena.

Experiencing things first hand can shed an entirely different light on the subject. Also, you have a better idea of whether you have been given an accurate accounting of what has taken place. You might determine that the biggest problem going on is an overactive imagination. You might decide that there really isn't a case there at all. You might also decide that you are dealing with fruit-loops. There is also the possibility that you will decide that there is something more serious going on than you first expected. This is also the time when you can assess what equipment you need or don't need. During one case, I realized that it would have been helpful to have had a couple more motion detectors handy. That meant a trip to Radio Shack. Lastly, you can assess the behavior of the investigators and offer constructive criticism, if needed.

Skull sessions are serious discussions about the phenomena encountered. Having said that, the sessions are also an outlet for the tension every investigator experiences. They will often end up being extremely funny. Enjoy them. Allowing yourself to laugh and have fun balances all of the unpleasant stuff. It is an important defense mechanism for an investigator. In situations of great stress, it is quite common for nervous laughter to occur, sometimes inappropriately. (I am the king of inappropriate laughter.) After discussing the serious aspects of the case, the tendency is to discuss the lighthearted ones. If anything humorous happened that day, (and something almost invariably does) you can bet that it will be discussed in the skull session. For example, let us say that you are sitting around a table with other investigators and members of the family. You have just witnessed something quite frightening and everyone's nerves are on edge. Then suddenly, seemingly out of nowhere, the family cat jumps onto your lap. You let out a startled scream before you realize what just happened. I guarantee you everyone there will crack up and you will be the subject of great barbs at the skull session. Laughter is a good thing. The tension and fear need to be released and humor is the best way to do it. You can burn out quickly if you do not inject a little humor into the situation, or you make the mistake of taking yourself too seriously. You have to be able to laugh. It breaks up the tension and it helps you relax as well. In a good skull session, that is what happens.

Another reason to hold this session is to correct any major problems that took place in the previous investigation. If there was a situation where one person refused to carry out an assignment, get it resolved here. One thing that can ruin an investigation is dissention between investigators. You cannot have that in someone's house. I should point out that it is important that you not let these sessions become "bitch" sessions if there have been conflicts between investigators. You will find that you do not always agree with everything that other investigators believe. There is room for disagreement and that can and should be discussed before anyone goes back into the house. The important thing is to work out any problems or kinks before the next trip to the site. This brings us to the next topic: your equipment.

THE INVESTIGATOR'S EQUIPMENT

You have no doubt seen television programs of paranormal investigators walking through some famous haunted location. Those shows are quite popular today and I for one love them. Although they never have much of a conclusion, they are fun to watch. It is common on those shows to see an investigator walking around with a Gauss meter. Upon seeing this, many amateur investigators will run out and buy one of their own. They are quite useful if you know what to do with them and what the readings mean. More often than not, a scholarly looking investigator will explain how he is getting "unusually high" readings of electromagnetic energy fields. They may also say how they have found "anomalous" temperature readings. More times than not, they will basically shrug their shoulders and say things like: "These types of readings often signify "paranormal activity." They may even be so bold as to suggest that a spirit is behind their odd readings. That is pretty much where it ends. These shows are for entertainment more so than anything else. Call it informative entertainment. They are usually about a haunted hotel or the Winchester house or a lighthouse or two. These places will stay haunted because there is no reason to try to stop the haunting. Many establishments even go so far as to advertise their ghosts. It is all in fun and it is great for ghost hunters because they can have a good time and do so safely.

On some programs, you will see an actual case where the haunting is not so fun and not so benign. On these shows, you will hear the same stuff about anomalous readings and the investigators may even suggest that there are nasty if not evil spirits behind the phenomena. Unfortunately, they rarely have conclusions and they rarely follow up on these cases. You are left to wonder whether the hauntings ever stopped. You will almost never hear the word "demon" associated with those cases. All that having been said let us take a look at the equipment you see on those shows and others that can be used and what it all means.

During the initial before site skull session, there is usually a discussion of what equipment is available and how to use it for those who are unfamiliar with them. Most investigators have their own equipment. What usually happens is everyone pools their equipment during the investigation. Organized groups may have equipment that belongs to the group. Either way, there is a considerable amount of equipment available. You can spend as much or as little as you want. Some of it is more useful than others. Let us review some of the equipment available.

In our gadget filled world, there are many devices available to the paranormal investigator. This has made investigations more scientific then ever before. We are able to offer scientific evidence to support our claims. It is not *absolute* scientific proof but it goes a long way towards backing up our assertions regarding the phenomena taking place. This does not convince everyone in the world of mainstream science that ghosts exist but it makes it harder than ever for them to issue out of hand denials.

Digital cameras and camcorders, combined with computers and scanners allow us to see images not seen by the naked eye. Electromagnetic field detectors or Gauss meters measure the amount of electromagnetic energy present. However, they are not ghost meters. What we know is that when spirits manifest themselves, they create an electromagnetic energy field. Both the scientific community and the spiritual community agree on that fact. However, the source of that energy is in dispute. To a parapsychologist, the unusual EMF's are the cause of the activity although they cannot pinpoint the source of that energy. To those who believe in hauntings, it is the spirit that causes the activity and the resulting EMF is a byproduct of that spirit. Therefore, a high reading on the Gauss meter can give you an idea that something is about to happen or is happening. In that sense, they can tell you where to take some pictures. However, many things can generate electromagnetic fields. Fluorescent lights, overhead power lines, TV's, computers, and microwaves (even when they are off) all create these fields. Therefore, it is very important to take baseline readings in all areas of the house. These baseline figures will vary from room to room. You need to spend about ten minutes per room to get a good baseline reading. Once you have established that, you can begin to look for higher than normal readings. More so than any given number, you want to look for spikes in the readings. A reading of ten milligauss does not indicate the present of a spirit. However, if the baseline for that room is two milligauss, you now have to start thinking that something is going on there. When you are not out doing investigations, you can always use your Gauss meter to see what level of electromagnetic energy is coming from your microwave and TV. I have been in houses where I recorded very high EMF's and subsequently took pictures. In many of those cases, I got good shots. At one case, I picked up some mid-range readings and one of my team members picked up an orb on his digital camera. He then shot another picture across the basement and he picked up many orbs. As I walked to that area, the Gauss meter went nuts. That is a nice piece of evidence. However, there have been times when the high readings produced nothing. So here we had a moving electromagnetic field and that is significant since there are not too many natural explanations for that. It becomes a nice piece of evidence. You can get great pictures this way. To further confuse things, I have sometimes gotten great pictures when the meter registered nothing. Just the same, it is a useful toy.

Another very useful item on the market is the night vision scope. It allows you to see images with almost no light whatsoever. This is a great device to have because most of our work is done in the dark. It is not uncommon to see a spirit through the scope, an image you may not have been able to see with the naked eye. It also makes it easier to sit a dark room for hours. The thought of sitting in the dark unnerves some people. (Most, to be honest about it.) Having night vision equipment takes away some of the anxiety. I keep expecting to see an eyeball looking back at me through the scope one day. It will probably happen too since it is a fear of mine. Things we fear often have a way of happening. Talk about unnerving. These scopes are still expensive but they are well worth the money. There are three types of scope referred to as first, second, and third generation. In short, first generation scopes are the early models. Each new generation scope is advanced from the previous one. First or second generation scopes are fine for what we do. Third is overkill. Forget the night vision goggles. They are great but very expensive.

So, just what do we need to conduct an investigation? Well, to get started you need yourself and maybe a camera. What I am saying here is that if you are in a haunted house and the refrigerator is doing a slam dance in the kitchen, it is safe to say that something is going on. However, if you want to document and attempt to offer proof of the haunting, certain things will help you accomplish that goal. Obviously, equipment can be very costly. It is certainly not necessary for you to have all of the equipment mentioned here. Excellent investigations are conducted without all kinds of expensive equipment. Most investigators acquire equipment over time to cut down on the pain, er, cost.

Just get what you can afford. There are obviously the basics, flashlights, batteries, and spare bulbs. As far as the flashlight goes, I do not recommend using the one that has been sitting in your car's glove compartment since the Eisenhower administration, unless you check the batteries and the bulb. You do not want to be caught in the dark on an investigation. You should always have a pen and paper handy to record your observations. Another basic item that you do need is a tape recorder. It does not really matter what kind you use, although digital recorders are the new rave. Obviously, you can use it to record audio phenomena but you also need it for your interviews. I often dictate into mine when I am on a case. At times, it can be kind of funny to play it back. For example, on one tape, you can clearly hear me saying the time and what room I was in. Then you can clearly hear a bang and me saying: "Shit!" when I banged me knee on something I did not see in the dark. Dictating can result in EVP's and they are a way of staying sane and passing the time. Let us examine some other types of equipment.

Camcorders are an obvious choice. Today, there are many good camcorders that have built in night vision equipment. Adding an infrared illuminator will allow you to record in near total darkness. To me, that is amazing. It is a wise idea to have a tripod as well. If there is considerable activity occurring, holding it in your hand is fine. However, if you know that activity often occurs in one particular spot, having the camcorder on a tripod can make things easier. Along with camcorders, cameras are necessary. If you can afford a digital camera, so much the better for the investigation. A digital camera results in instant gratification. This is because you can see the photograph you have taken within seconds on the camera display screen. Any camera will do, however, even throwaways. It is always a good idea to use more than one camera. Catching phenomena on more than one camera eliminates the possibility of faulty film or development problems. Do not go crazy and run out, and spent $1,000 on camera equipment. It is not necessary; any camera will do. In the days of yore, infrared film was used commonly on paranormal investigations. It is a little pricey but still well worth using. Besides, you haven't lived until you try loading your film in the complete darkness of your closet. With faster film, better cameras, and improved development techniques, we are able to get pictures now that we would not have imagined a decade ago. One quick but important note: be sure to document and organize your photos so that you don't find yourself having to go through three zillion pictures looking for the one good one. Yep, I am guilty of that.

It is a good idea to buy a digital thermometer. Temperature changes are a good indicator of activity. The best choice would be one where you can take temperature readings indoors and outdoors. You can pick these up pretty cheaply at an electronic supply store, such as Radio Shack. Laser and infrared non-contact thermometers are a great idea. You can simply point and shoot and get an instant reading. This is perfect for those times where there is a sudden rise or drop in temperature. If someone suddenly complains of a chill, point and shoot and see whether there is a temperature change. That can be important. If the temperature to the left of so and so is 72 degrees and to the right of that person it is 50 degrees, you again have a significant piece of evidence. In addition, you can actually follow moving temperature fields. This can clue you in as to where a spirit might be hiding. It can also serve as a warning sign that activity is about to break out.

While you are there, you might want to look at motion detectors. They have inexpensive, portable ones, which can come in handy in an investigation. They usually work on a passive infrared basis so they can alert you to a manifestation without your being present in the room. It also enables you to set "traps," meaning you can take an area of noted activity and set up a camcorder. When it goes off, you know to take pictures and check equipment readings. I worked on a case where I believed that the spirit came up from the basement through one particular closet. This was based on unusually high electromagnetic readings in that closet. What I did was set up several motion detectors along the path from the closet in question to the bed in that room. If I was right in my assumption that the spirit moved along that set path, each motion detector would trip in sequence. That is exactly what happened. That brings up the question of why a spirit would use such a path. I really cannot answer that question. It makes no sense to me. You would think that they could move about any way they want. I do not see why they would be limited. Maybe it is just a matter of choice. The spirit may simply feel comfortable going one specific way. Perhaps the spirit was afraid of going any other way. However, it does lend itself to the argument that spirits, albeit invisible, consist of mass. *Something* made the detector go off. I actually tried an experiment to test the theory of spirits having mass. In this one house, the spirit would often come to the victim if she asked it to. What I did was set up motion detectors along the floor and have her call the spirit. As soon as she felt something, the detectors would go off, once again in sequence. I did this several times and it worked each time. I do not know who appeared to be more stupid, me for calling the spirit or the spirit for coming when I called it. For some, it is hard to imagine how something they cannot be seen can have mass. My answer to that is that there are many things that cannot be seen but can be measured. Radio and television waves cannot be seen but they can be captured and recorded. The same is true for cellular signals. Dogs can hear frequencies that we cannot. Perhaps our eyes work the same way. There may well be things all around us that we cannot see. That does not mean it is not there. Still, those things do not have mass.

Video surveillance cameras can be very useful as they enable you to monitor activity in more than one place at a time. If they are hooked up to a VCR, you may be able to get some great activity on tape. This, however, is a costly endeavor. However, if you are going to dream, then dream big. You can cover a lot more ground with cameras. Having a PC at home is also great as it allows you to keep large files on a small disk. In addition, if you have a scanner, you can really enhance your pictures. It can also be hooked to other things like a computer. With the right program, you can analyze sounds and images.

Geiger counters and radiological survey equipment can also be used on an investigation. These will measure the amounts of gamma and beta radiation in an area. Ghosts do not give off radiation, thank God. If they did, I would surely glow in the dark by now. What ghosts can do is manipulate the energy in the environment and confuse the detectors. Again, these are nice devices to have but are not critical to an investigation. Consider purchasing some walkie-talkies. There is a good chance that you will have investigators in different parts of the house. You will want to be able to contact the other investigators in case you get into trouble or are witnessing phenomena that you may want the others to see or record. Not only that, it makes you feel less isolated if you have one. Just knowing that you can communicate with the other members of your group can reduce some of the nervous jitters associated with working by yourself. It also enables your co-workers to periodically check in with you to make sure you are safe. In addition, it cuts down on the boredom when nothing is happening. Two-way radios can be quite expensive. For that reason, you need to shop around. You do not need radios that have a range of two trillion miles or eighty-four channels. Keep it simple. Again, Radio Shack offers some affordable ones. All you want to do is be able to communicate with your team.

Failing that, you can get body alarms that you can use in case of a problem. Some of the models make a hideous noise that could serve as a panic button. Some have a built in red light, which comes in handy if you want to get someone's attention without deafening everyone within a two-mile radius. You can pick these up pretty inexpensively. Another inexpensive trinket is a baby monitor. You can put them in rooms where you have no coverage. This can alert you to activity breaking out there. It is a cheap but effective way of covering a large area.

You can use many devices, depending on finances. None of the devices are absolutely necessary to a given investigation. You can add equipment a little at a time. It can run you a good amount of money. Also, if you have friends working with you, you can all pitch in and buy equipment. If you are working as part of an organization, chances are that they will have many of these things. For the most part, investigators buy their own equipment but if the equipment is part of an organization, you have their resources available. Here is a piece of advice: make sure that your equipment is clearly marked with your name. You do not want to lose any of your stuff. Since many investigators bring the same equipment, you want to make sure that you are taking your own stuff home. I have a checklist that I use on investigations. By doing this, I know for sure that I have everything I brought with me. It is a good idea because you will most likely be dragging after sitting up all night and thus, it is easier to forget something.

While the things I am about to mention do not fall under the category of equipment, they most definitely belong in your tool belt. They do not cost much but they are necessary when you are investigating a potentially haunted house. You should always keep holy water on your person. In addition, you should have a religious cross (assuming you are a Christian) and keep some prayers handy. If the situation gets critical these are the "equipment items" that will be the most useful. Many investigators will look down on religious items. There are those who believe that there is no place for religion when it comes to hauntings. Good for them but I know what has worked for me and I really do not care what some people think. My advice is to have them. I have gotten out of a few jams with those items. Besides, like foxholes, there are no atheists in haunted houses. I think that part of the reason why people shun the religious aspect has to do with those individuals who see a demon in every corner. They feel the need to create rituals designed to exorcise every spirit around. It can be ridiculous sometimes to see someone try to exorcise the benign ghost who once lived in the house. Not only will the ritual fail, but you can look pretty stupid. The human spirit who once lived in the house has for all intents and purposes the right to stay there. Trying to chase it out is unnecessary and very hard to do, if you can do it at all, that is. Still, there are those who try. They make everyone else look bad.

One last word on equipment, play with it beforehand and make sure you know how it works. You do not want to waste valuable time on an investigation reading an instruction manual. It slows things down and looks unprofessional. Besides, most people do not take full advantage of all of the features their equipment offers. So take the time to play with it and make sure you understand how everything works and what the readings mean. I have seen people get very excited about some anomalous readings only to find that the machine in question was set to a test mode. Also, you need to experiment with your equipment so as not to look stupid. I was recording with a night vision camcorder one time and it appeared that every so often, lights would appear to float by. Well, we thought that our spirit was trying to communicate with us. Needless to say, we asked a bunch of questions. Some, It appeared, were answered. Then I made a remarkable discovery. Dust, when floating around in the dark can be picked up using night vision equipment. So, what we were doing was questioning dust. Ugh! Make sure that you have all of the supplies you need for your equipment. That means having extra batteries and having tapes for you recorders. You also want to have extra film with you. You never know when something might break out. If that happens, you will be kicking your own butt for a long time if you missed something. I am a believer in Murphy's Law. If something can go wrong, it will. You will see great activity when you have no film. You will hear EVP's galore when you forgot to bring extra tapes. It is some law of the cosmos, I think. It is always good to be prepared.

SECTION 2:

Basics Of An Investigation

INVESTIGATOR OBJECTIVITY

In many instances, investigations determine that there is a natural explanation for the activity reported. Spirits are not always behind the phenomena. Whenever you find yourself dealing with a family that believes they are being haunted, you must be very careful in how you approach the situation. People can convince themselves that they are being haunted. Here is how it happens. One member of the family begins to notice what appears to be a paranormal phenomenon. Maybe it is strange sounds coming from the attic. They become afraid and try to avoid the attic. As their fear mounts, they become convinced that there is something more going on. Now, they begin to focus more and more on sounds coming from the attic. Many of the things they are hearing are quite normal and have been going on for years but they never paid any attention to them. Now, their generalized fear gives new meaning to the sounds. They are colored differently.

Now that they are convinced that something is amiss up there, they begin trying to convince other family members that they are haunted. At first, the other members of the family totally discount this possibility. They will tell the one scared family member that he or she is imagining all of this. However, a seed has been planted. At some point, different things begin to happen that are questionable. Now a second family member starts thinking about the possibility of a haunting and that maybe she was right after all. It does not take much for doubt to creep in. This person is now obsessed by every sound he hears. Slowly but surely, other family members start wondering if maybe something *is* wrong. Now the problem begins to spread.

This can reach a point where the family starts to convince each other that there really is a problem. Their fears gather momentum and take on a life of their own. They all begin to notice peculiar things. Before you know it, they are convinced that their house is haunted and undoubtedly by something malicious. Some people refer to this as an example of "mass hysteria." Personally I do not like that explanation and I think it is an unfair label. Rather than mass hysteria, it is a case of misreading distorted natural phenomena. However, sine they now believe they are haunted, each sound is compounded. Also, once you start looking for something, there is a better than even chance that you will find *something.*

However, you have to be very careful here. You have to look for as much scientific data as possible. What you are going to find when you interview them are many exaggerations. Tales will be told that are more exaggeration than fact and you may be told about a few things that really did not happen at all. The family is not doing this on purpose. It is not a case of them lying to you. You will find they really believe their story. Memory is faulty and when you add terror to the mix, it can get confusing. We have to sort through the data given to us and try to make a determination whether to investigate the situation or not. Most of all, we have to be very careful about what we say to the family, especially during the infant stages of an investigation. Since they are convinced they are being haunted, they will look at everything you say and jump on anything that even sounds like you agree with their assessment. They will read into everything, guaranteed.

When I begin taking information from a client, I have what I call the "exaggeration factor." What I do is discount 25% of what I hear. Again, the family does not do this intentionally; it is just that when you are frightened, things seem larger than life. Noises that have been heard a million times suddenly sound ominous when you are frightened and looking for things. And as I said, if you look for anything long enough, you are sure to find something.

(First Meeting With The Client)

After you initially meet the victims and gain their trust, you will find that they are looking to you as their savior. After all, they reason, you are a psychic investigator and are sure to solve their problem. That puts unnecessary pressure on you if you let it. Try to avoid that. At this early stage, you do not know if there is a problem or not. You have an idea but that is all you have. What you do not have are facts. What compounds this dilemma is that the family is looking to you for validity. They want to hear you say that a ghost is present. It takes a lot of the onus off them. They have probably been questioning their own sanity. However, to have a psychic investigator reach the same conclusion as they have, gives them considerable relief. It gives them instant validation. They have gone through the stage where no one believes them and they feel like the person who has car trouble that never happens when they take it to the mechanic. It may make a horrible noise all of the time but it somehow fails to happen at the garage. I think there is some kind of cosmic law about that. So just knowing that you are taking them seriously is a great lift for them. It takes away some of their pressure immediately.

What we have to remember is that we should never give a diagnosis until we have done a thorough investigation. This is true in cases where there seems to be nothing going on and it is just as true if there is something happening there. Also, when talking to the family, never offer guesses, for example, do not say things like "well, it sounds as if you have a poltergeist here." Before you offer that, make sure you are correct because they are sure to take the ball and run with it. It is not a case of them wanting to be haunted, it is just that they are looking to you for validation of the problem that they have been experiencing. If you are not careful, you will give them a name for what they believe is happening. That makes the problem stronger. One important point is that when you give them information, it is hard to take it back. If they think the problem is something serious like a poltergeist explosion, you will have a hard time getting them to believe anything else. That is why I bristle when some investigators throw the "demon" word around. Once a victim is convinced that they have a demonic infestation on their hands, it is incredibly hard to convince them that the problem is really a human spirit. Even overwhelming evidence can fail to convince them. Once a seed has been planted, it is hard to change it. Another essential point is never give them a lot of terminology to digest. They do not need to know all about "Equipmental Transcommunication." It will suffice to tell them that you are trying to capture voices on tape. Do not tell them about an incubus or explain what demons can do or what they can expect to happen. It is very easy to teach people how to be haunted. I can almost guarantee that if you mention that demons do this or that, at some point down the road, you are going to be told that it happened.

It is the same principal as dealing with hypochondriacs. A friend of mine would end up getting whatever I had or would tell me stories about how he had the same thing a few years earlier only it was so much worse when he had it. I actually had a situation where I complained of pain in an organ that I made up. My friend also suffered from that same condition a few years ago and it was horrible. Oh, how he must have suffered! So, you have to be careful what you say lest you create an "illness" for them.

This is not the case in every investigation. You have to be sure there is a problem before you begin giving out a lot of information. Be honest but be vague. I always tell clients that I want to be absolutely sure before I say anything. I also tell them that since there are so many possibilities, it would be unfair to slap a label on it. Once you see for yourself that phenomena is occurring, there will be plenty of time to discuss specifics after gathering adequate evidence.

Never Be Judgmental

When you are dealing with someone who thinks they may be haunted, never sound judgmental and never scoff at them. For example, do not say, "That is ridiculous; I've never heard of any such thing." The only thing you are accomplishing when you do that is alienating the person who came to you looking for help. Do not act disbelieving. Do not immediately think that Mr. so and so is a wackadoo. He may be but you are not going to know that until you collect more data. Never have a preconceived notion one-way or the other. Obviously, you may have some idea as to what is happening but until you know something, tread lightly. Be professional and be supportive. Even if you do not think something is there, choose your words carefully. You never want to lie to them but you also do not want them to think that they are crazy either. It is a delicate balance and a difficult road to walk.

Carefully Observe Your Client

When you begin interviewing, you have to play close attention to your clients. Do they make eye contact? When they tell you how frightening the situation is, do they seem sincere? Is what they say congruent to how they act? Do they appear stable? You have to be careful, especially when you first meet someone. If there is never eye contact, you have to wonder if what they are telling you is true. If they are laughing when they tell you how scared they are, that should raise some doubts. What we are talking about here is someone who really seems to be having fun with the situation rather than having nervous laughter. Always look for sincerity and congruency. For an example, please read the stories in the Lighter Side of Hauntings. As far as the question of stability goes, anyone who really is being haunted will seem somewhat unstable. This comes from being under tremendous pressure. It would be quite normal for them to become shaky and fearful when they are describing terrifying phenomena. You should expect that. How they answer your questions tells you a lot, too. When they tell you how their cousin Abby is a werewolf who chews on the furniture, the chances are pretty favorable that you are dealing with someone who is mentally ill.

Evaluating Evidence

Keep in mind that many of the incidents reported can have natural causes. This is especially true when it comes to sounds. Houses, especially older ones, do creak and groan. Hot water heaters make some strange noises. Mine sure does. Animals do scratch objects. Mine sure do. If you find the water heater standing upside down, or the entire house is filled with pounding noises in the walls so bad that the whole house shakes, you probably have a problem. If there are gouges three inches deep and two feet long in the door leading to the basement, it is safe to say that you are on to something. Let the evidence paint a picture. Never jump to conclusions.

An object crashing to the floor is a type of occurrence that stands out, especially if it is a religious one. However, when this is reported to you, you must ask when that happened and under what circumstances. Does this always seem to happen when your laundry is in the spin cycle? Is there a train station nearby and if so, do these objects fall around the same time that the 7:30 train from Podunk whizzes by? These are important things to know. Do you have children who like to frighten each other? You may be terribly upset because every so often, the sound of a slamming door wakes you up. The next thing you know, you hear footsteps in the hall outside your bedroom. On a number of occasions, you got up, looked in the hall, and saw nothing. You then went to each of your children's rooms and found them to be sleeping soundly. This is a ghost, right? Maybe ... but it might be little Johnny, who is trying to scare the crap out of his sister. Johnny slams her door, runs back to his room and fakes sleep so he will not get in trouble. Consider all possibilities but keep that information to your self until you have the evidence to support your belief.

Of course, if you go into little Johnny's room at three in the morning and you find him levitating above his bed, then a prank can be ruled out. You just have to try to find a natural cause for any activity that is going on. In far more cases than not, there are rational explanations. Hauntings, while they do happen, are quite rare. It seems that everyone you meet has a ghost story or two to tell. That makes sense since spirits are all around us and when they can, they like to interact with us. However, the truth is that very few people are haunted. Most of those people would not recognize a ghost if it reared up and bit them on the ass.

A Haunting Can be Staged

Another thing you have to be aware of is fraud. People will stage a haunting. They may do it for different reasons, such as playing a joke on the investigators. They may think that this is a way to make a fortune through book deals. Good luck. They may simply be trying to discredit you. I do not want to sound paranoid here but there are many people in this world that will do nasty things. You have to be on your guard against this. Once your reputation has taken a hit, it is extremely difficult to regain it. Therefore, look for microphones, projectors, and the like and watch closely any individual who always seems to be around when things start flying. If something flies across the room and you noticed a quick movement from someone near where the object took off, be leery. This one is tricky because in cases of poltergeist phenomena, one person is often the trigger and as such, will be around when most activities take place. In addition, in poltergeist cases, objects have a tendency to move when you are not looking directly at them. You often see the movement out of the corner of your eye. This also happens in cases of RSPK. You have to be careful and follow your instincts.

Sounds Are The Least Reliable Evidence

As a rule, sounds are the least reliable types of phenomena. All houses creak and moan. An occasional bang is normal. This is also true of some scratching sounds. When you start hearing voices, that is an obvious sign that something unusual is going on. Screams and crying are also good indicators. Of course, you have to rule out the possibility that the sounds are coming from a neighbor's house. Repetitive banging in the walls is another sign of a haunting. However, many sounds are completely normal. One of the most difficult parts of your job is determining which sounds are normal and which ones are not normal. Look for continuation and patterns. One solo knock may mean nothing since it could be anything. However, three straight knocks can be harder to explain. Another problem with sounds is that it can be hard to determine the direction they came from. I live in a mobile home that has windows everywhere and there are times when a sound appears to have come from the rear, left side of the trailer when it actually originated from the front, right. Unless you are an acoustics expert, and I sure as hell am not, it can be hard to determine the origin of the sound.

In true hauntings, sounds seem to come from everywhere and nowhere at the same time. For example, you may hear crying. To you, it sounds like it is coming from the kitchen but when you get there, it sounds like it is coming from the living room. You never seem to be able to pinpoint it. When it comes to sounds, try to get them on tape. Needless to say, you are most likely to hear a sound when your tape recorder is in another room. (Another cosmic law, I fear.) Also, it seems that things never seem to happen when you have tape running. I should also point out that sounds do not always record. I was in a house where there were reports of loud knocking coming from the walls. It never happened when I was there but I believed what I was being told. Well finally one day I was there when the knocking started. I even had a tape recorder in my hand at the time. How perfect, right? Well I turned it on and began recording. When I played the tape back later that day, there was everything on that tape except for the banging. That did not come out. Such is life, I guess. There are times when all you get on your recorders is two hours of air. Still, it is worth the try. I have gotten some amazing things on tape.

Another time, I was at a house where a woman was supposedly channeling a spirit. There were quite a few investigators present and there were four camcorders operating. There were also two audio recorders running. When the spirit was commanded to give us its name, we all heard something garbled. One by one, we played or tapes back only to find that on all six machines, the answer skipped leaving only a high-pitched sound. So much for that idea.

Visual Evidence is More Reliable

Visual evidence is much more reliable. Yes, your eyes can play tricks on you but as a rule, you either saw it or you did not. Sounds, on the other hand, can be caused by anything. In addition, memory of sounds can be faulty. That creaking noise in the attic sounds sinister. Have you heard it before? You might not be so sure. You will not forget the appearance of an apparition though. Where you do have difficulty with visualization is that two people may see different things. On the other hand, one person sees something and another one does not. Why that happens is open to speculation. Perhaps the entity can control who sees it. My feeling is that some people just happen to be on the right frequency. Whatever the cause, this creates confusion and that confusion makes it hard to determine the validity of the sighting. Just the same though, catching an apparition on videotape is one hell of a piece of evidence, especially if you are talking about an apparition.

Obtain Adequate Physical Evidence

This is why you need as much physical evidence as possible. Always take pictures, even if you do not see or feel anything. Also, use more than one camera. If you do end up picking up something, getting it on two cameras rules out the possibility of defective film or a defective camera. Using a Polaroid instant picture camera is a good idea. For one, it provides instant gratification by seeing the photograph in minutes. For another, it is much harder to "doctor" a Polaroid picture. This is important when it comes time to prove, or disprove the phenomena all of you saw. Digital cameras are great because you get the instant gratification plus it is easy to store a lot of photos. Plus, you can delete those shots that show nothing. In that sense, they pay for themselves because you do not need to have film developed. You will also want to use tape recorders, video cameras, thermometers, an EMF detector, Geiger counters and any other equipment you have access to.

Remember, the idea is to find the cause of the reported phenomena, natural or not. You need to use everything you can to make a determination. Do not be afraid to say that there are natural causes for the phenomena, even if the client seems disappointed. The reverse is true also. No matter how scared the client may be, if something *is* there, you must tell them about it. You would be putting them at great risk if you did not. Again though, you do not want to speculate on what is there; just tell them that *something* is there and you will try to determine what it is.

Evaluating Evidence Objectively

The most important thing is to be objective. Gather the evidence, study it, and let the evidence make the determination. Bear in mind that your own senses are part of the evidence. Listen to your instincts. They are probably right most of the time but they are just a part of the process. Should you find yourself in a situation where all of the physical evidence points one way and your instincts another, review the evidence again. Do not be afraid to consult with other investigators, even if they were not part of the investigation. They will appreciate the request and they will look at the evidence from a different perspective. Many a mystery has been solved using this method.

Some investigators make the mistake of wanting to experience paranormal phenomena so badly that they tend to read into things. In other words, they try to create something out of nothing. You really cannot afford to read into anything in this business. Sure, it is cool to get great evidence and it is cool to have a really good story to tell your friends but it has to be real. It is one thing to exaggerate a situation where you stayed in a haunted hotel but it is quite another thing when you are trying to help a terrified family. You really have to play it straight. Was that really a growl or was that a sound that came from the heating system? Are you really sure? Well, maybe it was just such and such. Be sure. I have been embarrassed many times in my early days by mistaking normal sounds for something paranormal. If you are sure that you heard three loud, paranormal knocks, you can tell that to the family. However, if it turns out that the sound came from the refrigerator like it always does when it cycles every twenty minutes, then you look foolish. "Oh, right. Yes of course it was the refrigerator." You can also lose all credibility that way and sometimes never get it back.

There are times when you find yourself caught in a difficult situation. You have evidence that just is not conclusive. It could be this or it could be that. In that instance, the best thing you can do is be honest. Do not lean one-way or the other. It could be a situation where you need to gather more evidence. It could also be a situation where you will never know for sure. That does happen from time to time. In a case like that, the odds are that no one is in danger. If there were something dangerous operating in the house, you would likely have had numerous outward manifestations that pointed to that. If there are none, be honest with the client and offer to check in with them from time to time. Also, let them know that they can always call you if trouble does start. If the client has been describing outward manifestations but you have not seen anything, it is best to recommend further investigation. There are cases that start off slowly but pick up in intensity. There are also cases that take a long time to develop.

At some point though, you may have to withdraw if nothing happens over a long period of time. You cannot live with the client if nothing happens over the course of several sittings. Of course, that does not mean that if nothing happens the first night, you should abandon them. The thing is that you have to be reasonable towards them and towards you as well. Sometimes the best you can do is teaching them what to look for and how to protect themselves if something does happen. The door is never completely closed. You can always go back in if the activity intensifies again. I have left cases where all activity ceased after several investigations. However, several months later, the activity started up again and I went back to work. It happens that way from time to time and for any number of reasons. You can always go back in at a later date should that be necessary.

DIFFERENT ROLES OF THE INVESTIGATOR

The main role of an investigator is to investigate the phenomena and try to find a way to stop it, if that is warranted. In some of the simpler cases, there may be actions you can take to end the activity. In the bad cases, you may need to call in qualified demonologists. Often in those cases, you must try to get the religious leaders of the victim's particular faith in to help. That can be difficult bordering on impossible, in some instances. Unfortunately, many in the religious fields are as close-minded and ignorant, as are many scientists. There are great leaders in all faiths and there are great scientists so this is not a blanket condemnation. Unfortunately, this is a business open to ridicule by people who know absolutely nothing about the field. Therefore, at times it can be very hard to get help. There is a cute statement said about St. Jude, the patron Saint of the impossible. It goes like this: "The difficult, we will do immediately, the impossible will take a little longer." Keep that in mind when you are dealing with close-minded pastors, priests, rabbis, or parapsychologists. Also keep in mind that many in the religious field simply do not know anything about hauntings so when you go to them for help, they really do not know what to do. I have made suggestions to priests and have had good results with that. Of course, they were opened minded priests. That is the key.

Attributes Of A Successful Investigator

We know that we need to be professional, open-minded, kind, sincere, and perhaps most of all, objective. That has all been covered. What we need to do is take a closer look at some of the other roles we often must play. Before we get deeply into this area I want to point something out. I have heard poorly trained investigators say things to the effect of "I'm not a psychiatrist" or "I'm not here to do therapy," or other equally ignorant thoughts. If that is your opinion, my suggestion would be to stay home and leave the investigating to more dedicated investigators, the types who care. I am not suggesting that we should start counseling people on their interpersonal relationships or their desire to quit smoking or some such thing. However, you do have to be willing to listen to their haunting related problems and you need to lend them support. Of course, you have to know your limitations and not overstep your boundaries. To be an outstanding investigator, you must possess the following personality traits:

1) Faith.
2) Kindness.
3) Empathy.
4) A strong desire to help other.
5) A strong will.
6) One big heart.
7) Courage.
8) A willingness to make sacrifices.
9) Sincerity.

There are probably many more investigator attributes that are helpful but the above nine traits are a must. Believe me when I tell you, you will use all of these traits at some point in your career. It is hard to imagine working a case where you do not use all of the above. If you cannot muster these, you do not belong in this field.

Primary Goal Is To Help The Victim

We must always keep in mind that our number one goal is to help the victims. Sure, we want to learn, experience, and grow in knowledge but those are secondary objectives. Sometimes all we can do is lend the victim support and educate them. There are defenses such as the use of sacramentals and prayer. Evil activity can be stopped using religious means. Coping skills can be taught. If you teach them well, you can make the haunting much easier for them to deal with. To the victim of a haunting, this is huge.

Chances are that the victims of a haunting have little or no idea how to behave. We need to educate them in this area to prevent them from doing things that will actually cause far more harm. One thing that often happens during a haunting is that one adult or another will inadvertently challenge the invading entity. They may yell something like: "Fight me you SOB and leave my family alone!" Trust me, at some point in time he will get his wish and he *will* lose. Mortals stand no chance against immortals so we cannot let that happen if we can avoid it. I have listed some "do's and don'ts" for the victims that is given to them upon beginning the investigation. They cover almost everything. We must also reinforce the items on the list. People have a tendency to forget things. This is especially true when you are dealing with the unnatural stress of a haunting.

Counseling The Client

Teaching them the "do's and don'ts" is one thing but there is another area where we can be invaluable. This is where we become counselors and our main job here is to lend all the support we can muster and teach them some defensive skills and some coping ones as well. Surviving a haunting is way beyond difficult. Even with our beautiful English language of more than 500,000 words, it is all but impossible to adequately describe the terror of a full-blown haunting. We can read about it repeatedly but if you have never experienced one either as a victim or as an investigator, you cannot fully appreciate or understand the absolute horror of a haunting. Just letting the family know that you believe them can make a huge difference in their lives. Knowing that other people have endured and been freed from bad hauntings can make a huge difference as well. Again though, if you are not a psychiatrist, confine your counseling to only haunting related stuff. For example, it is fine to suggest to the family that they get out for a night to escape the haunting but I would not start a weight-losing seminar or a twelve-step program to solve their other ills. Common sense should dictate the degree, scope and nature of your help.

Describing A Haunting

Let me attempt to describe a bad haunting for you. The reality of it is way beyond my ability to describe but I will do the best I can. The first thing that a victim undergoes is a sense of confusion. Remember, in the early stages of a haunting, many things happen that go unnoticed. This is what gives the invading entity time to become established. As time goes by, the victim slowly begins to notice things but shrugs them off or rationalizes them. It may be furniture that is not in place. It may be the magazine that keeps moving around or the door that you always find closed but do not remember closing. After a while, you begin to make mental notes about these things. You may tell yourself, "I am going to make sure I keep this door opened." Later, of course, you find it closed.

This is where the confusion begins. They may begin to doubt themselves. A common thought is: "I must be losing my mind?" Guess what? They are not loosing it ... yet. Once they start becoming confused, they are now expending energy that an invading spirit can begin to feed off of. Remember the circle, the stronger it gets, the more it can scare you, which in turn gives it more energy to use against you. We are talking about a calculating, cunning entity. It knows what you fear and it knows how to hurt you psychologically. For this reason, anything you can do to make the victim less afraid will reduce the power of the evil spirit.

(The Infestation Stage)

As the haunting begins to intensify, a sense of unreality begins. By now, the victim knows that something is going on. With that realization, fear becomes the operative emotion. We know how spirits love to feed off fear. This is the infestation stage. It creates a new feeling for the victim. The victim begins to suffer a sense of disassociation. Think back to a time when someone particularly close to you died. When that happened, didn't your usual surroundings suddenly seem alien to you? All of a sudden, as you went through first the stage, shock, then the grieving stage, those things that usually made you feel comfortable now look so different. You seem to lose interest in the things that used to make you feel comfortable. The chair that you always sit in while watching TV may now seem cold and alien. You probably also felt disassociated or cut off from the people around you. It is as if for a short time, you no longer fit in your old world and you certainly do not fit in the outside world. In fact, with that passing, your old world ceased to exist, as you knew it. It became a totally different world for you. Yes, many of the things *looked* the same, but how you viewed and perceived them became different. We only begin to recover from our grief when we begin to accept that new world with all of the changes that the passing of our loved one created. We do not forget them; we just slowly accept the new world that now has a void in it. That is how we heal. We are not reverting to our old life; we are forced to create a new one.

(Learning To Cope With A Haunting)

This is what happens to the person being haunted. Their world has changed and no matter what happens, their world will never be the same again. Yes, they will cope with it, especially with your help. The fact remains that their world cannot be the same. They feel terribly isolated. They then find it difficult to be around their friends and relatives. These people no longer belong to the same world as they do. Here they have their friends at work talking about the ball game while you are worrying about a ghost. You find that you cannot relate to your friends anymore. How do you compare the importance of a ball game to a haunting?

Consequently, they become more distant and aloof which only makes them feel even more isolated. Here goes the vicious cycle again.

It always seems that everyone has a ghost story but the truth of the matter is that most people really do not believe in ghosts as actual entities that can terrorize them. For the person being haunted, it only adds to the problem because they probably have no one they can talk to about it. They are faced with the skeptics who will ridicule them and tell them to stop "being stupid." Therefore, lending support can be critical. Just the fact that you believe the victim provides a boost to their spirits. They no longer feel as alone and they no longer feel as if they are losing their mind. It is amazing how much of a relief it is for them to find someone who really believes them. They have probably discussed their problem with those who were closest to them. It is not just the skeptical friend they have to worry about either. In many cases, they run into trouble with even their closest family members. Too often, instead of the support so necessary to help them deal with their situation, they are told that "they are imagining it" or that "they are scaring themselves." This makes them feel increasingly isolated as their support system crashes and burns around them. Now they find themselves in a situation where they are afraid to mention their problems to the people they have always been able to count on. How is that for feeling lonely? Sadly, in many cases, relationships that were damaged are never repaired. In that sense, the suffering goes on far longer than the haunting.

You will often hear a huge sigh of relief when you tell them that you believe their story. Not only do they feel less alone, they now feel that they have someone who is on their side. This will often give them needed courage to fight the terrible battle they find confronting them. You have to jump on that. Take advantage of anything that makes the victim feel better because the better they feel, the stronger they become. And of course, as they grow stronger, the invading entity weakens. This is the first positive step in the battle. The victim now feels like they can fight back. You will sometimes see such elation on the part of a family when they see the investigators come in. It is almost like the cavalry coming over the hill to rescue them. It is nice to see the look of hope on their faces.

The Terror Stage

The next stage for them is the terror stage. This is where things begin to get really ugly. They begin to wear down from the activity and the pressure they are facing. They begin to fear for their lives and sanity. They lose sleep. Sometimes they stop eating. If they work, the strain starts to show there. They become less productive, more argumentative. This creates work problems. They begin to fear going home. Therefore, nowhere feels safe. They feel totally besieged because they are. Their whole life is different. The spirit's grip starts to become a stranglehold. Their lives are turned upside down. Terror becomes the operative emotion. In short, they live in constant fear.

As the haunting progresses, they start to become frustrated and they begin to feel helpless and hopeless. Eating habits change, sleep becomes a problem. Soon, depression sets in. So too does apathy. As that happens, the entity gets stronger. In extreme cases, thoughts of suicide may set in. Even death may seem better than to live in constant fear. A negative spirit more than welcomes suicidal thoughts. It is a sure sign that he is winning the war since it is bent on destroying all that is good, especially that which is made in the image and likeness of God Himself.

Educating The Victim

In addition to being supportive, we must begin to educate them. The first thing we must do is to convince them that hauntings do in fact happen. It can be very comforting for them to hear that many others have been haunted and they have survived it. This helps to take away some of the sense of unreality they have been experiencing. It also makes them feel less alone. Remember again, the better they feel, the less power the negative spirit has over them. Momentum is very definitely a factor here. Make sure you explain to them how the negative spirit derives its power from them.

They are experiencing something that does not fit in their model of the world or too many others for that matter. You have to realize that they have felt alone and isolated, probably for a long time. Ghosts are not supposed to exist in the real world and they surely aren't supposed to terrorize them, right? Once they see that spirits do exist and that they sometimes interact with us, a burden is taken off their shoulders. Their newfound knowledge of spirits and how they work takes away much of the sense of shock they have been feeling. It also serves to empower them. That gives them the strength to fight back effectively.

Defending Oneself Against Attack

The next step is to teach them ways in which they can actually defend themselves. Give them some prayers to say. Explain how effective holy water is in protecting oneself. Teach them about the God light. Help them to build their faith in God and in themselves. Show them that these things can be combated. However, let them know that they can expect retaliation. Also, let them know that the more the entity retaliates, the more they have to retaliate in turn. The entity wants to damage them any way it can. If it could, it would try to destroy them. (Even if it is not a demonic haunting, the human spirit has its own agenda and will work in much the same was as a demon, with obviously less results.) That is the ultimate goal and it is that simple. It is going to continue to accelerate whether they fight back or not. They need to know that they have to fight back. The negative entity is not going to feel sorry for them and leave them alone. It just "ain't gonna happen." That being the case, go down swinging. However, they also need to know that they can win and that they will win if they trust in God.

Changing The Environment

Another thing to tell them is to make the environment as inhospitable to the spirit as possible. Negative spirits want recognition. With recognition comes fear. For this reason, they need to try as hard as possible not to give it that recognition. Start cutting off its food supply. If they need to talk about strategy, they should do it outside the home.

There are other ways of making the environment less demon friendly. Tell them to fill the house with love ... yes, love. Evil spirits hate love!

They hate all positive emotions but especially that one. They are trying to split the household, turn one against the other. The family cannot let that happen. Family members should make a special effort to get along with each other. Forget the petty problems. Their actions should show that they love one another. This can be very hard when your nerves are dangling over the edge but it is a very effective form of self-defense. They should openly talk about God in the home and do so in a positive way. They should talk about how God loves His creatures. And how God will always defeat evil. Most of all, they should pray. God will answer their prayers. It may take awhile but He will answer them. A good idea is to brighten the place up with flowers. Play religious music; play upbeat music. Have friends come over for a prayer group. (By the way, that is particularly effective in most bad hauntings.) Laugh a lot. Throw a party. Anything that promotes a positive environment will help. Make the home a place where evil does not want to be. Just do not give in.

The Investigator Can Become the Victim

In short, we must do everything in our power to help them. We will have to be their "rock" at times. When we feel that they are wearing down from the battle, we must give them the support they need. We need to remind them that they are not fighting alone. If they need a shoulder to cry on, lend them one. If they need to vent their emotions, do not take it personally. Always remember what they are going through. You will have to make some sacrifices, for sure. You may be called on for support on a day in which circumstances in your own life leave *you* in need of support. Try to be there for them. You may have to give up a sizeable amount of your free time. That can be a tough one. It can become a juggling match. You are trying to do everything possible for the victims but you cannot do it at the expense of yourself. You will have to make sacrifices but you cannot stop your own life in the process. There will come times when you need to back off. It is, quite simply, a matter of survival. You are of no value to these victims and future victims if you end up losing yourself. Burnout, and I mean serious burnout can occur if you are not careful. They need you, so try to be there for them whenever you can. Remember though, your family needs you too. If the negative spirit cannot destroy the family it has chosen, it will gladly settle for destroying yours. Do not fight the battle to the point where you become the victim. It is a terrible balancing act and sometimes there is no safety net.

There is always the possibility you may begin to feel resentment towards your clients. This is especially true when you cannot see an end to the investigation. You may start to resent the time you are missing with your family. You may notice the negativity they are beginning to feel. Sometimes, the family will lash out at you in frustration. Then you start to think that you are doing a thankless job. Here you are, giving up your life for them and they are giving you the hard time. Take a step back and remind yourself what they are going through. I have been there and I redefined the meaning of the word irrational. When you begin to analyze it objectively, you may see that your resentment is a result of the frustration you are feeling because the family is still suffering, despite your best efforts.

Your Goal Is to Help Others

A haunting is not easy on anyone involved. Nerves are frayed, tempers grow short, and patience ebbs. Always remind yourself of the reasons why you have chosen to get into this field. The likelihood is because you want to help people. When things become rough, keep reminding yourself of that goal. Keep *your* faith strong. Keep in mind the advice you have given to the client. It applies to you as well. Pray for help and guidance. Divorce yourself from the investigation from time to time, unless you want to end up divorcing your spouse. In order to help them, you have to be alert and you have to be sharp. Your thinking processes have to be clear at all times. Solving a haunting can be like a game of chess. To succeed, one must be able to think several moves ahead. You also have to be strong because the victims are watching you and they are in a sense feeding off of you. If you appear tired or disgusted, that will set the tone for them. Never underestimate the psychological role in a haunting. Investigations take time. In many cases, it is a marathon, not a sprint. If you try to sprint through a marathon, it will be a short outing for you. Pace yourself, no matter how hard that can be for you when you know a family is suffering. Remember that you are going to need to be around for the finish. You see, you need to play several roles for yourself too. Most of all do not lose faith in yourself and do not give in to self-doubt. Remember that you may be under attack too.

There will be times when you need to get away from the haunting and that is a necessary thing. The brain is designed to do what is best for the host and will let you know when it is time to back off a bit. You should not feel guilty about that at all. Again, you are of no value to the victims if you end up in a psychiatric hospital yourself. Besides, that will *really* ruin your reputation. "This ghost guy, wasn't he in a psyche ward for a time?" Just imagine telling a psychiatrist that your problem is a ghost or demon. One suspects that he will put you on medication. When you tell him that you hear disembodied voices, he will increase your medicine. If you protest too much, plan on a long stay at your nearest psychiatric center. The moral of the story is to step back when you need to. In truth, you have to play quite the balancing act at times and as I said before, you often have to do that without a safety net. It can be difficult but it can be done.

OUTLINE OF AN INVESTIGATION

Paranormal investigations are multifaceted. For that reason, it helps to have an outline, or guide, to ensure that all of the things that need to be done are done in the most logical and timely fashion. Plans do not always go the way we expect them to and rare is the case that goes by the numbers. Many times, we have to improvise. Time constraints, travel and the availability of the investigators or the client will often dictate how the investigation develops. However, in a best-case scenario, you will have an orderly progression from one step to another. With that thought in mind, let us look at a basic outline of an investigation. (Some assembly required.)

1) **Initial contact made between the client and investigator.**
2) **Initial interview is set up to discuss the phenomena.**
3) **Do a walk through of the home.**
4) **Send in photographers and do detailed interviews. Draw up diagram of premises.**
5) **Set up the investigation with the family and investigators.**
6) **Check equipment and set up assignments. (Skull session.)**
7) **Have a light trance medium, LTM, do walkthrough.**
8) **Do walkthrough with your Gauss meter, Geiger counter, radiological survey meters, thermometers, if you have these things, and record baseline figures.**
9) **Take additional photos of known areas of activity.**
10) **Periodically monitor equipment and fill out activity reports.**
11) **Work with client about coping skills and defenses.**

12) Have post investigation debriefing. (Skull session)

13) Make recommendations to family and assist them in getting outside help if needed.

(Steps Of an Investigation)

Okay, there you have it. Once the initial contact is made between the client and the investigator, a preliminary interview is set up to discuss the phenomena that have been occurring. Personally, I think it is better to do this away from the house, if possible. This is not critical to the investigation and often is difficult to arrange due to time constraints and/or investigator availability. In regards to the steps that follow, many of these items can be done in stages but you will probably find that this is rarely possible. For that reason, I will detail these steps under the premise that these steps are all being done on the first night of the investigation.

From the initial call, you will have determined how many investigators will be involved. This is determined by the size of the premises and the degree of the problem. If it is really bad, you may decide that you want to double up into teams instead of having everyone work individually. It is important to note that you do not want to have too many investigators involved; you will be banging into each other and you can pretty much count on no activity taking place.

On the night of the investigation, the investigators, with the exception of the light trance medium should meet at a prearranged place for a skull session. Mc, Donalds is often a popular place for these meetings. Our organization has had more meetings in various McDonalds than you can imagine. Here, you can discuss the case and you can then go to the house as a group. One of the funniest things to me is seeing the reaction on the faces of the people nearest to you should they overhear your conversation. Now that can be hysterical. Upon arrival at the home, one of the investigators should do a walk through of the home to get an idea where the activity is strongest. He can also grasp the layout of the premises. The next step ideally, would be to send in the photographers. While they are taking photographs, conduct the detailed, formal interviews with the clients. If you have a light trance medium available, he/she can do a walk through the home. This is one of the things that can be done before the day of the investigation, although again, this is not critical, just nice.

At this stage, you want to draw up a diagram of the home. You can then take an overlay of plastic and highlight in red the areas of activity. You can put little numbers on the overlay and write up reports of what type of activity is there. This comes in very handy when you reach the point where you set up assignments. In a perfect world, this will have been done already.

Now you come to the point where you want to set up the investigation. What you want to do here is discuss the investigation with the family involved and the investigators. Here is where you decide how you want the family and investigators to interact. Unless the situation warrants otherwise, I believe it is a wise idea to have some interaction between the family and the investigators. This helps set up a desired rapport and it also gives you the opportunity to educate the family. However, you have to judge the situation on a case-to-case basis. There are clients who are a pleasure to work with. They will be involved with you but give you enough space in which to work. However, there are others who will cling to you to the point where you cannot get anything accomplished. They make it difficult for the investigators to talk to each other. When that is the case, you have to be careful what you say to each other since the odds are that the client knows very little about hauntings and if they hear someone mention the demon word, you can have a problem on your hands. You will also have the clients who will follow you every place you go, jabbering away. Others will sit you down and talk for hours. You have to try to be as diplomatic as possible but you eventually have to get the actual investigation started. It can be a fine line that you are walking because you want to lend support but at some point, you have to get down to business. Then there are the ones who want the investigation to be a party. You will read more about that in the chapter on the lighter side of hauntings. Ugh!

Next, you can brief the investigators on the information you have gathered so far. The discussion will focus on the results of the interviews, and the diagram of the premises. It is important to have a team meeting before going into the location. You want your investigators to know what they may be facing and you want to establish a strategy. This is a favorable time to set up assignments based on each member's strengths. You can also discuss where to set up camcorders and other equipment. If an investigator has any fears or concerns, this is the forum in which to discuss them. Thus, a plan of action is formulated before the investigation begins. One note about plans of action, they often need revision no matter how well they are planned. You will often find yourself "winging it" as the night progresses. Organization is a key in an investigation. Every action has to be done in an organized fashion. However, you have to be flexible as well. The better prepared you are before going in, the better your results will be.

Equipment and Light Trance Medium

This is the point where the LTM should do her walk through to see what she can discern. This can save you valuable time and it can give you a clue about how to proceed with the investigation. Even with the best LTM, you still have to do a full investigation because you need documentation. This is crucial should you need outside assistance. If, for example, you have to go to the Church looking for their help, the information from the psychic will carry very little weight, if any at all. You need much better evidence. Still, the LTM can help you get the evidence needed, if she can read that particular house.

Once this is done, you will begin to set up your equipment. Depending on what you are using, you need to get baseline figures. What you are trying to determine is how much of a particular type of energy is ambient. Once you determine what the average is you then monitor your equipment and look for changes. Now, I must point out that you are not looking for a particular reading. Unfortunately, there is no scientific standard where a reading of such and such indicates there is a spirit present. What you are looking for are any changes in the amount of energy in a given area. This could indicate that a spirit is manifesting although it does not conclusively prove it. However, it does support the theory that manifestations alter the various fields of energy in a given location at a given time. While you need baseline readings throughout the home, it is especially important where you have activity reported in different areas. Once you have baseline readings, you will then set up your equipment in the area of the most activity. This is where having a LTM can save you so much time. The LTM can give you an idea where to set up based on her discernment of the home. Most investigators have some discernment abilities so if you do not have a LTM available, you can follow your instincts. Obviously, if the activity takes place in a particular part of the home, that is where you will set up. You should now take more photographs in the areas where the family says activity has taken place.

Monitoring The Equipment

Once you are set up, you need to monitor your equipment. If there is no activity going on and you do not feel or sense anything, you probably want to record your energy and temperature readings every half-hour or so. You may find that energy, be it electromagnetic, beta or gamma often starts to build during the "psychic hours," between 9 p.m. and 6 a.m. If activity does break out, it is important to record any changes in the ambient energy fields and temperature in the area of activity. In most cases, energy fields become much higher when there is some form of outward manifestation, such as poltergeist phenomena. You will often see the room temperature drop significantly during periods of activity. Again, there is no specific reading that indicates a spirit's presence. An electromagnetic field reading of 6 milligauss only means that there is more of that type of energy present than if it read 4 milligauss; it does not prove a spirit is present. Therefore, the point is you need to look for any change, not necessarily a specific one. If something is going on, you need to take as many pictures as possible and have a video camera running. If you are alone when this happens, as is often the case, do the best you can. (Remember cosmic laws.)

Taking Photographs For Evidence

Throughout the night, it is a good idea to take photographs every so often using different cameras. This is something that you should always do if you feel anything at all. You will go through a lot of film this way but you may also capture some important images. It is worth the cost. That is what makes digital cameras so good. Although they are expensive to buy, they pay for themselves very quickly on an investigation. They are really worth the cost as well. Of importance is cataloging your data especially when it comes to pictures. At the start of an investigation, and on each subsequent night, take a small chalkboard and record the date, time, location and camera number. Once you have done that, take a close-up picture of the board with each camera. You should also do this every time you change the film. If you use the same roll of film on different nights, take the chalkboard picture at the start of the investigation for that night. The benefit of this is it makes it much easier to keep track of your film once you have it developed. If you are investigating a house with a lot of activity, you will be surprised at how many pictures you will take. Keeping track of it all can be a logistical nightmare. Another advantage of taking a chalkboard photograph is that you can get an idea of which camera is giving you the best shots. It also helps eliminate any problems with a particular camera. Never use the same roll of film on more than one investigation. You never want a mix up. All you need is to come up with a great picture only to discover that you cannot tell which investigation it came from. If you still have shots left at the close of an investigation, just develop what you have.

Keeping Activity Reports Current

Another important step is to keep your activity reports up to date. Always make sure that you have logged the day and time on you activity log. Record keeping is extremely important. You will have many completed forms after an investigation that must be filed in chronological order. You need to be able to determine any changes in the activity. In addition, you have to keep in mind that if outside help is needed you must be able to present an open and shut case to the organization you are contacting. You will meet a lot of resistance when you seek help. It is important that everything be in order and presented in a professional manner. Not only does it benefit the particular case you are working on, it also helps the outside organization develop trust in you and your investigation team. This can make future requests easier. Clear, concise reports make it easier to study the case at some future date, should you wish to. I like to take hauntings apart when things are slow. It gives me something to do when I need my paranormal "fix" and I learn a lot from those reports that sometimes helps on another investigation. Activity reports and record keeping are presented in more detail at the end of this chapter.

The Summary Report

At the end of each day or night of an investigation, you should write a summary report. Remember, you need to report anything that may be helpful, even if it is just a feeling you experienced. Obviously, if there was a lot of activity, your report will be lengthy. Always try to write your report right after the investigation has ended. You will probably be too tired right after the investigation but get to it as quickly as you can, preferable first thing in the morning. This way, the information will be fresh. Time makes us forget things. Plus, data can accumulate quickly on an investigation. Also, write your reports legibly. Much of the information on these reports will end up being entered into a computer, should you have one. (And you should, if you can. You can store tons of information on a single disk.) That is time consuming enough without having to strain to read every line. Laptops are great because they are obviously portable. What I sometimes do is bring mine with me on a case and if things are slow, I work on my reports while I am still in the house. It makes things easier.

Help The Client Develop Coping Skills

Once the investigation is underway, you can begin the process of working with the clients to help them develop coping skills. You will also teach them defenses. This ongoing process never stops as long as you are there. You want to establish a good rapport with the client. As I said earlier, do not be afraid to be a little lighthearted here as you do not want to appear unapproachable. Just make sure that you take your work seriously. You don't want the investigation to turn into "Animal House" but you also do not want to appear as if your underwear is a few sizes too tight. The message you want to convey is that you are a professional and very human. Let them see the human side of you. As always, it is a balancing act but let your common sense dictate your behavior.

Keep In Contact With Others

You should always keep in contact with the group leader. If you have been assigned to a particular location and you desire a change, it is okay to leave for a while. It is always a good idea to bring food along with you. In some investigations, the client will provide you with anything you could possibly ask for and then some. On others investigations you have to fend for yourself. It seems that .if you bring lots of food with you, they will have a banquet set up. If you bring nothing, they will have nothing for you. There is one drawback to mention here. Investigations can play havoc on your diet. You will find yourself eating all kinds of junk food. Smokers always smoke more too. This is especially true when you have reached the boredom stage of the investigation. (And you always do.) A lot of Devil Dogs (no pun intended, they are a favorite of mine.) and potato chips are consumed on a slow investigation. An overnight investigation can seem very long, especially if you are not used to being up all night and you need to be as sharp as possible in the event, something does happen. For this reason, if you need a break, take one. If you are sick of sitting in one place, ask for a switch.

Many investigations are boring in that often nothing happens. Thus, you often have to find ways to amuse yourself. I have been on some investigations where the investigators had a ball. Between crude jokes and hilarious accounts of other investigations, you can laugh until it hurts. You need to act professionally but you should not be an automaton either. I have seen a number of practical jokes played. You just need to know where to draw the line. Investigations are usually 90% boredom and 10% pure terror. You need to be ready to deal with both.

Should activity begin to occur in the area where you are assigned, contact other team members. If you are using a walkie-talkie system, call in asking for assistance. If walkie-talkies are not used, use your personal body alarm, if you have them. These cute little devices, which are quite popular with joggers, can prove to be very useful in an investigation. They are little battery-operated devices, which work in two ways. They have a flashing red light, which you can turn on by flipping a switch. This is helpful if you want to get another investigators attention quietly. This is useful if you are in a room where you have video or audio recording devices running. The other feature is a very loud alarm, which you activate by pulling a little pin. Other investigators who may be in other parts of the house can hear this alarm as well as the people in neighboring counties. They are also inexpensive and can be found in many sporting goods stores.

When activity breaks out, you want as many people around as possible. For one thing, it makes you feel better to have a number of people around you, the old safety in numbers idea. The other benefit is that the more people that are around, the more witnesses you have to a given occurrence. Also, you have more people to record the phenomena using the various forms of equipment you may be using. It can get hectic if you are by yourself when something happens and you have to check three gages, one thermometer, one video recorder and a camera to boot. Of course, in some cases, you may find yourself standing frozen with your mouth wide open. That happened to me one time when I saw a table levitate. I was smoking a cigarette at the time and I sat there staring at the table in disbelief. The damn cigarette burned right down to my fingers and I did not even register the pain. (At the time, that is. I sure as hell did afterwards, I can tell you that.) It was not fear that got to me; it was just so amazing to see.

Never Put Yourself In Jeopardy

Never put yourself in jeopardy. If you feel threatened, leave the area. There is a difference between being frightened and feeling threatened. After a while, you learn to distinguish between the two. If you feel threatened, leave the area. There is no shame in this as long as you do it right. Running up the stairs screaming is a no-no because that frightens the client. Just leave quietly. Your group leader will certainly understand and so will the other investigators, unless they are new and ignorant.

Anyone who has worked a bad case will certainly understand. We have all been frightened at one time or another. Anyone who says they were never frightened either lied to you or they had no pulse. The important thing is how you react to the fear you feel. When you are frightened, you have to fall back on your training to get you through those tough moments. Again though, there is a difference between feeling frightened and feeling threatened.

Working With Fellow Investigators

Investigations can take some time and it is much better for all parties concerned if you can have the same investigators around from beginning to end. New blood is sometimes welcomed but it is important to have continuity in an investigation. A revolving door of investigators does not look good to the clients and it makes it difficult to run the investigation since the team leader has to constantly brief the new investigators and a lot of time is wasted going over the same material time after time. Continuity is important. To help accomplish this, you have to avoid burnout by not being terrified from day one. Burnout means a revolving door. Communication is also very important. Report anything you think is noteworthy to your fellow investigators. Even if you think it is minor, report it anyway. It may coincide with something that happened to the others. Skull sessions are a very big part of an investigation. The group should always keep the lines of communication open. Events that seem insignificant can turn out to be very significant later. Also, keep the lines of communication open with the client. Very often information will come out in casual conversation that is important. Always listen carefully. In a sense, the interview never really ends.

After A Night Of Investigating

At the end of the night, carefully pack up your equipment unless it has been decided to leave it there for another night. If there are young children in the house, you may not want to do that. Many investigations take several days if not longer. Often there is no activity at the beginning of an investigation. Do not be discouraged by this. If the place is haunted, you will eventually see activity.

It is wise to have a debriefing session soon after an investigation. This is not always possible on the night of the investigation since everyone is usually tired. However, it helps to have one at some time before you go in again.

Those are the basic steps to an investigation. There is no one right way to do an investigation. Every investigation is different and different investigators like to use different approaches. However, the goal is always the same. At this point, we should take a closer look at the activity reports and record keeping.

Activity Reports and Record Keeping

One of the things that are important to an investigation is accurate documentation. Should a situation arise where help is needed from religious leaders or those in the scientific field, you must be able to prove conclusively that there are supernatural or preternatural phenomena occurring. Record keeping is very important. At some point in time, you may be asked to produce proof of something that happened in a given situation. In addition, you may want to find out something that happened on a given night that will help to establish a pattern. Whatever the reason, it is very important that we keep accurate records.

Activity Reports Record Phenomena

Activity reports are used to record any phenomena, which has occurred. They are also used as a log even when there is no discernable activity. For example, if you are assigned to monitor certain equipment, you note the readings at specified intervals. For example, you may be assigned to the electromagnetic field detector, (EMF) and the digital thermometer. The assignment may call for taking a reading every 30 minutes. You would record the time and meter readings on the report.

There is another use for the activity report. Should you get a feeling or a hunch, you would write that down on the report. You could then take photographs. In this instance, it would be a wise idea to record the camera used and the frames as well. The entry would look something like this: *23:05 had a feeling of being watched. Strong! Took pictures of general area. Canon, frames 18,19,20.*

There are two benefits to this notation. One, you may be able to document an occurrence of some sort. When the film is developed and you find some anomaly on the photograph, the occurrence is documented. We know when the photograph was taken, who took it, and which camera was used. From these records, we can determine whether a particular person, a particular location or a specific camera is getting the best shots. The second benefit is that it validates the discernment abilities of the individual involved. When that person felt that something was there watching him, the camera confirmed that he was right. You then develop a trust in the discernment ability of that person. In addition, this builds that person's confidence. This can be important where you have a situation where so much is based on feelings and senses as it so often is.

While there can be a formal activity log, a legal pad will do just as well. All you need to record is the time, what was going on, or equipment readings, if nothing was going on. List the people who were present, if there was some form of paranormal activity. You should also list any feelings or sensations. Do not hesitate to record something that may turn out to be nothing. As with the client's journal, it is better to have 10 entries that are nothing than to miss out on 1 item that is important. Besides, if the investigation is going slowly, this will give you something to do, which will help you retain your focus or regain it if you lost it, not to mention keeping you awake.

Determining Activity Patterns

Should there be activity, it is important to note everything that happened, equipment readings, and any sensations felt. Obviously, if something is manifesting in the room, you do not stand there and write down everything you are seeing. Get the equipment readings if you can. Take photographs if you can. After the event is over with, you can then add a detailed description. Again, note on your activity report who was present at the time the activity began. This should include both members of the client's family and the investigators. From this information, we can look for a pattern. Are the same family members or investigators around when activity breaks out? This can be extremely important. Equally important, we may be able to determine that very little activity takes place when certain people are around. Once you have answered all of those questions, you can begin to look for the "why" of the situation.

Seek Solutions At Skull Sessions

Most likely, you will look at the "why" during your post investigation skull session. For example, if a pattern develops where one particular member of the family is always present during outbreaks of activity, you can begin searching for why that person is being targeted. If the phenomena is mild, you may be dealing with recurrent spontaneous psychokinesis, (RSPK) mind over matter. That person may hold the key to ending the activity. If a certain investigator was always present, you would look to make sure that person is around as much as possible during subsequent nights in the home. Place him where most of the activity is noticed. If there is a certain person around and there is never any activity, it could mean that whatever is causing the activity does not want to expose itself to that individual. If that person is a family member and you suspect RSPK as the cause of the activity, you can tell who seems to be causing it and who may be preventing it from happening. If you are dealing with an entity, this could be because the entity either fears this person or feels very calm around that person, thus stopping or preventing the activity from breaking out. In that case, you might not want that person around while you are trying to collect evidence. The point is that you can tell a lot from the activity reports.

Documentation And Record Keeping

As an investigation unfolds, there may be a shoebox filled with documentation, such as photographs and written accounts of manifestations. Paper somehow seems to reproduce itself at alarming rates sometimes.

The next critical item is record keeping so you can find important items when you need them.

If you are in a "hot" house, that is one where there is a lot of activity going on, you would be amazed at the amount of paperwork that is generated. There will be many photographs and activity reports up the whazoo. Keeping track of them and organizing them in a coherent fashion is critical. There is no single way to do this. Different people have different systems. You can use whatever system works for you. It really helps if you have a friend or relative who can help you with that task. There are some people who may want to help you in your investigation but they may be afraid to actually go into a potentially haunted house. If that is the case, they can help you with the record keeping. Believe me, you will see just how valuable that person is to a case. Remember when I said that everyone's role is of equal importance?

Organizing Photographs

Where you have photographs showing phenomenon, such as psychic fog, mist like shapes, orbs or whatever, an excellent idea is to file them in a three ring binder using plastic photo holders. The advantage to photo holders is that they protect your pictures. In addition, some of these holders have slots for the negatives as well as the pictures. They are somewhat expensive but for what they do, they are well worth the cost. That can make life much easier for you down the road. To me, nothing is worse than having to look at two thousand negatives when you want to make a copy of a good picture. On the back of the photograph, write the date, the time the photo was taken, who took it and what camera was used. You should also assign it a document number so it will be easier to keep track of it. Again, there are many different ways to organize your material. Feel free to use whatever method works best for you.

Starting An Index of Your Records

Start an index of all of your records where it appears you recorded unusual phenomena. You can list the activity report number, the picture number, and record where those items can be found. You will have an excessive amount of photographs that do not show anything but you want to keep them as well. Use them as comparison shots or for later reference. If you have a hit, or an anomaly on one of your photos and you have a good comparison shot, it is a good idea to keep the two together. You can then file the rest of the photos in a file box or other container. Just make sure you put in dividers so you can keep all of your sets separated. File the negatives with the pictures. You never know if you will need a negative later and like I said, you do not want to search for them.

Another thought on photographs. If you do get shots showing anything unusual, make at least one copy of that shot, more if the family has expressed a desire to keep them. If you feel you may need outside help, you will need a copy of all "hits" for that purpose. If you like to keep a scrapbook of special shots, you may want another copy. You also do not want to wear out your negatives either. Should you have to go outside for assistance, the organization you go to may want to see the negatives to ensure the pictures were not tampered with. If that happens, get something in writing saying the negatives must be returned to you. If the organization insists on keeping them and you determine that you really need their assistance, you may have to agree. The number one priority is getting help for the client. If you have to lose the negatives in order to do that, so be it. You have to keep your priorities straight but do whatever you can to resist that.

Preparing Your Report

In most investigations, you stay up all night. You are pretty tired and drained when you get home. The last thing you want to do is write up a report of the night's events. However, it is important to write one up as soon as possible, certainly before you go back to the location.

This has two advantages. First, it is wise to write your report while everything is still fresh in your mind. Second, you do not want yourself to be swamped with reports that need to be written. If this is a case where there will be multiple trips to the site, reports can back up in a hurry. Further, if you go to the site a few times before you write up your report, you may get confused about what happened and when. There may be a steady progression to the activity and it is important to be able to draw a time line. However, there is only so much time in a day and if you are working for a living, which means most of us, you can only do so much. So, if you have not been able to write up your report before you go back to the site, always jot down notes on the next night. Do not forget that you will want to have all of your reports ready at the next meeting of your group.

The Client's And Investigator's Journal

Clients are always encouraged to keep a journal. This is important for a number of reasons. The investigators can check the client's journal for patterns and it prevents things from being forgotten.

It is a good idea for investigators to keep a journal also. It can be important to know what is going on in the investigator's life in regards to investigations and the possibility of discernment powers developing. We are not looking for personal information, only information relating to their investigations. The reason for this is because investigators sometimes find phenomena breaking out in their own homes. This could mean they are followed from the site. It may also serve as a warning. Of course, sometimes things just happen for no apparent reason. Phenomena will sometimes occur as a sign that an investigation is coming up. Whatever the cause, experiencing phenomena in an investigator's home does happen from time to time. Paranormal investigators can truly say that they bring their work home with them. So, let us take a look at that.

Activity In The Investigator's Home

If the activity in the investigator's home is severe during an investigation, you will want to discuss the situation with him. Then, the two of you or the group can get together and try to come up with a solution. If the problem is severe, it may be a good idea to remove the investigator from that particular case. A lot of that is up to the investigator. If he has a family at home, it may be an excellent idea for him to remove himself if he feels there is a threat towards his family. If the activity is not severe, you may just want to reinforce the need for that investigator to protect himself.

The investigator's journal sometimes comes in handy on investigations where not much is going on. Just as with the client's journal, everything that may be related to the case should be noted. This just may be a vague feeling that the investigator is not alone or that he feels that he is being watched. If activity does start happening, the journal may hold the key to a case solution.

Record Your Dreams

In addition, it can be important to keep track of odd dreams. They may have a hidden message in them. During sleep, people are much closer to the astral plane. According to scores of people who have had near death experiences, as well as psychics who have communicated with spirits, it appears that at the moment of death, our spirit leaves the body and travels to the next level of existence. While the final destination of the spirit seems to vary, most agree that the spirit enters a tunnel, which links the physical plane to the next level. This plane is known as the "astral plane." At that point, it appears the spirit has the choice of moving forward to the next plane or remaining on the astral plane. Many believe that during deep sleep, we may be in that astral plane ourselves. For that reason, spirits can sometimes communicate with us during our sleep.

In addition, all nightmares should be recorded. Keep a pen and paper hand next to your bed so that you can jot down your dreams and nightmares when you first wake up and before they start to fade away.

You can also use a tape recorder for that purpose. Your dreams may tell you something about the case you are working on or even possible future ones.

(SUMMARY)

It all amounts to keeping all of your records complete and up to date. When you start to get backlogged, it is easy to misfile something. You can also overlook something that may turn out to be important. It can all seem overwhelming but it really isn't. The more you do this kind of work, the easier it becomes. You will know where you can take shortcuts. The thing of it is that it can be very hard to find a good EVP if you have to go through hours of tape, especially when most of the tapes consist of nothing but air. The same is true for camcorders. That is overwhelming and it can drive you to distraction. The same is true with photographs. Try to stay as organized as possible. It will make your investigative life considerably easier.

THE INITIAL INTERVIEW

People will come to you seeking help in numerous ways. One is through the Internet or E-mail if you are on line and have a web page. Another is through the telephone, often from word of mouth referrals. Once you have established a reputation or gotten some exposure, you receive many cases through the mail. Whatever the method, the most important part of any investigation is the initial interview. Before you can even consider an investigation, you must ask yourself the following questions:

1) **Are the phenomena they described investigable?**
2) **Does the person contacting you sound sincere?**
3) **What do they want you to do for them?**
4) **What do they expect as the final outcome?**

Only when you have satisfied the preceding conditions can you agree to proceed further.

Is The Phenomena Investigable?

You will come in to contact with many people who will think they have a problem when they do not. An example of this would be when a distraught parent gets in touch with you because they think their 8-year-old child is possessed. When you ask them to describe why they feel that way, they might tell you that Johnny is behaving in a bizarre manner. (although what 8-year-old doesn't?) When you ask them if there are preternatural or supernatural events taking place such as items moving on their own accord or are there terrible smells without an apparent cause, or does Johnny speak in a language that he could not possibly know, they tell you "no." They may then go on to explain how he seems to "have a mind of his own" and "he shows no respect" to his elders. At this point, you need to tell them that if they really think something is wrong with him they should think about counseling before jumping head on into supernatural beliefs. Of course at this point, the distraught parent will scream at you and say something like "Don't you know anything about the devil? My little Johnny has the devil in him, can't you see that!" At this point, a line I once heard on some TV program comes to mind. I haven't been able to find the author but the line goes: "There is a devil, of that there is no doubt but is he trying to get in us or trying to get out?" Anyway, you need to try to explain to her that demonic possession is extremely rare and it is the least likely scenario. Furthermore, you can explain that the problem sounds behavioral and that it is in their best interests to rule out all natural causes first. Explain to them the damage that can be done to a child it he/she begins to believe that "the devil is in them." This may or may not satisfy her but this is the only safe course you can possibly take.

I did a case where the mother of an 8 year old was convinced that her child was possessed. The call came in on Saturday and it was decided that we would go over to the house on Sunday. Well, there was an emergency call later on Saturday so my partner took a ride over there to calm things down. On Sunday, my partner and I went there to get an idea of what was going on. Almost immediately, red flags went up. For openers, the apartment was a mess. I am not talking about an item or two being out of place; in this house, there was garbage literally piled a foot high in every corner. The same was true of the kitchen table. This was a place where I really did not want to sit down, which worked out well because the only thing to sit on was a plastic cooler. Anyway, on top of the pile on the kitchen table were two books that dealt with the ritual of deliverance. (This is a sort of mini-exorcism.) We immediately grew concerned about the mental state of those who lived there. I think it is safe to say that most people attempt to clean their house before they ask strangers in. Furthermore, reading books of that nature scares me. It leads me to believe that they may have talked themselves into believing that the child was possessed. To make matters worse, the girl in question kept dousing herself with holy water. That alone told me that the child was anything but possessed. One of the major symptoms of demonic possession is a revulsion to sacramental objects. Holy water certainly qualifies. There is no way, none, nada, that possessed people will pour holy water on themselves.

Another thing I found odd was that the father of the child remained in his bedroom watching TV while we discussed the situation in the kitchen. That sent up more red flags. He only came out when he decided to blast my partner and I for running around and screaming about demons being in his house. We were the only ones who did not believe that there were demons in his house. I was tempted to tell him that no self-respecting demon would dare live in a house that filthy. However, I restrained myself. To make a long story short, there were no demons there, just a disturbed family. We found out that the girls was on medication for a mental illness. That was no surprise. The thing that most surprised me was that the parents were *not* on medication. Something was wrong there. This brings up a good point. In many cases, you will find that one family member believes that there is a problem while another does not. That can be a hairy proposition. If all parties are open-minded about the situation, I do not mind working the case. However, if there is going to be a conflict, I will generally stay away. The job is hard enough when everyone is on the same page. It is almost impossible to do when there is constant conflict. That is where I have to draw the line. If one party in the house does not want investigators around, I will not take the case. It is a lose-lose proposition and I think it is nuts to get involved in that type of situation.

There are many people out there who really do believe they live in a haunted house and some of them are right. A very important point to note here is that you often have to do a balancing act between asking them what they feel they are experiencing and telling them what symptoms could occur. It is possible to teach people how to be haunted. Believe it or not, you can also teach a ghost how to haunt a place too. When talking to them for the first time, be very vague about what often happens in a haunting situation. Make them tell you as much as possible about their experiences without coaching them. If what they are describing sounds like something quite natural, explain to them why you feel that way. If you tell them what types of things can happen, they will most assuredly call you somewhere down the road and report the very things you mentioned to them in the earlier conversation. It is not that they are trying to fool you; they really do believe there is a problem and they will do anything they can to convince you of that. Explain to them that while hauntings do occur, they are relatively rare, especially the bad ones.

Obviously though, you will get calls where the person contacting you will describe phenomena that does indeed seem to indicate a problem. When you have satisfied yourself that the phenomena sounds real and that the person talking to you sounds sincere and sane you can then set up an appointment to discuss the matter further. One very important rule: never diagnose the situation over the telephone. Just because they are describing a haunting does not mean there is one. You must always get as much information as possible and try to observe as much phenomena for yourself before you can accurately determine whether there is a bona fide haunting going on or not. People do have a tendency to exaggerate at times so be careful about what you say. Always remember my 25% exaggeration factor.

Is The Party Contacting You Sincere?

Once you get an inquiry, you must determine whether the person sounds sincere. It a sad fact that there are many people out there who are mentally ill. You can expect to get more than your fair share of inquiries from people who have a delusion about being haunted or who are hearing voices or seeing things that are not there. What makes this a difficult situation to discern is that that many people who are being haunted will sound hysterical when they first contact you. They are undergoing something so traumatic and stressful that they are being driven to the point of psychosis. It may take several discussions with them to determine what may be a real haunting as compared to a psychotic break. It can be of great help to you if you have some background in the mental health field. Use common sense. Ask yourself if the things that are being reported are consistent with the types of things that happen in a haunting. If the person should divulge to you that he/she is seeing a therapist, this should send up a red flag. It does not mean that you should just summarily drop them but you need to be very careful. You can ask their permission to speak to that therapist although that is both tricky and risky. One important note, the mental hygiene laws are very strict regarding a therapist talking to anyone about a client. Your client must sign a consent form to release information form, which must be given to the therapist before he/she will talk to you. Even with this, you may have a hard time getting any information about your client. At best, the therapist may be artfully vague; at worst, the therapist may accuse you of feeding into their delusion. It is the proverbial "Catch-22."

A woman who sounded very credible once contacted me. She spoke well; she was articulate and obviously well educated. Everything seemed fine until I asked her what the problem was. She then went on to explain that she saw John the Baptist in her shower curtain every morning. Okay! On a few occasions, she also claimed to see the angel Gabriel. I have heard of crystal gazing and crystal balls but nothing about shower curtains. One wonders who or what would appear if she changed the curtain. Of course, in this day and age, she could probably make a killing selling the shower curtain on E-Bay.

Just to confuse things even further, it is common for people who are mentally ill to be targeted by the demonic. They are easy targets because no one will believe anything they say. The illness they are being treated for probably has many symptoms similar to haunting phenomena. Of course, when they tell this to their therapist, they will simply be given stronger doses of medication for their troubles. So, as a paranormal investigator, you have to be very careful when dealing with potentially mentally ill people.

You always have to worry about what the mentally ill person will say about you, should you take a case involving them. It is potentially dangerous to begin with and you can easily be accused of something if you spend time alone with someone who is mentally ill. The last thing you need to do is be accused of something terrible. It is sad to say, but you really have to stay away from them when it comes to investigating a case.

What Does The Client Expect?

Once you have decided that an investigation is warranted, you need to determine what they want you to do and what do they expect as an outcome. Do they want you to bring in a psychic or have someone called in to cleanse the house? Are they searching for some magical way of ending the problem or do they want a serious investigation? People will sometimes believe that the only way to solve their problem is with some form of ritual, whether it is done by a priest, shaman, or psychic. A huge question you must ask is are they looking for publicity? The majority of the time, publicity is the last thing a serious paranormal investigator wants. It can disrupt your investigation terribly if not totally ruin it. The media will turn the investigation into a circus and the public at large will descend on the family in droves. You will find you own credibility constantly questioned. The family will find no peace and they will eventually realize that the human factor is causing more trouble that the supernatural one.

If the family or person informs you that they have been in touch with the media, red flags should go up in your mind. They have to have a reason for going that route. It could be something simple like they did not know where to turn and they figured the press would know. It could also be that they are looking for publicity either to make themselves seem important or to land book or TV rights. If either of those two possibilities are correct, you will be doing yourself a great favor by declining the investigation.

What Outcome Is Expected?

The last thing that must be considered is what do they expect as the outcome. There is no way you can guarantee that you can stop the problem, assuming that it is a problem that needs to be stopped. You can guarantee that you will do everything in your power to stop the problem. You can call in someone with more experience or a member of the clergy. However, you cannot guarantee the outcome. You even have to be careful in promising clergy involvement because that is always an unknown. Very often, the clergy will not want to get involved in what appears to be a haunting. This can be especially true with the Catholic Church. Whether or not to investigate a paranormal situation is up to the Bishop of the Archdiocese. Your parish priest may or may not believe you. If he does, he may contact the diocese for you. If he does not believe you, you will have to do that yourself. Then, depending on where the family lives, your problems may just be beginning.

Sometimes, the client will tell you that they don't want to get rid of the spirit at all; they just want to know more about it. I would not touch that with a 10-foot pole. There are people who enjoy having a ghost around. Some people will ask you to just convince the ghost not to bother them. I do not get involved in behavior modification for the spirit world. You have to make sure you know *exactly* what they want and then you have to decide if it is something you can or want to do. Only you can make that decision. You will find that there are some cases that are simply not worth taking.

Interviewing Those Involved

Once you have decided to investigate, you will need to interview all of the people involved. It is wise ideas to videotape the first interview. Admittedly, it can make both you and the client a little nervous. However, it serves a good purpose in that you can refer to it again in the event something was said that you did not take notice of at the time it was said. Relying on memory can be disastrous, especially if you are me. It can also help eliminate people who are inclined towards fraud. People do not usually lie as easily when they are being taped. However, if they object, it is sufficient to audiotape the interview. If they object to that, you have to wonder what is going on and that should send up a red flag. Proceed with caution. They may fear that the interview will go public. If that is the case, you must assure them that is not your intention. Always explain to them why you want to tape them. To be honest, no one has ever refused when I have requested taping.

Once you start, you need to get as much information on any occurrences as you possibly can. This is an ongoing thing. When you first talk to people, they will be nervous and are likely to forget things. Also, frightened people tend to remember only the most frightening things when they are under the pressure of questioning and that means a lot of small stuff gets forgotten. The problem is that the small stuff could well turn out to be something really important. As we all know, we always remember things later that we should have said. For that reason, I have made up a questionnaire, which should be helpful. It is not an exact science so there may be things going on that are not covered in the questionnaire. There are some questions in there that you may choose not to ask, depending on the situation. Again, be careful when it comes to leading them. Let them tell you as much as possible in their own words. This questionnaire can be found in the appendix section of this book. You need to get as much information as possible, so always make your clients aware that they can add things to what they have already told you. In fact, you should encourage them to talk with others involved in the situation and try to remember items that were missed.

Background Data and Belief Systems

The next step in the interview is to get some background data and an idea of their belief systems. This can go a long way towards finding out the critical question of why they are experiencing unusual phenomena. It can also help you determine what you are dealing with. Are they religious? Do they believe in demons and devils? If so, do they believe that it is easy to fall prey to them? That leaves you to wonder whether they are convincing themselves that there are demonic forces at work. You will often find during initial interviews that your client is nervous, especially when you are taping them. Even in times of great stress, people are always acutely aware of how they might look and sound when recorded. For that reason, you may want to do several interviews. It also helps to have other people from your team do follow-up interviews. Sometimes women prefer to talk to other woman, sometimes not. The same is true with males. The trick is to keep the interview as casual as possible. You will find that being casual helps establish rapport and that leads to trust. Trust leads to more detailed answers to important questions.

Be Positive and Supporting

Since the initial interview is your first real contact with the family, you need to be as positive and as supporting as possible. First impressions always count but probably more so here. You do not want to say or do anything that might offend them or make them think you do not believe them. Also, never act condescendingly or say anything accusatory. You need honest answers so let them feel that they can confide in you. Try to act as natural as possible. To me, a good interview is one where there is a good flow of conversation with a lot of information mixed in and with a little bit of laughter. The more relaxed you and the client are, the better the interview and the more information you will get. In the beginning, always interview everyone separately. You want to get as many difference perspectives on the situation as you can. Plus, you don't want one person to say something that will capture the other person's attention and have them forget something important. When the initial interview is done, encourage all of the parties involved to get together and discuss the situation. You can collect valuable information in this informal setting. It does not hurt to tape this either but you can decide that on a case-to-case basis. With me, I tape everything.

Again, what you are trying to determine from the initial contact is whether they person sounds sincere and if the problem they describe is something that warrants an investigation. You are not trying to determine what the problem is at this point. Meet the caller for the first time away from the home, if possible. This is not always practical but it can help. Meeting them in a setting away from the house will cut down on the influence of whatever might be in the house. Someone who is being haunted may not be able to give you objective answers to your questions if they are sitting in a room where there may have been terrifying activity the night before. They may focus on things that happened only in that room as opposed to things that happened elsewhere. Try to get an objective a rundown on the situation. Remember my 25% exaggeration factor.

Of course, time and distance can dictate how you are going to do the interview process. If I feel, based on the initial contact that the caller sounds sincere and there does appear to be a haunting taking place and that the family involved is in danger, I will throw all of the rules out of the window and try to get in there as quickly as possible. It is not a perfect world and things rarely go the way we would like them to go. Always keep "Murphy's Law" in mind. Hence the need for flexibility.

Give The Client An Overview

Meet the person away from the house if you can and discuss with them an overview of the investigation. Do not discuss specifics yet but give them an idea of what to expect. Let them know how many people you might bring in and what equipment you will be working with. You can even explain what some of the equipment is for. If you have it, give them some literature explaining the process in a bit more detail. They can take that home with them and read it at their leisure. This takes some of the uncertainty away and that can make your first night of the investigation a little easier and possibly more productive as well. Encourage them to ask questions. What I always tell a client is to ask as many questions as they can and if anyone else they talk to have questions, they should write them down and I will do my best to answer them when I see them. This, I have found, puts them at ease. At this point, either go back with them to do the formal interviews and look around the house or set up an appointment to do that at a later date. Remember, at this early stage, we are just collecting information. From that information and what we will gather later, we can go about planning and setting up the actual investigation.

Listen Carefully To The Client

You have to pay close attention to what they say and how they say it. Look at their body language. There may be hidden clues in there. For example, if you ask if there is any form of abuse, physical or mental going on in the home, the woman may answer "no" but she may also look away from you when she says that. That would be a red flag. The same would be true if you asked about whether she or someone else has dabbled with the occult. The verbal answer may be "no" but again, look for the hidden clue. Suddenly looking down at the ground when you ask that question may well supply you with the true answer. Of course, some people have difficulty making eye contact under normal conditions. That is something I am occasionally guilty of. So, when you first start talking to a person, although you are asking general questions, look at their posture and whether or not they make eye contact. Make a mental note of that. This could establish a baseline from which to evaluate them. After a short time spent with them, you will get an idea of who makes eye contact and who doesn't. That bit of information can come in handy later on. If one person always makes eye contact and two weeks into the investigation, the person looks away from you when you ask them a question, you now have some reason to believe that the answers may not be truthful. What you need to look for is changes in their body language when they begin to answer the more detailed questions.

Congruence In Answering Questions

Whenever you do any kind of interview, you have to look for congruence. Does someone tell you that they are relaxed while they are wringing their hands? If so, what do you think is the honest answer? Do you believe the client when they say that they slept fine while you see bags under their eyes? The list can go on. If you come across incongruence, don't automatically assume that they are being deceitful for a negative purpose. They may not be lying to you to cover up for something bad. What you tend to come across with people who are being haunted is that they do not want to appear weak in front of you. They will make every attempt to look strong. Also, if there are children around, they have to put up a good front in front of them. I have to agree with that. Where I mention that we cannot let the client see fear in us, a parent has to do the same thing with their children. It is even more important for them to act strong in front of the children than it is for us to act strong in front of the client. At least with adults there is some rationalization going on. With children, most of that is missing. For that reason, it is better to exclude them when you are going to be discussing the haunting with the adults.

In addition, while an adult can be scarred by a terrible haunting, it is much, much worse for the children to be scarred. Again, an adult can rationalize much of the horror away. The child does not have that ability. Plus, a frightening incident is viewed differently by an adult and a child. The effects are much worse for the child because the terror they experience as children changes how they develop into adults. While an adult will have difficulty long after the haunting has ended, the child will have that terror with them for a much longer period of time. So, always make sure that what is being told to you matched what you are seeing. Communication consists of much more than words.

To better understand this, let us take a look at the components of human communication. You would think that communication is made up of words. That is true, but only to a small extent. Believe it or not, words only account for 7% of human communication. Amazing, right? So many people say so much and yet they really say nothing. So what else constitutes communication? Tonality and body language is the answer. Tonality accounts for 38% of human communication. The remaining 55% is body language. Therefore, whether we are talking about a paranormal investigation or something else, make sure you "read" the person you are talking to. So, whether it is a client or another investigator you are talking to and they tell you that they are not frightened, make sure you look at *how* they say it.

Are there going to be times when you get fooled? Sure, it may happen at some point. That is why it is important to learn how to read people because that way, you can keep embarrassing episodes to a minimum. There are people who like to pull pranks. There are people who are out for profit only, regardless of whether it is at someone else's expense. There are also mentally ill people out there so you really have to be careful.

GETTING STARTED

Now that you have gotten the initial interview out of the way and you feel comfortable in your decision to start the actual investigation, you need to give the family some instructions. These instructions will help make it easier for you to determine what is going on, and hopefully, stop the problem. Instruct the family to get a 3-section notebook. In one section, ask them to list anything that they feel may have happened that they think may have been of a supernatural nature and the approximate date when this occurred. I do not expect them to know exactly when something occurred; I just want to get a starting point or a baseline period. An answer such as "I think that was 2 or 3 months ago," is fine. Ask them to put as much information down as they can remember. If they think uncle Fred was present when something happened, then have them put that down.

Recording The Past Happenings

Now bear in mind that at this point the items mentioned may or may not be paranormal. It may well be something quite normal or it could be partly imagination. What we need to do at this point is try to figure out when things began happening. Typically, in a haunting, happenings start slowly. Many little incidents go unnoticed. For example, you are sitting on the sofa reading a magazine. The telephone rings and you drop the magazine on the coffee table and get up to answer the phone. When you are finished with the call, you return to the sofa and discover that the magazine is no longer on the table where you left it. You think to yourself something to the effect that: "I could have sworn I left that magazine on the table." Then you see it sitting on an end table by the telephone. At this point you probably chide yourself for being absent minded and go about your business.

Now in many instances that is all there is to it, simple absentmindedness. (Something I have perfected.) The same type of things happens with sounds. Maybe you hear a scratching sound coming from the basement. You immediately write it off as some little animal and forget about it. In many cases, these are the types of things that will happen in the early stages of a haunting. While they may be natural, they could indicate the start of something. In the early stages of a haunting, many things are missed because they are thought to be coincidence. Conversely, in the full-blown stages of a haunting, you have the case where you really did do something absentmindedly but now you automatically assume it is your ghost doing it. Sounds that are natural in origin may now sound ominous since they are being colored by fear. It makes things confusing.

When Did It All Start?

Remember though, the goal here is to try to determine when this all started and what types of things are going on. By asking them to write down anything they remember helps the investigator get an idea of when it started and what it did in the early stages. Our memories tend to be clouded, especially when we are scared. Under the best of circumstances, memory is faulty. Still, try to get as much information as is possible on the early happenings and then try to sort out what is probably normal from what might be paranormal. To do this, use a weighing system. This will be discussed in detail later in this book. In short, the investigator sits down with all of the parties involved and tries to decide what seems to be normal and what seems to be paranormal. This process is usually done during a calm period when the client is most likely to use objective reasoning. It is pointless to try to score an item right after some frightening activity just took place. Under those circumstances, everything looks paranormal and ominous.

This is hardly a foolproof method because of reliance on the client's memory. Therefore, a lot of client material may be questionable. However, it is better to get 75 items that are normal than to miss one that is not. The starting point is that important; it really justifies all the extra work.

Recording Everything New

The second thing to do in their notebook is to record everything new that happens. Ask them to do this in as much detail as they possibly can. Have them record what happened, where it happened, when it happened, under what circumstances, and who witnessed it. Also record the time, date and if possible, the weather conditions. Also, ask them to make a note if there is something special about a day, for example, is it someone's birthday or was it on the day one of the children was receiving a sacrament. This seems like a lot of work for them but each of these areas can be crucial to the investigation. It is critical to look for patterns. Patterns are so important that they will be presented in detail shortly.

Keeping The Family Informed

Of the utmost importance is keeping the family informed. They should know exactly what is happening and why it is being done. Do not be afraid to answer their questions. However, you do not want to tell them that you expect to find a demon running around when you have no evidence whatsoever to support that claim. Always remember the rule: what do we think, what do we know, and what can prove? We are only going to tell them what we can prove. It is okay to speculate on occasion but you have to be very careful in that area. You may not be able to prove something yet but you may know what is going on. Let me use an example because this is a sensitive area. If much of the activity appears to be centering on religious items, crosses being inverted or destroyed, for example, then you may want to consider the demonic. However, if not many of the conditions for demonic activity have been met, you may know that you are dealing with something other than demonic. If there is some evidence that seems to cross the line, you can then speculate that an inhuman spirit may be present. However, do not volunteer that speculation unless you feel sure that the family is in danger. Danger is the key word here. Even if you are not 100% sure that it is demonic but you have a reason to believe that someone is in immediate danger, you are then almost forced to speculate.

One example where you are almost forced to speculate would be a situation where no one is able to sleep due to constant activity such as someone being touched at night or the children being threatened or some such thing. In order for the family to get any sleep, it may be wise to have everyone sleep in the same room. Making a change like that is telling the story without any words but if the situation is that severe, it is understandable to speculate. However, you have to remember that there is a difference between keeping them informed and causing them to panic. It would be horrible to have them believe that a demon from hell is running around their home when it turns out to be a simple case of RSPK. You have to be sure in your own mind and have some proof to support your theory. It stands to reason they are scared enough to begin with or they would not have come to you in the first place. Should there be an entity of some form operating there, it is already feeding off of their fear so we do not want to add unnecessary stress. It is also a good way to ruin your reputation as an investigator and even ruin your organization. Always make sure brain is engaged before letting your mouth fly.

An Extreme Measure

I want to point out something here. The idea of having everyone sleep in the same room can be a good one if you have serious outward manifestations and people starving for sleep. Any parent would want to sleep in the same room as their children when things are bad. Any frightened child would like to sleep with their parents. That makes perfect sense. However, you have to be careful with that. When things are severe, it can work out fine. The problem is that you have to pick your spot carefully because there is no going back. Once everyone has the safety of strength in numbers, no one is going to want to split up later. That is why I never recommend that in the early stages of a haunting unless the manifestations are extreme and dangerous. It can almost become a crutch of sorts and you have to remember that one of our goals is to help make the family stronger and less afraid of their circumstances. However, that is an individual choice the victims have to make. In extreme cases it is a good idea.

Interpersonal Relations

Always be respectful of the property of your client. If they are a non-smoking household, then do not smoke there unless they tell you it is all right to do so. If you go outside to smoke, do not drop cigarette butts on their lawn. Do not leave soda cans and candy bar wrappers around the house. If you are doing an overnighter, do not raid their refrigerator unless they have invited you to do so and then be fair about it. It is recommended that you bring food and beverages with you on an investigation. Also, be professional at all times. It is fine to have fun on an investigation. In fact, you often do. The interactions between the investigator and the client can be hysterical at times. There is nothing wrong with that. A few funny ghost stories can go a long way. You just have to remember that these people came to you for help. You need to treat the serious matters seriously. Really, this is all common sense. Unfortunately, common sense is not all that common.

The next step in the investigation is to begin the detailed interviewing process, which we will look at in detail. That is where you start trying to figure out what you are dealing with and why it is happening in that house to those particular people. Before doing that, let us look at the importance of patterns to get a good idea what types of questions to ask.

Determining Patterns of Activity

One of the most crucial parts of any investigation is determining whether or not there is a discernable pattern to the activity. A pattern is anything that happens repeatedly. It can be something that happens quite regularly such as weekly or daily or it can be something that happens rarely but does repeat itself. Determining a pattern can conceivably answer the four big questions facing the investigator. Once again these questions are:

1) *Is something there?*
2) *What is it?*
3) *Why is it there?*
4) *If the spirit is human, who is it?*

Examples of Patterns

Here is an example of a pattern. Let us say that the client tells you that six times in the last 3 months she has seen an apparition in her living room. When you question her in detail, it comes out that all six sightings occurred on Thursdays. What does that tell us? In and of itself, possibly nothing. However, it may give us a starting point for investigating. Did something happen to the previous resident that caused such emotional pain that her energy has been somehow burned in the environment? This is called a "psychic imprint." If we can determine that on a Thursday night years ago, the woman living in the house waited nervously for one of her children to come home. Later, she learned that the child was killed in an accident. The terrible worry and emotional trauma this woman suffered could have left an energy imprint by that one window where you always see the apparition. It is possible that what you are seeing is nothing more than energy recording or imprint. There really is no ghost. Problem solved.

Let us say that this scenario does not fit, that there was no traumatic event and it does appear that you have an actual entity there, then what is the value of knowing the pattern? Well, if we know that it appears every Thursday at 1 a.m., then it makes it very easy for us to be there and collect pictures and other data. This input is very useful in determining what is there and ultimately to help us to get rid of it, should that be necessary. If we know that every fourth Wednesday something may happen, it gives the researcher the time to prepare for whatever it is.

The investigator can set up his equipment in that particular area. It also gives him/her the chance to bring in others to witness the phenomena. In this case, the pattern can serve as an early warning system.

Patterns Must Be Recorded Over Time

Patterns can be hard to determine and to make any pattern useful it must be recorded over time. Sometimes you get lucky and things will start happening right away. However, that is not the norm. That is where the journal you have asked the client to keep becomes so important. Determining a pattern can and usually does take time. For that reason, the quicker the client begins keeping a journal, the sooner we can begin to figure out what is there and why it is there. Now this is not a neat and orderly world in which we live and there are many instances where there just does not appear to be a pattern.

Actually, the lack of a pattern can tell you a lot too. The randomness of the activity could mean that you have an entity, either human or inhuman, that chooses when and how it will act. In some cases, the spirit might single one person out for abuse and it may completely ignore another. It is showing that there is an intelligence of some sort behind the activity. Any signs of intelligence behind activity is proof that there is an entity present.

Look For A Common Denominator

In many instances, certain types of phenomena will occur on certain days. How does knowing that rapping's take place every Tuesday help us? Well, what we would do is see if there is a common denominator involved. Does the husband go bowling every Tuesday night? That tells us that whatever is there may be trying to scare the wife when it feels she is most vulnerable. Negative spirits do not play fair. The woman may automatically feel more frightened when she is alone and we know what spirits love for dinner: fear. In many instances, the males in the house will scoff at any mention of supernatural happenings. They will say things like "you're imagining this, or do you see what you're doing to yourself?" Because nothing happens to them, or at least nothing that stands out or is recognized, the males will almost invariably disbelieve the one who reports the incidents. Over time, the male usually finds out the hard way that the female was right but that can take a long time to develop. The invading entity knows this and will pick up its activity on the nights he is not home just to make her look hysterical. It is part of the spirit's strategy and it enjoys the game. Therefore, it is not enough just to know when things will happen but also to know who is or is not home at the time of that particular activity.

Weather Conditions Are Important

Weather conditions are also important. In many instances, people have reported smelling ozone before a ghostly manifestation. Of course, many people also smell ozone just before a thundershower. There is a big difference obviously and it is important to know which is which. Spirit activity tends to occur more often when there are electrical storms or thundershowers. We often get great pictures during electrical storms. Of course, taking outdoor pictures in the rain is not a good idea because even if you do get a good shot, it is automatically suspect because of the rain. Perhaps the spirits know how to use the natural energy to manifest. It makes sense if you think about it. We know that there is a rise of electromagnetic energy when a spirit manifests. The more energy it has available, the stronger the manifestation will be. It might affect the duration of the activity. By knowing this, you can better prepare for your investigations.

Activity Can Form A Pattern

It is important to know where in the house manifestations occur. It may be throughout the house or it may be in just one room. There can be a pattern to the actual activity as well. Does this always happen before that? For example, does the pounding in the walls always precede an apparitional manifestation? That is important to know. Does it start in one room and move to another? Again, that is a good piece of information to have. Does the intensity level vary from room to room? Does it always start around the same time? Does it always end around the same time?

Again, it can serve as an early warning system and it gives the researcher time to set up equipment and otherwise prepare for the activity.

What Patterns Can Tell You

Patterns can tell you a lot about what is going on in the home. It can help you determine if anyone is being targeted. That in itself can point you in a particular direction. Maybe that person is suffering from depression and an invading entity is feeding off that illness. Maybe someone had cursed that person and he really believes in it. Possibly that person was actually involved in some form of occult practice but was afraid or ashamed to admit it? Maybe that person always says a Rosary on a particular night. An invading spirit may take exception to that. If it does, then you have a good piece of evidence and that can help make a case for the spirit being demonic. However, it could also mean that you have a human spirit who simply hates the Rosary, perhaps because she or she was once forced to say them all the time. That is where you have to look at the other evidence you have gathered up to that point. These are all possibilities. In addition, this is all if the activity is preternatural or supernatural. Patterns can also help you determine that the phenomena are of natural causes. If one person appears to be targeted and another one is always around that person, you may be able to develop a case for RSPK based on some unspoken hostility between the two parties involved. Again, the possibilities are infinite.

Look at the journal the client's family has kept. Their memory of past events, before your arrival, will be faulty but if they remembered that the banging in the walls always occurs on Tuesday, that claim may be confirmed now that they are keeping the journal. Once there have been established patterns, you can then look to find reasons why those patterns keep occurring. That can lead to solving the case. The point is that finding patterns can make the investigation more productive and it can also play a huge role in understanding the problem and in possibly finding the solution to it.

PROTECTING YOURSELF

As a paranormal investigator, you will be putting yourself in danger to some extent. Granted, there is little risk of being hurt physically but the mental attacks are common and can be very effective. While every possible step is taken to eliminate or minimize the risk, at some point in time you will need to defend yourself. There is an old saying, "If you jump into the fire, expect to get burned." Knowing how to protect yourself is crucial. What many do not realize is that you also need to protect yourself at home, at work, and in your car. Protection is not limited to just the site of the investigation. You have to realize that by the nature of your work, that is becoming involved with the spirit world, has its own peculiar concerns. Since spirits are not hostage to the physical world as we are, they can move to anywhere they want. That means that they can most certainly follow you. This is true if you are a caseworker who puts himself on the front lines or if you simply like to go to haunted locations to take pictures. If you go looking for spirits, they will go looking for you. That however, does not make it dangerous. It is simply something you have to be aware of and take steps to avoid if you feel it might be a problem.

Protection Prayers Start At Home

There is a have a tendency to forget to do protection prayers at home before going on an investigation. Between the excitement of the investigation itself and checking all the equipment to ensure that everything is present and in working order, prayers can be forgotten. Keep a little checklist with the equipment and let the last item on the list be a reminder to say a protection prayer before leaving home. Granted, you may not need it but in many cases you have no idea what you may encounter and as the old saying goes: an ounce of prevention is worth a pound of cure. Besides, it might save you from some activity in your own home.

Paranormal investigators are sometimes "marked individuals" if they have worked on demonic cases. When dealing with the demonic, in some cases, activity may break out before an investigation with the intent of sending you a warning. The message is simple: stay out of it. In addition, once you enter the investigation, retaliation can often be expected. How severe the retaliation is depends in part on what is doing it, how strong it is and how well you have protected yourself. Demons do not like the people who are threatening to them. In that regard, they are no different from us. Just about any paranormal investigator you meet will have a story or two about attacks that they have endured. These attacks are not of the life threatening variety but they are serious just the same. They will also tell you how they were successful in repelling the attack, or protecting themselves once it started. I personally recommend saying the Rosary before going on an investigation. Of course, that is a Catholic prayer and that may turn many people off. Pray in a manner in which you are comfortable but I have done many cases, the good, the bad and the ugly and I know what works for me.

An Investigator Must Believe In God

Protection starts long before an investigation begins. Whatever your religious beliefs are, it is important that you do believe in God, in whatever form that your particular beliefs call for. There is one God; He just goes under many different names. Since you will be dealing with things of a spiritual nature, you should have a good spiritual foundation to fall back on. Pray to God as a matter of routine. He wants to hear from us even when we are not in trouble. For that matter, He wants to hear from us more when things are going well. Another key is to live a good life. If you are a mean, hurtful person, you are going to get yourself in trouble as like attracts like. Believe me, what goes around most assuredly comes around. We all sin and we always will sin. That is the nature of man. The key is to try hard to be a good person. For most of us, this takes some work. The last thing you want to do is go into a house infested by something nasty and find out that it is attracted to you. Oops!

Bless Your Home And Family

Once you know you are about to begin an investigation, pray hard for God's help and protection. Before you leave your home, it is a good idea to bless it. Always use holy water. It does not matter what your religion is holy water has been proven to work. It will cut down on some of the activity that might take place in your home. Also, always say a prayer of protection for your pets. They can be the subjects of attacks too. If a demon cannot get at you because you have protected yourself well with prayers, it may decide to go after the ones you love. When you ask God for protection, do not pray only for your own protection. Ask God to protect all of the people and things that are important to you ... your family, your friends and your pets. Do not worry; God charges the same amount, no matter how many things you are asking Him to protect.

Bless Your Vehicle

When you get into your car, bless it also. You do not want any uninvited guests riding with you. There have been many stories of investigators looking in their rear view mirrors only to see an uninvited guest staring up at them from the back seat. This does not help your nerves. Investigators have been pinched or touched by unseen forces going to or from an investigation. You might just get away with having to endure horrible smells on your ride but even that can shake you up a bit. In extreme cases, there have been reports of drivers encountering phantom vehicles or phantom people designed to cause an accident. This usually only happens to demonologists who work the worst cases but it is always better to be safe than sorry. Besides, it might help your car to start. It is not uncommon for a car to have problems starting up during investigations.

Do Not Take Anything For Granted

When you have done an investigation and you did not experience any overt phenomena, that does not mean that nothing was there. We have all gone on investigations where we felt that nothing was present because there were no outward manifestations of any kind and your senses may not have picked up anything. We eventually send our rolls of film to be developed and pretty much forget the investigation. When we finally get around to picking up the pictures, we are shocked to see all kinds of anomalies. Something was there all the time only it did nothing overt and we may have missed some things that were less obvious. A common mistake that is often made by experienced investigators is they get careless and take it for granted that nothing was there. They are often so used to actually experiencing phenomena that they forget to take the proper precautions when they do not experience anything. This can lead to trouble. The lesson is never taking anything for granted.

There Is One Universal God

Your prayers and blessings do not have to be long-winded elaborate rituals. You do not have to be up for three days so you can fast before the investigation so you can say all of your prayers. They can be quick and simple. After leaving the sight of the investigation, repeat this routine. Always play it safe, if there is nothing-unnatural going on, you have not hurt yourself by praying.

There is no one right religion. As a Roman Catholic, I do not have the arrogance necessary to think that this is the only true religion. In fact, that is an absurd notion. I believe strongly in Jesus Christ and He is the one I pray to for help and protection. I have prayed to Mary and several saints too. My point is this; church authorities would have you believe that if you are not Catholic, you are not saved. Born again Christians can be even worse. Somehow, I do not think that was

Christ's message when He walked among us. He never said you have to be Catholic. He said you have to believe in Him and His Father. Are Jews, Muslims, and people of other religions all condemned to eternal fire? Somehow, I do not think so. My feeling is, if you worship God, in whatever form your religious beliefs dictate and you are a good, caring, and loving person, you will have no problem entering Heaven.

This is not meant to sound like an indictment against the Catholic Church. Believe me, that is not my intention. I am a Catholic and I very much love my religion. I just think that many of the leaders need to read more about Jesus and cut down on the prehistoric thinking that still permeates the religion. There are scores of wonderful people in the Catholic Church just as there are in all religious faiths. Unfortunately, there are some ignorant people too. You need to focus on the good ones and pray for the others. Never in history has the church come under such fire as it does today. Never has it done more to deserve it. Just the same, the church is not God.

Having said all of that, it does not matter whether you pray to the Catholic God or the Muslim God. He is the same God. The important thing is you must believe in God and you must call on Him for protection. He will answer your prayers.

At some point in time, everyone loses his or her faith to some degree. That is part of the human condition. It is when this happens that you have to pray the hardest. You have to pray, asking God to strengthen your faith. If you are suffering from a lack of faith, it would be very dangerous for you to be involved in an investigation and most certainly, a possibly demonic one. You are extremely vulnerable if you meet the demonic when your faith is shaky. Like all bullies, the demonic picks on the perceived weakest victims and believe me, it knows your vulnerabilities and it knows what scares you. Believe me, God will still protect you. He is not losing His faith in you just because you may have lost your faith in Him. If your faith is weak, do everyone a favor, especially yourself and avoid any investigations until your faith becomes stronger. Here are some of the ways to protect yourself in this field. You have heard it all before but it is important to drill this into your head so here we go again.

Prayer

Pray according to your own religious beliefs. Prayers do not have to be long-winded, formal affairs. In a pinch, you can improvise. There are many wonderful protection prayers available to you. Several of the prayers are listed at the end of this book. However, it is appropriate to say any prayers you feel comfortable with. God listens to all prayers, not just the formal ones. If you have a favorite Saint, ask his/her help. St. Michael the Archangel is a good one to pray to. He has long battles and already defeated Satan. Since you do not know what you might run into, he is a good choice to pray to. Say prayers both before and after an investigation. I know of some investigators who will try to attend Mass on the day of an investigation, especially when they feel it is a bad one. Others try to have a priest bless them before the investigation. It is certainly added protection and well worth the effort in my opinion.

Holy Water

No matter what your religious beliefs are holy water works. It will repel an attack whether your religion believes in it or not. I have been asked many times why this is so and whether that says something about religion. I will leave it up to the individual to draw their own conclusions. Use holy water whenever you bless something. Also, make sure you have it with you on the investigation. If activity breaks out and you or someone else comes under attack, sprinkle the holy water while commanding in the name of God that the evil entity stop. It works. I always keep a small bottle of holy water in my car just in case something should pop up, so to speak. It never hurts to have it with you.

Put Yourself In The light

Surround yourself in a force field of "God's" light or the "white" light if you prefer. Picture yourself in it any time you go into an investigation and use it whenever you feel you are being attacked. If you find yourself feeling uncomfortable at any time, do this. It is a very effective tool.

Christians refer to this as the "Christ" light. Many non-Christians use the idea of the aforementioned "white" light. God will gladly protect all of us and you need to believe this. Do not ever let any members of the clergy tell you different. You would not believe some of the things I have heard attributed to some members of the clergy of various faiths.

Carry Or Wear Religious Objects

Wearing a cross or a medal is very effective. Again, this works for non-Christians too. The Saint Benedict medal is a good one to carry as it has exorcistic powers. (St. Benedict was an exorcist) Also, a Padre Pio medal is a good one to have. Demonic forces often attacked Padre Pio throughout his life. Consequently, his medal is known to have strong protective qualities. Relics are particularly effective; Rosaries are too. It is always a wise idea to carry a cross with you. The size does not matter. One word of advice, if you wear something around your neck, you may want to keep it under your clothes. Should the chain break, you do not want to lose a precious cross or medal. One thing to note, religious objects should be blessed by a priest to make them the most effective. I am sure that unblessed items have a value but it is better to have the blessing done.

Have A Strong Belief And Confidence In God

You must have confidence that God will protect you. You need to believe this. He will always protect his children. If you do not believe this strongly, you will have less confidence when you try to do something in God's name. In addition, low confidence makes you an easy demonic target. While I was teaching a class in the supernatural, a woman commented to me that I must have extraordinary faith to do this work. I began to explain to her that my faith was no better or stronger than hers was. It may have been less for all I know. Then I said something that bugged her out. I remarked that if faith was all I had to protect me in a demonic haunting, I was as good as dead. Well at that, my partner did a double take and for that matter, looked stricken. Well, I enjoyed the shocked faces for a few seconds then, I explained myself.

I told the class (and my stricken partner) that human faith is extremely fleeting and easily lost. Everyone at some time or another loses their faith. It may happen after the death of a loved one or it may happen after a trying time at work. I am sure there are a ton of other times when we lose our faith. The point is that faith is a human emotion and if the only thing protecting me is my human emotion, I am a goner. What enables me to do this work and do it fairly well has nothing to do with my *faith* that God will protect me. What protects me is *knowledge.* It is my knowledge that God will protect me that makes the difference. There are no ifs, ands or buts about it. God will protect me, even though I try His Divine patience. It is not my human faith. You have to believe that too if you want to stay healthy and somewhat sane doing this work. That, however, does not mean that there won't be trying times because there will be but I know I will be protected.

Command It To Leave In God's Name

If you find yourself confronted by something evil, command it in the name of God to leave. If the command is in the name of God, the entity must leave eventually. Be forceful! This is no place to be meek. You may have to repeat it several times and I can almost assure you that the activity taking place might increase for a short time but that is a test of wills. The battle is usually won by attrition. It is almost a game to see who blinks first. Continue to repeat the commands even if things become louder. That can be critical because the negative spirit will test you and if you back down, it will be extremely hard for you to stop future problems because it knows that you can be "backed down." Stick with it even when things get louder. Remember that all commands must be made in the name of God. Believe it or not, those commands actually hurt the spirit. They may be bullet proof but they are not omnipotent.

What If You Do Not Believe In God

I have had people ask me what they should do if they do not believe in God. That is a tough one for me to answer. I have never yet met an investigator who did not believe in God. I have met many who do not practice any religion but they all have a belief in God to some extant. My assumption is that you would have to try to "gut it out" if they are in a dangerous situation. On a normal, fun type of investigation, I can assume they would not have any problems. If however, they found themselves in the middle of a demonic case, I honestly do not know what they would do. I cannot understand how someone could believe in a spiritual world and have some kind of belief in a higher power.

Use Common Sense

Do not put yourself in unnecessary danger. If your senses are telling you that you are in danger, immediately say a prayer for protection. Also, do not be afraid to leave the area. There is a difference between being a coward and being smart. There is no reason to try to be heroic. Yes, you need to gather evidence but if items are flying all around your head, it is a good idea to duck. Yes, you want to get the great picture. However, you do not want a close up picture of the lamp that struck you in the head. There will be times when you just know you need to leave an area. Pay attention to those feelings. Your senses are telling you something for your own protection. You can always go back later.

Try Not To Be Afraid

We know that demons feed off of our fear. However, we need to realize that if we allow ourselves to panic, we may cause ourselves harm. Always try to keep your wits about you. This is not the easiest thing in the world to do. You will be scared, as long as you have a pulse, that is. The trick here is not to panic. Fear is a good thing. It gives you extra strength and it makes you sharper. Just do not let it take control. Fall back on your training when fear begins to strike. You must always remember that these spirits can be stopped. Everyone has their little tricks to help them cope with fearful situations. One of mine is to think of the religious song, "Be Not Afraid." There is a line in the song that says: "If you stand before the powers of hell and death is at your side, know that I am with you through it all." (The "I," of course being Jesus.) I have thought of those words on many an investigation. It works.

Do No Personally Challenge Evil Spirits

You have heard it before and I'll say it again. Do not personally challenge a demon or other evil spirit. Remember that any commands you give must be in the name of God. It is not you versus the demon. We cannot win a battle by ourselves. In anger, it is very easy to challenge an entity. This is always a concern when it comes to the client who is trying to protect a loved one. Sometimes investigators, having developed a bond with the client, can fall into this trap too. I have come close a few times in demonic encounters and I have actually done that with human spirits but it is very dangerous. Even with humans, it is still risky. You don't know what is behind the human spirit.

Never Respond To An Disembodied Voice

If something calls you from an empty room do not go in there. You never know what you may be walking into. There could be any of a host of dangerous conditions waiting for you. For example, if a voice from the basement tells you to go down there, you may hit a broken step or it may decide to push you down the stairs. It may wait until you get to the bottom and turn the lights out on you. Who knows what can happen then? The only exception to this rule is if someone else in already in that room. There is the chance that they are in some kind of danger so that is grounds for going in. However, never enter an empty room if you are called into it.

Look Out For Each Other

Always be alert and watchful of the clients and other investigators. Look for any signs of duress. They may be under some form of psychic attack. You might see them "zone out," where they stare off into space for several minutes. They may be suffering from horrible images playing in their minds. They may be experiencing something physical. Make contact with them and make sure they are okay. Also, look to see if someone seems on the verge losing it or succumbing to fear. An arm placed around someone or touching their shoulder can go a long way if there is something happening to them. If you watch out for them, they will watch out for you.

Work As A Team

Always keep your fellow investigators informed of your moves. If you plan to go down to the basement, for example, let another investigator know. This way if activity breaks out down there, someone knows you are there and can come to your aid. While paranormal investigators rarely get hurt, it is still a high-risk profession because of the mental attacks. By following the preceding simple rules, you will find that most investigations are completely safe. Safety is always your number one concern. Always remember that you cannot help anyone if you end up injured or burned out. Always cover each other's backs.

SOME TRICKS OF THE TRADE

Over the course of your paranormal investigating career, you are likely to find yourself in some unusual situations. When you think about it, everything that has to do with this field is a little on the unusual side. How many people do you know who sit in cemeteries at 3 a.m. waiting to take pictures of things they cannot see? How many people do you know who spend a Saturday night sitting in some dusty attic, in the dark, waiting for some long dead person to appear? One last question: how many of them are sane? I will leave that answer up to the readers.

It is a safe bet you will find yourself in some scary situations as well. As a professional called in to investigate reported paranormal phenomena, you do not want your client to see fear on your face during an investigation. Now, most investigators do not scare easily to begin with. If they did, they would have chosen a different profession. However, there are times when activity will break out that is downright frightening. When this happens, you never want the client to see how scared you are. No matter who you are or how long you have been doing this, you will find yourself in a situation that will frighten you at some point. If this has never happened to you, it is likely you have never been in a demonically infested home. If you have been and you never felt fear, it might be a wise idea to check your pulse. You cannot be taught to have no fear but you can learn to deal with it and take some of the bite out of it. What you have to do is mask that fear around your clients.

To a certain extent, you cannot help but show some signs that you are afraid. That can be a helpful thing in that it lets the family see your human side. However, no matter how scared you are, the last thing you want to do is lose your composure. During a particularly serious haunting, sometimes people do lose their composure. Investigators have cried, although that is rare. More common is the old handshaking phenomenon. Yes, that happened to me once. There is no shame in this. At some point in time, it has most likely happened to just about everyone. For those who can honestly say that this has never happened to them, they might just check that old pulse again.

What you want to do is remain as calm as you can. The family is looking to you for help and you want them to feel confident around you. One of their more potent weapons in their battle against evil forces is hope. They see you as their hope and it is important that you help that hope grow. How you carry yourself has a lot to do with that. Again, it is okay for them to see your human side but at the same time, as an investigator, you are trained in dealing with unusual and often frightening phenomena. If you witness something frightening and pass out, that is not going to give the victims much confidence in your ability to help them. In theory, you have some experience in dealing with those types of occurrences; therefore it is reasonable to say that you should be somewhat composed. The question now is what can you do to ensure that you handle a frightening situation in a professional manner.

How To Handle A Frightening Situation

People generally become frightened for two reasons: they are dealing with something they do not understand and because they have a concern for their safety. To a child, getting their tonsils out sounds horrifying! Think about it, from their point of view, someone who they do not know and cannot trust is going to shove a sharp object down their throat and cut out a part of them. They are obviously scared for their safety. In addition, they are looking at being in a hospital, away from their friends and family. They are facing the unknown and this is very unsettling. Now, to an adult, a tonsillectomy is probably no big deal because the adult understands what is about to happen and has no real fear of the unknown because he knows that he will survive the procedure. Hopefully. Probably, the only frightening part for the adult is the bill that will follow. So what is my point?

Training Helps Us Conquer Fear

The point is this; through our training we know what we may be facing when we do an investigation. Going in, we know all of the possibilities. We sure do not like what we may experience but we do know what it is. That should help eliminate the fear of the unknown factor. That leaves us with fear for our safety. This is a tougher nut to crack because this fear is a valid one and one that is necessary for our survival. If someone does not have any fear for their safety, they become reckless and that is how you get hurt. That is true in any endeavor, whether it is driving, swimming, or investigating. It is most certainly true when you may be dealing with evil spirits. The fact of the matter is you can get hurt and in many ways. For that reason, you need to fear for your safety, to a certain point. That is what keeps you sharp and safe. However, you cannot let that fear cripple you. Before you walk into any investigation, whether it is a possible haunted house or a cemetery shoot, you have to know how to protect yourself and you have to use that knowledge. Your fear for your safety is a warning to protect yourself. Heed that warning. You have already learned different ways in which to do that. Again you cannot be taught not to experience fear but you can learn how to deal with it effectively.

Your mindset before going into an investigation is very important as well. If you go in believing that God will protect you, and He will, then your fear factor is diminished. On the other hand, if you are unsure about God's protection and you walk into an investigation that way, you are opening yourself to attack from any evil spirits. They will gather strength from your fear and use it to create more fear. It has been said, "faith can move mountains." It also protects you. You must realize that God will protect you. Believe that! If you go into a potentially dangerous situation believing that, you will walk out in one piece. You also have to realize that it is extremely rare for an investigator to be hurt, physically, anyway. Therefore, as frightened as you may be, realize that you will survive the situation. You may decide never to go back but you will walk out with your various body parts intact. As you become more experienced, you will find that this will become easier. In many cases, it will come automatically.

Pray And View Phenomenon Clinically

When activity breaks out, do not be afraid to say a silent prayer. That can be very effective. It does not matter what prayer you say, just say whatever comes to mind. Another helpful trick is to focus on your role. For example, if you are assigned to a camcorder and doors start opening and closing, it will help you immensely if you focus on getting the activity on tape. Do not consider the activity of the door as something terrifying, look at it clinically. See it not as something frightening; see it as phenomena to capture. It sounds like a head game and it is. However, it is a successful head game. It really does work.

Let Your Training Guide You

Along the same lines, another helpful item is to fall back on your training. You know what to expect. Therefore, you are not surprised by the activity that may be occurring. That gives you an advantage. However, you have also been trained in how to deal with the situation. You need to fall back on that training. This is how police officers, firefighters, and doctors all get through their rough moments. They know what they need to do and they focus on that. I call that "task saturation." Well, that is what you should do as well. Pay attention to the equipment assigned to you. If you are focusing on the equipment, you are not focusing on your fear. Also, look around you and observe the others in the room with you, both clients and investigators alike. How do they look? Who needs help? It is amazing what a hand placed on someone's shoulder can do for their fear. Do not put your arms around them because that conveys a message that you are physically shielding them from the activity. That is a nice gesture, to be sure, but they may be in that situation again when you are not there to hold them. What you want to do is show them that you are supporting them but at the same time, you want them to learn how to deal with their fear. They can learn that from watching you deal with your own fear. When someone is called in to help, it is important to see how he or she handles fear. The best thing you can do is lead by example. If the experienced investigator does not panic, that sends a message to the newer investigator that things are under control no matter how wild things seem to be.

There are other methods of dealing with frightening phenomena, such as thinking about loved ones when things get rough or disassociating from the experience. You have to be careful with the latter one. What you have to remember is that we have a job to do. If you are focusing on ways of surviving a difficult situation, you are not focusing on the task at hand. Again, you are a professional and that is the message you must convey to the client. You cannot afford the luxury of looking scared out of your wits and you cannot look like you are frozen in shock. If that happens, they may start to think something like: "if the professionals are scared to death, what hope do we have?" In addition, they may flat out lose confidence in your ability to help them. That will feed their feelings of hopelessness and helplessness in the situation. Our adversary will notice that in a heartbeat. Always remember that a huge part of this battle is a head game. The client's confidence weakens the opponent and their fear and other assorted, negative emotions strengthen it. Also, do not kid yourself, your composure sends a message to the evil entity too. It is telling it that you are not going to fold under the pressure. That can make a big difference in an oppressed house. It can also make a big difference on future investigations as well. Much of our business is through word of mouth. If you develop a reputation as someone who is cool under fire, that can help the confidence and hope level for another family. Also, it does not hurt to have a demon see that you are strong. You may come across one of those little darlings in a later investigation. If it knows that you are not terrified of him, he may not bother testing you again. Grab every advantage you can. There usually are not many there for the taking.

Always keep in mind what you are doing and why you are doing it. Once you have gotten to the point where you feel you are ready for an investigation, you pretty much have an idea what to do and how to handle the frightening activity you may witness. As you gather more and more experience, this becomes much easier. This is intended for the particularly bad haunting that arises from time to time. Fortunately, those are rare. Some investigators never come across a demonic haunting at all in their careers. Then again, some investigators get several of them. There is no way to figure it. If there is a rhyme or reason to it, I have yet to see it.

Being Ready For An Investigation

Before you do any investigations, you must be sure that you are ready for it. Do not just jump into one for the sake of being able to say you did it. Simply reading this or any book does not fully prepare you to begin investigations. There has to be a certain spiritual maturity involved. You have to be at peace with yourself and you have to be mentally prepared to deal with dangerous situations. Investigators should be brought along slowly. Where possible, they should start out with cases of human spirits. Ideally, they will begin to experience phenomena gradually. This builds their tolerance for frightening phenomena. Think about it. Imagine a situation where an investigator goes on his first case and it turns out to be a demonic infestation. This poor guy may have never experienced anything paranormal. Now, on his first case, he finds himself being slapped or sees a five hundred-pound freezer get thrown around a room. There is a good chance that will be his *only* investigation. If you are a member of a society that does investigations, the directors should consider this when scheduling assignments. Baptism by fire is not the desired way to go. Some may argue this is the only way to weed out those who cannot do this work. My feeling is you can lose some potentially good investigators that way. They may have what it takes but it has to be nurtured slowly.

In addition, you have to be positive that you are doing this for the right reasons. The only valid reason for doing this type of work is having an honest desire to help someone who is greatly in need of help. If you are a thrill seeker or are just doing it for kicks, you could find yourself in a world of trouble. There is nothing wrong with doing this work for the sake of spiritual growth. There is also nothing wrong with going on ghost hunts for the sake of adventure. There are hundreds of haunted places where you can safely do this. Pick up the National Ghost

Registry. You can do cemetery shoots. However, there is a difference between going into a haunted site where there is little or no danger present and going into a situation where you may encounter a demon or at least a nasty human spirit. This work is not for thrill seekers.

This can be a humbling profession. Arrogance, cockiness, and a "know it all" attitude are three sure fire ways to run into trouble. Arrogant investigators usually are not in a position to help the victims deal with a haunting. If you feel that "it's not my job to counsel people," do everyone a favor and pick another profession. Let me tell you, it is a big part of your job. You are not going to magically remove the invading spirit. Therefore, you must do whatever is necessary to help the client.

Cockiness gets you into trouble too. No one likes to work with someone who is cocky. A lot of time in investigations is spent sitting around with other investigators. Having a cocky person sitting next to you all night is not pleasant. Believe me, I know. The "know it all's" are also a problem. No one knows it all. Obviously, as the author of this book, I must know it all, right? Let me tell you, before this book made it to print, several of my colleagues read it so that they could give me comments. We never know it all. That type of attitude can get you hurt on an investigation. Injuries to investigators are rare but when they do happen, it is usually because the investigator made some mistakes. You may be 110% sure you are dealing with a human spirit and no amount of discussion will make you change your mind. So, you go into a room and start waving a cross around to get rid of the human spirit. Unfortunately for you, there is an inhuman spirit at work there and you just ticked him off. The next thing you know, you are in the middle of a firestorm due to your religious provocation. Oops! So, heed my warning, you do not know it all.

What it all boils down to is you have to make sure you know as much about what you are doing as possible and why you are doing it. Then, realize that others know a lot too. It can be a rewarding field and it can be a difficult one if you make it that way.

PATIENCE IN INVESTIGATIONS

One key trait you need in an investigation is patience and lots of it. Investigating the paranormal is usually 90% boredom and 10% terror. You have to keep in mind that in many investigations, outward manifestations do not occur right away, if at all. This is especially true in the early stages of the investigation. You may have been told some of the odd things that have been going on in the house and you just cannot wait to see it for yourself. This is only natural. The fact is, you do not know what is there and whether there may have been some exaggerations in the reports. (There almost always are, even though they are usually not intentional.) Then, even if there is something there, it may not want to expose itself, at east not quickly. It may decide to wait until it determines who you are and whether you are a threat to it. So, you might find yourself sitting vigil for a while.

When you are asked to work a case, you are generally filled with excitement and a sense of anticipation. You will usually try to find out all of the details possible. Your group leader will fill you in on this prior to your entering the location in question. If the investigation is well organized, all of the investigators are briefed before going in with the exception of the LTM. It does not always work out that way but that is the ideal. In some instances, especially when you hear about an investigation in a classroom setting, there may not be much known about the case at that time. Should that be the case, the group leader is responsible for getting as many details as possible and relaying that information to you before your arrival on site.

Once you know as much of the story as is possible, you are generally eager to get started. You may spend days thinking about what might be there and wondering how you are going to react when the activity takes place. You might start thinking about what pictures or videotape you may get. Some investigators run through various scenarios that might take place. They may spend hours thinking about the questions that they want to ask. Friends of the investigators may hear so much about the upcoming investigation that they get excited about it. Other friends may hide at the sight of their investigator friend. The point is a lot of anticipation precedes an investigation. Generally, try spending the night before the investigation checking equipment to make sure it is in working order. Also begin packing everything that may be necessary for the investigation. Make sure there is a generous amount of spare batteries and tapes on hand. Investigators will often call each other the night before the investigation. The longer it has been between investigations, the more excited you get. Many investigators report having difficulty sleeping the night before the investigation. That anticipation continues right up to the moment you leave for the site. Finally, the day arrives and off you go.

While you are on your way to the site, your mind races. You go through all of the possible scenarios you can envision. Generally, nothing ever happens the way you picture it, at least not in my life. Finally, you get to the house in question. Your excitement threatens to boil over. You go in and immediately begin setting up your equipment. If you are doing interviews, you dive headfirst into them. Once you are in there for a while and all of the excitement wears off, you are left with the anticipation. That stage lasts for a little while. At first, you become acutely aware of every sound. Is this it? Am I going to see some exceptional phenomenon now? It does not take long before you find yourself thinking about how you wish something would happen. All of the excitement and anticipation that has been building now starts to work against you. Here you are, thinking to yourself how you wondered if you would be scared only to find out you wish something, anything would happen. Do not be discouraged. Boredom is a big part of the job. It affects both the experienced investigator and the newcomer. The experienced investigators do better with this. They expect things to start slowly and they usually have contingency plans.

Interacting With The Family

One way to deal with the boredom is to interact with the family requesting your help, assuming they choose to be around during the investigation. One word of caution, when you are discussing the situation with members of the family, do not tell them anything without proof. This can be difficult when they start pressing you for an answer but you have to stick to what you can prove. They may ask you to speculate about the origins of the phenomena they have described. Here, you have to be artfully vague. Obviously, you do not want to alienate them by not answering the question but you have to word your response carefully. Tell them that there can be many causes for the phenomena they describe. Point out how you do not want to say anything because you do not want to look silly if you are wrong. Then try to toss in a funny story about a past investigation where you looked like a fool, for one reason or another. Make one up if you have to. The trick is to say all of this in an upbeat way so they do not think you are just trying to avoid the issue. This can be very hard when they are describing how little Johnny was levitating around the living room the night before but in a case that extreme, it is easy to speculate. However, if the occurrences are not so well defined, speculating can hurt the situation. You cannot be sure how much of what they told you happened the way they described it. There is the fear factor and the exaggeration factor to consider. It makes things seem worse than they are. You can really scare the wits out of someone if you start talking about possible demons running loose in their house. As a rule, the client is not informed until the evidence has been reviewed and discussed. The exception to that would be if a spirit materializes and throws the kitchen table at you. That would be a tough one to dodge.

It is common for your client to ask you for some ghost stories. Children especially love to do this. The poor parents are scared witless about the whole thing but little Johnny wants to be scared out of his pants. If you happen to have any scary stories, it is probably best that you avoid telling them. People can be suggestive to begin with and people who believe they are haunted are overly suggestive when it comes to scary stories. As much as little Johnny begs you to tell him a story and as happy as he appears when he hears it, you can bet that he will have a difficult time sleeping that night. Mom and Dad are going to love you for that. If you have a funny one or two, those are the ones to talk about. Everybody appreciates a good laugh and this allows the client to see you in human terms. It also helps pass the time, which is no small feat on some investigations.

Interacting With Other Investigators

If you are assigned to work with another investigator, the time goes by quicker. Idle conversation with another investigator is fine. Be careful, though, if you are within earshot of the client. You do not want to be talking about the "so and so" case where you saw the headless kangaroo hopping in the basement. Client's love to hear what the investigators are talking about. They are hoping to hear something that will confirm their suspicions. It is not that they want to be haunted; they just want to find someone who believes them and does not ridicule them. They also want confirmation that they are not insane. Believe me, that is a consideration. The clients may walk in halfway through the conversation and think that the spirit of the three-headed rat you are talking about is living in their food pantry. You just have to be careful about what you say and where you say it.

You might want to bring a book with you. It can cut down on the boredom factor. Of course, it may also make you sleepy so you have to take that into account. I used to believe that you should not bother bringing reading material since the majority of the time you will find yourself sitting in the dark or near dark. However, you can pick up a book light and that solves the darkness problem. They are inexpensive too. On one investigation I did, I was sitting in the basement waiting for something, anything to happen. Finally, I took out a book I was reading on the dangers of Ouija boards and read that for a while. You just have to stay alert and look around often to make sure that you do not miss anything. That would be my luck; I would be reading while a spirit is posing for the camera just three feet away. Either that or just as I put the book down, some form of demonic creature would be staring me right in the eye. If you are working with equipment, you should always check on that every so often. Whatever you do, be prepared to move if anything does happen. If something starts to materialize in the corner of the room you are sitting in, have that camera ready. You would really hate to miss that exceptional shot. You may not get too many chances.

Teaching Coping Skills

One thing you can do while you are waiting for something to happen is establish a rapport with the client. This is also a good opportunity to begin teaching them coping skills. You have to keep them general. You cannot start telling them how to deal with a demon if there is no evidence of one. You can show them they are not alone and explain how these things are a part of our convoluted, wacky world. You can give them hope, no matter what they may be experiencing. Advising them to have holy water handy is always a good thing to do. If they are Christians, you can give them some protection prayers. You can talk about the God light. These are all things that apply whether you are dealing with a human spirit or a demon. Just do not say anything that they can read into.

Let them know that others have faced the same problems and have beaten them. Let them know that their lives *will* get back to something resembling normal. When times were rough for me, my mother always told me that: "This too will pass." She was always right. Help them to believe that. Tell them stories of successful cases you have worked, if you had any, that is. Avoid telling them horror stories because that can have a profound affect on them. Keep everything positive. That will help them more than you know. Praise them on how well they have handled the situation. Build up their confidence. That too is so important. Confidence can go a long way in a haunting.

You do not have to sit frozen in one spot. It is fine to get up and move around a bit. Actually, you should, the last thing you want is to have a muscle cramp up on you. If you are working an assigned area with a partner, make sure that he/she knows when you are going. If you are going down a basement or some other place where you will be isolated, tell them where you are going. (No, this does not include the bathroom and you do not have to ask permission to go either. "Do you have to do # 1 or # 2?" is not required) However, you do not want to be caught alone should serious activity break out and no one knows where you are. In addition, you do not want to scare your partner half to death when you suddenly reappear. Try not to appear jumpy and do not spook yourself. By that, I mean do not let your imagination run wild. Picture this scenario: you are sitting in the basement with a partner. While you are sitting there, you hear a sound off in the far corner. You and your partner look at each other and slowly move in the direction of the sound. Remember now, it is probably dark down there. As you reach the corner, a black figure suddenly jumps out. The next thing that happens is the two of you set a land speed record getting up those basement stairs. Following you is the black figure, Muffy, the pet cat. Can you imagine how that would look to the client! Hey, these guys are afraid of a cat! What are they going to do when the see a ghost? Of course, on the positive side, you will have a funny story to tell the next client.

Being patient is not the easiest thing to do especially when you are doing something as interesting as investigating a possible haunting. If you think about it, how many people do you know who spend their free time investigating ghosts? It probably does not rank too far up on the average person's list of hobbies. However, when you are sitting in a house waiting for something to happen, your patience is tested. Many an investigator has fallen asleep while waiting for something to happen. Believe it or not, this tends to happen more with more experienced investigators. The reason why this is so is that the experienced investigator will have developed some degree of discernment. That investigator will know if something is about to happen, although this is not fool proof by any means. Pounding in the walls has dragged some investigators from their sleep. That is an awkward way to wake up, to put it mildly. The other reason is the inexperienced investigators are so keyed up waiting for something to happen that you could not get them to fall asleep if they tried.

Never Let The Client See Impatience

You have to be careful about letting the client see that you are impatient. This is a tough time for them and if they see you are inpatient, it can make them feel guilty on top of everything else they are dealing with.

One of their fears is that nothing will happen when the investigators are present. As we know, that is often the case. This is a problem for the victims because they are probably questioning their sanity to begin with. When nothing happens, they start to feel worse. For that reason, it is important for them to see that not only are you patient but that you expect things to be slow, especially in the very beginning. The better you are at that, the easier it becomes for the family. Remember that our job is more than just hunting ghosts. Our job there is to help the family, any way we can. How we carry ourselves and how we act can help or hurt them. You always want them see you as a patient, competent investigator, even when you are ready to stick pins in your eyes to alleviate the boredom.

Now, while you are trying to stay sane, you have to be alert. In many instances, little things may happen that might go unnoticed. It can be something as simple as an ashtray moving a couple of inches. Sometimes it will be something like a door slamming closed. You have to be alert. Remember, finding patterns to the activity are very important. Not only that but you may only get minor activity. You do not want to miss it. Everything that happens on site needs to be documented by the investigator. So, be aware of every little occurrence that happens. Often times, minor activity is a warning sign of bigger things to come. For that reason, you want to be alert to every possible sign. That ashtray that barely moved may herald the moving of a table or a lamp flying across the room. By catching that one little sign you may be able to set up your camcorder in that area and catch the big thing, if it happens. Sometimes, investigators will watch TV. That is okay if the family has no objection to it. Just keep the sound down low and do not fall asleep, no matter what you have to do to prevent it. If you feel sleep coming on, get up and move around. That always helps.

Do not make the mistake of trying to make things happen, even if you have been sitting vigil for hours. By that I mean do not do anything to provoke a response from whatever might be there. Only the most experienced investigator or demonologist should try that and only when absolutely necessary. If you are doing a fun expedition, there is no reason to provoke anything. It will have no affect on a benign spirit so in that regard it is a waste of time. Should there be something negative around, the last thing you want to do is risk stirring up a hornet's nest. So why then would you ever use provocation? The demonologist would use that in a situation where the entity in question will do nothing while he is there but as soon as he leaves, the demon retaliates against the family. In that situation, he really has no choice but to try to bring everything to a head. However, if you do not know what you are doing, you could set off a chain of events that you have not prepared for and the family will suffer. So, will you. You cannot force things to happen. All you can do is wait it out.

You never know what will happen during an investigation. Events may start out quietly and then all kinds of things may happen. There are as many variables as you can imagine. It is not uncommon for there to be no action at all in the early stages of the investigation. Sometimes several nights will pass without an incident. That is always a possibility and you need to know that going in. It is not all activity all of the time. Sometimes it is all *inactivity* all of the time. This can be hard to deal with. However, it is one of the negatives that comes with the job. I have found though that patience is almost always rewarded. Keep that in mind when you are working what appears to be a slow case. You never know what is about to happen. Just when you think the night has been a bust, you find a voice on your tape or you get a good picture on your digital camera. Things often happen when you least expect them too. That has happened to me numerous times and it has happened to every investigator I have ever talked to. It is part of the game, so to speak.

Again, this is a little easier for the experienced investigator than it is for the overly eager new one. The experienced guys (or gals) know that boredom comes with the turf and they have ways in which they deal with it. Whatever you do, the trick is to remain patient. Also, it is important not to pull out too early. If you have been sitting around since 9 at night, stick it out until 6 a.m. That can be difficult but the last thing you want to do is shut it down early and miss something important. I have heard of many cases where a bunch of friends would go to a reputedly haunted location and sit there for three or four hours. Finally, one or two of them decide that they have sat around long enough and write the night off as a loss and leave, only to find out that a half-hour after they left, their friends were visited by some form of spirit and they were able to capture clear voices on tape and also catch a few balls of light darting around on the camcorder. Believe me, you will kick yourself for days after that. You just never know when something might happen. If you are working for a client and you pull out early and something does happen, not only have missed a chance to document phenomena, you may have lost some credibility with the client. That can be difficult to repair.

You have to keep in mind that if there is something-paranormal happening in the house, eventually things will start to happen. In addition, you have to realize that your investigation may eventually determine that there is nothing going on. That does happen from time to time. Cases that sound like true hauntings often are not. Keep in mind the reason you are there is to help them and proving that nothing is there is a way of doing that. Most of all, be patient no matter how hard that can be. It just may pay off in spades.

DOING A CEMETERY SHOOT

During the times between investigations, paranormal investigators will often go to cemeteries at night to take some pictures. Why would they want to do that? Doing a cemetery shoot is sort of a mini-investigation in a sense. You would be surprised how many good pictures of spirits you can get in a cemetery. These pictures can range from a small point of light to the odd shapes of elemental spirits, if you are lucky enough to catch them. Elementals are nature spirits. They are regarded by many as being cousins to the Angels. These spirits represent the four elements, fire, water, earth, and air. These spirits often appear in pictures as squares, rectangles, and hexagons. "Ghost" globules are common in cemetery shots. These appear as circles which are either almost transparent or a deep white. In many instances these globules, or "orbs" as they are sometimes called, will appear as perfect circles. I have seen many that have what looks like comet tails behind them which makes it appear as if the are moving quickly. To be captured on film with a tail, they would have to be very fast indeed. Scientifically speaking, these different shapes are balls of energy. It is not the spirit you see in the pictures, it is the energy, most likely electromagnetic. Either that or all ghosts are circles.

You will sometimes see what appears to be a fog. It may be amorphous, having no definite shape, or you may be able to make out a shape. This can sometimes be like staring at clouds. If you look long enough, you can see anything you want. Sometimes though, there are very definite shapes to them. I have seen a photograph of what is almost unmistakingly the shape of an Angel. You could clearly see the body and wings. Is it really an Angel? I personally took a shot that distinctly resembled a demon. You could see the face and you could also make out ears and what looked like horns on its head. If that is what demons really look like, no wonder they are always angry. However, it could have been anything. Just what is this fog like mist? It is an electromagnetic energy field. The amazing thing about these mists, as well as the items described in the first paragraph, is they are often not visible to the naked eye.

Sometimes when you take a shot, you will see little pinpoints of light. They are referred to as "sparkles" and you will usually see many of them. Keep shooting because you will sometimes get great pictures around them. They appear to be another form of energy. On a case once, my wife took pictures outside of the house. In every one, there were sparkles galore. The funny thing was that when we got that film back, none of those pictures came out at all. The ones before them and the ones after them were fine but those with the sparkles were blank. You may find that happen to you on a cemetery shoot as well. What you don't get on film can be as telling as what you do get. Sometimes you batteries will die; sometimes your film won't develop. When I was teaching classes on the supernatural, we would always take a field trip to a local cemetery for a shoot. Since the cemetery we always went to was so large, we would split up into small groups. On one such trip, I turned my gauss meter on and after a few seconds, it started blasting away. Everyone immediately started taking pictures. A few seconds later, the meter slowly stopped, its battery dead. The same happened to my camera. Unfortunately, the same happened to everyone's cameras. The other groups all got great pictures. The moral of the story is that you don't want to be in my group on a cemetery shoot. I have seen some interesting pictures of streaks of light taken in cemeteries. They seem to be fairly common.

One note, there is a theory in parapsychological circles that basically says that these pictures are a result of telepathy on the part of the photographer. The idea is that the photographer, hoping to get good shots actually unconsciously imprints the image on the film. That may explain some shots but I really do not believe it explains them all. I would think however that if your mind was capable of imprinting on file, you would get something more exciting that orbs. Still, it is an interesting theory.

A Cemetery Apparition

If you are very lucky, you may actually capture an apparition on film. Apparitions are spirits who appear the same way as they did in life, only they are most often translucent. This does happen although it is somewhat rare. There have been many cases where an apparition actually appears in the cemetery, visible to the naked eye. Again, it is rare but it does happen every now and again. There was an apparition in the cemetery where my parents are buried. This took place in broad daylight. While kneeling on my parent's grave, cleaning away grass cuttings, I noticed movement off to my left. There, about 30 feet away was a woman bending down and clearing the grass cuttings away from another headstone. This woman was wearing a dark blue, floral print dress. I watched her for a few seconds wondering what her relationship was to the person buried there. Did the grave belong to her spouse, or could it have been her parent's grave and so on. I turned back towards my parent's grave. The funny thing was I had not noticed her when I drove up. The cemetery is flat and you could easily see one section from any other. At one point, she turned and looked at me and smiled. It was a warm smile ... a kindly smile.

A few seconds later, I saw her arranging a flower box in front of the grave. I thought this very odd because I had not seen a flower box before. It just sort of appeared out of nowhere. The flowers in the box were quite beautiful. There were bright marigolds and some geraniums too. I soon returned my gaze back to my parent's stone. However, something inside me told me to look back over there again so I did. The woman was gone! In the span of about five seconds, that woman, who looked as solid as me, had just vanished. As I said, this cemetery is on flat ground. Even if she had immediately stood up and took off on a dead run, she could not have gone more than about five feet. Even if she had, she would have been visible and I surely would have heard her. I immediately jumped up and started frantically looking around. There was no one around in the entire cemetery. I then realized too that I had not seen any cars parked in the cemetery. There were not too many places around that were within a reasonable walking distance. Okay, so maybe this lady likes to walk. However, since my parents grave is right on the corner lot, she would have to walk past me to get to the entrance. That did not happen. I decided I had to walk around the cemetery. If she was there, I had to find her. Well, it is not a big cemetery so it did not take too long to walk it. There was no sign of the lady. Finally, I walked back to my parent's grave. Lying before the headstone was a single geranium flower. I stood there in amazement. So, you never know what you might see at a cemetery, even in broad daylight.

That brings up a good point. Many interesting photographs have been taken in the daytime. So, you can get daytime pictures but the odds are better at night. The psychic hours are between 9 p.m. and 6 a.m., with 3 in the morning being the peak time for night photographs. For many people cemeteries are frightening. If you are squeamish though, try a few daytime shoots. You may get something and it may help you get over any fear you might have of being in a cemetery. Many a good picture was taken during daylight hours.

Psychic Photography

Can anyone get good pictures in a cemetery? Yes they can. Some people are gifted with the ability to get great shots almost anywhere they go. These people are known as "psychic photographers. I have been given this gift to a point. I do not know why God would choose to give me this precious gift, but I have to assume He pretty much knows what He is doing. God knows I don't. I have been very lucky in that I started getting great shots right from the start. I am like a kid on Christmas morning every time I see an exceptional shot. Believe me, I am always appreciative when I am successful. You should be too.

My belief is that while being a psychic photographer is a gift, you can develop the ability as well. Everyone has psychic abilities. In many cases, those abilities are drowned out by everyday life. Others block themselves by not believing in their existence. You have to be open to the possibility. The people who are born with this gift all have a few things in common. For one, they believe in the spirit world. If you do not believe in the spirit world, then you are blocking yourself off from them right from the word go. Secondly, you must be open to the experience. When I go into a cemetery, I leave myself open to any spirits that may be there. Before we go any further, let me make one thing perfectly clear. When I say that I leave myself open, it does not mean that I am allowing a spirit to enter me. You should *never* allow a spirit to enter you. *Never!* When I say that I am open, I am saying that I am listening, in a sense, to the cemetery and allowing myself to pick up the vibrations that are all around me. Were I to sense something negative, I would shut down immediately. That has happened to me before. When I get that odd feeling that it is a good time to leave, I listen to that feeling and follow what it is telling me. Who knows for sure what would go wrong if I ignored it but there is no reason to find out. There are plenty of other times to go out and do a shoot. It is better to be safe than sorry. There is no point in taking unnecessary risks. Besides, with my luck being what it is, I would probably get "skunked" or something equally hideous.

What is also very helpful in developing this gift is believing that you may get your shots. Remember that spirits are energy. So are we and so are our thoughts. The laws of physics teach us that energy of one type will attract energy of a similar type. This is the "like attracts like" theory. If you go into a cemetery believing that you may get something, you are giving off positive energy. That positive energy creates a particular type of vibration. What this does is it attracts spirits because they can tell from your vibration that you believe in them. If, on the other hand, you go in with a negative attitude such as "I never get anything," you are sending out negative vibrations, which probably chases them away.

Let us say that you have decided to do a shoot tonight. You take your camera and head out to your local cemetery. You are excited and feel positive that you will get some great pictures. After walking around a bit, you start shooting. After that roll is used up, you load up another one. That one is shot too. The next morning, you cannot wait to get the film developed. Off to the mall you go and race right into one of those 1-hour photo places, which are so named because they usually take two hours at the minimum. Now you wander around the mall trying to kill those two-hours that seems to be 2 million minutes long and you do so while trying not to spend you next three paychecks. Finally, they are ready. You pay the kings ransom that it costs to have photo's developed in one hour. In your excitement, the little envelope gets ripped apart and you look at the pictures. Nothing! Nothing except a bunch of headstones ... no globules, no mist, no apparitions, nothing. You just sat in a cemetery until 2 in the morning, avoided many different breeds of nocturnal animals, became insect food, spooked yourself, and paid all this money and you have absolutely nothing to show for it. Welcome to the world of psychic photography!

One of the most important rules is you must be patient and persevere. People who have been doing this a long time often never get a great picture. Do not let that statement depress you. With better film, better cameras, and better development techniques, people are getting pictures like never before. Here is a positive thought. Once you get a "hit," you usually keep getting them. It seems that getting that first one can be tough but once you have broken through, you have automatically opened yourself up. That is exciting. Be prepared to use a lot of film. I mentioned earlier that I have been very lucky in getting good shots on a regular basis. Still, I may take anywhere from twenty four to sixty shots and come out with two or three hits. That is a successful shoot. Again, this is where digital cameras are great. If you don't get a good shot, you can simply delete that picture. Plus, there is the instant gratification factor. Anytime you get a hit, even just one, you have been successful.

Equipment For A Cemetery Shoot

One of the most often asked questions is about equipment. I mentioned earlier that a cemetery shoot is a sort of mini-investigation. There are many things you may find useful. You can bring a camcorder if you want in the hopes of capturing an apparition on tape. I do not usually do that because those cases are very rare. In addition, I do not like to lug all kinds of equipment around unless I have a reason to believe that something may happen. If other investigators tell me that a particular cemetery has been active, then I might take a camcorder in. Otherwise, you can take a camera or two along with a tape recorder to the cemetery.

There have been many reports of people picking up voices in cemeteries. The best thing to do is pick a spot for the recorder, someplace where you will be able to find it easily in the dark and just place it down. Leave it there for a good half-hour or so. Your might want to use a recorder that tapes continuously as opposed to a voice activated one. I have a great one with a super amplified mike that picks up just about anything. The problem with using the voice activation feature outdoors is that the starting and stopping of it every time a car passes by makes it annoying as hell to play it back. Of course, the problem with letting it run constantly is you end up having hours of "air" to listen to, depending on the amount of noise in the cemetery. This makes it very difficult to stay focused when you play it back. If you are working inside a house, the voice activation is a good feature.

Other little tidbits you can bring are a pad and pen just so you can jot down some notes. In one instance, my wife started taking pictures. When she was done, she told me to finish out the roll. A notation was made of what frame the camera was on. That way, if something came out, we would know who took the shot. In addition, one time a few of us were doing a cemetery shoot. We took a bunch of shots. Then we decided to do a little experiment. We pictured a white, God light encompassing the entire cemetery. We made a note showing where we had started the experiment. We then finished taking pictures. When we got all the film developed, we saw that we had gotten a few good hits. What was quite interesting was that all of the hits occurred before we did the light experiment. We got nothing afterwards. Another thing you should do is jot down the frame number if you feel something. It may turn out to be nothing but if you get something, it shows that your feelings were right on. So, in short, always carry a pen and paper. If you have a night vision scope, bring that with you. You never know what might pop up. In addition, if you have one, bring an EMF detector. Since it is widely believed that when spirits manifest, they create an electromagnetic energy field, the meter may tell you where to shoot. Do not feel that you have to rush out and buy these things though. You will get plenty of pictures without them.

The next biggie is about the type of camera you bring. Polaroid cameras are great. They let you see what you got or did not get, right away. If you are going to take many shots, they will run into some money. Auto focus cameras are the best. A friend of mine has some very expensive equipment. Despite that, he has not been very successful with it. The reason for that is we do not see what we are shooting at most of the time. Therefore, if you focus in on a headstone for instance, you will get a very good shot of that headstone, nothing more. With an auto focus, you just point it in any direction and shoot. The fun part is that you do not even need to look through the viewfinder. Those good old throwaway cameras work well too. Of course, if your budge allows it, pick up a digital. You have instant gratification and it will ultimately pay for itself in the long haul. Plus, you never have to worry about running out of film, especially if you have the type that takes a soft disk. Just keep a few disks handy. With those, if you do get something, you can copy it to a disk right there and give it to whoever you are working with.

Always bring a flashlight. The last thing you want to do is trip over a headstone or slip on a depression in the ground. Cemeteries are not the most level places in the world. After a class at a psychic society, a few of us decided to do a shoot in a nearby cemetery. This particular one had been very active and some great shots had been taken there. We had a new student with us so I thought it best that she stay near me. After all, I was Joe Cool, paranormal expert. We started walking into the cemetery and I asked her if she had ever done a cemetery shoot before. She told me that she had not. As we walked, I started explaining to her that "the most dangerous thing you have to fear in a cemetery is..." before I finished the sentence, I tripped on a headstone and fell flat on my face. Looking up at her, covered in mud, I finished my statement, "tripping over headstones." She laughed so hard I thought she was going to have a seizure. I took some ribbing for that one. I have heard some people say that if you want to get great shots, you should ask the spirits to allow themselves to be photographed. I don't really know whether or not that works but it is worth a try.

(Protecting Yourself In The Cemetery)

Is it dangerous to do a cemetery photo shoot? No, not if you use common sense and follow a few basic rules. If you say protection prayers, there really is no danger, outside of natural occurrences, such as falling or twisting an ankle. Still, there is a need for caution. The fact of the matter is you can run into any kind of spirit there. For that reason, you should say a prayer for protection before going in. I personally always say the St. Michael prayer before going in and I also say a prayer asking God to let all of the souls there rest in peace. Furthermore, you have to remember that this is the final resting-place for those buried there. It is consecrated ground ... sacred ground. You need to be respectful. For that reason, always address the souls there. Inform them that you mean them no disrespect and that you hope they are at peace.

Before you go into a cemetery for a photo shoot, it is a good idea to check out the area during the day. Get an idea of the size and the terrain as well. Also, look for signs of activity. Does it look like it gets a lot of traffic? In addition, look for odd symbols on any rocks there. Check the trees too. This is especially true if it is an old cemetery and one well hidden from the road. This can make for an ideal site for your photo shoot as you can do your thing with no interruptions. It is also an ideal site for satanic practices. Yes, they are alive and well. You have to be wary of the organized Satanists and the local teenagers who are dabbling, as well. Whatever the type, you do not want to run into them. So, if you hear chanting or see fires lit, keep on driving. Nothing good can come out of a meeting with them. If the area is involved in satanic practices, you will get some wild shots there but you have to be smart about it. Just be careful and do not forget to say prayers for protection.

Always Listen To Your Feelings

Another area we should cover is listening to your feelings. Some people are gifted with the ability to discern. Actually, everyone has it but it is more developed in some than others. Discernment, in a sense is actually being able to read and understand energy patterns. Everybody has had the experience of entering someone's home and being greeted warmly. Yet, despite the warm greeting, you can just sense that something is wrong. It may be something as simple as sensing the couple just had an argument. The phrase that many people use is they "got bad vibes." Well, that is exactly what you felt. You were picking up the vibrations that were a result of the energy given off by the couple that was arguing.

That is discernment. When this happens, you may get the feeling that you should leave. You are right, you probably should.

We have all had instances where we got a bad feeling about something. Often we are right. This is another example of discernment. The point is that it is always a wise idea to pay attention to your feelings. This is especially true when it comes to bad feelings. If you find yourself in a cemetery or any other place for that matter and something tells you to leave, then leave. We have those feelings for a reason. Call it intuition or call it your Guardian Angel but heed the warning. You are not acting like a coward. It is not about courage, it's about not being stupid. Also, pay attention to nature. If you suddenly hear that all sounds stop, be wary. In the presence of evil, animals and insects will remain very quiet. They may be smarter than we are.

Once in the cemetery, set up a base of operations. Make sure you keep track of where you place your equipment. The last thing you want to do before you leave is search in the dark, especially if you decide to get out in a hurry. Take your time, if you can afford to. Give whatever presence is there the chance to see that you mean no harm. You will be surprised at some of the photographs you get. When you rush in and rush out, you usually do not get much of anything. Take shots of some of the headstones. This can show the age of the cemetery. Some of my shots are of graves that were filled in the 1700's. Background shots just add to the shoot. In addition, it has been said that you will sometimes see a face on a headstone. It is believed by many that these are the faces of the people buried there. Of course, there is no way to prove this if the person was buried in 1851. Personally, I have never gotten any shots like that. One word of advice about shooting headstones: Taking a shot on those beautiful, shiny, polished headstones does not work so well. All you will get is a flashback. If you have fast enough film to avoid using a flash, those headstones are as good as any.

When it comes time to leave, say a prayer for confinement. You do not want anything following you home. Again, I usually say a prayer asking God to let all the souls there be at peace but I say the confinement prayer to keep them there. I am very appreciative to them for letting me get some pictures but not so appreciative that I want to see them in my living room at 3 in the morning.

(Recording Your Activity)

Doing a cemetery shoot is a great way for someone starting out to get established. If they are scared, this can help them overcome their fear. It may also make them realize that this field is not for them, if that is the case. Better to find out in a cemetery than on an investigation. When you get your photos back, make sure you mark where you got them. Also, your should note the time, the weather conditions, and who took the pictures. You would be surprised how quickly pictures can add up. Besides that, how can you tell one cemetery from another, should you forget to mark them. One suggestion is to use the first shot on the camera film to mark the name and location of the shoot. Use a small chalkboard but you can use anything to accomplish this. Always note the location, time, and weather conditions. Of course, that does not do much for you should you get pictures from different cemeteries mixed up.

When you get those hits, do yourself a favor and keep those pictures apart from the rest. When you get the chance to show off your prize, the last thing you want to do is go through 300 pictures. Besides that, you may want to keep a scrapbook of your pictures. Do the same with the negatives. It is even more important with them. You may want to make copies or enlargements later. Imagine having to go through a whole bunch of negatives at once. By the time you find the one you are looking for, the chances are pretty good that you will be extremely tired and possibly blind. (Not to mention insane.) Another idea is to keep comparison shots with your hits. If you have a shot of a particular area taken at 2:05am that shows nothing but you have one of the same general area taken at 2:30am, it adds credence to the hit.

When you get some really great shots, you may want to write a short story about them. It makes for interesting reading later on. It also helps you to remember that particular night which will come in handy when you are showing your pictures to your friends and family. After awhile, you may find that you have been to so many cemeteries that they all become a blur. Then again, maybe not. It is sometimes funny how we remember certain things. You may look at a picture and suddenly remember all the details. You may not remember your children's names but you will remember such and such cemetery.

If you plan to be in the cemetery for a while, you may want to bring snacks or coffee with you. If you do, make sure you clean up after yourself. If you smoke, do not leave butts all over the place. Remember that this is the final resting-place for those souls. Always respect that. Bring a folding chair or a beach towel with you. The ground will eventually get wet once it has reached the dew point. Do not bring your recliner but do bring something. You may as well be comfortable. Do not feel that you have to stay there all night. You do not want to rush in and out but you do not have to camp out there either ... play it by ear. One caution on smoking: do not take pictures anywhere near where you have been smoking. Cigarette smoke looks quite similar to fog. If you do not want you pictures called into account, don't smoke at all in the cemetery.

Contact The Local Police

Before you go to a cemetery for a shoot, do yourself a favor and drop a letter off at the local police station or at least call them. Most cemeteries close at dusk. If you go in anytime after that, you are technically trespassing. You probably won't get in trouble if the police show up but it can be a little embarrassing when you have to explain why you are there. The police can give you a ticket if they want. Again, technically, you are trespassing. Bring photos taken from other cemeteries. That way you can show them to the police. That may help convince them that you are not a vandal. The sad truth of the matter is that people do desecrate cemeteries. If you have any form of identification linking you to a paranormal society, bring that too. Always make sure you have some form of identification with you.

Another advantage of notifying the police is that you do not have to get paranoid every time you hear a car nearby. If you are sitting there worried about the police seeing you, it will be hard to concentrate on the task at hand. In addition, it changes your vibrations, which may keep the spirits away from you. Moreover, you do not need the interruption. For the most part, the police are reasonable about this. They will pretty much leave you alone. In some cases, they may show up and tell you to leave but that is rare.

What you want to put in the letter is your name, address, and telephone number so they can get in touch with you if they do not want you there. Then, you want to tell them that you are a paranormal investigator and you are doing research on cemeteries and would like to do a photo shoot in whatever cemetery you are going to. Let them know what time you plan to start and what time you think you will finish. Be polite. Bring a copy of the letter with you when you go on the shoot. If the police do come, you can show them that. You can make up a form letter if you want. Just leave the name and address blank and fill it in before you send it. Using a form, especially if it is on letterhead looks professional. Moreover, it may make them think that other police departments let you do this they may be more inclined to let you do it too.

If you are planning on going into a cemetery affiliated with a Church, it may be more difficult to get permission. The proper thing to do is get permission from the Pastor of the Church. Good luck. If you do get it, try to get this in writing. This way you can show that to the police if they come. You may find, however, that the Pastor will not give you permission. If that is the case, do not go to that cemetery. That is a sure way to get a ticket for trespassing. There are many cemeteries around, so do not push it. There is always somewhere else to go.

Some of the older, country cemeteries are good ones to go to. For some reason, you usually get better pictures in the older cemeteries. I am not sure why that is. You would think you might get better pictures at new gravesites, since the spirit of the recently deceased might still be around and the sadness of that person's passing is still fresh. However, I have never gotten a great shot from a fresh grave. Like many things in life, this does not figure.

When you go on a shoot, do not do so if you have been drinking. If you are slow mentally, you are leaving yourself open to whatever spirit might be there. Evil spirits like to hang out in cemeteries. I would guess that they like all of the negative energy found there from all of the mourners. Remember, energy cannot be destroyed so it is likely still there long after the mourners are gone. If you think about it, no one is ever happy in a cemetery. So avoid alcohol. If by some rare chance you do come across something negative, you do not want to be half-tanked.

In addition, if you are drinking, you increase your chances of falling over a headstone.

There are always skeptics who will debunk any photo you have. They will blame camera straps, rain, snow (even in July with some of them) fog, humidity and on and on. All I can say is that I have taken thousands of pictures in my lifetime and the only time I get orbs or fog is on something that is paranormal related. I have never gotten orbs at an outdoor wedding. Ditto for fog or misty pictures. If you make sure that you are taking the pictures properly, that is not in the rain or with a cigarette hanging out of your mouth, you have every right to be proud. Skeptics are skeptics. You can never convince everyone of anything and you really shouldn't try. So, just don't go to a cemetery on a rainy, snowy or foggy night. The pictures you get are more than likely to be of natural origin. They may look similar to paranormal ones so it is easy to get them confused. If you can get there just before a thunderstorm, you might get some really good shots what with the electrical activity. Once it starts raining though, you may as well go home. Anything you do get is going to be suspect anyway.

Some people feel that it is disrespectful to take pictures in a cemetery. Frankly, I do not see anything especially wrong with it. Certainly, you should show respect for the dead since the cemetery is their final resting place. However, merely being there to take pictures is not being disrespectful. There are people who like to jog in cemeteries. I have seen more than a few people eat their lunches in cemeteries. There is nothing wrong with that either. I doubt very much that the spirits would mind. Hell, when I kick the bucket, if I see people taking pictures near my grave, I will put on a show for them, if I can. As with everything in life, use common sense. If you behave properly, there is no disrespect in taking pictures in a cemetery.

SECTION 3:

Anatomy Of An Investigation

WHAT TO LOOK FOR

Remember, when you go into an investigation, you are trying to determine three things. You need to determine if something is there, what it is, and why is it there. You can add a fourth: if you are sure you are dealing with a human spirit, that being who is it. Later, you will see a listing of many different types of phenomena and what type of spirit causes them. It is not perfect by any means but it will help make things a bit clearer. For now though, let's take a look at some of the things that you need to look for before you determine whether or not a spirit is responsible for the activity.

In many cases, there are natural causes for a seemingly unnatural phenomenon. There is always the possibility of an over active imagination. That does happen. There are some people who are frightened when the subject is ghosts and hauntings. They may see something frightening on television and eventually convince themselves that they have a ghost on their hands. Others simply mistake natural phenomenon for supernatural phenomenon. We do not know this until we investigate. While you never want to do anything that would make the victim think you do not believe what they say, you do need to have something of a "show me" attitude, directed at the spirit, not the client.

The fact that you are doing an investigation at all means that something was said during the interview process that lead you to believe there may be something paranormal going on. The key word there is *may*. Based on those interviews, you may have strong feelings about what may be going on although in many cases, you are not presented with enough information to formulate strong feelings for what might be there.

However, you also have to take into account the possibility of unintentional exaggeration. When people are frightened, things seem much worse then they actually are. In addition, it is easy to spook yourself. Ask any paranormal investigator. We all know how the mind can play tricks on us. Bear in mind too that with the number of scary books and movies available, people who are experiencing some problems will sometimes let their imagination go wild. There are many suggestible people in this world. In some cases, they are taught how to be haunted. You also have to be wary when it comes to the family being victimized.It is not at all unusual for family members to convince each other that they are being haunted. People describe some wild stuff. In one case, I was led to believe that several different family members experienced particular occurrences. Later, I asked one family member to describe an event in full detail only to find out that she had not actually seen it herself. It turned out that only the son had seen it. After further discussion, it was determined that only the son had seen *anything*. That was when I learned the lesson that you have to interview everyone individually. After that is done, then you can talk to everyone as a group.

The point is simply that you need to do a thorough investigation in order to make any determination. That can take some time. It is the rare case where you walk in and immediately observe phenomena that conclusively proves the presence of a spirit. In the majority of cases, it may take several overnighters before you observe anything, let alone everything. So, even if you think you know what the problem is, let the evidence speak for itself. If there really is a serious problem, something will happen soon enough. A very important point has to be made here. Obviously, if a family is experiencing trouble, they want to know what is going on as quickly as you can tell them. Be very, very careful what you tell them and when. You should never make a judgment based on anecdotal evidence. Memory is faulty at best and never forget the exaggeration factor. No matter how nice the family is and no matter how clear-cut their descriptions are, you have to observe the phenomena for yourself. It is almost impossible to make a rational determination based solely on someone's memory. Memory is just not reliable enough. It is also easy to delude yourself.

Furthermore, if you do observe phenomena yourself or get a report from another investigator, you cannot rush your judgment. The family may be hounding you, however, you have to be sure. Witnessing one or two odd occurrences is not necessarily enough to go on unless the event that took place was indisputable. If you see the 87-year-old grandmother doing cartwheels up the stairs, complete with walker, then you may have something. If you see the families 4x4 doing wheelies in the driveway with no one in it, that would be acceptable evidence. Witnessing one or two glasses breaking is not enough evidence.

It can cause untold suffering if what you tell the family is wrong. It will hurt them severely and you may find yourself being sued in the process. Never arrive at a decision until you have done a thorough investigation, analyzed the evidence and have discussed the results with your team leader. If there is a debate between team members, take a closer look at all of the evidence and try to come to a consensus of opinion. Make sure you have that worked out before your next trip to the house. Also, never let the victims see a split in the group. That will make the investigation look like a farce.

What Should You Look For?

The things you need to look for are outward manifestations. Simply put, an outward manifestation is any event that can be called paranormal. Doors and drawers that open and close without any physical means would be evidence of this. So would any sightings of spirits. Sounds, smells and unnatural cold would be examples of outward manifestations. The family described outward manifestations to you. If they did not, you would not be there, right? What you want to do is take the information you are given and look at it item by item. Suppose they tell you that they hear doors opening and closing at night. They also tell you that doors that were locked at night are found open in the morning. On top of that, they keep hearing scratching coming from the attic and there is a terrible smell in the basement. Furthermore, every so often, they will find their Blessed Mary statue, which they keep on a shelf in the living room, facing the wall instead of facing the room. They also go on to describe various sounds they hear at night, creaks and groans and the like. Then they tell you about the pounding sound they sometimes hear. Okay, you have a sound starting point. There is obviously enough there to warrant an investigation. Your first step should be to take each item and look for a possible cause.

If you are with a few other investigators, you can give each investigator an item to check out. First, consider the opening and closing door problem. You need to try to determine whether it is always one door or every door? After talking to the family, you find that they do not know for sure. The best actions to take are look at every door downstairs and see if they all close properly. After doing that, you may feel satisfied that all of the interior doors are in good shape. However, you do find that the storm door outside of the house does not fully latch unless you pull it tight. If you let it close on its own, it does not catch. At that point, have a family member go up to their room with an investigator. Make sure all TV's and radios are off. Go outside and try opening and closing the storm door. A few minutes later, the father agrees that is the sound he hears. Excellent, that is one item taken care of.

While you are doing this, another investigator is looking at the door that seems to unlock itself. After tinkering with it for several minutes, he reports that he cannot find any rational explanation for it. The lock appears to be working properly and there is no obvious sign of damage. Okay, there goes one in the other column. Next, you go up to the attic. A close inspection shows some evidence of scratch marks along the baseboard. Maybe we have something here. It is going to be a tough one because it could swing either way. However, you have physical evidence. Make sure you take a picture. At that point, I would place that in the category of a natural occurrence, although you may want to leave a question mark next to it. You check the basement next. Yes, you smell it. It definitely smells like something dead. Now you are sure that you have a good piece of evidence. However, a thorough check of the basement reveals a deceased woodland creature hidden behind a stack of boxes.

The next item to check out is the moving Mary statue. While you are outside giving the poor woodland creature a decent burial, one of the other investigators is looking into the statue problem. There does not appear to be any way that the statue can move on its own. It turns out that it is heavy. You kick around a number of possibilities but none seem reasonable. These become wait and see items. Now you have two occurrences that are of natural origin and two that are questionable.

There is also that one that could go either way. As far as the creaks and groans heard at night, they can be anything. All houses make noise. When you are scared, all sounds are magnified. Unless they are describing a particular sound, something like laughing or crying, it is hard to tell.

Their last major complaint is what they are describing as pounding. This one, you have to wait on. What they describe as pounding might be more of a knocking sound being exaggerated. You have to hear it for yourself in order to be sure. That being the case, you set up your equipment and play the waiting game. The first night passes without a sound. On night two, the Mary statue begins to vibrate. Two investigators watch as the statue turns towards the wall. They see nothing that can account for the phenomena. Now you have trained investigators who have witnessed what appears to be a significant outward manifestation, one that could point to the demonic since it is a religious item that is involved. You can bet they are psyched. Within a span of thirty seconds, the eager investigators take many photographs. The family feels a sense of relief now that something they reported has been witnessed. After many debates, mom goes downstairs to finish her laundry. A short time later, the investigators see the statue move again. This time, one of them puts his hand on the shelf and feels the vibration. As soon as Mom comes up from the basement with her laundry in hand, the investigator rushes to tell her what he just witnessed.

Suddenly, a thought comes to him. After both instances of the vibrating shelf, Mom has come up with laundry. He asks her where the machines are in relation to the shelf in questions. His heart sinks when she tells him that the washer is directly below the living room. They try an experiment. They do another load of laundry and guess what, when the machine goes into the spin cycle, the statue does its dance. Just like that, their one piece of solid evidence has been explained. Imagine the embarrassment the investigators would have felt had they told the family that the moving statue was the result of a demonic spirit. Say goodbye to your credibility also. The rest of the night is uneventful. At daybreak, the investigators pack up their equipment and leave. They instruct the family to keep them informed of any new occurrences. Perhaps feeling a bit dejected, they leave the house.

Later that week, the team leader talks to the family. He finds out that the pounding happened two nights ago. He is also told that one of the children saw a shadow in her room. The team leader informs the family that he will be back on Saturday night and the investigators will try again. On Saturday night, they focus their attention on the child's room. Sure enough, they see a shadow move across the room. They also realize that it looks like a tree. Going to the window, they see the branches of the tree outside move. Another occurrence explained. That may cause the investigator feel a bit disheartened. Somewhere around 2 a.m., the investigators begin whispering to each other that they are pretty much convinced that there is nothing wrong in the house. Looking a little disappointed, the team leader begins jotting notes, which he will use for his final report.

Just as one of the investigators starts to nod out, she hears a clicking noise. Looking up, she sees the locked door open. She remembers that this was the door they could not explain. Slowly she stands up and starts to make her way into the living room to tell the team leader. Just as she enters the room, the pounding starts. Tremendous banging reverberates throughout the house. Stunned, the investigators look at one another. Suddenly, they hear a scream coming from upstairs. As a unit, they charge up the stairs, two steps at a time. Locating the source of the scream, they enter the child's room. In the corner, they see a black mist floating towards the nearly hysterical child. Moving with a speed that she herself could never imagine, the investigator scoops up the child, never taking her eyes off the black form hovering nearby. They flee the room.

See how confusing an investigation can be. The above scenario is an over simplification but it shows what can happen. Just when you think you know what is going on, something happens to make you rethink your position. In many cases, evidence swings one way to the other numerous times. It illustrates the reason why you should never tell the family anything until you are sure yourself. The timeline on the above story could have been much longer. There may have been many nights spent in the house without anything occurring. Another thing to realize is that hauntings can be subtle. It is not wild, full-blown activity 24 hours a day. Weeks can often pass without any noticeable activity. Then, unexpectedly, things start happening again. For that reason, never consider a case as being completely closed. You never know what the future holds. Cases that look simple can become complicated in a heartbeat. Cases where you are sure that no spirits are present often turn into complicated cases. You just never know.

Even when you observe phenomena yourself, you have to be careful. Be sure to document the experience and do not jump to conclusions. Memory is faulty at best so do not rely too heavily on it. Also, try not to read too much into a single experience. Something may happen which looks as though it may be the result of inhuman spirits but one such occurrence may be an aberration. Wait and see what happens next. When you hear whispering, look around for radios. This is especially true if you cannot make out what is being said. The possibility always exists that there is a radio on in the room above or below where you hear the voice. Sound travels in funny ways. It is very easy to mistake normal sounds you hear for paranormal sounds.

Should you see signs of a spirit present, do not overlook the possibility that it is benign in nature. People always think of hauntings and evil when they see a spirit. It may not be evil at all. Do not assume that it is. When sighting what appears to be a spirit, look closely for signs of intelligent activity. Also, determine whether the spirit reacts to your presence. You want to eliminate the possibility of a psychic recording. (Energy imprint.) Keep a constant eye on any equipment you have with you. Look for sudden temperature changes. If you have an EMF detector, record the readings if there are any variances. Gather as much physical evidence as you can. Should rapping or pounding take place, try to record the sound. If you see items shaking due to the pounding, focus your video camera on those items.

As I said earlier, do not be too quick to diagnose the problem to the family. Obviously, if you were sitting with them when some form of phenomenon broke out, it would be impossible to get away without saying something. You have to acknowledge the event; just do not be quick to say the phenomenon was caused by an evil or demonic force. The odds of that being the case are extremely low. You have to be sure first. Do your best to answer the question but be artfully vague. Again, I want to point out that you do not want to say or act in a manner that might make the victims think you do not believe them. Wait for all of the evidence to come in before you tell them anything concrete. In the end, you will be doing everyone a favor.

Also, be on the lookout for any evidence of fraud. The type of things you would look for are microphones, tape recorders, projectors, etc. People will try to fake a haunting for one reason or another, usually for some form of monetary gain. Along that same line, be wary of pictures that were run off a computer. It is not hard to create pictures of just about anything you want if you have a scanner or a digital camera and a little bit of knowledge. This is not to say that you should discount all such pictures, just be wary. Look at the whole picture.

When investigating items that fall of tables and such, look for wires. Ditto for doors that open and close. Also look for magnets in unusual places. You would hate to think that anyone would go to those lengths but it has been known to happen. Be careful if the contact starts talking about going to the press. You do not want to get involved in publicity. Be wary if you hear the client talk about what a great book their case would make, especially if they say that multiple times. Yes, they may be sincere but they may also be looking for a way to make a few bucks. Listen closely to what you are told. You can usually tell when someone is trying to take advantage of you. Ask yourself if the contact looks frightened. Remember what I said before about congruence. That is one of the best indicators of truth. Listen to the way he talks to you. Is what he is describing and the way he is describing it congruent?

Look for signs of mental illness. Unfortunately, you will come across many people who are mentally disturbed. If one person is always the focal point and no one else ever hears or sees anything, warning bells should go off. You would have picked that up in the interview process but always be conscious of the possibility. Also, if your interviews did not show a cause for the possible haunting, try to analyze the phenomena with an eye on the possible cause. Does this occurrence fit in with the laws of attraction or invitation? Could it be that you have an opportunistic spirit on your hands? Looking at the evidence this way makes it easier to determine whether it is paranormal or not.

The Importance Of Being Thorough

The most important thing to remember is to be as thorough as possible. Sloppy investigations are dangerous. You will not only ruin your own credibility but you can be doing damage to the people who need your help. Once you have all of the facts, you can make a determination about the situation. Is there something there or not? If there is, what is it? Once you have answered that question, you need to look into the steps necessary to eliminate the problem, if that is warranted. We will cover that in detail in the next section but it is very important that you have done a thorough investigation. If the results of your investigation showed a demonic presence, you will most likely have to get outside help. How easy or difficult that will be may be determined by how well you investigated the situation. Make sure that your final report is clear and well written. That report will be used when you go for help. It has to be objective and it has to be professional. A poorly written report may make it difficult to get the proper help. On the other hand, you can gain a lot of credibility by doing it well and that may make future cases much easier to work.

Be Able To Prove Your Theory

Make sure you are able to offer proof for any of claims you may make. Do not exaggerate anything in your report. Do not make any speculations ... stick to the facts. Whatever outside source you go to will likely do its own investigation. However, if you have done a thorough job, you may save them a lot of time. When it comes to the family being haunted, time is of the essence. If you can save just one week, you have done a lot. If your investigation was well done and presented in a professional manner, you may save considerably more time than that. Make sure you have all of your evidence filed in a manner, which makes it easy to find things. You are not going to give all of your evidence away but you want to be able to produce it when requested. Just a note: when you do produce evidence, whether it is pictures or tapes, always keep the originals. It is costly to make copies of everything but it would be catastrophic to lose them. Evidence has a way of getting lost or damaged

... especially evidence of anything demonic. It is also very difficult to get so never take a chance. It is always better to be safe than sorry.

ALWAYS BE TRUTHFUL

If you are asked to give a verbal report, do not embellish anything. Just as with the written report, always stick to the facts. If you are caught in just one exaggeration, it makes the whole rest of the report suspect. Be sure to present yourself in a professional manner. Dress properly, make eye contact and speak confidently while avoiding sounding cocky. If you are asked a question you cannot answer, be honest about it. It is fine to say that you do not know. No one has all of the answers. I remember one time when I was teaching a class on the supernatural and a student asked me a question that really had me stumped. I hemmed and hawed a bit and finally answered: "I haven't got a clue." Everyone got a kick out of that. Never offer an opinion as fact. If you are asked for an opinion, give it. Just do not ever offer an opinion as a fact. I have seen first hand the damage that can be done when an "expert" tells a besieged family that there is something demonic running through their house when there is no evidence to support that notion. If you declare that there are demonic forces at work, you are far more than likely to be wrong than right.

Demonic hauntings are rare and I cannot say that enough. I know that much of this book talks about the worst case scenarios but that should not be taken to mean that you are likely to come across one. My feeling is that if you are prepared for the worst and nothing happens, so much the better. Always err on the side of caution. Be sure that you know what you are dealing with before you diagnose a problem. Once you establish a reputation as professional investigator, you will find that it becomes easier to get help. The reverse is also true. If you have established a poor reputation, getting help can be extremely difficult, bordering on impossible. For that reason, always make sure your work is top notch. Keep in mind that all it takes is one mistake and your whole report, if not your investigation, goes for naught. The ones who will suffer the most are the victims. Never forget that the reason we do any of this is to help people. You need to do everything you can to help them.

WHAT YOU MIGHT ENCOUNTER

It is time to discuss what types of things you might encounter while doing an investigation. Citing examples from my own experiences and that of others I have known will hopefully help do this. Needless to say, you have a good idea of what you might find. You know the different types of spirits that are out there and there are only so many things they can do. Bear with me though. Many things can happen on an investigation. They range from equipment failure to assault by demons. (Rare!) Some of the things are funny; some are terrifying. Some are just flat out amazing.

The most memorable event for me was the first time I ever saw an object levitate. I have seen things far more horrific to be sure but this had me amazed. You know that levitation takes place but to see it yourself is unbelievable. You are taught certain laws of physics. You are taught that there is no such thing as a rising fastball or levitation of objects. Personally, I think they are wrong on both counts. I sat and watched as a small table levitated about one foot off the ground. It moved slowly, very slowly in fact, but it did rise. Once it reached its peak, it seemed to hover for about 15 seconds and then just dropped to the floor. The witnesses sat there in stunned silence. Oddly enough, I was not frightened. More than anything, I was shocked. I kept mumbling to myself something about how this cannot happen. Well, it did. The whole night took on a surreal quality. I felt disassociated, as if I was watching myself watch the table rise.

Smells And Psychic Cold

One of the more annoying occurrences you will eventually encounter involve smells. There are times when you are sitting in a room and all of a sudden, there is the horrible smell of decaying flesh or rotten eggs. No matter how hard you try, you cannot find the source of the smell nor can you get rid of it. It is a very effective strategy on the part of an evil spirit because it can clear out a room in a hurry. And you thought uncle Joe had a flatulence problem! I often seem to come across ghosts with gas problems. These smells can be so bad you may well vomit. Lovely, right? There is no escaping it either. I have tried putting pleasant smelling things under my nose but nothing works. You are stuck until it finally fades away. It may come out of nowhere, quite suddenly at times. It can end just as suddenly. Believe me, this falls into the category of the unforgettable. You need to smell it just once to know what I mean. I should make a point here. While the stench associated with hauntings can be horrible, it is not necessarily a given that a demon is behind it. This is one of those items that I am not 100% sure how to categorize. (And you thought I had all the answers.)

I can make a good argument that it is a demonic phenomenon because a human spirit would not be capable of creating an odor, especially a foul one. On the other hand, it is not at all uncommon to smell the perfume of a loved one in situations where it appears that the loved one has come back to visit. There is a tremendous amount of anecdotal evidence that loved ones *can* come back under some circumstances. These visitations tend to occur during periods of great stress and in some cases, when there is a big event that the loved one would have been very excited about, were they still alive. It might be a wedding or baptism or something of that sort. If that type of smell can manifest, why not a foul one? The argument can be made that the pleasant smell is simply a byproduct of the spirit; it is not something that the spirit knows how to make. Most people do not carry around the smell of a sewer so the foul odor would have to be generated consciously. That would seem to be outside the realm of the human spirit. Did I confuse you enough? Good, now we are on a level playing field.

Psychic cold is common experience in houses where there is paranormal phenomena occurring. There are really two different types of psychic cold, although they both feel the same. In one instance, a materializing spirit or one who is attempting to bring about paranormal phenomena, draws the energy it needs from the environment. In this case, the actual room temperature will drop. You will see the drop on your thermometer and you will also see your breath. The drop in temperature may be quite sudden and dramatic. You may find that the heart of the house is always cooler than the rest of it. That too, shows up on a thermometer. In the other case, the spirit or force will draw its energy from the people present. When this happens, you will feel extremely cold but your room thermometer will not register the change. There seems to be no way to warm yourself up when you are faced with this type of psychic cold. It should be pointed out though that in cases of extreme stress, people have been known to feel cold even when the temperature is recorded as being hot. In those cases, you will shiver although the temperature says it is seventy degrees. The same happens sometimes when you are very tired.

So what is this telling us? Well, if you have a drastic drop in room temperature and there is no natural cause, that is, there is no drop in the outside temperature and no cooling system has been introduced, then you have an occurrence that defies the known laws of physics. Notice that I say: "known." With the advances in science, it is possible that one day we will have a natural explanation for this type of phenomenon as we have for others. If you and others suddenly feel very cold and the temperature has not changed, that tells you something right there. At that time, check your instrument readings if you are using any. Your EMF may react to coincide with the temperature change, even if your thermometer doesn't.

If you are in a haunted house, there is a good chance that you will see something unusual. You may well see lights flickering around the room. They can be colorful, although for some reason they are often blue. Sometimes they are white lights that blink on and off, almost like Christmas tree lights. In some instances, they will shoot across the room. At other times, you will see what appears to be an arc of electricity. Actually that is exactly what it is, an arch of electricity. While these lights can be frightening, they can also be quite fascinating to watch. I have heard people describe them as "awesome." They certainly can be. Your eyes may play tricks on you. You may see something one minute and have it be gone in the next. To confuse things, you may see something and the person sitting next to you may not. In many cases, you will see things out of the corner of your eyes only to find nothing there when you turn you head. This can happen in either eye but in cases of evil entities, you will most often see it from the left eye. You may also see an apparitional manifestation of some sort. This can range from an amorphous mist like thing, to a cloven hoofed demon. I will discuss this further in the next section. Sightings can be quite frightening, especially when you know you are dealing with something evil.

(Being Touched and Sounds)

Worse than a sighting is to be touched. If you see something, you can move away from it. Being touched by something unseen will unnerve you in a hurry. Touches can range from a light brush against your skin to being pinched, scratched, bitten or even punched. I worked a case not long ago where the spirit pulled my hair one two occasions. In both cases, it was a light tugging; there was no effort to cause any pain. It was simply an attention getter. It worked. Also, there were several occasions where I felt a hand on me. At one point, it started to run its hand up my leg. (I have this odd habit of acting irreverent at the worst times. I also get a case of the giggles from time to time.) My reaction to that was to tell the spirit that we did not know each other well enough for that. The touching stopped and never repeated it even though I was there many times after that. Maybe it felt it was wasting its time on me. Most of the touches you feel are attention getters. Of course, it must be pointed out that the severe physical attacks such as being bitten or punched only happen in the most extreme cases of demonic infestation and they are rare. Thank God!

Also particularly unnerving are the various sounds that often occur during a haunting. You will sometimes hear what is referred to as "rapping." This can be like a knocking sound. In some cases, it is more accurately described as pounding. It usually comes from the walls or the ceiling but I have found that the sound seems to come from everywhere, including the floor. You will actually feel the vibrations or shock waves. Items will fall off walls and shelves. The furniture you are sitting on may shake or move to the pounding. These poundings can be inhumanly loud and fast. I remember an instance of pounding that was unbelievable in its speed and loudness. Long after it stopped, I tried to duplicate the speed of the poundings. I knew I would not have been able to duplicate the loudness of it but I thought I could duplicate the speed. Wrong ... I could not even come close. Nor could anyone else who heard it. It sounded like an automatic weapon being discharged, only louder. Oddly enough, the neighbors all around us did not hear it.

Fairly common is knocking on the doors. When you answer it, there is no one there. The knocking may come in threes. This is often a sign of evil or demonic spirits. They sometimes do things in threes as a mock of the Trinity. This type of knocking is more annoying than frightening, unless you are alone in the house, that is. When you are alone, that knocking gets to you very quickly. Okay, now to show you how the mind works, you are afraid to open the door for fear that something evil might come in. Think about it. The damn thing has been torturing you all along and it can come and go as it pleases, door or no door. Yet, you are terrified at the thought of opening the door. Part of that, I guess is the fear of some horrible looking entity waiting for you on the other side of the door. Here's Johnny!

You will sometimes hear your name called. In fact, something may call you to go into a certain room. Do not do it unless there is someone (living) in there. If there is something evil there, it sure does not want to sit down and socialize with you. Do not listen to it. In many instances, you will hear whispering. In my experience, you can never quite make out what it is saying. What feels like air brushing against your ears often accompanies this. That bothers me no end. It is also infuriating that you cannot tell what is being said. Of course, that may well be a good thing. I doubt that the disembodied voices are discussing your hair color.

There have been many reports of people hearing growling. I have had that pleasure. You want to become paranoid? That will do it for you. Trust me, you never forget it. Screams and crying are common in a haunted house. The crying can get to you, especially if you are sensitive. It can be heartbreaking. You hear that and you want to help whatever it is that is doing the crying. It can really tug on your emotions. This can be a ploy on the part of a negative spirit although that is not always the case. However, they are quite capable of playing head games and they have an almost startling proficiency at it.

Laughter is something else that you may experience. It often sounds diabolical. You will not forget that either. It is very unnerving. You know something is around you somewhere and you can hear it laughing at you. I think I like the growling better. Of course, there have been many reports of people hearing a room full of laughter coming from an empty room. This usually happens in places like hotels. It may well be an energy imprint from the past. Animal sounds are very common in demonic or diabolical hauntings. (A demonic haunting is one that has a demon involved. A diabolical haunting has a devil involved. Yes, there is more than one devil.) Pigs are a favorite of the demonic although you may hear other animals. Goats get their licks in from time to time. You may find eyes staring at you from across the room. They are usually red and they will follow you around the room, if you stay in it, that is. Footsteps are also quite common. They may sound like human footsteps or they may sound like an animal with cloven hooves.

A note on footsteps, if that is the only phenomenon you are experiencing, do not take that to mean it is necessarily the result of an evil spirit. Benign spirits will produce footsteps too. I occasionally hear footsteps walking up and down my hallway. So has everyone who has stayed overnight or spent a lot of time there. However, there is nothing negative residing there. You have to see what other activity is going on, if there is any. Again, always be careful when dealing with only one bit of phenomenon. Still, even keeping that in mind, it can be very frightening to hear something walking towards you, be they good, bad, or indifferent. This is especially true if you are alone in a house. You may be sleeping in bed when you hear footsteps coming from your living room. You may initially believe that someone has broken into your home. That will surely send you into a panic.

In situations like that, people have been known to call the police. Once they arrive, needless to say, they find no signs of forced entry. It may happen again right after they leave. Trust me; that will shake you up to no end. It is one of the effects of a haunting… pure terror. Once you come to realize that it is not a person, at least not a *living* person, the terror magnifies. You cannot help but wonder what will happen if the spirit finally reaches you. In the majority of cases, nothing happens at all. In a lot of those cases, the footsteps often stop right outside the door to the room you are in. Just the same, the effect is terrorizing. Just ask anyone who has ever experienced it.

Poltergeist Activity

Perhaps the most amazing phenomena you will witness are poltergeist activities. It can range anywhere from a glass sliding slowly across a table to furniture being thrown around with great force. You may witness doors opening and closing, drawers doing the same. Items may rain on the house. These are called *apports.* They often appear as rock like items but they can actually be anything. There have been documented cases where live animals were the apports. Don't get this confused with the documented cases where small fish or frogs have rained down on a house. Waterspouts have been known to cause that type of thing. However, when fish are raining down *inside* the house, then you have a problem. Ditto for rocks. Holes may be punched in walls and pictures ripped from them. Electrical appliances may go berserk. Lights may go on and off or they may dim. TV's may turn on and off as well. Channels will often change while you are watching TV. Some people in the field refer to this as an *electronic* poltergeist. During an investigation, do not be surprised if your equipment fails to function properly, or at all. Batteries have a way of draining during poltergeist activity. That may be the source of some of the energy the poltergeist uses.

Sometimes cars will break down in route to an investigation. Cameras will fail. Sometimes the camera will work but when you get the film developed, nothing comes out. Water may appear out of nowhere. There have been cases where it has rained indoors. Some call this a *water* poltergeist. As far as I am concerned, the same spirit may be responsible for the water and the electrical malfunctions so do not get too caught up in giving the poltergeist a name. There are some who believe that there are poltergeists for all occasions. There is usually just one. I don't think there are trade schools for poltergeists. A poltergeist is a poltergeist is a poltergeist. If I have learned one thing in life, (and there are those who believe that is all I learned) it is to beware of labels. They have a way of coming back to bite you. Bottles of holy water may go flying around the room. This usually happens in demonic hauntings. Demonic spirits hate religious items; therefore they are often targeted.

Poltergeists Explosions Can Be Destructive

Poltergeist explosions can be extremely destructive. Treasured items may be smashed on the floor. A two-dollar ashtray may fly through the screen of your three hundred-dollar TV. In addition, items may be thrown at you. One piece of advice is when you get involved in what appears to be a serious case, advise the client that they may want to take precious items and put them somewhere safe until the haunting is resolved. In many cases, items thrown at you may hit you but with next to no force behind it. In extreme cases, however, you can be injured by thrown objects. Be alert to this. Your expensive equipment may be targeted. Nothing is sacred to poltergeists, even sacred items. This is always a sign of the demonic. Religious statues may break; crosses may be turned upside down. Rosary beads, which are perhaps the most holy item in the world, may break. This is a sign of a very powerful demon or a devil.

Poltergeists will be discussed at length later on but I want to point out that there are times where poltergeist activity is just than, the work of a poltergeist spirit. However, there are times when a demonic spirit is causing the activity. The difference is that poltergeist activity will eventually burn itself out and it has no real game plan. However, in a demonic haunting, steps must be taken to stop the problem because it will not stop on its own. Also, there is often a plan behind a demonic haunting. There is some goal on the part of the demon. That goal may vary but there is an intelligence behind what is taking place, it is not the random activity of a poltergeist.

Bi-location, a phenomenon where an item will appear in two different locations at the same time is commonly reported. Throughout history, there have been documented cases where people have been involved in acts of bi-location. The recently canonized Saint, Padre Pio was known to bi-locate on several occasions. Bi-location should not be confused with the spirit mimic. In some demonic hauntings, demons have taken on the appearance of a living person. An example would be a woman seeing her husband walking down the stairs to the basement when she just got off the phone with him. He is still at work, a full hour away. This is usually done to frighten and confuse a victim. It is a phenomenon designed to cast doubt on the part of the person who experiences it and it also creates a situation where it makes what the victim says unbelievable to the people he or she tells the story too. It is very effective when it comes to creating doubt and it can lead to a point where it drives a wedge between the victim and their families. Items may disappear and turn up somewhere else.

Objects that disappear and are not found are referred to as *asports.* If it turns up again, it was *teleported.* This can be particularly annoying when it comes to your equipment disappearing just when you need it. If you are lucky, it will turn up again. If you are really lucky, it will turn up again in the same number of pieces as it left. Amazingly enough, even large objects can be teleported. Doors have been teleported, as has furniture. Hopefully not the furniture that you are sitting on at the time. The weird thing about teleportation is that you never see the object disappear. What happens is the item is there one minute and when you turn around, it is gone. You do not see it leave and you do not hear anything either. It is not like "Star Trek" where you see it being beamed to another location. It is similar to poltergeist movements where you never actually see an item take off. You do see where it lands though, especially if the landing site is your head. If you do see it take off at all, it is usually out of the corner of your eye. Why that happens is beyond me. You would think it would have more of an effect if you saw the whole process.

Believe it or not, there have been documented cases where animals and even people have been teleported. For example, you take your trusty dog outside and tie him a tree while you go inside to vacuum the carpet. When you get back inside, you find the dog in the kitchen. In cases where people have teleported, they do not remember anything. He is sitting on the john one-minute and suddenly he finds himself on the couch the next. If you have company when this happens, let us hope you pulled your pants up before being teleported. This does sound unbelievable but there have been documented cases where this has happened. I do admit to being slightly skeptical of this myself but I have heard people I believe tell me that it has happened, if not to them, then to someone in a case they were working with.

Another thing you might encounter is less subtle. In a demonic haunting, it is common for the demonic force to "play with your head." You may experience unusual mood swings, such as anger, rage, and a host of other emotions. The same may be true of your spouse or children. If a demon can get you off a case, it will. It will use everything at its disposal to do so and it is not beneath going after your loved ones. If it cannot succeed in getting you off a case, it will then do whatever it can to make it as difficult for you as possible. That can mean equipment problems and it can mean family or other personal problems. It may also try to play "divide and conquer" in your household just as it does with the victims you are trying to help. It may well try to scare your children. The demon will be thrilled if your spouse begins to get on you for the trouble the case is causing in your own home. In addition, it may cause mischief, such as slashed tires or something of that ilk. Here you have a problem that could well have been done by a living person. Do you see how it can play with your head? The purpose behind this is simple: it wants to make your time there as uncomfortable as possible, partly because it enjoys hurting people and partly in the hope you will not come back.

It is common to suffer from severe nightmares while you are investigating a case. That can also happen just before and after one as well. Of course, nightmares can become a problem for investigators after a bad case. If the case was severe enough, those nightmares may last a long time. They may never go away completely. It is an unpleasant hazard of the job. Also, there have been numerous cases where investigators have gotten quite sick before or during an investigation. Another thing you might experience is phenomena breaking out in your own home. This often happens right before a case comes up, especially big ones. It may be a precursor of a case to come or a warning to you to stay out of one. If this starts to happen, deal with it immediately. Always have holy water handy and bless everyone in the house. Yes, that includes your pets too. Also, envision your home surrounded by and filled with white light and do not forget to use the St. Michael the archangel prayer. It is very powerful. There may be other things that I have failed to mention but I think this will at least give you an idea about what you might experience. The best rule to follow is "anything goes." Always expect the unexpected and you will not be disappointed.

WHAT SPIRITS LOOK LIKE

When you think of the word spirit, you do not imagine it as something that can be seen. After all, only the physical can be seen, right? All else would have to be an optical illusion at best or a hallucination at worst. However, spirits ... good and evil ...do occasionally appear to people. They take on different shapes and forms depending on what they are and why they are appearing. A ghost or a human spirit may be seen as a person, albeit a transparent one, although they are certainly not limited to looking like that. A demon on the other hand may appear as just about anything it chooses. Obviously, if it wants to scare you, (and a demon would; why else would it be around?) it will appear in such a manner as to do that. There is a theory that they know what you most fear and while choose a form that will accomplish your worst fears. From my own personal experiences, I can tell you that I firmly believe that to be so. I can also tell you that it is an effective strategy.

Throughout history, spirits have been portrayed in different ways. Everyone knows what Casper looks like, right? There is the infamous white sheet over the head routine. Devils have appeared as horned creatures and in many cases, demons took on a reptilian quality. You sometimes come across an old movie or two where the spirit looked very much like a person, albeit a misty one. I have seen ghosts portrayed as humans complete with rotting flesh. We can go on and on this way but the question is, just what do spirits look like? Well, some of the above mentioned descriptions are not all that far off. In fact, in some cases, they are right on the money. Let us take a look at the various types of spirits and how each one may be seen.

Human Spirits

In many cases, a human spirit may appear in much the same form as it did in life. It is usually not in solid form although that does sometimes happen. Many people have reported seeing spirits with defined features. In a large number of these instances, the spirit seemed to be transparent. In other words, while the spirit certainly resembled a person, you could see clear through it. These spirits have been widely reported to have no legs that can be seen. They usually appear from the waistline up, although that is certainly not always so. It is common for the spirits hair to move around as if there is a light breeze in the air. The same is true with the clothing they are wearing. I have seen this myself. On several occasions back in my haunted house, I along with many others saw the spirit of a woman. She was wearing a flowing white gown that appeared to be moving in response to a breeze. When she moved, the gown flowed some more. As is common with this type of spirit she did not walk ... she seemed to float. Although she did react to those of us who witnessed her, she never attempted to come towards us or otherwise threaten us.

Let me use an example. If she were to be appearing to me when someone walked into the room, she would turn around and look at that person. When she decided she no longer wanted to be seen, she simply faded away, growing lighter and lighter until she was no longer there. At that point, I shook my head and began questioning whether I really saw her or was it all my imagination? Despite numerous appearances over the years, I always found myself asking that same question. I want to point out something about that particular spirit. Aside from being frightened the first few times I saw her, I came to believe she was a benign spirit, possibly even a benevolent one. I felt she was watching over me since she most often manifested when I was either sick or injured. (And that was often. I had the worst luck in that house. Accidents and illnesses were frequent with me. I have since learned that many people suffering through hauntings experience that.) We had a spirit in that house that would cry and sob from time to time. I always believed that the spirit I saw was the one who did the crying. In some instances, the spirit that is seen is really a form of projection as opposed to it being a real spirit. You will read more about that later.

There are times when a spirit will appear exactly as it did during life. It will be as solid as you and me. There are scores of stories of people seeing deceased loved ones appear as alive as they had before death and in some cases even more alive than just before death. They are there one minute and when they finish their business, they suddenly just disappear. Poof! I have heard of stories where the spirit would appear bearing the same wounds that resulted in their death. It might take the form of a head injury that resulted from an auto accident or there may be burned flesh. However, in many reported cases, people who had been terribly ill will appear to a loved one looking fit and healthy. They may have been emaciated during their illness from something like cancer but when they appear in death, they look young and fit. Perhaps this is a way of the spirit showing a loved one that things are better for them now. Their pain and suffering is over. That can be very comforting to someone who watched a loved one waste away from some horrible disease.

A common experience, according to many stories I have read about, heard, and even experienced myself, has to do with seeing someone you know on the street. Sometimes, you just wave at them and they return your greeting. Later, you arrive home and receive a telephone call telling you that so and so died two days before. You profess amazement to the person you are talking to and you tell them all about the encounter you just had with that person. A little while later, after the shock wears off, you begin to question yourself again. I once experienced talking to someone who had just passed away, although I did not know that at the time. It is a startling but fairly common occurrence. There have also been many instances where people have seen very solid spirits who they did not know. This is not limited to a haunting alone. These apparitions will sometimes appear for other reasons. Perhaps it is to deliver a message? Perhaps it is a reason known only to the spirit?

Once I awoke to find someone standing next to my bed. This apparition was as solid as I am. I stared at this entity for several seconds. He was wearing a black pinstriped, three-piece suit with a gold pocket watch in his vest. The suit was of a style from long ago. He appeared to be in his seventies, with neatly cut white hair and he wore a well-trimmed mustache. Although he was staring at me, his eyes appeared lifeless. Many of you, I am sure, have seen people at the time of their death. They often have their eyes open but you can tell immediately that they are dead. Their eyes have a fixed, vacant look to them. I do not mean to be sarcastic but the phrase: "the lights are on but there is nobody home," applies. Again, I mean no offense; it just happens to be probably the best way to describe the look.

Back to my story, I watched him for several seconds, frozen at the sight, my heart pounding away. Suddenly, he pitched forward, stiff as a board and came crashing down on me. I braced for the impact, which I felt. It hurt and actually left a bruise on my ribs. He seemed to lie on me for a few seconds as I struggled to push him off. His body was very stiff and cold. I remember that today as if it just happened yesterday. Then, just like that, he was gone. I jumped out of that bed and charged out of the room. I woke my mother up and started to explain to her what I had just seen. I was talking a mile a minute and she was doing her best to calm me down so I could tell her what had just happened in something resembling a coherent way. As I was talking to her, the telephone rang. The call was from one of my uncles, informing us that my Grandfather had just died. After the wake and funeral, I spent a considerable amount of time looking at old pictures, trying to identify my visitor. I never did. Was this spirit a messenger sent to herald the passing of my Grandfather? It would seem so. As to why he chose me to appear to is anyone's guess. Perhaps it was a case where my brain was "tuned" to the right frequency? He may have tried to appear to other members of my family but they could not see him. That is as good a reason as any, I suppose.

Most of the time though, human spirits do not appear that solidly. As I said before, they are often transparent. From sight alone, it is hard to tell whether the human spirit you encounter is benign or evil. During my haunting, I saw another spirit from time to time. This spirit was also a woman and she too wore a white dress. She appeared to be considerably younger than the other spirit I mentioned. The astonishing thing about her was she was always engulfed in flames. Although she never appeared blackened or burned, the flames engulfing her did move. She and the flames were both transparent. When she appeared, we could see most of her body. She too reacted to us and she floated around as opposed to walking. I always felt very uncomfortable when she appeared. I found her to be very frightening, for that matter. Unlike the other spirit, I sensed this one meant trouble. I am not saying that she herself was definitely evil but I never sensed benevolence from her. If anything, she was probably a pawn of the demon that operated there. It may have puppeteered her. She may or may not have been harmful on her own. Perhaps it was the flames that bothered me. It is hard to imagine something in flames being a good thing. Was she a human spirit or an inhuman one? There is no way to be sure although I believe she was human.

Inhuman Spirits

When it comes to the inhuman spirits, things are a little different. For openers, demons are rarely seen, or rarely recognized as such when they are seen. It is believed that demons can take on virtually any appearance they choose. You name it; they can do it. However, they do seem to have some preferences. One of the most common depictions of demons is of a half-man, half-animal creature. It may have the head of an animal, the torso of a man and an animal's hairy legs. Very often through history, they have cloven hooves. They will sometimes appear with a goat's head. There are many depictions of creatures with bright, red eyes wearing ram's horns. Although hearing pig squealing is associated with the demonic, I have never heard of a demon appearing as one, except in the case of Jody, the pig demon of "The Amityville Horror" fame.

One investigator I know once saw a demon that looked human but was terrible decayed. I have no reason to doubt him on that. They do have the capability of appearing as a human, either the see through kind or the solid kind. I would venture to guess that this is their most common choice. That would explain why they are often not recognized as demons. When you are doing an investigation, that can confuse things a bit. You may see what appears to be a human spirit but in actuality, it could well be a demon. That is why I said earlier that it could be difficult to determine what you are dealing with by sight only. Obviously, if the spirit appears as a half-man, half-animal creature, you know you are dealing with a demon. However, they rarely make things so easy. Human spirits cannot take on the form of an animal. However, seeing the human figure does not tell you much. Could my "flaming lady" have been a demon? It could possibly have been one. To determine what type of spirit you are dealing with, you have to go more by action and intent than by looks.

Demons are androgynous, in other words they have no assigned sex. Although they are usually depicted as males, they can and do appear as females, if that suits their needs. An incubus, as you probably know, is a demon that will have sex with a woman. A succubus is a demon that will have sex with a male. However, it could be the same demon doing both. Demons will sometimes change appearances right in front of you. If you see an old hag one-minute and a small child the next, you are looking at a demon. This is beyond the realm of the human spirit. A common form of appearance for a demon is a black, mist like figure. Some people refer to this as a "shadow ghost," although I would not describe it that way. It is often amorphous, without definite shape. This shape can be translucent; it can also be solid looking. When I refer to the solid form of this spirit, I use the phrase, absence of light, as opposed to being black. We are probably just talking semantics here but to me, an absence of light is like looking at a void. This is my idea of a demon.

Again, it probably makes no difference how you describe it. You know what I mean, six of one and a half a dozen of the other. There have been many reported instances of headless or disfigured animals running around. This is another form demons like to take. Their aim is to horrify and disgust you and I would say this is an excellent way to accomplish that goal. Just a thought about the "shadow ghost." On several occasions, I have seen shadows, perhaps silhouettes is a better description. This is what I would call a shadow ghost. These usually appear in darkened rooms, although there would have to be some light. On the wall would be the silhouette of a person. Of course, the silhouette would move. That may not sound terribly frightening unless you are the only one in the room. Then it doesn't feel too good.

Before we move on, I want to run a theory by you. Back in my haunting, I saw some hideous forms. Those images will remain with me forever. But… there was always some doubt about what I saw. Those doubts were fostered by an exhausted, frightened mind. Lighting was poor and in some cases, nonexistent. Some of what was seen can be attributed to dreams. I am not denying that I saw those things; I am just saying that there was and still are some reasonable doubts as to what was there. Remember the 25% exaggeration rule. It applies to me as well. I have not met anyone who ever saw a demon in the form of a hideous creature. However, there are many accounts of people who have. The images I saw may not have been an actual creature clomping through the rooms. There is the strong possibility that the images I "saw" were actually projections sent to me telepathically. In a sense, it may have been a telepathic hallucination. The spirit planted that image in my mind to cause maximum fear. It was wholly effective. The spirit was there but the "creature" may not have been. I do not know for sure. However, I would love to hear from people who have experienced anything like that. Maybe together we can find some answers or at least understand the process better.

Angel Spirits

Having looked at the dark side of the inhuman spirit, it is only fair to look at the good, inhuman spirits. We know them as angels. For the record, demons are technically angels. Like the good angels, God created them. As the story goes, they chose to try to take over Heaven and we all know the rest. Anyway, if the bad angels or demons can appear as anything they want to, so too can the good angels. Therefore, they can be rock solid. However, they do not appear as mists like the bad guys do; they tend to prefer the human look. They too, are androgynous. Women often picture their angels as males; men do the reverse. Angels are always with us, walking the earth and performing great deeds mostly unnoticed and wholly unappreciated. We all know about our guardian angels but it appears that angels serve many purposes. The name "angel" means literally: "messenger." Therefore, they sometimes deliver messages from God, most of which probably go unheeded. There are recorded instances where in times of great trouble, someone will appear out of nowhere and save the day, whether it is in the form of protection or rescue.

It is quite likely that we see angels often but do not realize it. If you stop and think about it long enough, you wonder how many times you pass a person who seemed to radiate goodness and kindness. That person may give you a quick smile and move on. However, there is usually an extremely good feeling about the encounter. Could that person be an angel? It could well be. Those who study angels, *angelogists,* as they are now known believe that we all can see these loving creatures. Many experts believe that our own beliefs are essential to our being able to see them. However, there are enough cases recorded throughout history where even the biggest nonbelievers met an angel while they were in a time of great need. Do angels always appear human? The consensus is no. Angels often appear in the form of animals. They sometimes appear as the lovely, winged creatures depicted in so many books. Much of it has to do with your own concept of what an angel should look like. They appear to a person exactly as that person thinks they should so that person can believe that what they are seeing is, in fact, an angel. Whatever form they take, angels are always described as beautiful creatures that radiate love, kindness, and warmth. Of course, Satan and his legions would certainly disagree with that sentiment.

Do spirits take on other forms?

Yes they do. They sometimes appear as circles known as "globules" or "orbs." They may be perfect circles or they may be less than perfect circles. They may be perfectly clear or they may be white. Sometimes they are a solid white, other time they appear less dense. They will sometimes appear to be streaking upward with what resembles a comet tale. These globules are usually seen in photographs; they are rarely seen by the naked eye. Digital cameras are great because you can see these spirits in the viewing mechanism immediately after the photograph is taken. I once did a shoot with someone who had a digital camera. He found some spirits while walking through the woods. I rode his coat tails, so to speak and took some pictures with a 35mm camera where he had seen the globules. I got a couple of good pictures that day.

What exactly are these globules? I believe that these globules are actually balls of electromagnetic energy. Where the energy is coming together, you get the globules. Their density depends on whether they are forming or vanishing. They sometimes appear as an amorphous mist. Although not visible to the naked eye, these mists often come out in pictures. These mists or "psychic fog" as they are often referred to are electromagnetic energy fields. It is my belief that these mists are the results of the globule forming or vanishing. In other words, when the mist condenses itself, you get the globule. Sometimes you will see a face or some other shape in these mists. I have a picture that strongly resembles what to me appears to be a demonic face. As I mentioned earlier, I have also seen one that strongly resembles a winged angel. However, with most of them, it is like staring at a cloud or a Rorschach test. You see whatever you want or expect to see. These electromagnetic energy fields will register on a Gauss meter.

Nature Spirits

There are other types of spirits as well. The nature spirits, or *elementals* as they are called, photograph as squares or rectangular shapes of light. They can also be cylindrical in appearance. These nature spirits are said to be cousins to the angels. They represent each of the natural elements, air, earth, fire and water. These spirits are friendly but a bit mischievous. You are very lucky when you capture one of them on film. It is believed that wherever you have a plant, you have an elemental spirit who watches over it. These spirits do sometimes appear to people in their homes. They may take on different shapes, squares or triangles or others. They may be quite colorful too. They will sometimes float lazily around, just out of your reach. Consider yourself lucky when this happens to you.

Fairy lights are just that, lights. Seeing them in the woods is like looking at Christmas tree lights. They tend to blink on and off. While doing a cemetery shoot, my wife and a friend of ours were taking pictures. My wife asked me if I felt anything. I told her "Yes, I was feeling a lot of energy." Of course, who would not feel energy in a cemetery? However, I was more specific since I believe that "feeling energy" can be a copout answer. I explained to her that I felt we were being watched and that I thought we were "being checked out." My feeling was that there was something there that was as curious of us as we were of it. I did not fell threatened, however. There have been many times where I have sensed that there was something around that was less than thrilled with my being in a given place. This frequently happens on investigations. This was different. My feeling there was that the spirits around were simply as amused with our being there as we were about being there. Well, while sitting by a tree loading my camera, I felt something lightly brush my neck. It almost felt like a breeze but the touch seemed just a bit harder. When I looked over my shoulder, I saw a blinking light. It stayed on for a second or so then went out. After that, it blinked on and off again. After a few seconds, it stayed on and began to move lazily away. After travelling about thirty feet or so, the light went out. Nothing else approached me but I saw a spectacular light show in the woods where my little friend had gone.

(Other Forms)

Spirit energy can also take the form of an electrical arc. Usually bluish in color, these arcs of electricity will produce a sound much like the sound of static. On some occasions, it will appear as if you have an electrical storm in your house. Can you imagine seeing mini lightning in your bedroom? Wild, right? Of course, if you are being haunted, this light show is anything but appreciated. I have seen some good ones though. Since we know that manifesting spirits create electromagnetic energy fields, it would seem to make sense that they would appear in this form. Therefore, it is no surprise that spirits are often seen in many different forms, during electrical storms. You will get your best pictures then too. Of course, you might also get struck by lightening and become a spirit yourself. Just kidding.

Balls of light are common in haunting situations. They may be of any color and they will often shoot across a room. If they impact a wall, there is usually that static like sound. Although they usually fly overhead, there have been instances where they have been "shot," for want of a better term, right at someone. When touched by these balls, the victims often report having felt a shock. Many pictures of this type of electrical activity have been caught on film. This is also true of the arc and the lightning type of energy already mentioned. I do not think that this form of manifestation is done by choice. In other words, I do not think a spirit decides that it wants to be a ball of lightening today. It is most likely an unexpected and uncontrolled manifestation. This leaves you to wonder if maybe our physical world has a lot to do with how or even *if* a spirit can manifest. It would make sense because spirits are energy. It really stands to reason that atmospheric conditions would effect how energy is manifested. Does the same hold true for a haunting itself? Are you more likely to have poltergeist activity during an electrical storm? My guess would be yes. Would it affect how demons operate? There I would say no. I think that atmospheric conditions would affect how a spirit manifests although I am sure it has nothing to do with spirits intent.

(Photographic Evidence)

Do all of these many forms of spirits come out on photographs? Most of them do. These light shows commonly do. Ditto for the globules. Rare are the shots of ghosts looking like a person. There have been some really good shots published but like I said, getting those are pretty rare. I have never heard of anyone capturing a demonic form such as the half-man, half-animal creature or anything resembling a creature with a goat's head. I have also never heard of anyone capturing a headless animal on film. The shadow ghosts do sometimes come out. However, if there are pictures out there showing any other form of demonic creature, I have never seen one or met anyone that claims to have one. That does not mean they do not exist. If someone has such a horrific picture of a demon, he may well have chosen to keep it a secret. I just think that if there were a shot like that out there, someone would have published it by now. After all, it would be worth a fortune. After all, pictures of Elvis sightings make a fortune. Can you imagine a *real* ghost or demon? Still, you never know. I know that I have tried to capture spirits on film but all I have gotten are orbs and fog. I do have one where it appears that a skull is looking out from a door.

I am willing to bet that most, if not all of us have seen spirits at different times in our lives. The vast majority of those sightings have probably gone unnoticed. They may be around us all the time, both the good ones and the bad ones. Some protect us; others do their best to cause problems. Of course, there is no way to be sure. However, if you were to think back, you might just find that there was one time when you really did see something that just might have been a spirit. Maybe you thought it was just your imagination? Maybe you thought it was merely a coincidence? You never know.

I believe that if you are open to it and are observant, you will someday see a spirit, if you haven't already. Belief has something to do with it. I base that on the fact that almost invariably, those who believe in spirit phenomenon get some quality shots while skeptics often get squat for their efforts. Patience is important too. I have met many "ghost hunters" who have complained to me that they rarely if ever get good pictures. When I question them about it, I usually find that they often go in with the attitude that they won't get anything good. That kind of defeatist attitude may turn off a spirit or make him flee when the "defeatist" is around. The second most common thing I hear from people who have trouble getting shots is that they have little if any patience. You have to earn you dues. You cannot go into a supposedly haunted location, take a bunch of quick pictures and run out. You have to put the time and effort in. Sure, you might get lucky a time or two but by and large, the best thing to do is stay a while. Another thing is that you cannot give up if you are having trouble getting results. You have to stick with it. You don't always get hits every time you go out. It is like everything else in life, if you want to succeed, you cannot give up when things go wrong.

I had a friend who always got great pictures. In fact, he got them so often that it was almost annoying. After the one thousandth picture, I wanted to strangle him because I never got as many great shots. However, this man was very dedicated to his work. He went out often and he would stay in a location for hours at a time. I believe that an approach like that is sure to be successful. It certainly makes it understandable why he gets the great shots. I think there is a familiarity factor at work here too. I think spirits are simply drawn to this man because they can sense his commitment and therefore, they choose to cooperate with him. So basically, I think that you get out what you put in.

DISCERNMENT IN INVESTIGATIONS

In the first publication of this book, I had the issue of discernment and mediums combined into one chapter. However, I now believe that each area deserves its own chapter. By definition, discernment is the act of "perceiving" using the mind. What does that mean in the context of the paranormal? Well, if you are investigating a potentially haunted house, discernment can clue you in to what is happening there. If your powers of discernment are strong enough, you can get that information very quickly and accurately. What exactly is discernment? The best way to describe it would be to say that you *feel* something that you cannot explain through you normal senses. That sounds confusing so I will try to explain it using examples.

Suppose you walk into a room in a house you are investigating. As you enter it, you get a weird feeling that you are not alone. You look around and see that you are alone but the feeling persists. That is discernment to a small degree. Now let us say you start to feel nervous, even a little frightened. Not only that but you get a feeling that something bad is in the room with you. That would be discernment to a higher degree. If you were able to say you felt a number of presences in the room, that would be discernment to a much higher degree. However, now I am going to throw a wrench into the works. What if what you are feeling is just plain nervousness because you think the house may be haunted? That could certainly be the case. Is that discernment or have you just spooked yourself? How can you tell the difference? That is not easy at first.

Most people who have developed discernment ability will tell you that you know the difference. That reply is true but somewhat less than helpful. What you have to do is analyze your feelings. You can generally tell what is a fear reaction. We have all faced fear at one time or another. Discernment is a little different. You get a sense that something is wrong but it is not exactly fear. It is a nagging sense of something that you cannot quite comprehend. It is more a feeling that something bad may be present. When you are afraid, your heart beats rapidly, you begin to sweat, and you feel a sense of impending doom. With discernment, the reaction is far less intense. You will get the adrenaline pumping but it is not the same as being afraid. It may sound like a subtle difference but it really is not. Once you have experienced it, you will know exactly what I mean. With most people, it is a safe bet that they will have experienced some discernment ability before ever going on an investigation. They may not realize it and they probably do not believe it, but it is probably there. To be attracted to this field, you must have some degree of discernment. Often times, people will say they had a "gut reaction." Surprise; that is discernment. You will find that your discernment abilities will grow as you go on investigations. It is doubtful that you would suddenly develop it out of nowhere on a case. Once you know what it feels like though, you will not forget it. Then you will easily distinguish the difference between fear and true discernment.

Discernment Ability

Does everyone have discernment ability? The answer is yes. Most, if not all people do have the ability to some degree. How strong it is depends on several factors. For openers, you have to believe in it. The second factor is you have to use it. If the ability is ignored, it will fade away or at least become dormant. However, some people are gifted with very strong discernment abilities. They possess it to a point that most of us cannot reach and probably wouldn't want to. It can be every bit the curse as it is the blessing. However, while we may never reach the level of discernment ability that mediums possess, it is possible to strengthen your own abilities, as you will see later.

There are different types of discernment. Most people will tell you that they have experienced knowing who was calling them just as the telephone began ringing. This is actually a common form of discernment. Have you ever had a feeling that you should stop at the store on the way home and pick up something only to find out when you got home that your spouse wanted that very item? Again, that is a form of discernment. Some people have the ability to sense the presence of spirits. Many psychics are actually able to communicate with them. These people are known as "trance" mediums. These trance mediums can walk into a home and immediately tell if there are spirits present, and in rare cases, how many there are, and what type they are. This is of tremendous benefit to an investigation, providing that the medium is able to read that particular house. It can save a great deal of time and make the investigation process much easier. However, if a medium "misreads" the house, that can slow the investigative process down considerably. Unfortunately, genuine trance mediums are rare. What is not rare are the ones who *believe* they are trance mediums. You can find those by the dozens.

However, many people do have enough discernment ability to be quite useful in an investigation. In my own case, I have found that I can tell whether there are spirits present and I can also usually tell whether they are good or bad spirits. I do not have the ability to tell how many spirits are present and I cannot always tell if they are human or inhuman. There have been times when I was able to distinguish between the two but now I am not as positive. In addition, I cannot tell you anything about the spirits I feel. I cannot tell you who they are, how they died and what they want. I can just tell you they are there. Furthermore, I do not have the ability to communicate with them in the way that "trancers" do. Personally, I refer to my abilities as self-defense discernment. This came from living through a haunting. I developed just enough discernment ability to warn me when there was going to be a rough night. It probably has more to do with the Pavlov's dogs theory than any psychic ability. Experience anything long enough and through conditioning, you learn to anticipate it. Just don't ring a bell by me.

It is very hard to test discernment. For example, I mentioned that I could tell when there are spirits present. I have felt them and have managed to get some good pictures as a result. However, are there times when they are present and I do not sense them? Good question. How can you test that? There have probably been times when spirits have been present and I could not detect them. We all spend a lot of time being distracted by life. If I have ten things on my mind or I am very worried about something, I am sure that I am not in the proper mindset to pick up a spirit's vibrations. I would have to say that is true with most people.

Exactly how does discernment work?

All of life is energy and all of energy is vibrations. People with discernment abilities are able to interpret those vibrations. When we hear sound, we are interpreting the vibrations that sound is making. Some people have better hearing than others. The same is true when it comes to discernment. In my case, my brain is able to pick up enough of a spirit's vibrations to know that it is there. However, I am not able to interpret that spirit's vibrations enough to communicate with it. Some can. Discernment ability varies from person to person. Some are able to see images, others sense a presence, and still others communicate. There are people who only pick up positive energy, others who pick up only negative energy. Most people fall somewhere in between. A word of caution though: I have come across more than a few who make extraordinary claims.

There is a woman who is advanced enough to feel exactly where the spirit is in a given room. For example, she once told me that she felt something sitting between us. I took a picture and we did pick up an energy field. By the way, I should point out that I did not sense a presence at that time. Even when I do, I usually cannot tell exactly where it is. There have been times when I have felt surrounded by spirits. This has happened to me twice recently during cemetery shoots. In both cases, I got great pictures of huge energy fields. Discernment ability, like any form of psychic ability, seems to ebb and flow. You cannot always turn it on and off. For some people, it always seems to be there. For others, like myself, it comes and goes according to its own schedule.

(Strengthen Discernment Ability)

One of the important things to realize is that everybody has some degree of psychic ability. You are born with that. In fact, that ability is strongest while you are still in the womb. Consequently, discernment ability is quite strong in infants. Ask any mother and she will tell you that there are times when she knows something is wrong with her baby and sure enough, when she goes into the room, she finds she is right. Animals and infants seem to be able to communicate with each other. Have you ever watched the curious way that they stare at each other? Animals will often turn their heads as if they are trying to hear something. Children do that as well.

Have you ever watched a baby and an animal at the same time? How many times have you seen both the animal and the infant stare at a corner of the room? Then they would follow something with their eyes. I am willing to bet the answer is many times. It is a little unnerving, right? For the most part, the only way infants can communicate with their mother is telepathically. What happens later is that as their other five senses develop. The first sense, which for some bizarre reason we call the sixth sense, is used less and less. As the infant's mind begins to develop, they learn the laws of action and reaction. For example, I cry and Mommy comes, I laugh, Mommy laughs. Children are clairvoyant up until they reach between the ages of about nine through thirteen. Once they reach puberty, that clairvoyance begins to slip away. This is most likely due to the hormonal changes the child is experiencing. Some however, do retain some of that ability. I doubt it ever goes completely away. If anything, it is hidden.

Now, let us look at things you can do to make your own discernment grow. You should try to learn to meditate. This emptying of the mind's distractions allows you to focus on your nonphysical feelings. Remember that discernment is a sense. It is not physical. You can no more force yourself to sense something any more than you can force yourself to sleep. In fact, trying to do either only pushes you further away from your goal. Therefore, the first step is to try to meditate. There are many good books out on the subject and it would be a wise idea to purchase one. They will teach you systematically how best to do it. What I recommend to people is that they should "listen" to a room. In other words, sit in a dark room and listen for sounds around you as if you are waiting to hear something. This helps to change your focus from conscious thought. When you get proficient at this, you will find that feelings come more often.

The next step is to use your ability as much as possible. Once you start to develop some discernment, you need to use it or it will gradually lessen. Listen to a room or go outside and try to sense the presence of other forms of life. Obviously, you can hear insects but try to feel their presence. You may find this quite interesting. The next step is to pay attention to your feelings. If you get the feeling that you should rent a particular video as opposed to the one you had been planning on, follow your feelings. If something tells you to take a different route home than you normally do, listen to it. If you know someone else who usually goes the way you usually do, ask them the next day if they had any problems. You will probably hear how they sat in traffic for an hour due to an accident or a breakdown.

Follow Your Feelings

Get into the habit of following your feelings. They are usually right. I know that in my own life, every major mistake I have made occurred when I did the opposite of what I felt I should do. This is the old "listen to your head instead of your heart" thing and vice versa. The head is usually right. If you decide to use discernment ability in investigations, you will find that it will grow stronger the more it is used. The more exposure you have to the paranormal, the easier it will become for you to discern a presence. The repeated exposure sharpens your senses. In a short time, you will see surprising changes in your abilities. You almost cannot help developing discernment abilities when you are exposed to the paranormal. However, with power comes responsibility. If a spirit realizes that you have the ability to discern it, the spirit will often let you do it. In other words, it will make its presence known. This, in and of itself does not put you at greater risk than someone who cannot sense it. However, you have to be aware of what is going on. If at any time, you feel threatened or you feel something is telling you to leave, heed the warning. This is extremely important. If a person with no real discernment ability enters a house where a spirit is dwelling, it may well ignore that person as it feels that person poses no threat to it. On the other hand, if you go into that same house, the spirit may sense that you can feel it. Therefore, it may feel threatened by you. If that happens, it may well send you a warning. That warning may come to you as a feeling that you should not be there. If that happens, pay close attention to that feeling ... very close attention. We are not talking about feeling fear. Let me give you an example. It is not unusual for me to have some activity in my own home. This tends to happen more often when I am doing some work regarding the world of the paranormal.

During the course of writing this book, many odd things have happened in my home. They range from books going flying on their own, pictures and clocks becoming projectiles and on more than a few occasions I have sensed a presence in the room where I was writing. I have different ways of dealing with that problem. Many times, I will simply say the prayer to St. Michael. That often stops whatever is happening. At other times, I will play religious music. Sometimes my "guest" gets doused with holy water. However, there have been times when a mental "voice" would tell me that it was in my best interests to shut everything down and go to bed. I have learned that it is best that I listen to my senses. What would happen if I didn't? Who knows? It might be something like my computer locking out and eating my work. It may have been something else, maybe something more ominous. The point is that I listen to my feelings. You should too.

Now, I have to point out that it is a different story if you are working a case for someone who is being tormented by a spirit. In that situation, you have to be more aggressive and you do not have the luxury of leaving every time you get a "bad" feeling. If that were the case, you would not spend too much time there. After all, you are looking for phenomena. Here is where you need good discernment ability. There is a difference between the feeling that something wants you out versus something that wants to hurt you. If it is a negative spirit, you already know it wants you out. That much is obvious. However, if it is a demonic spirit and you sense a threat, unless you have trained for this type of encounter, you need to heed your inner voice.

You may find that if you do cemetery shoots, your ability to discern will grow as well. Spirits "hang out" in cemeteries so you can often sense them when you are there. This does not mean that you should spend all of your free time sitting in cemeteries. That would not be a particularly healthy thing to do. Too much exposure does not mean you will develop discernment abilities any faster. You can only go so far so fast. It is a nice feeling when you feel something and have it verified when you get the pictures back. It is a good way to validate and measure your abilities. Again though, if you start to feel that you should leave, do so.

Other responsibilities come with discernment. As you develop, you may find you can sense things about the people around you. I do not mean that you can read their minds but you may be able to feel things about them. Do not use your discernment abilities to try to read them just for fun. In a way, this constitutes an invasion of their privacy to the umpteenth power. It is morally wrong to attempt to read another person without their knowledge or consent. Besides the fact that it is wrong, you have no idea whether what you are sensing is correct. Besides that, it is a good way to see your abilities diminish. When you begin focusing on people, you are cutting off your ability to sense the spiritual world. I knew someone who was steadily developing discernment abilities. I watched with fascination as this person developed. At one point though, this person figured out that there are some people who are easily read. What happened was that person began to become more concerned with discerning the physical realm rather than the spiritual realm. The result was that the ability to discern the spiritual realm steadily diminished.

In that case, fortunately, the person involved was young and once the focus went back to the spiritual aspects, the discernment started coming back. Had that person been older, that may not have been the case. Usually though, it is the young person who experiments with their abilities. With age, in most cases anyway, comes wisdom. What is that phrase, "youth is wasted on the young?" Realize that discernment is a gift and it must be used in a responsible manner.

It is hard to gauge how strong your ability to discern will become. Not everyone can become a trance medium, of course; not everyone wants to. Being a medium is a gift from God. I am not talking about all of the people who claim they can predict your future, for a fee of course. This is not a blanket condemnation of all psychics by any means. You just need to be aware that there are many frauds in this world. This is true of any industry. There just seem to be more in this industry than in others. Why is it that psychics never win the lottery?

I think it is reasonable to expect that you can develop a useful amount of discernment, if you work at it. Certainly, your belief systems play a huge role. If you are open to it, your development will naturally be faster than someone who continually denies they have it. Some people either deny they have it or are afraid of it. Your motives seem to play a big role too. People who work on it for the sake of using their abilities for good purposes generally are far more successful than those who are want to use it for personal gain. As I have said, it is a gift from God. He knows what is in your heart, even if you do not. If your purpose in developing it is for the good of mankind, I think you will be quite surprised with the results. Always remember the "like attracts like" principle. It applies to all areas of life, not just the spiritual world.

Do Not Be Afraid Of Your Abilities

You should not be afraid of your abilities. Some fear that they will be overwhelmed if they are exposed to the negative energy in a haunting situation. That can happen in some circumstances involving negative spirits. In most cases, that is not a problem. If you should start to feel overwhelmed with sensations, simply leave the area. Most experienced investigators can shut off their discernment sensations. In most cases, the ability to discern comes with the ability to shut it off. Yes, there are situations where you will want to shut it off. That will come naturally to you so do not worry about it. Your mind has a built in shutoff. It will automatically block the energy if it becomes too much for your mind to handle. Remember too, if the feeling becomes too intense or threatening, it is a good idea to leave anyway. I have never heard of anyone being overwhelmed by discerned energy, except on one demonic case I worked on. During an exorcism, an experienced investigator "opened up," that is he wanted to see if he could sense the presence of the demon before the exorcism was completed. As it turned out, the demon was still present and the investigator began to feel lightheaded and almost overwhelmed by the sense of evil present. At that point, he was removed from the team in order to clear his head. The priest performing the exorcism blessed him when it was all over and there was serious harm done to him. What he did was learn a lesson.

It can be a different story with trance mediums, especially the deep trancers. Since spirits actually communicate *through* the medium, their senses can be overwhelmed. They may be overwhelmed with a sense of sorrow depending what is coming through. They may be overwhelmed with a sense of evil if there was something demonic around. In the majority of cases, the trance mediums snap out of the trance when things get too dicey. In some cases, they do this voluntarily. In other cases, it happens on its own. There really is no danger in using your discernment abilities in an investigation, whether it is at a local cemetery, on a ghost tour or the average investigation.

One last thought, do not listen to all of those people who will ridicule your abilities. There are some very close-minded people out there and they all like to criticize. Ignore them. Nothing you can say will convince them anyway, so do not waste your time trying. People like to make fun of things they do not understand. There are also people out there who are jealous of anyone they feel possesses something they do not. If individuals would take the time to try to understand and learn about it, they might be pleasantly surprised to find out that they too have it. Unfortunately, for some, it is easier to scoff than to take the time to learn.

Belief And Confidence

Do not forget that belief is a factor. So is disbelief. If they can make you doubt yourself and your abilities, it will hinder your progress. This is not to say that they are necessarily doing this maliciously, in many cases, they just do not understand. Do not give anyone the power to hurt you or retard your growing processes. People can say things that may make you doubt yourself but the bottom line is that words are just words and it is you that doubts yourself, not the spoken words of others.

Evil spirits themselves will try to create doubt within you. You need to be aware of this. It is part of their strategy and they do it well. Do not fall into their trap. Do not doubt yourself. If you have the ability to discern, you have it. It is that simple. You cannot suddenly lose it so do not put pressure on yourself. Always remember that it is a natural ability. There is no reason to try to force it. Have confidence in your abilities and don't let doubt dissuade you. So, go ahead and work on your learning process. You could well be opening yourself up to a wonderful and enlightening world. It is a world that can be extremely exciting. You will find that it will be a fun gift to use, as long as you respect it and do not abuse it. I am sure that it will prove to be a very useful gift as well. It can help you in many different ways in your life, not just with investigations. Don't count on winning the lottery though. Play around with it and test it. You cannot hurt anything. As with all things, use it for positive purposes and you will do well with it. Now, let us take a closer look at mediums and the role they can play in an investigation.

MEDIUMS IN INVESTIGATIONS

(Mediums Communicate With Spirits)

Mediums are people who have the ability to sense and communicate with spirits. While both men and women can be mediums, the majority of them are women, although that is starting to change. For example, when it comes to famous mediums or at least those with good P.R. people, men are slowly taking over. George Anderson started the ball rolling and then you have James Van Praagh. Sylvia Browne then stepped into the limelight on the woman's side and the new biggie is Jon Edward. He has his own television show although the others mentioned have had their share of TV exposure. I will give you my opinion on those types of psychics later in this chapter. For now though, we want to look at the role of mediums in haunting investigations.

For the sake of saving me from using him/her a trillion times, I will refer to mediums in the feminine "her." Do not be offended guys. In the preceding chapter, you have seen the role discernment plays in investigating hauntings. Obviously, mediums have more discernment that other people. However, their role in a haunting investigation must be clearly defined and their strengths and limitations must be gauged before one is brought into a haunting situation. In addition, the investigator needs to have some idea of the problem when he makes the decision to call a medium in. You also need to determine what outcome you want and have a clear strategy of how to best achieve that outcome. Depending on the medium, they can help or hurt that outcome.

In most cases, mediums communicate with human spirits. They are able to sense inhuman spirits as well but they usually do not communicate with them. Even if they have the ability to communicate with inhuman spirits, it would be extremely dangerous for them to attempt to do so and the team leader must know that. Besides, nothing good could come from it. I need to point out that we are talking about negative, inhuman spirits. Many people can and do communicate with angels, which we know are also inhuman spirits. So, for that matter, are elemental spirits and some people are gifted with the ability to communicate with them.

It is believed that most people have the ability to communicate with angels. Some people are gifted with a strong ability but for most people, they need to *learn* how to communicate with them. In the truest sense, that would mean we all have the ability to become mediums. While I think it may be possible, I tend to doubt whether most people could really learn to communicate with human spirits to the degree where there is an almost open dialog with them. However, what we are going to concern ourselves with now are those people who have that natural ability and how they affect paranormal investigations.

Light Trance and Deep Trance Mediums

As we discussed before, there are two basic types of mediums, light trance (LTM) and deep trance mediums. Before we go any further, it should be pointed out that each medium's abilities might vary. As with discernment, there are different levels of abilities. Light trance mediums are the more common of the two. Both types are able to sense spirits and both can communicate with them, although to a different degree. The way they do it, however, is different. In the case of the LTM, they go into a light trance state. This is very similar to a hypnotic state. They may be somewhat unaware of their surroundings but their consciousness is still there. It is lying just below the surface but their consciousness has not been displaced. If a person is in a hypnotically induced trance, they may seem to be far away but if you ask them to do something they are adverse to, they will come out of the trance state in a hurry. They may not seem conscious but trust me, their consciousness is there. If a medium is in a light trance state and someone yells, "fire," they will come out if it quickly. However, once they slip into the trance state, the spirit can begin to communicate *through* the medium without actually being inside her. That is an important point. The spirit is using her to communicate through her. It is not actually *in* her. A good way to describe it is *mega-discernment.* The light trance magnifies the natural discernment of the medium. In effect, the medium has become the messenger. Suppose there is something the spirit wants to tell someone in the room. The spirit will place the words in the medium's consciousness. The medium will then pass the message on to the person for whom it was intended. They may come out of the trance not remembering much of what they said while in the trance state. Once the medium is out of the trance, she usually feels drained. Therefore, the light trance medium serves as the messenger between the physical and non-physical plane.

Things are a little different with the deep trance medium. In their case, what happens is the spirit wishing to communicate will actually go into the deep trance medium. The spirit will then communicate directly with the person it wants to contact, using the body of the medium to do that. The risk is greater for the deep trance medium because they are allowing the spirit to go into them. For that reason, the deep trance medium must be sure who or what she is dealing with. There is always the fear that whatever goes into them may not want to leave. This is obviously a huge problem if the spirit is demonic. For that reason, I strongly feel that deep trance mediums should not be used in a demonic haunting. If you know going into a case that there is a demonic spirit at work, I see absolutely no point in using a "trancer," as I like to call them. You cannot reason with a demon. If it were a reasonable creature, it would not be there in the first place. You cannot convince him to leave so why put a trancer at risk? Therefore, it serves no purpose whatsoever.

In a case where you are not sure what you are dealing with, the medium should be able to tell what is there in fairly short order, assuming that she is developed enough to do so and is able to read the house. Once you know that you have a demonic or diabolical haunting on your hands, you should not use the medium any further. Now I need to point out that many mediums will fight you on this, especially experienced ones. I have told a few of my fears that something evil might get inside of them and in almost all cases, they tell me that this is not likely because they can "shut it off." That may be true although I was involved in an exorcism of a medium that had been improperly used on a demonic haunting. I have mentioned that incident to a medium but her feeling was that the person in question was probably not developed enough to handle that situation. My reply is that I have no way of knowing who is and isn't capable of dealing with that situation. As a team leader, I am not going to take a risk of that magnitude. I guess you have to look at each situation and know the medium in question before you make the decision to use one or not use one. I did see a case where a medium was used in a demonic situation. She channeled the spirit and sure enough, it decided to stay. An exorcism had to be performed. There is much less risk when using a light trance medium in a demonic situation since she is not going to let a spirit inside of her as the trancer does. Remember, a LTM is basically someone with a mega-discernment.

Another problem is that in some cases, the medium will go into a trance state spontaneously. This can be very frightening for the medium, as well as those around them. I was driving with a trancer one time en route to a case we were starting. On that trip, she was driving since she knew the area well. There we were, on a highway doing about 55 when she suddenly shook her head side to side and began speaking in voice quite different from her own. Then she bean yelling. I thought to myself that this would be a hell of a way to end my life. Fortunately, the trance was momentary and she was able to drive through it. For that reason, it is important to have someone who has experience with trances or hypnosis on hand in case things go wrong. In a haunting situation, things can go wrong in a hurry. This sometimes happens to the light trance medium as well, although it is not as common or as serious. If they slip into a light trance state, they can often get themselves out of it. Still, there should always be someone on hand with the proper experience any time a medium is at work. Although extremely rare, a light trance medium can slip into a deep trance state. Of those I have talked to, none have enjoyed the experience and they do everything possible to prevent it from happening again. Once the deep trance medium awakens, she will usually not remember anything that happened while she was in the trance state. She will also feel drained mentally and may be physically weakened as well. They will often seem groggy for an extended period, depending on the depth to which their trance took them and the amount of energy the spirit used during the communication.

(Mediums Assist In Investigations)

Having said all of the above, whether they are light trance or deep trance mediums, they can be extremely helpful to an investigation. If you have one available, they can, in some cases diagnose the problem very quickly. (You must still do a full investigation. There is no substitute for that. You can never be sure if what they are getting is accurate.) Should you find yourself in a human haunting, their assistance can make the case easier to solve. As you know, when you begin an investigation, it is important to brief your team before going into the home. I have belabored that point well past the point of death already. If the medium has not gone through the home already, they should not be part of the briefing meeting. When the medium does go into the home, you want them to tell you what they sense is going on. If they have been part of the briefing, they would be going in already knowing what had been happening and where the activity had been. What this does is create a situation where their "feelings" may be influenced by what they have been told. If they know that something happened in a given room going in, you cannot be sure whether their findings are accurate or not. I know that in the past, if I told an investigator that there had been activity in the basement, they would automatically be frightened when they went down there whether there had be any trouble down there or not. They *expected* trouble down there so they *looked* for it. The same is true for the medium. If they *look* for something, they may feel it whether it is there or not. Again though, I have had arguments with mediums about this point also. The point is that you want them to go in objectively. This is not done to test the medium. We want to make sure that the information they received or perceived is free from any preconceived notions that would jeopardize the efficacy of their findings.

At this stage of the investigation, we need them to confirm, if possible, the information we have been given by the client. If it is at all possible, you would like to have the medium go in before the investigation begins. This way, you can get her input, which you can use for your skull session before going on site. This way, you may have a favorable idea what to expect. You will also have an idea where the energy is the strongest. This makes it easier to get evidence since you can position your people and your equipment in the place where the activity is most likely to occur. In some cases, the medium may not be able to go in early. If that were the case, they would do a walk through while the interviews are being done and the equipment is being set up. They usually go through the house by themselves. This way there are no distractions and it makes their reading more effective. However, I leave it up to them. If they are uncomfortable being by themselves, I suggest having the team leader stay with them. Either way, I believe that someone should be nearby, just in case something goes wrong. The energy the medium may pick up can be quite intense. Even so, experienced mediums prefer to go through the house alone. Just be aware of where they are at all times.

Once the medium is finished with her tour, you should talk to her without the family being present. What you want to do is compare the medium's information with the information you learned from the family. The medium may have felt strong energy in a particular hallway. If the family had mentioned that hallway to you also, it validates both the family's reporting and the medium's sensing. Negative spirits will often try to confuse the medium. They will also do what they can to hide themselves from her. If you can substantiate the medium's findings, you know they are able to read the energy correctly. In other words, the spirit is not succeeding in confusing her. Once you know this, the medium can then alert you to activity before it starts, allowing you to reposition your team and equipment. If the spirit is human and benign, it may bug the medium. Once is has someone who it can communicate with, it may not want to let go. This can be annoying for the medium who is trying to figure the case out. However, the medium may be able to come up with a way to help the spirit cross over. If the spirit is inhuman, you can then start approaching this as a haunting as opposed to an investigation.

At this point, you still do not want to tell the family anything about the medium's findings. Always feel that you need to gather evidence, clear-cut evidence before you make a determination. If you are dealing with a very experienced medium with a proven record of accomplishment, you might be less hesitant about revealing her findings. Still, telling the family prematurely can cause great harm if she is wrong. You have to be sure of what you are dealing with. A particularly nasty human spirit can be mistaken for a low level, inhuman one. You do not want to make that mistake.

If you are dealing with an inhuman spirit, you need to expel it as quickly as possible. If you are treating it like a human spirit, you are giving it time to dig in, thus making it harder to expel later. In addition, it is getting the opportunity to inflict more damage on its victims. By treating it as a human spirit, you may end up provoking it by blessing the house. Blessing the house is a good thing to do with a human spirit but not such a good thing to do when you are dealing with the inhuman variety. So, long before you tell the victims anything, you need to be sure. I understand that by now, you want to gag me every time you read that. Just the same, it is important.

In addition, if an inhuman spirit is causing the haunting, you may end up needing to get the church involved. As much as you have learned to trust your medium's findings, the findings may well not be acceptable to many outside sources. It certainly would not be acceptable to the church. They are going to insist on documentation of the phenomena and lots of it. The advantage you do have is that your medium, through discernment, can tell when things are about to happen and where it is most likely to happen. This gives you a good chance of getting your documentation quickly. Again, once you know that a case is demonic, it is not a good idea to keep a deep trance medium around so get your documentation quickly.

When working with a trance medium, aside from the initial walk through, you should keep close watch of her. You do not know what they are experiencing or sensing. You always need to look for signs of distress. This is particularly important with deep trance mediums. Since spirits actually go into them, the potential for trouble is greater. If they are experiencing difficulty, they may not be able to call out for help. If they do look like they are in trouble, you need to try to rouse them quickly. This may or not be hard to do. With a light trance medium, calling their names or gently shaking them will often do the trick. With the deep trance medium it can be harder to do. Persistence pays off but you want to rouse them quickly if there are any signs of distress. I have told them things like: "Stay with me," or "come back to me." You can also tell them to think about loved ones or really anything that might awaken their conscious mind.

As I mentioned earlier, a medium may be able to help an earth-bound spirit move on. Of course, the spirit must be willing to do so. In case of an evil spirit, this would not be possible. It does not want help. What it wants to do is create turmoil and it will not leave easily. If there is an evil spirit causing the problem, especially a demonic one, once the medium has discerned its presence, no further contact with that spirit should be attempted. For that matter, the medium should resist any attempt by that spirit to communicate. It is not going to listen to reason so there is nothing to be gained by communicating with it. If anything, it would be trying to create more confusion and cause more harm and it will have no bearing on getting rid of it.

Another advantage to having a medium present is she can also tell in some cases, when there seems to be a change in the spirit's demeanor. In other words, if the spirit is going to retaliate for some reason, she may be able to notice that and warn everyone in advance. If the spirit is getting stronger, she may be able to sense that, as well. She may be able to sense that it is listening and may be willing to cross over and leave. That, of course, only applies to the human spirit. So, in short, there are a lot of advantages to having a medium present in an investigation.

There are, however, some negatives to using a medium in an investigation and we may as well discuss that now. It is my belief (and I have been working in this field forever) that a medium may not be able to read every house. I think there are situations where they may misread a particular house and that can cause as much trouble for the investigation as a good read helps it. Mediums are just like everyone else. They are affected by the daily events in life and they are subjected to the same fears and anxieties and problems of life as anyone else. An argument can be made that they have more to worry about than most people since they can sense things that we cannot. We may think our boss is annoyed with us; they know. Ditto for problems with relationships. People: don't ever cheat on your psychic spouse.

The point here is that a medium may have a lot of things on their minds when they go into a case. If they are worried about something major in their life, their ability to read a house can be clouded. That only stands to reason. Also, spirits will sometimes try to fool a medium, especially one that wants to stay where it is. This applies to human spirits as well as the bad guys. If you are dealing with an experienced medium and one that has a lot of experience in haunting investigations, a human spirit may have a hard time fooling her. I also feel that there are situations where the medium will misread the house for other reasons. I base this on the fact that I have worked with several different mediums that I have developed a trust in. There have been several cases where I have had two or three mediums involved in the same case. (Talk about torture!) In some of those cases, I was given different information by each of the psychics. Some of this is to be expected since each person is interpreting information from a different perspective. However, there have been times where the information was so different that it was obvious to me that one of them was misreading the situation.

Solving The Problem

There is a way to tell whether a medium can read a particular house. What I like to do is give them two pieces of information. One piece of information is true; the other is false. What I do then is look to see whether they disagree with anything that I told them. This sounds confusing or maybe I am making it sound confusing so let me explain what I mean. I worked a case where there was pretty much the same amount of activity all of the time. In this house, things always started up around 8pm and like I said, remained steady all night. What I told the LTM was that it always started around 8pm and it usually stopped around 10pm. After that, I waited. Well, sure enough, come 8pm, she told me that she was "sensing " something. Okay, good. Maybe she was reading the house, maybe not. She may really have been feeling something or she may have been "feeling" what she expected to feel. However, the real test came at 10pm. Shortly after that, she came to me and told me that she knew that I said that it should stop at 10 but that she was still feeling things as strongly as she did at 8. Since she refuted the false evidence, I knew she was getting a good read. Had she told me around ten that everything had stopped, I would have to conclude that she was not reading the house properly.

In still another case, I told her that there was a lot of activity in the master bedroom every night but none in the living room. The part about the master bedroom was false. Sure enough, she came to me after being in the house for two hours and told me that she felt absolutely nothing in the bedroom. Had she told me that she did, I would have to say that she was not getting a good read. However, her observation was correct. Thus, I knew she had a good read on that house. I need to point out that I am not trying to test her to see if she is good. I know she is or she would not be there with me. However, I firmly believe from experience that all mediums cannot read every house. So what I am doing is testing her ability in *that* house, not her overall abilities. By the way, I never tell them that I am testing them. For one, it would hurt their feelings; for another, it would defeat the purpose of the test.

Working with mediums can be a bit touchy. While they can be helpful, they can misread a house. That can cause you to lose time. It can also frustrate you when a medium tells you information that you know to be wrong. Some will argue with you until you are blue in the face, no matter how much evidence you present to them. This is not to say that *I* am always right but the evidence usually speaks for itself. In order to be a good medium, the person has to have a strong personality and they have to be very confident in their abilities. However, that confidence can become cockiness and there are some who mistake themselves for the case. I have been lucky with the mediums I have worked with although that is not to say that everything is always rosy. In addition, mediums can be very temperamental. That can cause some problems on an investigation, especially one where the client is especially vulnerable to information.

There are times when a psychic will blurt out what they felt without considering the context the information should be put in. Calling a spirit "very dark" is not helpful to a family that is sure there is a demonic force at work. They may take that information the wrong way. The medium should first talk to the team leader and formulate the response. Maybe all you have to do is qualify the information. "The spirit seems to be dark but it is human." In that case, you are saying the same thing but what a difference it makes because there are no hidden inferences. Also, depending on the medium, you might run into trouble with the client. If the medium makes a statement that the client refuses to believe, the inexperienced medium may well engage in an argument with the client. For some reason that I will leave up to the sociologists to discover, female mediums often run into trouble with female clients.

Another problem is that a medium will sometimes say something that is flat out irresponsible. For example, there may be a house that has a human spirit in it. The medium may come in and find that it is human. Good. She may determine that the spirit is Uncle Ron. That is good too. However, she may tell the family that uncle Ron is here because Aunt May is about to die. Whether it is true or not, and it may well not be, why would you tell someone something like that. The medium may get huffy and say something like: "Well, that is what I saw!" Maybe it was but is it wise to tell someone that? Let it suffice to say that it is Uncle Ron.

"Professional" Mediums

This is a subject that I do not like to touch but since I am always asked about it, here goes. There are many mediums out there today who have lots of published books out and television shows and the like. I am not going to get into names here. The question I am always asked is whether they are for real or not. To be perfectly honest about it, I don't know. I have not studied one and I doubt any of them would let me study them anyway. They claim to communicate with spirits of deceased loved ones. Maybe they do. However, I am skeptical for a few reasons. I have seen many programs on these psychics and I have found that they always say things that are so general that they can fit anybody and just about any situation. Once they have a "hit," it seems to me that they "fish" for information and the next thing you know, they have Uncle Mortimer on the line there and that "everyone is doing well." Then you hear something like: "Is there a Ron? I'm hearing Ron or maybe it's Don? Yes, it is strong but it may be John. Does that name mean anything to you?" Eventually, he or she is going to hit a name that you know. Then you hear stuff like: "I am feeling pain in the head. Was there a head injury involved in the passing?" When the person says no, the psychic will reiterate that "feeling in the head." Now he person being read feels bad and tries to find *anything* involving the head and they may remember that Ron/Don/John once suffered from migraines. Before you know it, the psychic has said very little. All he did was lead the person in the conversation and it is the person being read who does all of the talking. And of course, everything over there is always "just ducky." Granted, being in a studio and having a huge audience must make them nervous but I have never heard a reading that really impressed me.

The next thing that bothers me is when I hear how much many of them charge for a private reading. Some of those readings go for $500 or more, per person for a one-hour reading. If there is a party of four for that reading, it is $2,000 for an hours work. Everyone is entitled to make a living but it becomes ridiculous. What really bothers me is when I hear them say that they "only use their gift to help people." If so, why the usurious rates? Amazingly enough, there are often waiting lists of up to a year or more to see one of them. I just feel bad because the people looking for the reading are already vulnerable and since there are unscrupulous people in every other profession, there must be unscrupulous psychics too. Unfairly capitalizing on the grief and suffering of others is unconscionable in my opinion.

It is possible that they do have a gift and there is no doubt that many of their clients end up crying at the end of the reading but I don't know how much of that has to do with the clients feeling wonderful that "so and so" is happy or how much of that is sadness and grief brought about by trying to remember their loved one. It is difficult to read tears. Taking advantage of grieving people is nothing new in our society and it has been going on since the dawn of man and will continue until we have finally accomplished destroying ourselves. There are too many instances of fraud and no one is more vulnerable that someone who is grieving and not seeing things clearly. I would like to talk to some of the clients a day or so after the readings and see what they have to say then. Maybe then I could give you a better answer.

POLTERGEIST OR RSPK

While sitting on the edge of my bed talking to my girlfriend, we heard some odd sounds in the next room. Suddenly, a walkie-talkie that had been on top of the mantelpiece flew across the room. The sudden movement startled me. I sat there in stunned silence, my heart pounding away. I slowly turned towards my girlfriend and asked her if she saw what I thought I saw. She did not have to answer. The color of her skin told me all I needed to know. A few seconds later, the battery-operated radio began to squelch. Obviously, it must have been turned on by the fall. I walked over to it and bent down to pick it up as it squawked away. When I got my hand around it, I realized that the battery compartment was open. There were no batteries in it! (From: 316- A Ten Year Odyssey of Terror. C 2000-T. Cooney)

There are many areas in paranormal research that lead to debate between parapsychologists and demonologists but none more so than the phenomenon of the poltergeist. This one issue has managed to split those two disciplines right in half. It is the single most studied area of the paranormal and it is still the least understood. To make matters more confusing, there are many aspects that are agreed on by the two disciplines. Rather than make it easier to understand, it simply leads to more confusion. On top of that, I am going to muddy the waters a bit by adding a third possible scenario. So, let us take a good look at this troubling issue and see where it leads us.

Poltergeist Means Noisy Ghost

Okay, let us start with the basics. The term "poltergeist" originated in Germany. It means, literally, noisy ghost. It is believed by many that a poltergeist is a spirit that has the ability to manipulate the environment in such a manner that results in its ability to move objects. How it does this still remains a mystery but move objects it does. One theory I used to believe in was that objects were moved by a process known as "solidification of the air." The idea would be that the spirit or agent somehow made the air solid enough to cause movement. This would almost sound like a wind effect. However, I should think that this could be measured somehow. Right off the bat, we see a split developing between belief systems. That split is centered around the word "spirit." Let us take a closer look into this.

The Poltergeist As A Spirit

Demonologists and spiritualists (those who believe that spirits exist and can interact with the physical plane) believe that poltergeists are a form of spirit, a very destructive spirit at that. During a poltergeist explosion, holes can be bashed in walls, heavy items will move with amazing speed, and objects can be thrown around. In some of the more horrific cases, *people* have even been thrown around. In my mind, I do not consider that to be a "true" poltergeist manifestation but you will read about that shortly. Electrical appliances are a favorite target of the poltergeist. They seem to enjoy turning items on and off. They also seem to enjoy changing the channel while you watch TV. In a very short period of time, a poltergeist can cause total chaos in a home. Unfortunately, during poltergeist activity, cherished and expensive items are often destroyed. In so many instances, homes are left in states of unbelievable shambles.

There are certain things we know about poltergeist outbreaks. For openers, attacks seem to come out of nowhere. Life is routine and predictable one day and the next day, war has literally broken out. For example, on Saturday, you are lazily reading the paper on the couch. On Sunday, you are running down the street with your pants around you ankles because something pinched you on the butt while you were contemplating the mysteries of life on the bowl. On the positive side, this phenomenon usually stops just as inexplicably and as suddenly as it started. Most attacks are short lived. True poltergeist outbreaks rarely last longer than a month or so. It is rare for them to last near a year. However, there are situations where this phenomenon is merely a stepping-stone in the strategy of a haunting. In my mind, although much of the phenomenon is the same, stepping stone occurrences are not true poltergeist phenomena. In haunting situations, there are usually some signs of warning, some precursor of what is to come, although they are sometimes so subtle they are missed. I told you that I was really going to muddy the waters a bit.

We also know that there is a trigger or agent around whom the phenomenon appears to center. What this means is that activity will take place only when a particular person is present. While it can be anyone, in the vast majority of cases, the agent is usually a girl who is entering puberty. The belief is that due to all the hormonal changes taking place in the child, she is giving off powerful energy that is attractive to the spirit in question. In other words, the spirit is feeding off the child's energy. Once her body and mind begin to adjust to these natural changes, the energy that she is producing reverts to something closer to normal. What this is essentially doing is cutting off the "food" supply of the spirit. It then leaves, presumably to find a place better suited to its needs. This shows a small sense of intelligence behind the actions of the spirit. It has a game plan that it follows. If this food supply is cut off, it will find another. There are, however, numerous cases on record where adults are the agents for poltergeist activity and although rare, the phenomena may continue over a longer period of time. So what does that do for the above theory?

While much of the phenomena consist of objects being thrown around, there have been some wild, documented stories of truly bizarre happenings. There are many cases on record where stones or other items rained down on a home. As we know, these stones are called apports. Actually, any item that appears out of nowhere is called an apport. There are documented cases where the apports consist of living creatures. (Remember waterspouts.) Often, apports are found to be made up of hair, bones, and teeth, not to mention some other form of bodily fluid. In some cases, jewelry makes up the apport, if you are lucky. Unfortunately, it is rarely diamonds and gold. The opposite of an apport is the *asport*. This is where an object disappears completely. This can also happen during a poltergeist outbreak. Other strange things may happen, as well. While this may sound totally unbelievable, there have been some instances recorded where rain actually fell *inside* a house.

(Recurrent Spontaneous Psychokinesis)

Okay, that is the story on poltergeists for now. What is "RSPK?" RSPK is recurrent spontaneous psychokinesis. In short, it is mind over matter. The theory is that in RSPK, there is a person, call it a trigger or agent, who is actually causing the phenomena, albeit unwittingly. It is the power of the person's mind working to manipulate the moving object. It becomes a case of the repressed emotional energy suddenly venting itself, much like a steam valve. The trigger is the one actually causing the phenomena. If that person is feeling serious resentment or even hatred towards one person in particular, that person can become a target for the activity. The trigger does not do this consciously. He or she has no idea that they are behind the activity. In fact, since they are always present when the events take place, they are usually the ones most frightened by it.

In the majority of cases where parapsychologists feel RSPK is exhibited, the agent is usually a female entering puberty. Does that sound familiar? The parapsychologist's theory is that the hormonal changes occurring in the child's body result in her putting out a particular type of energy. The idea here would be that the hormones and associated changes in body chemistry would affect the brain in such a manner as to create the psychokinetic effect, the movement of objects by no apparent physical means. These episodes of RSPK can be very destructive. They are also short, usually lasting about a month or so. In these cases, they say as the girl's body adjusts to the changes taking place, the energy put out returns to normal and thus, the phenomena ceases. Confused yet? Let us see if we can confuse the issue some more.

Parapsychologists have been able to duplicate RSPK effects under controlled, scientific conditions. They have been able to test those who they identified as the agent with some interesting results. These results cannot be discounted. During these experiments, they have been able to witness examples of RSPK. However, they readily point out that in these experiments, only small objects have been moved. This, they feel, is due to the unease of the subject. The combination of being away from their natural environment and having to deal with a bunch of strangers who constantly surround them, is altering the type of energy they are putting out. Instead of putting out the type of energy necessary to manipulate large objects, they are putting out "nervous" energy. Since we really do not know how it works, this would seem to make as much sense as any. Just the same, you would have to think that there would be *some* evidence of large objects being moved. Someone would have to be able to accomplish that, even if by accident.

So where does this leave us? Both of these theories offer reasonable explanations for the movement of objects. In addition, they both offer reasonable explanations for the type of person who triggers the phenomena. Lastly, they explain the cause of the short duration of the phenomena. Obviously, since scientific studies have been done under controlled, duplicable conditions, there can be no doubt that RSPK exists. You cannot argue with scientific studies, which have been rigorously controlled and duplicated. RSPK is a scientific fact. Therefore, that explains the phenomena, which was thought to be poltergeist activity.

Well, not entirely. There can be no question that RSPK is a sound, fundamental principle. The facts speak for themselves. However, several things stand out which cannot be explained using the RSPK theory. Remember apports have been known to appear, rain has fallen indoors, and live animals mysteriously turn up. These things cannot be explained by science. While it appears that man can move objects using the power of the mind, he certainly cannot *create.* Therefore, there is no scientific explanation for the apports occasionally seen. In addition, you have the situation where the poltergeist activity is a stepping-stone for a more serious problem. Again, science cannot help us there. The other item than bears mentioning is that there have been hundreds of experiments done on individuals who have displayed RSPK abilities. These have been done by notable organizations, such as the Rhine Institute. They have been done under the ever-vigilant eyes of organizations such as the American Society for Psychic Research.

The results are quite interesting. While they have seen instances of RSPK, the movements of the objects used were slight at best. In addition, the objects were all very small and light. No one yet, under any circumstances, has displayed an ability to move a heavy object and furthermore, none were able to move an object with speed or force behind it. This would make sense. We know that human spirits have the ability to move light objects; therefore, it is only reasonable to assume that a living human would be able to do the same. Now we know that in poltergeist explosions, kitchen tables have done their best Rockette's imitation. In addition, objects are known to move at great speeds and with considerable force.

Because of this, there can only be one conclusion, RSPK does exist and so too, do poltergeists. Probably the best way to distinguish the two is to take a good look at the type of object that has moved and the speed of that movement. I also think that it is helpful if you can look at the occurrence and see if there appears to be any intelligence behind it. My feeling is that RSPK instances are random bursts of energy. There is no intelligence behind the activity. What you have is a sudden burst of energy, which may be strong enough to knock small items off a shelf or slam a door shut. In poltergeist situations, there does appear to be some intelligence behind the activity, although that intelligence is limited as opposed to the intelligence of a demonic spirit. In comparison, poltergeists are not the sharpest knife in the draw. Unfortunately, whatever intelligence there is behind it, is usually in a destructive form. Instead of a random burst of activity, one or more persons may be targeted. In addition, an item may change direction in order to strike someone. This, however, is more likely to occur in the stepping stone case, as you are about to see.

If you are dealing with RSPK, is there anything you can do to stop the activity? Well, here we go again. As with the poltergeist, if you can identify the agent, you may be able to stop the phenomena from occurring. Very often, there is some unspoken hostility on the part of the agent. That hostility may be directed at one or more members of the family. Identifying the agent and the primary target can clue you in to the problem. Resolve whatever dispute there may be and the problem may stop. However, in many cases, counseling the agent can make the problem worse. There is always the risk of causing that person embarrassment or igniting hostility.

Stepping Stone Poltergeist

I have mentioned what I call a stepping stone poltergeist. My belief is that in a stepping stone case, you are dealing with a flat out, full fledge demonic or diabolical spirit. It really is not a poltergeist at all. For many, this is a hard concept to accept. Many people find it hard to believe that there is such a thing as a demon in our age of wild technology and advancing science. After all, many of them say, we know so much more about the brain than we ever did before. And right they are. Unfortunately, our advanced knowledge of the brain cannot account for poltergeist manifestations, RSPK and certainly not demonic and diabolical infestation and possession. In some cases, fear may play a role. It may be a fear of demons as something that cannot be combated or it could be a fear of death itself. It may be a fear that we have very little control over our existence. In other cases, it may bother people to have to accept that religion and spirituality are indeed valid. There are scientists who would rather believe that we came from the "big bang" theory or that we are a sophisticated ape. Maybe we are. I wonder just how sophisticated we really are?

Back to the stepping stone theory. In this scenario, what you have is a serious haunting, one that is going to progress to extremely dangerous levels. This is the rarest of all hauntings and by far the most dangerous. The likelihood is that it will start off slowly and subtly. You may at some point see an apparition. Shortly after that, the poltergeist explosion begins. A big tip off is the appearance of an apparition. In true poltergeist hauntings, you do not see apparitions. Once the explosion starts, it will escalate and it will endure. Objects will fly around, often directed at someone or *everyone,* for that matter. Those objects are capable of causing harm should they strike. As with the poltergeist and RSPK scenarios, one person may be the trigger or agent. However, in a demonic or diabolical haunting, that trigger can also be the target as well. You have to be on the lookout for that. Since everyone experiences problems in this type of haunting, you may not notice that one person is being targeted. However, in most cases, someone is. One way to tell is by looking at the early stages of the haunting. The person who first experiences the haunting is often the target. However, like everything else in this field, it is not always so black and white.

In many hauntings, the first person to experience phenomena is chosen because he or she is *perceived* by the spirit to be the weakest link. It will bother that one person to cause confusion in the home and to start family splitting. Well into the haunting, one person may bear the brunt of the haunting and it may not be the first one that was picked on. In some cases, the real target is not even a family member; it may turn out to be someone who is called in to help the family. It may be the investigator, the demonologist or the priest who is eventually called in for help. Of course, just to make things easier, there may be no one targeted. This is your equal opportunity haunting.

When there is one person targeted, you have to look for the reason why. Again, it may be because that person is perceived to be the easiest mark. However, it could also point you in the direction of *why* the haunting started. For example, the person being targeted may have done something like using a conjuring book and brought the spirit into the house. It may also be that the spirit was there but dormant and was awakened because of a séance or some other form of divination. While that may be something to look for, you cannot jump to conclusions and immediately start blaming the one singled out. That person may well be innocent and is simply unlucky.

And The Conclusion is...

I am sorry to have to disappoint you but there is so much we do not know about spirits and the capabilities of the human mind. We use so little of it in our day-to-day existence. Why do spirits do what they do? Why do we use such a minute percentage of our brains? Can we grow to understand the spirit realm? What secrets lie dormant in our brains? There are just so many questions, there is so much that we have no answers for, as yet anyway. I think that someday soon, many of these questions will be answered to some extent. I do not think we will ever have all of the answers. In order for that to happen, it would take tremendous cooperation between parapsychologists and demonologists and the researchers in between. It would take serious, open mindedness on all sides. Sadly, to this point that has not happened anywhere near often enough. However, that is not to say that it will not happen in the future, although I have my doubts. Life could be so easy if everyone tried but there are too many egos at stake. Living in this information age, we strive to find answers to things that have puzzled us for centuries. I would say the chances are good that you will see more cooperation between the two disciplines, assuming they can check their egos at the door. Then again, that may well be next to impossible.

Are Poltergeists Dangerous?

The answer is sometimes. In true cases of poltergeist manifestations, objects thrown at someone may fall short of the mark. Sometimes objects will strike them but with almost no force behind them at all. Fortunately, the item merely makes contact and falls harmlessly to the floor. This is not to say there is no harm done to the person mentally. I do not care how deeply you believe a thrown object will not hurt you. Having a knife come your way is going to unnerve you. There are going to be deep psychological effects. It is not like you can walk in the door and call out, "Honey, I'm home!" as you dodge the table lamp headed toward your face. Besides, even though twenty things bounced harmlessly off of you, you never know when one might make contact and be harmful.

In stepping stone cases however, people can and do sometimes get hurt. Objects will land with considerable force. The glass that shattered against the wall may shower you. The books that fly off the shelf may rain on you. You may even find yourself being hit by the unseen intruder or you may be the object slammed against the wall. Stepping stone poltergeist activity can indeed be quite dangerous because in truth, you are dealing with a demonic or diabolic infestation. The big question is how do you tell the difference between the two types? In stepping stone cases, there has been some kind of warning as I mentioned earlier. In addition, the activity in the home progresses gradually. In the true cases, the poltergeist activity comes out of nowhere and is immediately apparent. It is a small distinction but it is easier to recognize than you think. If an object falls just short of hitting you, it is probably a true poltergeist attack. However, if the flying knife cuts you, it is a good bet you are dealing with a stepping stone poltergeist, which is likely to be demonic in origin. Are all poltergeist outbreaks demonic? The evidence would suggest yes. While a human spirit may be able to move light objects around, only an inhuman spirit could throw a sofa around. If it is inhuman and it is destructive, it must be demonic in nature. Surely a good inhuman spirit, the angel, would not destroy things or try to hurt you. However, although it may be demonic, a true poltergeist is not on par with the type of demon that is seen in horrific hauntings. The true poltergeist would seem to be a lesser demon. For that reason, the explosion is usually short-lived.

I have begun to wonder about the possibility that horrific hauntings may belong solely to diabolic spirits, in other words, devils. If that were to be the case, then poltergeists would be what we now consider the demonic. That is almost too neat a distinction. It would then suggest that there are a lot of diabolical spirits around and that does not seem likely. Like I said, that theory would fit too well.

How To Stop A Poltergeist Outbreak

What can you do to stop a poltergeist outbreak? There really is no good answer to that question. As I have said, true poltergeist explosions are of short duration. Still, with the destructiveness involved, a short duration is more than enough time to destroy everything that has meaning or value to you. What we do know is that blessing the house will often make the problem considerably worse. If anything, this would offer proof that the spirit behind the activity is demonic. If that were the case, blessing the house would be akin to religious provocation. Thus, there is a retaliatory attack on the part of the spirit. Where that leaves us is without a solution and I would hate to think that is the case. However, by all indications, it is. If you are able to identify the agent in the home, working with him or her might help. I think that would be more likely the case with RSPK than with a poltergeist. If you try to get him or her to think in a very positive manner, that may help. This is not say that she is necessarily thinking negatively. She may not be. It comes back to the old create a positive environment theory. If there is some kind of mental conflict going on, when that is resolved, the activity might end. Of course, if mental conflicts cause objects to fly around, my home would be a launching pad. If the problem turns out to be a demonic or diabolical infestation, exorcism may well be the only answer to the problem.

Summing It Up

If we compare the ideas between the two disciplines, we will see what appears to be black and white. One group says it is a spirit behind the activity. The other believes it is a mind over matter issue. One represents the spiritual, the other the physical. However, while life may be black and white, it is the shades of grey that we have to muddle through.

What is agreed on is the following:
In Cases of RSPK and "true" poltergeist manifestations,

1) There is an agent or trigger around whom the activity centers.
2) That agent is usually a female between the ages of 11-16.
3) The phenomenon is usually mindless bursts of energy.
4) Objects will often strike people but have little force behind them. (Unlike stepping stone poltergeists where the objects do cause injury. It is one of the ways in which the two can be distinguished.)
5) There are unusual concentrations of electromagnetic energy when the manifestations take place. (Although the source of the two is disputed. To the parapsychologist, the unusual electromagnetic fields are what cause the movement of objects. To the demonologist, it is a spirit that causes the movement with the electromagnetic fields being a byproduct of the spirit. A parapsychologist cannot explain the source of the energy field.)
6) Apparitions are not seen.
7) The outbreaks are usually short lived.
8) The activity occurs without warning and ends as inexplicably as it started.

9) They are destructive. (Extremely so in poltergeist explosions)
10) There is no real way to stop the activity. It must burn itself out.

Where does that leave us? Truthfully, it leaves us nowhere. Whatever the cause of the poltergeist manifestation, there are some things that do not make sense. If the agent plays a role as it most certainly seems to, why then are there so few outbreaks of poltergeist activity or RSPK? Surely there are many disturbed, pubescent females out there, certainly more so than can account for the relatively small number of outbreaks. Also, why does it usually revolve around a female? God knows that there are millions of pubescent males out there. Talk about raging hormones. Here is another point to ponder. If hormones can cause paranormal phenomena as a result of changes in the brain, you would have to think that extremely disturbed individuals would be able to move tanker trucks. God knows that we have no shortage of extremely disturbed individuals. We seem to breed them quite well. That tells you much about our society and the times we live in. Also, what then do you make of those times where an adult is the trigger or agent? If a poltergeist spirit is involved, why would one type of person be singled out over another? This singling out process makes sense only in the stepping stone type of manifestation. There a person is singled out because she is perceived as a weak link and that is typical of the strategy employed by a demonic spirit. There is still so much we do not know. What we do know is that we don't know. All of our explanations fall very short of the mark, especially those dealing with RSPK. If you want to read a great book on the subject, try to find: "Poltergeist- A Study In Destructive Haunting," by Colin Wilson and put out by Fate books. It looks at both sides of the issue in a clear and believable manner.

ARE ALL SPIRITS EVIL?

In a word: no. In two words: not hardly. There are many types of spirits we may and probably do encounter from time to time. There are human spirits; there are inhuman spirits. Then you have different classes of human and inhuman spirits. There are the elemental spirits or "nature spirits" as they are called. We hear the terms devils and demons. Everyone knows about evil spirits. What do you know about imps and fairies? Angels are starting to get a lot of press these days. They certainly deserve it. Then there are the poltergeists ...everyone's favorite. More books have been written about them than all of the other spirits combined. As you just saw, we still have so few answers when it comes to the poltergeist. This can all be very confusing. Yet, we do know a lot about the other types of spirits.

Many times, you will have multiple names for a particular type of spirit. This adds to the aforementioned confusion. But ... are all spirits evil? The answer is no, not all spirits are evil. Spirits are often benign and sometimes, quite benevolent. In addition, in some cases, spirits that may seem to be evil really are not. In those cases, we usually find a spirit whose actions are misinterpreted to be evil when in fact they are not. So with that thought in mind, let us consider the various types of spirits that are all around us and see which ones are evil and which ones are not.

You have read a great deal about the bad guys, so I am only going to touch on them. Human spirits are spirits who walked the earth at one time. If you were an evil person in life, the chances are pretty good that you will be evil in spirit as well. That makes sense, right? The reverse is also true. Good person, good spirit. Demons and devils are bad; we all know that. They are inhuman spirits, in other words, they have never lived as humans although they seem to want to. Okay, if they are inhuman spirits, then all inhuman spirits are bad? Not true. Remember, inhuman simply means that the spirit never lived on the physical plane. Angels fall into that category, right? Now we are going to confuse things a little. We all know that angels are good. Is that a fair statement? It may be fair but it is not true. Not all angels are good. Keep in mind that Lucifer, AKA Satan, was an angel. He still is for that matter. An angel is an angel, whether he is a good one or a bad one. You are still a human, even if you are the worst person in the world. The same is true of an angel. "Angel" is a classification, a title. Once an angel has been created, he is always an angel, even if he turns out to be negative.

Poltergeists are evil spirits and they are felt to be inhuman spirits. The reason why is because they are able to manipulate the environment somehow and that can result in extremely destructive behavior, as you have seen. There are different theories about how spirits can move things. As you have just read, one popular theory is that they move by means of "solidifying the air." It is believed that by using this means, they are able to move large or heavy objects. Human spirits can also move objects but they have to be small, light objects, usually about two pounds or less. A poltergeist can make your dresser do a great imitation of Gene Kelley doing "Singing In The Rain," complete with the rain. Human spirits cannot do that. They are limited to knocking small items off a counter or tipping pictures over and things like that.

While we are on the subject of things moving around, I want to point something out. Let us say that you are experiencing what appears to be a destructive phenomenon in your home. Is that proof that the force behind it is evil? Not necessarily. Let me give you an example. You have died and have passed on to the next level. For one reason or another, you decide that you need to communicate with a loved one. For arguments sake, we'll say it is a cousin who you were very close to. You somehow figure out how to travel through the astral plane and reach her home. Spirits do seem to have this ability. It is felt that they are able to move by thought. In other words, they think about where they want to be and they are suddenly there. Exactly how that happens is a mystery and one that will most likely stay that way. So anyway, you feel the need to communicate with her very much, so once you get to her house, you try to get her attention. The only problem is that you have not yet evolved enough to know how to do that. You may have tried to get through to her through her dreams. While she is having dreams of you, she is not getting the message. This would, of course, be very frustrating to you who has just managed the task of getting into people's dreams.

Once you are there in her home, the trick is to communicate with her. At this point, you see her in the kitchen washing dishes. You come up behind her and try to get her attention but you cannot. Not knowing what to do, you focus all of your attention on the glass she just washed. You try to move it but it is not happening; the glass will not budge. Concentrating harder, you find that that glass will move ever so slightly. She glances at the movement and then shakes her head as if she is wondering whether the glass actually moved or not. Your confidence begins to soar. You are getting there. Again, all of your concentration is focused on the glass. Suddenly, the glass moves. Unfortunately, it moves right off the counter onto the floor where it tests the theory that the whole is greater than the sum of its parts. In other words, the glass breaks into twenty trillion pieces, some of which will still be there two centuries from now. Oops!

Well, in a sense you were successful; you did get her attention. Congratulations! Of course, she is standing there whiter than a ghost, no pun intended. Frankly, she looks scared out of her wits. Of course, that was certainly not your intention. Now, in her mind, a file is being opened. In this file will go information about occurrences that are being labeled: "unusual." Now, if this is the only item in that file, no harm has been done. We have all experienced a strange event or two that has defied explanation. If nothing further occurred, the file ends up dying of loneliness in your head. However, if something else happens, it has the effect of the original action squared.

Later, you decide to try again. This time, she is sitting on the couch reading a magazine. On the coffee table in front of her, there is a glass of soda and an ashtray with a lit cigarette in it. Okay, the glass thing was a disaster so this time, you focus on the ashtray. Right off the bat, you are playing with fire. Literally. Anyway, to make a long story short, after several vain attempts, you are finally able to make the ashtray move a bit.

Out of the corner of her eye, she notices this. You might notice that she is frightened now although you are probably too busy concentrating on the ashtray to notice. That is too bad because that file she opened earlier just received an addition. Now, you may slowly become aware of the fact that you are scaring her, providing you noticed the shaking of her hands. Obviously, this is the last thing you want to do, so with that thought in mind, you press ever onward hoping to get her attention before you send her into the realm of complete panic. You concentrate on the ashtray and viola: you manage to knock it right off of the table. On the positive side, the ashtray did not break, thanks to the carpet. On the negative side, the lit cigarette rolls out of the ashtray and puts a lovely burn in the rug. Trust me, you are not endearing yourself to her. At this point, it is probably a good thing that you are already dead; otherwise she might well kill you. Her new file is expanding quite rapidly and now she has labeled it her "haunting file." You are two for two.

While she starts worrying herself to death, you go back to the drawing board and try to come up with a less disastrous way of letting her know that you are still around and that you still care. Just as she heads for bed, an idea pops into your head, assuming of course you still have one. This time, you will try your luck at moving the pillow. Surely she will know it is you and everything will be just great. So, just as she lies down, you try to move the pillow next to her. Unfortunately, you have some difficulty accomplishing this. To make matters worse, it appears that she has fallen asleep already, undoubtedly as a result of the sedative she took so that she could sleep in a haunted house. Well, now you know that your only chance will be to shake her pillow. With all of your newfound spiritual might, you pull on the pillow. Yes, you did it! It moved. Unfortunately for you, (and her) it moves completely off the bed, almost causing her to fall out of bed herself. She awakens to find her pillow flying across the room. The first thing she does after being released from the psyche hospital is call in an exorcist to get rid of your sorry ass. Ah, the best laid plans...

We can go on and on but I will spare you that. The point is that you are not an evil spirit, even though what you have done may make her think you are. What she is seeing is a trail of destruction when the problem is you were doing the only thing you knew how to do, or thought you knew how to do. Your actions seemed malevolent but they were not. All you wanted to do was communicate with her but you did not know how to and everything you tried served to make things worse. It is not that much different than being alive, is it? Instead of her being open to you, she is becoming convinced that she is being haunted, probably by a demon. Now, everything you do from that point on will be seen in that context.

Now the question is, how does one tell whether the activity is caused by an evil spirit or a benign one? You have to look at the duration of the activity and the intent behind it. One or two things cannot tell you much, unless they are extreme. As you just saw, it may be an attempt by a spirit to contact you. However, if it is an evil spirit who is causing the phenomena, it will continue to happen and it will likely get worse and worse over time. Right there, that tells you something. If the occurrences begin to escalate, you are probably dealing with an evil spirit. The good spirit is going to figure out quickly that what it is doing is not working. The evil one knows that it is working and will continue to put the pressure on. It will be relentless in its attempts to frighten you. In many cases, even those with poorly developed powers of discernment are able to sense evil. They may get goose bumps for no obvious reason or that may start to feel nervous all of a sudden. There is often some sign. One thing I have said to people is if you think you are being haunted, you are probably not; if you are haunted, you *know* it. That may sound like an oversimplification but it is accurate.

Friendly Nature Spirits

Let us look at some of the other types of spirits you may come across. You may have heard the term: "nature" spirits. These are sometimes called "undines." They are all around us, all of the time. They are also known as devas. Nature spirits are quite harmless and usually quite friendly if they can find a way of getting your attention. Since they were never human, you don't see quite the same foibles as in the example above. Your most common form of nature spirit is the "elemental" spirit. These spirits are believed by some to be the cousins of angels, although probably somewhat removed. Elementals come in different shapes and forms. When photographed, they may come out on film as square or rectangular shapes, as opposed to the circular orbs. They spend their time living in the woods and forests and watching over nature. If you have a houseplant, you probably have an elemental in your home. Like all nature spirits, they are friendly and quite harmless. They do like to have fun in their interactions with all living creatures, and towards that end, they are sometimes mischievous. These playful spirits can be observed in nature, if you focus on them and are lucky. Very often, farmers and gardeners see these magnificent spirits, although they probably have no clue what they are seeing. After all, these spirits are the ones responsible for the well being of whatever is planted so it stands to reason that they would try to interact with those who work the land. The best place to find them therefore is in the woods or any place where there is a significant amount of foliage.

There are four types of elemental spirits. The elementals of the air are called *sylphs*; those of earth are called *gnomes*. The elementals of fire are called *salamanders* and those of water are called *nymphs*. They have been around since the dawn of time. If you are a person who is open to them, that is, you believe in their existence and you make an effort to see them, then you may be quite successful, although it is not necessarily easy by any means. If you are able to gain their trust, they may even appear in your home, providing you are near woods or have plants there. They may appear as lighted shapes such as triangles and they may be of any color, although it is usually a bright one. They may float lazily towards you only to pull back when you reach for them. As I said, they also like to tease from time to time. Elementals fall into the category of inhuman spirits. You see, they are not all bad. As is true with life in general, the bad guys always get the press coverage.
****

Angels Are Messengers Of God

There is a lot of talk these days about angels, especially guardian angels. There have been some compelling stories about these messengers of God, as they are known. Most cultures and religions believe in these heavenly creatures. Just as with other forms of paranormal phenomena, there is no way to scientifically prove their existence. However, some very credible people are reporting encounters with these beautiful creatures. From all reports, these experiences are life altering in a positive way. Many believe it is our birthright to see angels. It is said that through meditation and visualization techniques, one can see their guardian angel. That must be a great experience. I have at times felt them around me although to this point, I have not been able to see them. I only get to see the bad guys, I guess. Those who report encounters with them describe them as all loving and non-judgmental. God knows we need that in this world. Angels may appear as people so it is possible, even likely that we have all encountered them without realizing it. I am sure that if you sat back and really thought about it, you may remember a time when you met someone, however briefly who gave off a radiance that was well above what you normally encounter. It may just have been a sense of peace or love that emanated from that person. Of course, there is no way to prove it was an angel but the possibility is there. Perhaps you found yourself lost somewhere and seemingly out of nowhere, someone appeared to help you. That could have been an angel. Think about a time where something happened where you cannot believe that you were not killed or seriously injured. That may have been the work of an angel. That brings up the question of discernment. I am sure you have had an experience where "something" told you to go home a different way only to find out later that something terrible happened on your usual route. That could be discernment, which we have already talked about. It might also have been an angel at work. Perhaps that is what all discernment is?

Encounters with angels have been reported throughout history. In fact, they have been reported in every culture and to people of every religion. Some of the most compelling reports have come from people who have had brushes with death, through illness or through injury. Yes, they will even appear to someone who does not believe in them. In all cases, they have described these beings as beautiful and loving creatures. Angels are androgynous; in other words, they are neither male nor female. However, when they appear to humans, they do take on a sex. This is most likely because they choose to appear in the form that we feel comfortable with. If, in our minds, we expect angels to be female, that is how they will appear to us. However they appear, encounters with angels are always intensely beautiful experiences.

(Imps, Fairies And The Like)

Folklore has given us other terms. We have all heard of imps, fairies and leprechauns. They would most likely fall into some of the categories mentioned throughout this section. In the minds of many, these spirits do not exist. The problem, I think, lies in semantics. There are many different names for the same type of spirit. These names vary, depending on the culture of those reporting them. This is one source of confusion. Another confusing factor is how a given type of spirit is defined. For example, look at the term "imp." You may read in one book that this is a minor demon. Take another book and you will read how it is a childlike spirit. Under this definition, an imp is harmless, although somewhat playful and mischievous. Take your pick. We know there are elementals. It is within the realm of possibility that "leprechauns" fall into this category. That could be something of a stretch. A pretty big stretch at that.

You will run into this problem with several of the spirits mentioned. This creates a lot of gray area. There is no one, central, defining source of information. Throughout recorded history, different people have created different names. Sometimes, those names have overlapped. Even today, demonologists will use one definition for a spirit and parapsychologists will use another. Psychics will use yet another term. It does make things difficult. However, we cannot clear up century's worth of confusion in this book.

There are growing numbers of people who believe in spirit guides. These spirits are gaining recognition through the many books available on angels and psychics who are able to communicate with deceased spirits. There is no clear-cut answer as to whether these spirit guides are human or inhuman spirits. Based on the literature available, it would seem it that the answer is both. It is believed by many that when we die, we may be able to choose to be spirit guides for the sake of others. Pity the poor one that gets me. Whatever they are, the theory is that they are with us for guiding us in our spiritual growth. They are not, however, our guardian angels. Therefore, it would seem, we are blessed with two spirits to help us. If that is so, why do we continue to make so many mistakes? Well, the answer to that is simple, we were given free will to do what we please. Our angels and spirit guides will try to influence us to do good but we still reserve the right to mess things up, if that is what we choose to do. We have the old inalienable right to screw up our lives if we want to. Maybe the little old voice in your head is coming from outside of your head? Could be.

Have you ever done something you knew was wrong but you did it anyway? It is a rhetorical question, I know. I am sure the answer is yes. Well, is it possible that you knew it was wrong because that is what your helper said? It is food for thought, isn't it? It makes you think a bit. Will we ever fully understand the spirit world? I would have to say probably not. However, that is not what we are trying to do here in this chapter. The purpose here is to determine whether all spirits are evil? I think we have answered that question. The most important point to learn is that not all spirits are evil. Fortunately, the vast majority of spirits you are likely to meet are indeed quite harmless. In truth, you are far more likely to meet good spirits than bad ones. Most encounters with spirits are positive in nature. Of course, you never know for sure if a person you meet on the street is a spirit. It could possibly be. Luckily for us, you have a much better chance of seeing an angel than a demon.

WHY HAUNTINGS OCCUR

Determining why hauntings occur is important because the reason it happened could tell you what type of spirit you are dealing with, if you have not already been able to determine that. For example, if someone bought a book on witchcraft and began trying to conjure something up, that would tell us that we are dealing with a spirit of the occult. In all likelihood, we are dealing with an inhuman spirit, in other words, a demon. If there does not seem to be a cause for a haunting, it could be that the spirit is indigenous to the location. In that case, it can be a human or an inhuman spirit. Equally important, knowing why it happened can give you an idea about how to make the haunting stop. Obviously, if you determined you are dealing with a spirit of the occult, which was caused by a satanic ritual, you know you are going to have to go for outside help, probably to a religious organization.

Sometimes there are clear-cut reasons for a haunting. Again, it may be something that was conjured up in some kind of ritual. Sometimes you have to search for the cause. In some cases, you never really find out why it has occurred. That can be because the victims are not telling you everything for fear of embarrassment or ridicule. Other times, you may have some clues but they do not really seem strong enough to account for the phenomena taking place. Then there are those cases that really do not have an apparent cause. It is always possible that something took place a hundred or more years ago. In some instances, people are tested because they are good people. This is especially true with demonic hauntings. The demon attacks precisely to hurt a person who tries to live his or her life according to God's wishes. In reality, it is an attack on God Himself.

In this chapter, we are going to see various ways that people come to be haunted. Sometimes the victim does something, albeit unintentionally to cause the problem. In others, the person is victimized because of his/her lifestyle. They create a perfect breeding ground for the demonic. In many of these cases, the victim has no idea that they actually did something to bring on the situation. If there is a positive side to be found here, it is that if they stop doing whatever it is that attracted the entity, it may well leave. It all depends on the reasons why it started the haunting in the first place. Let us take a close look at the three biggest reasons for hauntings. After that, we will look at some other reasons why a haunting may take place.

The Law Of Invitation

There are a number of ways in which people literally invite demons or evil spirits into their lives. This may sound preposterous to you but in actually, it happens quite often, although it may not be intentional. One of the biggest culprits is the still popular Ouija board, although for less hysterical reasons that you are sometimes given. What happens is two or more people put their fingers on a planchette and ask questions in this board game. These questions are directed at a spirit, sometimes that of a deceased loved one. This planchette begins to slide across the board, which has letters and numbers on it. The planchette, supposedly guided by a spirit, spells out the answers. Now, this sounds simple enough. At first glance, it seems harmless. However, you have no idea what force is guiding this movement. One thing any experienced investigator will tell you is that spirits lie. Often. In fact, they are pretty good at it.

When people begin playing the game, they usually say something like: "Are there are any spirits out there who wish to communicate with us?" Sometimes the answer is yes. The problem is that the people involved have absolutely no idea whether this spirit is good or evil. In many instances, the spirit is evil. Now, look at this scenario. You have just invited this spirit into your home. Whether good or bad, you said, "Come on in." The thing that is most interesting if you think about it is that no one would invite someone they do not know into their house, even though they can see the person. Why then would you invite in something you cannot even see but may also be extremely dangerous? In all fairness, many people who use the Ouija board do not really believe that there is anything unnatural speaking to them. They assume that the board is being controlled by one of the users. In many cases, that is true. However, that is not always the case. Often spirits do manipulate the board. They are not necessarily all bad but how do you know the difference? That is the dilemma. You also have to keep in mind that evil spirits are liars. If you are trying to contact Uncle Mortimer, an evil spirit will gladly play the role of Uncle Mortimer if that is what it takes to be invited in. Once it is in your home, you have a problem. There is a very good chance that it will not want to leave.

Children are especially vulnerable to their influences. This is felt to be due to their closeness to God. Jesus Himself was happiest when surrounded by children. The devil knows this. Lonely children often treat the board much like a companion. A spirit may begin talking to the child through the board and thus becomes her friend. She may wait all day, anxiously looking forward to conversing with her "friend." A good point needs to be made here. Whether or not it is a spirit, this type of obsession is unhealthy as it retards the child's social skills. Anyway, the spirit may say such nice and kind things to the child. It may really boost her self-esteem. Often, it proclaims itself to be the spirit of a child who once lived in that home. Ultimately, after winning the child's trust, it will ask if it can appear and stay in the home. The child naturally says yes. Now you have a haunting. Are all the spirits you may contact necessarily evil? No, they are not but since you do not know what type of spirit is communicating with you, do you want to take the risk?

In all fairness, there is another point of view on the Ouija board. There are many in the scientific world that believes the board is controlled by the collective unconscious minds of those using it. This is called *automatism*. There have been some heated debates on this subject. One point to ponder: many of those who subscribe to the theory of automatism agree that it is still dangerous. Their reasoning is that there is information in the unconscious mind that the conscious mind is not yet ready to handle. In addition, it is possible that if someone at the table has some pent up hostility towards another player, that hostility may show itself through the board. That can obviously be a problem. Whatever the vehicle, Ouija boards are notorious for using the foulest of language. ("Monsters from the id?" if I can borrow a line from one of my all-time favorite movies.) This is something to consider when it comes to children using it.

Another potential danger with Ouija boards is that some people become obsessed with using them. I have seen cases where it gets to the point where they will only make decisions after consulting the board. I don't care whether there is a spirit controlling the movements or whether it is automatism or space aliens for that matter, you cannot let a board game become the ruling factor in your life. Besides, no one has ever gotten winning lottery numbers from a Ouija board.

One argument made by proponents of the Ouija board is that millions of people use them and if there were any truth to the negative possibilities, millions of people would be haunted. That is true enough. The thing to note is that in many cases of the most severe hauntings, the Ouija board seems to be one common denominator, the "gateway" you could say. The point is that you can be playing with fire. You can make the argument that you can safely use the board if you ask for only "positive" spirits to come in or you can say a prayer for protection. That is what many people do successfully. An excellent book, which explores both sides of this debate, is "Ouija, The Most Dangerous Game" by Stoker Hunt. (C 1985, published by Harper and Row.)

Another way of inviting spirits in is by using Tarot Cards. The reasons why are less clear than with the Ouija board but the results can be the same. It probably has more to do with intent than anything else. The fact that you are trying to find "occult" or hidden information opens the door to the spirit world. If you look for spirits, they will look for you. Automatic writing is a phenomenon in which you hold a pen or pencil in your hand over a blank piece of paper. In many instances, the pen will begin to write. (Not when I have tried it.) There are those who feel that a spirit is communicating through the person holding the pen. One piece of evidence that would seem to support this theory is that the handwriting is usually noticeably different the person's own. In addition, in many cases, a right-handed individual will write with his left hand. If this theory is true, by doing this you are allowing something to write using yourself as a vehicle and that is potentially dangerous.

Again, there are those who feel that automatism is behind this too; the theory being that it is the subconscious mind is trying to communicate with the conscious one. That may very well be so. In fact, I would think this theory probably accounts for the majority of messages received. The thing is, again, how do you know what you are dealing with? If it turns out to be an evil spirit, you may have invited it into your life.

In all fairness, I do think a point needs to be brought up here. There is a danger in trying to blame everything on evil or demonic spirits. Not everything that happens can be blamed on the work of evil forces. Automatism does exist. If we try to blame everything on the supernatural, we are being just as pigheaded and are just as guilty of seeing through tunnel vision as those in the scientific world who reject out of hand, the possibility of the supernatural existing and accounting for the phenomena so often observed. In addition, people will use the idea of evil spirits as an excuse for their own misdeeds. We must realize that we are responsible for our own actions, regardless of how much temptation is used against us. It is very easy to blame our bad actions on evil spirits. In addition, I point this out because there is a real danger in "seeing a ghost in every corner." True hauntings, while they are more common than many believe are still relatively rare. However, they do happen and the Laws of Invitation are valid. We must take great pains not to invite the unknown into our lives. It is a lot easier to than you would think.

Another form of violating the Laws of Invitation would be trying to achieve personal gain using spells, magic, or witchcraft. Many people talk about practicing "white" witchcraft as opposed to "black" variety. Now I see books on "green" witchcraft. What is next, gold? How a spell or ritual is used does not alter the fact that some force is behind it. How can you tell what force that is? Evil forces have been known to do what may appear to be a good thing if it serves their overall purpose. It may just be "throwing you a bone" so to speak in return for your devotion to it. Many people, especially younger people buy books on ritual magic in the hopes that they can cast a spell to make them more popular. These lonely, shy people feel that they do not fit in this world and subsequently isolate from their peers. This compounds their problem. They certainly are not trying to bring evil into their lives. They do not want to hurt anyone. All they want to accomplish is a positive thing, to make themselves better. The problem is that they are extremely vulnerable to evil forces. They are easily misled by what looks to be a positive force. God does not promise miracles. He gives them willingly when the time is right. Spells and magic have nothing to do with it. I also want to make another point here. I am not knocking people who practice "Wicca." However, there is a danger in dabbling with things you know nothing about. This is what can happen when a young person runs to the local bookstore and picks up a book on spells. He does not know what he is doing and that is what can hurt him.

There are those who very willingly invite the demonic into their lives. These are Satanists. They perform ceremonies that are designed to call up demons. They are sometimes successful. I have mentioned before that Satan and his legions are not going to do our bidding. If they do anything at all that we want, you can bet that there is something in it for them. We are fools if we think we can harness the power of beings that are inhuman. They are not subjected to the laws of humans. Sadly, many people do not realize this. They actually worship Satan and often do the most abhorrent, evil things. The hard core Satanists will stop at nothing to please their "god." They will sacrifice animals and they will sacrifice humans, especially children. Rape, torture, and murder are all part and parcel for the organized Satanists.

What about the teen Satanists? They represent a huge problem as well. They listen to their "metal" music, dabble with rituals and slaughter animals while being in a drug induced fog. These people have no idea what they are dealing with. They are playing around with forces that hate all human beings, even the ones who worship them. These forces will destroy these dabblers just as quickly as they would anyone else. Satan has no loyalty to man. There is also a danger when it comes to fantasy games such as "Dungeons and Dragons." In many cases, the most vulnerable members of our society play this game. Many young people, especially those bored with the everyday realities of life find that these games make them feel alive. They consider their fantasy life better than their real life. Perhaps in some cases, it is. It is often neglected and abused children who find these games fun and exciting. They do not know the dangers. Swords and sorcery may or may not be harmful to a balanced individual but in the hands of the loners and those with no self-esteem, there is a great danger. If nothing else, these games can become an obsession. Cults of any kind are potentially dangerous both to the individual involved and to those around them.

While we are on the subject of fantasy, I just want to mention something. When The "Harry Potter" series became popular, I saw a television program where the moderator was interviewing some people who felt that this series was a serious detriment to children. Since it was a Catholic program, I took an interest in it, although admittedly, I missed several minutes of the program. Anyway, a short time later, a friend of mine suggested that I write an article saying how terrible Harry Potter was for our children. Since I really did not know all that much about the series, I figured I had better do some reading on the subject so I went and borrowed a couple of the books. Here I was, ready to battle evil forces! You know what, I found absolutely nothing wrong with them whatsoever. My conclusion was that if this series turned children on to reading, so much the better. There is a difference between reading books and seeing movies and turning yourself into a fantasy character.

What it all pretty much boils down to is that you have to be extremely careful about anything that is occult related. Take a stroll into just about any bookstore in your local mall and you are likely to see a section referred to a "New Age." New Age today was plain old occult yesterday. In this section, you will find many books on Astrology. You will also see many books on UFO's and alien abductions. However, take note of all of the books on spells, witchcraft, and tarot cards. You will be surprised at the number of books available on these subjects.

There is a large demand for these books and they do sell. I am not saying that purchasing books of this type will guarantee a haunting. What I am saying is that practicing the spells in some of these books can get you into trouble. What starts out innocently enough can become a big problem down the road. There is no way to gauge who will have problems and who will not. In some cases, just having such a book can cause problems although I would think that to be an unusual occurrence. Obviously, not everyone who plays with a Ouija board ends up haunted, although most people have a good story or two to tell about their experiences. The same goes for spells and magic. The thing is that in so many of the serious cases of hauntings, these items were used. They may or may not have caused the haunting but they surely did nothing to help the situation either. Something was contacted and that something accepted the invitation. It then chose not to leave. There have been so many cases where this has happened, too many to write off as chance or coincidence. It is just not worth the risk.

Another example of using the laws of invitation would be the person who tries to put a curse on someone else. For that curse to be successful, assuming it can, a demon would have to carry it out. Therefore, in sending a demon out, you have invited it into your own life. It may do what you want it to do but trust me, you will pay the price. You are nuts if you think you can control these things. There are times when someone will attempt a "spell" or something similar as a means of protecting themselves. That means using evil to fight evil. All I can say is that if I have learned anything in this long journey through life, it is this: When evil fights evil, evil wins. In addition, hating God is another form of invitation. This one could actually fit in this category and in the next one, which is "The Laws of Attraction." If you hate God, you are certainly pleasing His adversary. In that sense, you are inviting it into your life, even if you do not do so intentionally. Just by hating God, you have opened yourself up to evil influences. You do not even have to believe in evil. Let us look at how this one works.

The Law Of Attraction

The laws of attraction can be summed up in three words: *like attracts like.* That may sound like an oversimplification but that really is all there is to it. Like attracts like. What this means is that positive forces attract positive forces and negative ones do likewise. When you look at it, it all seems so simple. It is, up to a point, that is. However, while there are actions that are obviously good, some actions are unintentionally negative. Therefore, we need to look at the things that we do that are actually negative. You might be surprised by some of the things mentioned.

People who set out to kill others are obviously, evil people. So are child abusers and molesters. They do evil things therefore it is logical to assume that they will attract evil into their lives. The same goes for bigots and others filled with hate. Like attracts like. If a person if filled with hate, he is going to attract spirits who are filled with hate. That makes sense. The thing to remember is that evil spirits and demons are going to want to spend their time in an environment that is friendly to them. Yes, they will sometimes pick on the best our world has to offer. They do that to hurt God. However, if they are looking for a place to stay, they are going to go where they feel most at home. They love anger, rage, jealousy, hate, and fear. Cruelty and meanness make them feel wonderful. To them, these things are the breakfast of champions. Where can they find a better environment to live in?

There is one point that is important to make before we go any further. Everyone who has ever lived has felt negative at some point in time. If you just lost your job and you are wondering how you are going to pay your rent, I do not care who you are; you are going to feel negative. That is only human and it is not necessarily going to attract a negative spirit into your life, although you may sometimes wonder about that. We have all experienced periods where some thing went wrong and it started a snowball effect of other problems. Let us look at another example. If your child comes home from school with a black eye because the school bully beat him up, you are going to be very mad. Unfortunately, negative emotions are part of the human condition. Things do go wrong in life. Often. That is not what we are talking about here. We all get angry from time to time. That is not where the problem lies. The problem is with those individuals who are so angry that it begins to eat away at their soul. Being mad at your boss for criticizing you is normal. Letting it build up into a rage that affects your normal way of thinking is adverse to your welfare. You can become a walking time bomb and it is a horrible way to have to trudge through life. If enough negative energy is released often enough, negative spirits will most certainly be attracted to you. It is common sense.

There are people, good people, who have been dealt an unfavorable hand in life. Sometimes it eats away at them to the point where they become bitter people. They are not looking for negative forces, far from it. They just do not realize that how they *think* can control what they *attract*. Let us look at a couple of examples. Think of a day in your life where everything just seemed to fall into place. Maybe a couple of good things happened early in the day that lifted your mood. You go to work and hit almost no traffic. When you get there, your boss was in a good mood. Then, at work, you complete a couple of projects that have been nagging at you. Everything seems well. That is a case of positive attracting positive. When the first good thing happened, you gained some momentum. Your initial positive thoughts attracted further positive thoughts. Now think of the day when your alarm did not go off, you hit all kinds of traffic and your boss came in to work breathing fire. That will be the day when a project that you thought would be simple turns out to be a nightmare. Negative attracted negative.

There is more too. You will often find that many hauntings involve people with substance abuse problems. Relax guys. You can have that beer during the ballgame. What we are talking about here are those people who are addicted to one form of substance or another. The person who comes home night after night and drinks himself into a drunken sleep is a prime candidate for a haunting. Obviously, chronic alcoholism is a negative situation. Everyone knows that. While it is not true in all cases, in many, that person may well be verbally abusive to his family and he may be physically abusive too. Not only is he himself negative, he has turned his entire household in a negative environment. This is the perfect breeding ground for evil. It will feed off the constant negative energy being sent out by the occupants of that home.

People who are abusive to animals also run into problems. They too are God's creatures and He loves them as such. If you hurt any of His creatures, you are attracting a whole lot of negative things into you life. It does not have to be just physical hurt either. People who purposely try to hurt others in their jobs or relationships run into problems too. An example of this might be hiding the report your coworker labored on just to see him get in trouble with the boss. Criminals in general are prime candidates for trouble. Rapists, drug dealers, drive by shooters ...do you think they will have problems with the demonic? They may not necessarily be haunted but they are probably more compelled to commit a crime and it may be decidedly evil as well. Those who desecrate cemeteries run a big risk. There is another group too. These are the people who violate the body of someone deceased. I hate to say it but there are many necrophiliacs out there. That is pretty scary, isn't it? Necrophilia is an easy shortcut to demonic infestation and even possession.

Those who sacrifice people or animals run a double risk. Not only are they violating the Laws of Attraction, they are violating the Laws of Invitation as well. It is safe to say that anything that can be considered evil or intentionally mean would fall into this category. Again, we are not talking about the normal anger that is a part of everyday life. We are talking about negativism that is the commonplace way of life. In short, you can sum it up by saying that if you create an environment that is hostile or evil, you can expect that something evil may want to reside there. There are probably a hundred more examples but I think you get the idea. All you have to remember is like attracts like. You can make an argument that with all of the evil and negativity in the world today that there should be rampant cases of demonic infestation. Well, one thing to consider is that there are rampant cases of demonic interference. Infestation and possession are not the only ways demons interfere with our lives. If anything, they are the least likely way that evil affects our lives. However, the hate so many people feel and express may have its foundation in demonic interference. Certainly the rage we see would fit into that theory. Evil abounds today and it does not have to be in the form of a haunting. Of course, there are other reasons why a haunting may occur, as you are about to see. This may explain why one person attracts demonic interference while another find himself embroiled in infestation or possession.

The Law Of Opportunity

This law tends to be tied into the first two and may explain why some people run into problems and others do not. In that regard, it is really a sub-law although it can by itself cause a haunting without violating either of the first two laws. What this law means is that there are spirits on the prowl, so to speak, waiting for an opportunity to strike. They may fly around like vultures waiting for a carcass to feed on, although in this case, it is a human carcass. This could explain why two people can use a Ouija board, for instance, and only one has a problem. This can account for why one may use the board for years and years seemingly safely and suddenly develop a problem. In this case, there just happened to be a spirit looking for the opportunity to strike. The same would go for any of the Laws of Invitation or Attraction. The person who is getting results while doing automatic writing may actually be getting that information from his own subconscious. It may be a case of automatism. Then one day, the tone of the messages changes, as may the actual handwriting itself. In that scenario, there just happened to be an opportunistic spirit (spiritual vulture) looking for a place to dine out. It then comes across the automatic writer who has left himself open and it gets sucked in, so to speak. Ditto for the person using a conjuring book. He may be surprised that nothing seems to work for him and then one day, his "luck" changes. That "luck" could be the vulture and the success of his spell may be the start of something terribly evil taking over his life.

The same would be true in cases where there is an abusive household. The only evil at work may be in the form of interference until the vulture comes along and discovers an environment that it knows it can thrive in. The addict who has turned over his life to drugs may end up turning it over to the opportunistic spirit whether he knows it or not and whether he intended for that to happen or not. In most cases, he didn't. Of course, not only evil actions are required to become the victim of an opportunistic spirit. There may be a person suffering from the terrible affliction of depression or anxiety. That person, who finds so little joy in life, may attract an equally unhappy, opportunistic spirit into his life. Opportunistic spirits are by no means all demonic. There are many human opportunistic spirits out there as well. Also, the possible haunting that results from this encounter may not be evilly based either. The opportunistic spirit of a suicide victim may not want to haunt or hurt a living person; it may just want to find a place to stay with someone who is like him. Like attracts like is not always an evil encounter.

The Law of Indigeny

This is where you have the misfortune of moving into a house that is already haunted. The spirit of someone who previously lived there may haunt it or it may be that the ground the house was built on was haunted. There are many reports of haunted houses that were built over old cemeteries. It is also possible that the house or grounds were used in some form of black ceremony. One of the problems dealing with this type of situation is that it is not always clear why you are being haunted. Unless you like looking through tons of old records, you may never find out anything useful. Sometimes records were not even kept or were lost over the years. Also, there may be nothing in those records that explains the reason for the haunting.

To confuse matters even more, the people who lived there before you may not have been haunted. In many cases, a haunting will only affect certain people. This may be due to their ability to experience it. In other words, the previous residents had very little psychic ability and were therefore not particularly susceptible to the forces there, try as they might to reach those people. Some people are just more prone to being haunted than others. Always bear in mind that while houses can be haunted, so too can people. They may be haunted wherever they go. In other cases, spirits or demons may lay dormant for years and wake up when you begin making major changes in the place or you do something to bring it out.

Let us pick on the old, abused Ouija board once again. (It is almost unfair but it makes for a good example because so many people use them and can thus relate to it.) You may be a person who has used the Ouija board for years without any negative consequences. You may have used it in many different locations as well and fortunately, never ran into an opportunistic spirit. However, six weeks after you moved into your new house, "odd" things began to happen, things that never happened before in all of the years that you had used the board. What happened in that case? Well, perhaps you had a dormant spirit residing in the house and by using the board, you awakened it. That certainly was not your intention. After all, you had no idea that the spirit was even there to begin with. It can be as simple as that. So, in that regard, the Law of Indigeny can also be a sub-law in that it can explain why the Laws of Invitation or Attraction became factors. They were empowered by the spirit indigenous to the location.

How do you know if a house you are planning to move into is haunted? You probably do not know. Unless you have the power to discern, you are out of luck. Let me say this though, I have gone apartment hunting over the years and I have walked into many places where I could tell immediately that something was wrong. I cannot say that I always knew that it was haunted but I could tell that *something* was wrong. There may have been a tragedy associated with the place or simply a lot of sadness there. That does not always mean that I would not recommend the place because joy can be brought to a home that was once filled with tragedy or grief. However, I can usually tell whether it is something that can be changed. Simply feeling a spirit presence would not rule out moving there. It is the *kind* of spirit that I sense that matters. I can usually tell if the spirit is negative, whether it is human or not. I have been in some places where I just knew immediately that it was not a good place to move into. I have even gone house or apartment shopping with friends at their request for that reason. I remember when I bought my beautiful trailer. The first thing I did when I was looking at it was "open" myself up and see whether I felt anything negative. I didn't. I then asked my mother to look at is as well because she was even better than I was at feeling negativity. She agreed with me that it felt "good" so I went ahead and bought it. (I have never regretted that decision.)

You may find that you get a bad feeling when you walk into a house or apartment. This has happened to people who will tell you that they do not really possess psychic gifts. If you happen to know a psychic, he or she may be able to tell you. If you know one, it may be a good idea to have him or her check the place out before you buy it. On the other hand, they can be wrong and you could conceivably pass up on a great buy because they thought that they felt something that may not have been there. It is a judgment call on your part. You can always have the house blessed by a priest before or after you move in. That used to be a common practice years ago but it is less seen today, sadly so. I know of one person who asked their parish priest to bless their new home and he told her that: "we don't do that anymore."

You may be thinking at this point that blessing the house could wake up and anger a dormant negative spirit living there. While that is certainly possible, the odds of that are slim since those situations are rare. If you look at the whole picture, the odds are greatly in your favor that the blessing will be a good idea. One positive note: in many states, if there have been reports of unusual happenings, the owner of the house and the real estate agent must tell you about that. They must tell you if something unusual happened there and if the house was ever investigated by paranormal investigators, you must be informed of that as well. Even if the house is rumored to be haunted, you must be informed before you buy it. If nothing was said to you and you buy it and it turns out to be haunted, you are well within your rights to sue both the real estate agency that handled the sale and the previous owner, providing that you can prove that they knew about it. Check the laws in your state before buying a house. Another thing, if you see a beautiful house selling for way less than the market value, be careful. There may be a reason why.

Other Possible Causes

Sometimes a haunting will occur because something is brought into a house that has a spirit attached to it. This item may be something you picked up while on vacation. It may be something that looks innocent enough, like a statue or figurine. That statue may have been used in some kind of occult ceremony. You may pick up a piece of furniture in an antique shop that was once in a haunted house. The spirit that haunted that house may have decided to go along for the ride. Is there anyway to know if something is attached to an item? Again, without discernment ability, the answer is no. If you are gifted in psychometry, which is the ability to read the energy of an object, you might know just by touching it. However, even if you do not have a lot of psychic ability, just being near an object may give you a bad feeling. If that should happen to you, stay away from it. The same is true of a house too. If you get a bad feeling when you walk into it, look elsewhere. Your guardian angel may be trying to tell you something.

Hauntings can also result from a curse someone put on the house or the person moving into it. I have a little trouble believing in this one but I cannot absolutely rule it out. Some bitter, hateful person who leaves a house may have put a curse on it so that all future residents will be haunted. They invited a demon to terrorize anyone else that lives there. They will pay for it but so too will the unsuspecting family that moves in there. A house may be haunted due to a tragedy that occurred there. Maybe someone was killed in the house. Perhaps someone took his or her own life in the house. That could definitely result in a haunting. There could be someone buried on the premises, or in the house. The land the house was built on may once have been used for satanic rituals. As you see, there are many reasons why a house may be haunted. In some cases, there is no explanation for a haunting. It can happen to the nicest people in the world. These people have lived clean lives, and were faithful to their religion. So why are they haunted? Sometimes the entity singles out the good people just to hurt God. He picks on these people because of their goodness. Why does God allow it? Well, He may allow it so that it will inspire others in a similar situation. He may do it to attract attention to the problem. There may be other reasons too. I do firmly believe that God does have a purpose, even if we do not see it. However, that may be small comfort for the family being terrorized.

THE WEIGHING SYSTEM

(The Type Of Phenomena)

Solving a haunting can be challenging and at times insufferably hard. In many cases, you have to play the role of detective. At other times, it is like a chess match. You have to have an idea of what you want to do and you have to think several moves ahead. At the same time, you have to anticipate the spirit's moves. You sometimes need to be a tactician and a brilliant one at that. If you are going to be successful, you need to know as much about the haunting as possible and try to figure out where it is going. The next item to look at is the system I use to determine what type of phenomena I am are seeing. Earlier, the importance of trying to figure out when the phenomena began to occur was stressed. In addition, the importance of detecting patterns was noted. Patterns can sometimes make or break a case. Finding that all-important pattern can be difficult to do especially when you have to go back and try to figure out when the haunting started. It can become complicated because many of the early warning signs were probably missed. For that reason, one of the things I have asked the client to do is to keep a journal of everything that is currently happening in as much detail as possible. Obviously, things that are happening in the present are obviously easier to rate than something that may have happened six months ago.

.You should have also instructed him/her to think back and list anything at all that they think might have been unusual. As I have mentioned earlier, many things happen in the early stages that go unnoticed. Many little things may have occurred that were a precursor to the onset of the problem. One of my most repeated lines in classes and lectures and letters I write to clients is that they should list everything they can think of because: "I would rather have 99 things that have natural explanations than to miss the one bit of information that has no natural explanation." That one thing may turn out to be huge. Later in a haunting, everything that happens is attributed to the haunting even when there are obvious natural causes. Memory is a faulty thing to begin with and a haunting adds a touch of fear therefore, you have a confusing mix of information. In order to classify current happenings and to be able to go back in time with some degree of accuracy, I use a weighing system. What I do is assign a value from 1 to 5 with 1 being the least likely unnatural thing and 5 being the most likely. For example, noises heard in the basement that sound familiar and are likely to have been caused by the hot water heater, would rate a one. If your living room table started sailing down the highway and got pulled over for speeding, that would likely be a five. It is really a common sense thing. This is not a flawless system by any means but it does help though.

Early in the investigation, things usually proceed slowly. During the wait for something to happen, I try to sit down with as many people as possible that were around for any of the activity that has taken place. This is where we take that journal and try to determine what happenings were really unnatural and which ones can be explained logically. What I like to do is use the weighing system. Initially, these sessions can take some time. Remember, we have asked the client to go back and write down anything that seemed odd. If the haunting has been going on for a while, you may have a considerable amount of items to discuss so this can take time. It can also be hilariously funny at times as everyone tells their stories about what happened to them and how they reacted. Funny is good in a haunting. It lightens the mood and it helps establish a good rapport with the family. Lightening the mood can be a huge weapon in a haunting. Trust me, the beleaguered family needs all of the help they can get. A night filled with humor can help the victims enormously.

Another good thing about assigning weights is that it is helpful to the investigators because they are getting a good idea of what had been going on prior to their arrival. Another benefit is in going over the items in question; someone may remember something that had been overlooked. This could turn out to be important. I feel it is best to conduct these weight sessions in an informal manner. Let it be an open forum where everyone feels comfortable discussing the various items in their journals.

(The Weighting System)

One: Most likely normal. Things here might be creaking sounds that suddenly seem ominous but are likely very natural, such as the house settling or the hot water heater filling up. These are all the little things that you never noticed before but are actually normal. Most likely, these are sounds that have been heard a thousand times. However, once someone thinks he is being haunted, every sound now seems ominous. For that matter, the person who thinks they are being haunted will actually start imagining things out of fear. This is where you see how our eyes and ears can play tricks on us. Of course, this is not done intentionally. Fear creates its own little world and it colors everything in that world.

Everyone has the tendency at times to do things so routinely that they are not aware that they are doing them. It might be something like moving the TV remote control from the coffee table to the lamp table while you are dusting. However, when you are experiencing a haunting, you see the remote on the lamp table and wonder how it got there. That can make someone think that objects are moving around by themselves. That would drive me nuts if I was being haunted because I am scatterbrained to the max to begin with. I could move my car two blocks and not realize I did it.

You might have something like a screen door that bangs shut seemingly by itself. Under ordinary circumstances, you would probably pay little, if any attention to that. However, when you are being haunted, that banging door is definitely a sure sign of the demonic. In actuality, it is probably a sure sign that the latch does not work properly. Again, your imagination can run wild with you and your mind can most certainly play tricks on you.

Obviously, when you sit down to discuss the situation with the client, you have to be objective about it. That has to be stressed with the client. You have to have a sort of "prove it to me" attitude in your mind. However, do not act that way towards the client; that will only strain the relationship between you. Just make sure that you do not read anything into what they tell you. Let the item stand and fall on its own merits. If you think something is most likely natural, don't be afraid to tell them that but never do so in an accusatory or condescending tone. They will probably be sensitive about it and if they do not know you yet, they may be wondering whether you believe them or not. I have had clients fight with me on some things. Don't argue with them. Try to be as reassuring as possible but mark on your own notes what weight you give to each item. Ideally, you would like them to agree with you because the less things that are unnatural taking place can reduce their fear levels considerably. It also makes them more objective when they come across new things. They sometimes become better able to deal with future frightening events as well. One word of advice, do not conduct this type of session right after an outbreak of activity. This will severely impede everyone's ability to be objective. It is always possible to change a weight if the situation warrants it. Something may have happened one time and consequently, you rated it as a three. Later, you may talk to someone else who experienced the same thing on three other occasions. Now, that item may rate a four. Once you have gone through everyone's journal, you do not have to keep going over it repeatedly.

Two: Could be paranormal but doubtful. When you are involved in a haunting, the natural tendency is to lean towards the supernatural. In other words, the benefit of the doubt goes to the unnatural explanation. This is the category where you begin to scare yourself. An example of this might be finding a piece of furniture slightly out of place. It is quite probable that you or someone else bumped into it and moved it. Another example might be finding knick-knacks slightly out of place. If your washer causes enough vibrations in the spin cycle, it can make it seem as if your knick-knacks are doing a little dance. Objectivity is especially important in this category.

Three: Could be natural but doubtful. This is a bit of a gray area as things that happen here could have a natural explanation but it is highly unlikely. An example would be your turning off the TV and then heading up the stairs to bed. When you get into your bedroom, you hear that the TV is on again. You know that you turned it off but it is possible that something explainable has happened such as, a pet stepping on the remote. Maybe your next-door neighbor has the same TV and his remote turned yours on. Of course, if it happens repeatedly then it is most likely a four. A book that keeps disappearing and reappearing somewhere else would rate a three. You could be absentminded, right?

Four: Likely to be paranormal. Things that are likely to be paranormal would be things like toilets flushing or lights that occasionally go on or off for no apparent reason. If it just happened once, it would probably not qualify as a four. If it keeps happening, there is a good chance it is a four. Repetition is a good indicator. A bathtub that fills itself up would rate a four, as it could be possible that the faucet leaked but it is highly unlikely. It would take a long time for a leaky faucet to fill a bathtub.

Five: No possible natural explanation. This would be a phenomenon such as furniture moving around a room or pounding in the walls so loud that the room vibrates. Objects exploding or seeing certain types of apparitions could be a five. Seeing a shadow would probably not rate a five unless it is quite defined and is seen often in different areas under different conditions. A door that slams shut would not be a five. It could have been caused by a draft. Doors that repeatedly open and close would be a five. Levitation of any kind would be a five. Furniture, which moves more than an inch or so, would rate a five. Needless to say, teleportation of objects or evidence of bi-location would constitute a five. Remember that the key here is that the occurrence must be unexplainable.

This system has helped me on many cases. It is a way of shining a light on a dark area. It makes everyone think and it helps the victims to see what is real and what isn't. There ability to be objective becomes stronger. They may no longer see all activity as being haunting related. That alone can alleviate much of their fear. Needless to say, that weakens the hold the spirit has on them. So, as you can see, a lot goes into these discussions and they are important.

STAGES OF A HAUNTING

There are many misconceptions when it comes to a haunting. It is probably one of the most misunderstood of all the oddities we are likely to come across in our lives. Much of what we know about hauntings comes from TV and movies. Everyone equates demonic possession with Linda Blair's pea soup vomiting and 360 degree head thing portrayed in "The Exorcist." While many of the scenes depicted in that movie were accurate, it is safe to say that there was a good amount of "poetic license" used. Of course, it was not meant to be seen as a true story so I should not accuse it of using poetic license. What I am trying to say is that many of the terrors shown there do happen at times but not quite the way in which they were portrayed in the movie. Did I confuse you yet? Good, because I sure confused myself.

Movies are made to entertain, not to instruct. They are made to make money and let us face it, gore sells. So does horror and depravity. If you look at today's movies, they are filled with nonstop blood and gore. There is rarely any plot at all, just lots of eye puncturing, disembowelment fun. The result is that people become more desensitized to violence and bloodshed. Therefore, in order to sell movies, they have to have more and more shock value. When you see ghost stories, they are often so distorted that they become unreal. The other thing is that there are very few true ghost stories. Even some of the true stories become distorted. "The Amityville Horror" is probably a true story but the reality is that much of what was shown was an exaggeration of the truth, so much so that it lost all credibility. Throw in all the sequels, which were not even meant to be true and you have a much-distorted mix. You may be hard pressed to find anyone who believes that was a real haunting.

Before we go on, "The Exorcist" was loosely based on a true story. The author, William Peter Blatty was studying to become a Jesuit priest and came across the true story of a case of demonic possession. That story became a book written by Thomas B. Allen titled: "Possessed- The True Story of an Exorcism," by Bantam books. It was a great book based on a diary made by one of the priests involved in the exorcism. If you can find it, buy the book; it is very well written. "Showtime" also put out a movie by the same name. It also was quite good and you should try to see it. The book and movie will give you a much better idea of what demonic possession is all about. Absent is all of the nonsensical gore and unreal feats caused by the demon. It also tells you a little bit about how the Catholic Church sees cases of possession. That will give you some idea of what to expect should you ever need to go to the Church for help.

In reality, a haunting is usually very subtle. As I mentioned earlier, it often starts off so subtly that the early signs are often missed. In addition to that, it is not full-blown activity all of the time. Days, weeks, and even months often pass with little or no activity. It is common for people to believe that it is over only to have it heartbreakingly start up again. Furthermore, a haunting has a natural progression. While there may be some exceptions, it usually goes through predictable stages. It is rare for a haunting to start out with full-blown activity. The exception would be a true poltergeist explosion. Initially, as an entity attempts to get in, activity starts up. As the entity begins to get stronger, the activity increases and becomes more blatant. Once you start to take notice of the activity and start fearing it, the invading entity now has a foothold. As your fear grows, the entity is able to feed off that fear and in turn grows stronger.

While you cannot look for the ghost in every corner, it is very important to recognize the early warning signs of a haunting. The earlier you recognize it, the better your chances of ending it. The more time the entity has to dig in, the harder it will be to stop it. There are defenses but time is a factor. Do not get me wrong, even if you are experiencing full blown activity, it can be stopped; it is just a lot easier to stop it in the early stages. Snuff it out in its infancy whenever possible. Saying a prayer for protection and blessing the house is a lot easier that an exorcism. But, and this is a big but, you have to know when to bless the house and when not to. Different people have different views on the stages of a haunting, and the terminology may differ somewhat too. You will always find that as long as you are in this field. There are no absolutes. One thing to note, the following stages can apply to a haunting from an entity that was *human* as well as one that is *inhuman.* In the case of a human spirit, it stops at the third stage. When dealing with the inhuman spirit, it may progress to all five stages. If you read different books and talk to different people, you may see these stages in a different order or there may be more or less that five, depending on the author. From my research and experience, these are the five stages of a haunting:

1) **Oppression:** In this stage, an entity has begun the process of haunting you. Whether it has always been there or not, it will now begin to exert itself subtly. The invading spirit is trying to get that all-important foothold. You may begin to notice little things here and there. Slowly but surely, the entity will begin to oppress you. It is trying to solidify its position in the home and it is now beginning the process of wearing you down. You will gradually notice odd happenings and often begin to question yourself. "Did I really see that?" People living in the home at this stage will often feel depressed, although they do not know why. That is part of the strategy. Depression taps your spirit. It makes you weaker and therefore more susceptible to the next stage of the haunting. At this point, it is possible to stop the haunting before it really gets started. Prayer is very effective as is blessing the house with holy water. If action on the part of one of the occupants is causing the problem, ceasing that activity may stop the haunting at this early stage. This is also true if the spirit is attracted to the home. If the attraction stops, such as chronic drug use, the haunting may end here.

2) **Obsession:** At this stage, things are happening that you know are unusual. You start to focus on it. There is no attempt on the part of the entity to disguise its actions. It wants you to notice happenings. It wants you to become scared and confused.

The activity picks up a notch and the entity will often play divide and conquer. By this, I mean the entity may torment one member of the family, usually the woman. It usually chooses women because they are naturally more psychic than men and are therefore more vulnerable. In addition, men, by nature are more skeptical than women. Therefore, the man will often try to convince the woman that nothing is going on, that it is all in her head. In addition, frankly, men have a tendency not to notice some of the more subtle occurrences unless they take place in front of the TV. I am kidding. You could say that the entity would be wasting a lot of its effort on men. However, when men do finally realize that there is a problem, they usually do not handle it as well as women do. Their instincts to physically fight to protect their family becomes a drawback since you cannot fight what you cannot see. Once you have reached this stage, it becomes harder to remove the entity than in the first stage because now it has a foothold. However, it can still be stopped with prayer. A blessing of the house may do it and having a mass said in the house most likely will take care of the matter. From here, we go to the third stage.

3) **Infestation:** At this stage, the entity is well entrenched in the home; it is literally infested. The haunting is now very strong and the activity is full blown. Yes, even the men admit to the problem. The spirit now makes no secret of its intentions. There is nothing subtle here; you are now being haunted. The entity is strong now and removing it will be very difficult. At this point, you are probably going to need outside help. If the entity is a human spirit, this will be the last stage but take no comfort in that. You still have a serious problem on your hands. Prayer always helps; no matter what stage the haunting has reached. If the entity is a human spirit, prayers and blessings of the home, especially by a member of the clergy may still be effective in stopping the problem. You have to be careful though when it comes to blessing the house. As I belabored this point before, blessing a house at this stage may provoke a demon. You really have to be careful. As a rule, human spirits want no part in a

fight with God. They know they cannot win such a battle. Still, they will try to bully you as much as possible. They may retaliate somewhat if you attempt to get rid of them but ultimately they will leave before getting embroiled in a battle with God. For this reason, it is extremely important that you fight this thing hard from the start. If you did not notice the earlier stages of a haunting, (and sometimes you do not) the quicker you combat the problem, the better.

Never make the mistake of thinking that you should defend yourself in stages. By that, I do not mean that you should attempt to find an exorcist the first time you cannot find your keys. I just mean that once you do know that you have a problem, attack it with everything you have. End it early if you can. This will save you a lot of grief. We will look at some of the ways to end hauntings in a later chapter. Most hauntings never get past this stage, thank God. Even where there are demons involved, they usually stay at this stage. However, if the entity is inhuman, that is demonic, it may progress to the next stage, although that is not true in every case. In case of an inhuman infestation, an exorcism will be needed to remove the demon.

4) **Possession:** Before we take a closer look at this stage, it must be noted that demonic possession is extremely rare. That cannot be stressed enough. It can happen, it does happen, but you probably have a much better chance of winning a twenty million dollar lottery. Another thing to point out is that a home may be "possessed." This occurs when your home is infested by a demon, so it is really called demonic infestation. I note that only because the solution for possession and infestation is the same: exorcism. A person in the home does not have to be possessed. The Roman Ritual, which is the Rite of Exorcism used by the Catholic Church, has been modified to apply to a location as well as a person.

In order for possession to occur, certain conditions must be met. For one, you would have to be dealing with a very powerful demon. Secondly, in order to possess someone, he would have to have been given some form of permission to enter the victim's body. No one can be possessed without his or her consent. Before we look at the how and why a person would give permission to a demon to possess him, I have heard of stories where a parent cursed their child to the devil. One such case became a book written by David St. Clair. It is: "The Devil Rocked Her Cradle." It was published by Dell books and it is a good one to read. However, I have to admit that I am not sure that I agree that possession can result from the actions of a parent. The sins of the father aside, I cannot imagine God allowing a person the right to give away the soul of an innocent. However, that may be naïve on my part. After all, he allows people to take other people's lives and if you assume that the soul of the child possessed in this manner goes back to God at the time of death, then it could well happen.

So, just why would anyone allow a demon into their lives? Well, it is not always a conscious choice or intention. A demon may trick you into giving it permission. (Nothing is beneath them.) Consider the lonely child who makes friends with the spirit it conjured up when playing with the Ouija board. The spirit, having gained the confidence of the child, may ask if it can go into the child's body for a little while just to feel what it is like to be alive again. The child may well say yes. Is this fair? No, of course not. The devil is never fair. However, the fact of the matter is the demon was given permission. There is no such thing as the age of reasoning when dealing with the devil. This can happen to an adult as well. We know that people can be fooled into letting a spirit take up residence in a house and they can be fooled into letting something inside of them. Again, intent is not an issue here. A demon will get inside a person any way it can.

Another way a demon may get in is by someone giving conscious permission. Believe it or not, people do this. They may be mentally disturbed or they may be seeking power. Whatever the reason, they allow possession to take place. In addition, someone who is practicing Satanism opens the door for possession to take place. Worshipping Satan is willingly allowing him into their lives, not to mention their body. People who use a conjuring spell are open to possession. This person conjures up a demon. That is his game plan from the start. It is safe to say that this person probably has no idea of what he is dealing with. He may think he does but he probably has no real clue. In short, he probably underestimates the demons power. He may believe that since he conjured up the demon, he can also make it go away. That may sound reasonable but it is not the way it works. Demons are not supposed to be in this world. God does not want them to have anything to do with us. He cast them out of heaven and banished them to hell. However, God gave us free will. If we use that free will to invite a demon into our lives, it will come in. The horrible part is that once it is in, we cannot just ask it to leave. It wants to be here. It has a choice, be here or be in hell. Which do you think it will choose? Once here, it will do everything in its power to stay here. The painfully shy person who buys a book on rituals and performs one designed to make himself popular may have just invited a demon in. The newfound popularity may be the result of a demon's work. You have to look at the spell and see who it was directed to. These are some of the ways a demon can get into us.

Although rare, it sometimes appears that good people are singled out as a target of the demonic. One possible reason for that is if you are a bad person, an evil person, you are already doing the devil's work for him. He does not need to possess you. Whether that person is possessed or not, he is already doing what the devil wants. There are sometimes cases where there does not seem to have been an entry point for the demon. Although rare, that does seem to happen. A number of things may have happened. A curse may have been placed on the person. A parent may have been involved in Satanism and promised their child to the devil. Sometimes, a person invites a demon in by giving up on his own life. He may decide he does not want to live anymore and spends his days laying on the couch and drinking himself blind. He may have unwittingly forfeited his life to a demon. If you will not run your life, something else may choose to do the job. There are people who willingly make pacts with the Devil. It sounds insane and unbelievable but it is true. There are many people out there in our world who get themselves into trouble by renouncing God and all of His works. Guess who steps in to fill the void? Then there are the times that we simply cannot explain. Maybe someone has been chosen as the vehicle in the battle of good and evil. That is one theory.

There is good news though. Whether you invited a demon into your life or not, God will expel the demon from you if you truly want it to leave. This is done through the ritual of exorcism. The person must renounce Satan and all evil. Once that is done, an exorcist can begin the process of expelling the demon in the name of God. (Or Jesus Christ if the exorcist is a Christian.) Believe it or not, there are some people who do not want to expel the demon. However much they are suffering, they may enjoy some of the things the devil is giving them. That can be wealth, popularity, or power. If the person does not really want to be freed, then the exorcism is doomed to fail. Indeed, the exorcist will probably chose not to perform the ritual in that case. The person has to want to be freed and he must be willing to work and work hard towards that freedom.

The rite of exorcism can take a long time and there are no guarantees of success. In some cases, many exorcisms are needed. This may be due to the strength of the demon. In some cases, it is as simple as the time is not right yet. There may be purpose to the possession that requires it to last awhile. Only God would know the reason for that. Also, there are two types of possession, full and partial. In full possession, the demon has completely taken over the individual. This is extremely difficult to reverse. The only chance is through the solemn exorcism but it is going to be one big battle. When dealing with this form of possession, there may be few, if any outward symptoms. Perfect possession as this is sometimes called can go unnoticed for what it is. I would have to say someone like Hitler was perfectly possessed. His actions point to possession, even if there are no outward signs or paranormal manifestations.

In partial possession, the demon does not have complete control. The victim retains some control over himself. Consequently, that person has the ability to renounce the demon, which has entered him. He can renounce any practice on his part that led to the possession and he can ask God to forgive his sins. In addition, he can ask God to expel the demon which makes things that much easier for the exorcist. However, no exorcism is easy. In this form of possession, there are usually noticeable outward manifestations. That is the tip off. Also, the person will seem sane some of the time and act bizarre at other times. This mimics mental illnesses but you have to look for the paranormal manifestations. You also have to look for things like a revulsion to religious articles or speaking in a language unknown to the person. The Roman Ritual lists the various signs to look for in a possible case of possession.

5) Death: This is the ultimate sin against God, destroying one of His creatures. For that reason, it is very rare for a death to occur. Once a demon crosses over the line between life and death, God will usually destroy it. The demon knows that. It does not want to be destroyed so it will usually stop short of actually killing a person. However, there are some cosmic loopholes it can exploit. For example, it can use one person to kill another. You would think this amounts to the same thing but it does not. The reason for this is that man has free will. He may be led astray by the devil but he always has the free will to choose. Thus, it is his responsibility, not the demons. In this day and age of not taking responsibility for our actions, that may be a tough pill to swallow. However, that is the way it works, right or wrong.

Demons can and do hurt people, physically as well as mentally. While they may stop short of physically killing you, they may try to make you kill yourself. Again, there is a free will involved, another loophole. Although the demon may be pushing you, if you chose to kill yourself, you did so using your own free will. As much as he may have pushed you, there was an option there. You have to wonder just how many suicides are the result of the devil's work? I guess there is no way to know the answer to that but I bet the numbers are higher than you would think. You also have to realize that the suffering involved in a possession takes a terrible toll on the victim as well as their family. If you are ill to begin with, for example, a person with a bad heart, death may result from the horror of the situation. The strain can be too much for the body to take.

Remember that possession is extremely rare. It should not be a first choice when diagnosing the nature of a haunting. Much harm can be done to a person who is convinced he is possessed. The strain on that person and their family is overwhelming. Many conditions must be met to even begin to think of possession. In addition to the many examples of the outward manifestations found in levels 1, 2 and 3, the possessed person would have to show abilities outside of the natural order of things. These may include super human strength, speaking in a language the victim has no way of knowing, or having knowledge about someone in the room he could not possibly know through normal means. In addition, this person would react violently to the touch of a cross or holy water. Physical changes will also take place in the body of the victim. Facial features may alter. He may speak with a strong accent. Strange marks may appear on the body, such as scratches or burn marks. Unexplainable foul stenches may be smelled through the house. Fires may break out spontaneously. The person involved may levitate or other objects around the house may do so, as well.

Again, possession is extremely rare and in order to further this thinking, many physical and psychological tests must be done to rule out any natural causes for the phenomena. You might think this absurd, especially in light of some of the manifestations taking place but you have to remember, we are not talking about the movies here. You may not see anything as dramatic as you did in the movie "The Exorcist." Remember too that some of the symptoms of demonic possession can mimic many mental illnesses. Before you can even begin thinking possession, all natural explanations must be exhausted first.

In addition, while I was studying hypnosis, we did age regression work. The idea was to bring people back to past lives. While I am still not sure about reincarnation, despite the evidence, I saw some very odd things happen. During one session, I saw the facial features of a very attractive woman turn decidedly masculine. Her skin seemed to grow older and more wrinkled and deep, dark circles formed under her eyes. Although I do not know how it was possible, her lips seemed to become fuller and her blonde hair seemed to darken. That may have been a trick of the light since the room was lit only by a small lamp. I actually moved quietly to a position where I could get a better vantage point. I saw what I saw. (After the session was completed and we all had to give an assessment, the instructor and two others agree that they saw what I saw.) Also, her voice deepened and she lost her natural accent, which was English. She spoke with a thick, German accent and she told quite a story, much of which was later verified. So, you never know. I still am not convinced in the possibility of reincarnation although it seems to make some sense. It also explains a lot. Perhaps my reluctance to embrace that theory is because it does not fit in with my religious training? Another reason is that I hope it is not true; I for one do not want to come back and do this again. Once has been more than enough for me, thank you.

Here are some final thoughts on the stages of a haunting. The time line on this can be very long. The early stages of a haunting could go on for years before it reaches the stage where it becomes obvious that something is wrong. In addition, I need to point out that even in a severe haunting, a level 3 or 4, it is not full-blown activity all the time. You may go through a particularly difficult few weeks and then the activity may stop for days, weeks, and even months. Blessing a house or having a mass said in it may end the problem completely or stop it for a long period. There is no science with a haunting. They seem to have their own rules, when there are rules at all. Again, I want to point out that a haunting is rare and an extremely bad haunting is beyond rare. Do not scare yourself to death thinking about it. As I have said before, I have known investigators who have worked in this field for many, many years and they never encountered anything demonic.

LEVELS OF A HAUNTING

(OVERVIEW)

You will find that there are different types of hauntings. In addition, the severity of a haunting can differ from one to another. Some human spirit hauntings are severe while others are mild. That can even be true to a small extent with a demonic haunting. A haunting involving a minor demon may be slightly worse than a bad human one while others are pure horror. Determining the type and severity of a haunting is no exact science. In many cases, the type and severity can be black or white. In the most severe cases, it is easy to tell what you have; there is also no doubt about the severity. In most cases though, the black and white will come together and you will be left to deal with the shades of gray. There are many of them. This is where you have to be careful. What you might do in a case regarding a benign spirit can have catastrophic results if you are dealing with a demonic spirit. There are certain things you can do in a case of RSPK that will cause you trouble if the problem is really due to a poltergeist. The reverse is true as well.

Telling a family that their problem is a result of RSPK and that they should ignore any activity that is going on can give an invading spirit a very strong foothold that later can cause great harm. Stopping a haunting in the earlier stages can be critical. However, going overboard can also be dangerous. People often do things in a haunting situation that actually exacerbates the problem, no matter how well intentioned those actions are. In addition, the longer an entity is left unchecked, the greater the toll on the victims and the more energy it then has to feed off of. On the other hand, telling a family that they have a poltergeist on their hands will cause them untold fear and misery that is totally avoidable. Imagine how frightened you would feel if someone told you that you have a poltergeist loose in your house. You would be absolutely terrified. It would affect every facet of your life. Imagine if that was unnecessary?

For that reason, I have created a guide intended to make it easier to determine the type and severity of a haunting, if indeed a haunting is what you have. It cannot and should not replace good judgment, common sense, experience, education, or intuition. Intuition by the way is often the best indicator, although you then have to prove that your intuition is correct. What this guide can do give you some parameters with which to work. A good parapsychologist, demonologist, or a light trance medium can probably tell fairly quickly if a problem exists and how severe it is. Still, that should never replace a good investigation because that is where the proof comes from. This scale gives you something to work with. It can give you a good idea of what you are dealing with.

In each level of a haunting, there are particular symptoms inherent to it. It is not necessary to have all of the particular symptoms present to determine the level of the haunting. Sometimes only one or two may be present. Again, we often deal with shades of gray. While the symptoms of a level two haunting have symptoms peculiar to it, it will also have symptoms of a level one haunting. A level three will have elements of a one or a two. In most cases, you will gradually move up the scale. Is it possible to suddenly have symptoms of a level four haunting without experiencing symptoms of a level one to three? Yes, it is possible but that is very rare. In that situation, it is possible that some of the earlier signs were missed although I doubt that you could miss level three symptoms. There is usually a steady progression up the scale. This is not to say that a haunting that goes from a level one to a level two will continue to progress. A haunting may reach a level two and never go higher. Almost invariably though, a level four would have exhibited elements of a one, two, or three.

Listed below are symptoms of paranormal phenomena that you are likely to come across in your travels. Also, it will tell you in which type of haunting you are likely to see them. This list will help you to determine the level and intensity of a haunting you are either experiencing or investigating. Like everything in life, it is not perfect. You may know of phenomena that are not listed here at all and you may experience situations where I have listed something under the category of a Level 4 haunting that you are seeing in a Level 3 haunting. Remember, this is by no means an exact science.

Still, I think you will find this list helpful. It provides you with a good baseline and it will make things a little clearer. In each Level, I will list the symptoms that are generally associated with that type of haunting. For the sake of brevity, I am not going to write the same symptoms over and over again. You can assume that all the phenomena associated in a level 1 haunting will be seen in a Level 2 haunting. A Level 4 haunting will consist of all of the items found in a Level 1, 2, 3 and so on. It must be pointed out that one or two symptoms do not a haunting make. Many, if not most of the items listed can have natural explanations. Never be too quick to blame the preternatural or supernatural until you have exhausted all possible natural explanations first. There are going to be times where the activity witnessed is so gray that it is easy to get confused. Always look for natural explanations first.

Levels Of A Haunting:

Level 1: Energy Imprint
Level 2: Human Spirit
Level 3: Poltergeist
Level 4: Evil Spirit
Level 5: Demonic Spirit

Level 1: Energy Imprint

A "psychic recording" or "energy imprint" is not a true haunting at all since there is no real entity involved. It is classified with a level only because to a person not familiar with it, it appears that a ghost is involved since it looks and acts like one. In a psychic recording, you will see what appears to be an apparition. It may be a misty looking spirit or it could appear solid. In actuality though, it really is not a spirit at all. A psychic recording is energy imprinted into an environment. We know form physics that energy cannot be destroyed but it can change form. The theory behind a psychic recording is that at some point in time, undoubtedly at a time of great stress, someone's energy was "burned" into the environment. An example would be a situation where a woman paced back and forth while waiting for her husband to return home in a terrible storm. It is a Thursday night and her husband always comes home early on Thursday nights. As this woman waited, her anxiety grew and grew. She probably had a feeling that something terrible has happened and no matter how she tried to convince herself that everything was fine, that feeling nagged at her. Finally, she learned that her husband was killed on his way home from work. Her anxiety and grief was so great that it became imprinted in the area. It is almost as if her energy became a motion picture.

Now, imagine that you are living in that house years later. You go downstairs one night at around 11:30pm. It is a Thursday night and a terrible storm is raging. You walk into your den and see this apparition pacing back and forth. The likelihood is that you think you are seeing a ghost. Most of us would, needless to say. You are terrified. You stand there for a minute in total shock and then you run like the dickens. That is a natural reaction. Are you really seeing a ghost? No, what you are seeing is that imprint being projected in that room. There is no actual entity there; it is a replay of what once happened. The terrible emotion that was felt by that lady became part of the environment.

How is it that you lived in that house for a year and never saw this before? Well, the right conditions have to have been met. It would have to have been a Thursday night and there would have to be a storm raging. In addition, it would have to be the same time. The conditions would have to be *identical* to the conditions at the time the recording was made. Perhaps you were never in that room at the same time and under the same weather conditions. In addition, you might not have been on the same frequency as that woman. What does that mean? If you look at a psychic recording as a transmission, in order to receive it you would need a receiver that is on the same frequency. This is why two people in a room see an apparition while two others do not see it. Their brains are not capable of picking up the transmission. Some people are just more open to things like that.

How do you tell the difference between a real ghost and a psychic recording? The best way to determine the difference is to see if the "entity" reacts to you. Of course, you need to stick around a few minutes to tell that. If the apparition does not react to you, it is likely a psychic recording. If it does react to you, then it is likely a ghost. Another way to tell is to see if there appears to be any intelligence behind its activity or is it just playing out a scene almost mindlessly. In addition, in a psychic recording, the apparition will continue to do the same thing repeatedly each time it appears. It will never deviate from that repetitious cycle. It is possible to hear sounds as well. The energy imprint is not limited to a visual phenomenon. You might hear something like a telephone ringing. Then the apparition, if there is one, may disappear. That might be followed by a scream or gut-wrenching sobbing. By the way, I have heard stories where there have been energy imprints of people still living. I am skeptical of that because there is only anecdotal evidence involved but the theory makes sense. Why would you have to be dead for the recording to stick? Let us take a look at the type of activity you are likely to see at that level.

Common Manifestations

1) Manifestation that appears to be a ghost but is actually a psychic recording.
2) Footsteps.
3) Crying or sobbing. It is rare but you sometimes hear words.

Level 2: A Human Spirit

When it comes to the human spirit, you have basically two types: you have the benign spirit and the nasty one. For that reason, I will list benign spirits as **A)** and the unpleasant ones as **B)**.

A) A benign spirit is any spirit that does not mean harm to anyone. This is by far the most common type of spirit and the one you are most likely to encounter. For that matter, you probably have encountered one but you did not know it was a spirit. Although they will sometimes do things that frighten you, that is not their intention. (Remember my examples?) More often than not, we are scared because we misunderstand the spirits intentions. Examples of this will be cited later in this section. There are usually two types of benign spirits. One is the playful type. This type usually acts like a mischievous child, which it could very well be. I refer to this type of spirit as an "imp," although some books consider an imp to be a minor demon. An example of the type of thing a playful spirit may do is tie your shoelaces together or remove them entirely. You will then find them in some unusual place like your freezer. These types of spirits account for some of those cases of invisible playmates that children often have. This is not to say that all invisible playmates are spirits. Any parent can attest to that. Sometimes though, the child really does see their invisible friend. Children are naturally psychic up to the age of around 12, which enables them to see these spirits more easily. As the child matures, that sixth sense begins to be replaced by the other five. In time, the child loses the ability to see its playmate. Again, this type of spirit means no harm.

Another example of a benign spirit is one who died tragically and is having trouble believing and accepting the fact that it has passed over. That spirit is stuck between our physical plane and the other realm. This is a spirit that can be guided to the light. This can often be done by a light trance medium and in some cases by those who were close to the spirit in life. You do this by telling the spirit to ask for a spirit guide to help it find the light. Very often, that spirit guide is a relative or close friend. In some cases, it can be a beloved pet. Once the spirit accepts the fact that it has died and it is guided to the light, the haunting phenomena stops.

Sometimes spirits are tied to the physical plane because they feel they have unfinished business to attend to. They may be worried about a loved one and want to watch over them. In some instances, they are held back because of reluctance on their part to leave behind some material things. They too can be guided to the light once you have figured out why they have chosen to remain. That can be the difficult part because you first have to figure out who they are first. After you have done that, you then have to figure out what is keeping them there.

Sometimes a benign spirit will frighten us. That is true but it is not necessarily intentional on their part. Having a door slam shut can certainly frighten you. Having a vase of flowers go flying off a table can be scary too. When these things happen, you may begin to think you are having a poltergeist manifestation. The phenomena are similar. What often happens though is that the spirit does not know how to communicate with you. This is especially true with a spirit that has just passed over. The spirit may panic when it realizes that something is not right. It has not been part of that plane long enough to know how to communicate with the living or the dead for that matter. It may try very hard to communicate but it just cannot do it. All it may be able to do is push a picture off a table or slam a door. This frightens you, which in turn makes the spirit want to communicate with you all the more to alleviate your fears. The more it wants to communicate, the harder it may try. Not realizing how to communicate, you get more activity that is just a burst of energy. That may be all that the spirit *can* do. It becomes the proverbial vicious cycle. At some point in time, the spirit may finally decide to leave on its own or after a spirit guide comes for it. A level 2 haunting is never evil or vicious. If there appears to be malevolent intent behind any activity, you are dealing with a level 3 haunting or above.

B) The flip side of the benign spirit is the one who seems to be on the nasty side. The type of spirit we are talking about here is not the evil human spirit. We will take a look at that type of spirit shortly. What we are looking at here is the spirit who will occasionally do frightening and even some out and out bad things but is not an evil entity like the ones we will see when we see the Level 4 haunting. This type of spirit is one who was generally unhappy while alive. He may have been short-tempered, grouchy and mean. His physical death has not brought him any new insight because he refuses to leave the earth plane. The house he lived in was *his* and in his mind, it always will be. So, when you move in, he views you as a trespasser and he will do everything in his power to get you out of *his* house. Fortunately, there really is not all that much that he *can* do to you. The majority of his antics are designed to frighten you or make your life so uncomfortable that you choose to leave. The key to dealing with this type of spirit is to not be intimidated by him. He cannot hurt you and once you realize that, the haunting will become easier to tolerate. The key to getting rid of him is to know who he is. If you can identify him, you may be able to convince him to leave. Sometimes the nasty human spirit will stop his pestering once he realizes that the people who moved into *his* house really love it. If you cannot find out who he is, it is still possible to make him leave. A psychic may be able to get through to him and convince him to depart. (We will discuss this at greater length in a later chapter.)

Common Manifestations

1) Moving objects.
2) Hearing a voice. (Voices are rare at this level.)
3) Seeing unexplainable lights.
4) Light knockings. This is not the pounding found in Levels 3 to 5.
5) Shaking or vibrations. (Usually mild.)
6) Child's imaginary friend is seen or heard.
7) Footsteps.
8) Small objects may break.
9) Odd odors although not necessarily foul. It may be more like cigar smoke or the like.

LEVEL 3: We have spent a good deal of time on the poltergeist so let's just do a quick recap. "True" poltergeist explosions can be very destructive although there are usually not physically dangerous. However, seeing objects precious to you destroyed can certainly inflict serious wounds to you mental state. Poltergeist manifestations are similar to RSPK although the objects moved can be heavy. Poltergeist type manifestations are sometimes indicative of stepping-stone hauntings. Poltergeists are believed to be lower demonic spirits. The destruction and bizarre activity often stops as quickly and inexplicable as it started.

Common Manifestations

1) Rapping. These are loud and tend to be fast.
2) Pounding in the walls. There is no mistaking this.
3) Objects that explode or suddenly fall apart.
4) Severe shaking or vibrations. These will feel much like an earthquake.
5) Apports. Things coming from nowhere.
6) Asports. Things that disappear.
7) Teleportation. Things that disappear and reappear elsewhere. (Most likely seen in a stepping stone case.)
8) Spontaneous combustion. Fires.
9) Plumbing leaks. These just seem to come from nowhere.
10) Toilets flushing by themselves.
11) Holes bashed in walls.
12) Furniture unexplainably breaking.
13) Furniture or other items that seem to arrange themselves.
14) Doors and windows which open and close by themselves.
15) Drawers which open and close.
16) Phones that ring but no one is on the other end.
17) Electrical appliances that turn themselves on and off.

Level 4: Evil Spirits

In this category, we are going to discuss evil human spirits. You may wonder why we would go from a demonic force in level three to a human one in level four. I will explain that shortly. In this level, we are not dealing with the nasty spirit that we encountered in Level 2. This spirit means business. It becomes what I call "a haunting with a purpose." Since it is a human spirit, it ability to hurt anyone is limited. However, it may try to get you to hurt yourself. They way it will do this is by trying to scare you into running up or down stairs where you may, in your haste, trip and fall. They will also try to trip you up, if given the chance. They can do severe harm to you mentally. The terror they evoke can cause severe harm to your psyche, which can, and often does, result in physical illness. Sleep patterns are destroyed and you find yourself feeling helpless and frustrated. This can lead to clinical depression. The evil spirit loves to feed off this.

Before we go any further, let us discuss the makeup of the evil spirit. In most, if not all cases, these people were very angry in life. They were mean, selfish, cruel people. Many people are under the misconception that when we die and cross over, we suddenly attain great wisdom and become kind and loving spirits. That is just not so. While some progress may be made at the time of passing, nasty people become nasty spirits. They just have a bigger audience now. A person who was good in life is not going to turn evil when he dies unless maybe he or a loved one is a victim of a terrible crime. If you had a situation where maybe an adult died while watching a loved one being brutalized, he may seek revenge on the ones who committed the crime although there is not much he would be able to do. It is also possible that a previously deceased loved one might come over and guide him across. The possibility also exists that the same thing could happen to someone who was evil in life. Being nasty in life does not *guarantee* that the spirit will remain earthbound as an evil spirit. He too may be guided across by a loved one.

The thing that makes evil human spirits so dangerous is because they often attract demonic spirits. Their negativity and evil intent draws demonic spirits like a chum line draws sharks. That is why I list them as being more serious than a poltergeist explosion. You are not really dealing with a demonic haunting, yet anyway. What does happen is that the demonic spirit or spirits will start to use the human spirit to do its dirty work. It will, in effect, "puppeteer" the human spirit. This is an effective strategy because the demon is safe from attack. No one is going to try to exorcise the demon because no one knows that it is there. With the backing of the demon, the evil spirit can do more to scare the victims. There are manifestations that you would not ordinarily see in a human haunting.

There are ways to combat them. Prayer is very effective. Sprinkling holy water is also very effective, as is having the home blessed. For the most part, these entities want no part in a fight with God and will usually depart once it starts to get a little too hot for them. However, it can be a long battle. You have to protect yourself as much as possible, especially against the emotional attacks they mount. You have to realize that they want to feed on your terror and any other negative emotion they can create. They try to wear you down. The weaker you get, the stronger they get. The stronger they get, the more they can wear you down. That is the game plan. You have to be alert to this and try your best to deal with it. Your belief in God will always beat them and you must keep that in mind. It will make you stronger and them weaker. In other words, reverse their game plan. I have mentioned before that blessing a house with holy water might provoke a demonic entity. It often will but that is when you have a Level 5 haunting. In this case, the demon is not actually doing the haunting. Instead, it has its new lackey to do that. Once the holy water starts flying, the demonic spirit will often leave rather than be realized. Once that happens, you are back to dealing with Level 2 type human haunting. However, in some cases, the demon will decide that it likes the situation and that is when you have a Level 5 haunting, which we will now take a look at. One last word on the evil spirit, I know this one sounds impossible but try your best not to give recognition to the spirit. That is hard to do when the TV turns itself on and off while you are trying to watch it. It is somewhat hard to calmly say, "Pass me the salt, honey, I think it just flew onto the porch". Still, you have to try. They love recognition because with recognition comes fear. Above all, try to remain positive. That is so important. Remember that your faith in God will overcome them.

Common Manifestations

1) Seeing "odd" visions. This is seeing something that suddenly does not look normal.
2) Experience severe nightmares or night terrors.
3) Unexplainable fear. This is usually a precursor to more serious events.
4) Writing on mirrors or on the walls. (Usually very foul language.)
5) Telephone calls with a voice on the other end. It usually threatens you.
6) Unexplained difficulty breathing.
7) Attempts to injure you by frightening you into doing something dangerous.
8) Unexplainable feelings of rage or sadness or depression.

9) Levitation of light items.
10) Threatening voices.
11) Unexplained sounds.
12) Unexplained distress in children or animals.
13) Observing children and animals that appear to be visually following something.
14) Animals suddenly becoming terrified and running away.
15) Animals suddenly growl or otherwise become protective.
16) Children or animals that react fearfully and refuse to go into a room.
17) Unexplainable temperature changes. "Psychic" cold or heat.
18) TV or radio channels change by themselves.
19) Heat or AC turns itself on or off.
20) Clocks stop working.
21) Alarm is manipulated so that you miss important functions.

Level 5: Demonic Spirits.

"Houston, we have a problem!" That pretty much sums up the level 5 haunting. In a level 5 haunting, the worst of all possible scenarios have taken place. You are now dealing with a demon from hell. There is no worse imaginable situation known to man. Demons are inhuman spirits, in other words, they have never lived as a human. Therefore, they are not subject to the laws of nature that restrict us. They are the fallen angels. Demons have one goal. That goal is to destroy, any way it can, *any* creature of God. That is its sole purpose. It will resort to anything to hurt you as badly as it can. It will fight dirty, it will exhibit cruelty unimaginable to even the worst mankind has to offer. While it is felt that a demon will rarely physically kill you, it will gladly accept your killing yourself.

There is some debate as to why demons cannot, or more accurately, rarely kill humans. The most common theory is that although they are not subject to the same laws of nature that we are, even they fear God's wrath. It is felt that if a demon were to kill a human, God would instantly destroy him. He may be God's sworn enemy but like it or not, he was created by God and can thus be destroyed by Him as well. It would seem then that there are some rules that a demon must follow. He can battle man and try to destroy him or make him destroy himself, but man has the ability to fight back. He can attempt to destroy a human's will, but remember, we do have free will and it is up to use to utilize it properly. We can and must resist the attack by a demonic entity.

Demons want to possess humans. It is the ultimate act of defiance against God. It wants to corrupt that which God made in His image and likeness. While demonic possession is extremely rare, it does happen. There are different levels of demonic possession. In partial possession, a person still maintains some free will. That will is under constant attack but it is still there. In perfect possession, the demon has totally taken over the human host. The individual now has no control over himself. Free will is gone. In the case of partial possession, it *may* be possible to free the victim using prayers of deliverance, depending on the strength of the entity. Deliverance rituals are similar to an exorcism but are a lesser version of it. In the case of full possession, the only way to combat it is through a solemn exorcism. Why the difference? The partially possessed person has an advantage in that he can renounce the demon and ask God for help. This is a great aid to the exorcist. The partially possessed person has the ability to battle for his life and his soul. Although at times, his will is suppressed, he still has that little bit in him that the demon has not taken and he can use that bit to ask for God's help directly.

The partially possessed person may function quite normally at times. Then, out of nowhere, the demon may rear his ugly head. Interestingly enough, the fully possessed person usually functions quite well. That is the strategy of the demon. Since he acts seemingly rationally, he can escape detection and that enables him to be able to carry out his evil deeds, whatever they may be. My belief is that serial killers and people without consciences are fully possessed. I often wonder how many people are locked up in mental institutions because they are possessed as opposed to being mentally ill. I am sure that it happens from time to time. In those instances, you would be talking partial possession. It is a double whammy for the victim because he may well be mentally ill and be partially possessed. To the treating psychiatrist, he represents a person not responding to medical treatment. Sadly, that person may rarely if ever be able to function in the outside world.

Demons are capable of defying the laws of nature. They can appear as anything they want. They can speak in a human voice. They can teleport objects, even make them disappear. They can levitate objects, including people and animals. They will produce horrible smells, destroy anything they so choose, and they *will* attack man. They are capable of inflicting bites, slashes, and burns. They will destroy religious objects. That, by the way is one sure sign of demonic involvement. The assaults they unleash are relentless. They will tempt you to do the vilest things. They are capable of making humans do unimaginably cruel and heinous things to each other. They revel in man's perversions. They are driving force behind some of the most atrocious of people and the things they do. Is there any doubt that Hitler was a demon?

Demons can be combated. The only way to combat them is through God. You must believe in Him and pray. Prayer is the only way to beat a demon. If you are a Christian, you must pray to Jesus Christ. Through Him, demons can be sent back to the fires of hell. Demons are bullies and they must be treated as such. Do not give them recognition! Do your absolute best not to discuss them in the home. Do not give them any advantages. When activity suddenly breaks out, imagine yourself in a God light, a protective light where the demon cannot get to you. Do not play its game. Give it as little recognition as possible. Try not to be afraid of them. That must sound impossible to do. Still, try not to be afraid. They are bullies and they want you to fear them. They want you to think that they are invincible. They most certainly are not. However as much as they like to think they are invincible, they are still creations of God, just like we are. God does not want them to destroy us. As long as we believe in Him and trust in Him, we can defeat them. When you believe that, you will find they are not as terrifying as they seemed before. Also, when activity breaks out, command them in the name of God to stop the activity immediately. Say this in as forceful a tone as you are capable of. You will also find that holy water can put an end to the activity. Use it.

In cases of possession, we know that the Rite of Exorcism is used. However, exorcism is also used to clear a dwelling from demonic influences. In extreme cases, an exorcism is the only thing that will stop the horrors. An ordained member of the clergy should perform the exorcism. Here is something you probably do not know: any Christian can perform an exorcism. While I would never recommend it, there is a biblical precedence. In Mark16, verses 15 through 17 Jesus says to His Apostles, "Go into the world and preach the gospel to every creature. He who believes and is baptized will be saved; but he who does not believe will be condemned. And these signs will follow those who believe: In My name they will cast out demons; they will speak with new tongues. They will take up serpents; and if they drink anything deadly, it will by no means hurt them; they will lay hands on the sick and they will recover."

According to the Catholic Church, any Catholic can perform an exorcism *in an emergency.* The key words there are in an emergency. Again, I would never recommend that you try to perform an exorcism yourself. Unless you are specifically trained to do this, you are inviting a world of trouble. Only specialized clergy should try this. This is the circumstance in which a demon or diabolical spirit may try to take a life. Eternal nothingness may be better than eternal damnation. Having said all of that, know that you can do it in an emergency. If worse comes to worse and a life is on the line, you do what you have to do. Bear something in mind; demons will retaliate when you attempt to stop them. If you bless the house, they may retaliate. If you call in outside help, they may retaliate. You have to know this. However, what is the alternative, give in to them? That is no solution.

Preparing The Family

Whenever I start a case, I always sit down with the family and give them a lot of information. I explain to them how hauntings work, what the strategies are and I explain what I can do and what I cannot do for them. I also explain to them that depending on what type of spirit we are dealing with, they can expect retaliation. Obviously, if something wants to stay there, it will fight. However, I also tell them that the spirit is not going to do anything in retaliation that it was not *already* planning to do. Evil spirits have no decency. They have no kindness. They are not going to say, "Well, these poor people are pretty tired tonight. Maybe I will leave them alone for a few days." That just does not happen. They are incapable of compassion. So, in that sense, all that is happening is that we are simply speeding the process up. We are just throwing off its strategy. Fighting a demon is a battle to the end. You are engaged in a war, pure and simple. There is no other way to describe it. There is no way to sugar coat it. It is a war. However, it is a war that you can win. You have to believe in that. You have to have faith. Only prayer and faith can stop a demon.

You also have to be willing to see it through. As an investigator, there can be no turning back if the situation gets hairy. Once you have engaged a demon in battle, you cannot walk away and hope that it leaves you alone. That is not going to happen. The evil spirit is not going to let you off that easy. You can expect that it will continue to bother you even after you have dropped the case. That is pone reason why I always stress knowing your role and not going beyond that. It may sound cool to your friends when you tell them how you are going to battle a demonic force. However, once you start that, you are in it until the end, whether you like it or not. For that reason, always make sure you are willing to go the distance come hell or high water. That is why you have to make an accurate diagnosis and then turn to the people who are experienced in dealing with that type of spirit.

While it would not be called possession, a house infested by demons would need to be exorcised. That is the only way in which to end the siege, although I should point out that in some cases where you are dealing with a minor demon, having a Mass said in the house may work. A demon infesting a house will attempt to possess someone if it is given the time to do that. For that reason, it is vitally important that you quickly identify a demonic presence. The more time it has to wear someone down, the better the chance that a victim will fall into possession. A person can only take so much before there is a breakdown in their will. Demons are very persistent. They are also bloodthirsty. If they detect that a person's will is beginning to crumble, they will pounce on that individual in a second. Such is the nature of these deplorable beings. They are parasites in the truest sense of the word.

Never Give Up

At some point during the war, you will feel tired and beaten. That is only natural. A battle with demonic forces can become a battle of attrition. However, you must not let this happen. As hard as it may be, you have to have the will to fight; you have to resist it. You always have to remember that demons have a game plan. You must have one too. They are cunning and they will stop at nothing to get what they want. They play dirty and so must you. Do not fight a demon on its terms; fight it on yours. Make your home a place where no demon wants to be. Fill your home with love and life. Once you are involved in a level 5 haunting, you have little to lose by fighting back.

Common Manifestations

1) Desecration of religious objects.
2) Dematerialization of objects, which are never found. (Often money.)
3) Teleportation of heavy objects. An example would be finding your couch in the attic.
4) Bi-location of objects. Two people are seeing something in different places.
5) Growling or other animal noises. (Pigs and goats are the most common.)
6) Finding hoof prints or other animal prints.
7) Finding fecal matter, urine or vomit with no apparent cause.
8) Sudden, unexplainable illnesses.
9) Destruction of objects precious to an individual.
10) Retaliation after attempts to combat it. (Prayers, investigations, holy water.)
11) Hallucinations, visual, audio, or kinesthetic.
12) Levitation of heavy objects, people, or animals.
13) Psychic sleep, where you cannot wake up a person, or an animal.
14) Twilight paralysis. This is where you are conscious but are held immobile. (This has happened to me in a demonic infestation but it

has also happened to me in a house where I was sure the spirit was human. More gray area.)

15) Rape by an invisible entity. (Incubus or succubus. Can be same demon.)
16) Being bitten, slashed, burned, by an unseen entity.
17) Seeing phantom animals, people or cars.
18) Deliberate attempts to injure such as tripping or pushing someone down stairs.
19) Being touched or caressed by unseen entity. (Often sexual in nature)
20) Hair pulling by unseen entity. (Strong)
21) Objects disappear then reappear in the same spot.
22) Lights that will not go on.
23) Telephone does not work when you attempt to get help.
24) Prevention of others to help you. (Illness, car failure, faulty phone, etc.)
25) Telephone conversation with someone, later you learn that he was not home.
26) Car will not start when you attempt to flee. (Yours or others.)
27) Car breaks down when someone tries to come to your aid.
28) Unexplained substances appear.
29) You are prevented from going to Church.
30) Pictures or other items ripped from walls.
31) Unexplained flooding in your home.
32) Finding blood splattered around.
33) Electrical appliances work when not plugged in.
34) Furniture or clothes shredded.
35) Religious objects disappear.
36) Cold water suddenly becomes scalding hot or vice versa.
37) Food rots even when frozen.
38) Plants or flowers suddenly die or will not grow.
39) Pets are injured or die unexplainably.
40) Foul odors, the source of which cannot be explained and cannot be stopped.
41) Scratching sounds, usually in the walls.
42) Finding claw marks on a door or wall. (Three claw marks are especially bad.)

To Sum It Up

Fortunately, demonic hauntings are rare. However, should you find yourself a victim of paranormal attack, there is hope. Of course, it is critical that you be able to tell the difference between a human spirit and an inhuman one. My hope is that this guide will help you determine that. It gives you some parameters with which to work. Again, you do not have to see all of the items listed take place to be able to make your determination. You might have a bunch of things that fit the level two category and only one that fits a level three. Don't rush to judgment. However, it can happen that only on item will take place that is in a higher category and it may well be an accurate assessment that it is indeed a higher or more serious haunting. You really have to look at the whole picture to be sure.

GETTING OUTSIDE HELP

(Human Spirits)

Once you have determined the problem, you need to look into ways to end the phenomena. How to accomplish that depends on what you are dealing with. If you are dealing with a benign, human spirit, you may be able to solve the problem on your own. Human spirits may remain earthbound for a number of reasons. They may feel they have unfinished business to deal with. They may be staying because they are watching over someone they love. In some instances, they do not realize they have passed over. This is often the case when they died suddenly and violently. They may be having a difficult time understanding their physical death or accepting it. Many times, spirits remain earthbound simply because they do not know how to fully cross over. We will look at this more closely in the next chapter.

If that is the case, you can try to communicate with it and direct it to the light. If you are dealing with a spirit that does not realize it is dead, you may be able to convince it that it needs to pass over. Having someone with discernment with you can make this much easier. That person may be able to communicate with the spirit directly. You can advise the spirit to ask a spirit guide to help it go into the light. Predeceased loved ones will often come back and help them. In many cases, that is all it takes.

A Negative Human Spirit

That is not the case when you are dealing with a negative, human spirit. Directing it to move into the light may not be effective at all. The negative spirit may have no desire to leave. In that case, prayer may be helpful. As a rule, negative human spirits do not want a quarrel with God. Once they are faced with prayer, they will often leave or at least stop the haunting. This may take some time and a lot of prayer but it is usually effective. Having the residence blessed by a member of the clergy and having a Mass said will often end the problem. A qualified demonologist may be able to do some things on his own to stop the problem but that is not something a paranormal investigator should try. When dealing with negative spirits, you always have to consider the possibility that you are dealing with a puppeteer.

Demons and Negative Human Spirits

There is another possibility when dealing with a negative, human spirit. In cases of demonic infestation, the demon will often use the human spirit's energy and make the human spirit do its dirty work. In that case, you have a big problem on your hands. The human spirit may not be able to leave even if he wanted to, which he might. Of course, in the case of a demonic haunting, the human spirit is the least of your worries. Getting rid of the human spirit will not stop the haunting. You are going to have to deal with the demon and that will not be easy. Depending on the power of the demon, there is a very good chance that you will have to seek outside help to accomplish that. If you are successful in getting rid of the demon, the human spirit will leave too. For that matter, he will probably have left before the demonic spirit was forced out. One the demon is under assault, its grip on the human spirit weakens and at that point, the human spirit usually takes off. I have never heard of a case where a demonic spirit was repelled only to have a human spirit remain behind. The likelihood of that happening is very small.

DEVILS

I will make this section brief. There has always been a debate about the hierarchy of evil. Is there one devil? Are Satan and Lucifer one and the same? Is there any way to answer these questions? That is actually the only one of these questions that I will answer and that answer is "no," there really is no way to tell. Each religion and culture, for that matter has its own beliefs on the subject. Much of what we do know about the evil hierarchy has come from the mouths of those possessed. Still, that is no definitive. Rather than go into a debate, I will tell you my theory and I will pretty much leave it at that. In the end, it really does not matter.

I personally believe that there is one main devil, call him Lucifer or Satan. I think he is one and the same. I also believe that there are several devils, although I think few, if any involve themselves in the affairs of man. Demons and devils are supposedly the fallen angels. I would then consider the devils as of the rank of archangel. It is only a title. Those archangels battle with the good ones. That is why I think they pretty much ignore man. That and the fact man needs no help in screwing up the world. We do that quite well all by ourselves. Thus, we need to be concerned with the demons. If it turned out that a devil was causing a haunting instead of a demon, the solution would be the same, exorcism. It would just end up being a tougher battle.

MINOR AND MAJOR DEMONS

There are different types of demons, minor and major. The minor demons can do only so much damage but that "so much" is unbelievable. By no means can you take them lightly. Make no mistake: a demon is still a demon. A poltergeist is a minor demon but we all know what they are capable of. They are capable of causing a considerable amount of misery. Major demons are very powerful and they are capable of inflicting a great deal of suffering. They are extremely difficult to get rid of. Expelling a minor demon is not easy either but comparatively speaking, it is, *easier.* The likelihood is that you will not be able to get rid of a demon on your own, whether it is a minor or a major one.

Prayer can help; there is no question about that. It is possible that you can get rid of a minor demon through prayer but it would be extremely difficult. Do not try to do it on your own. Demons retaliate and if all you succeed in doing is making it angry, you are in for big trouble. Part of the problem is that it can be very difficult to tell whether it is a minor or major demon. If you are wrong and try to get rid of a major one without the proper help, you are opening yourself up to a world of hurt. You may be anyway.

Is It A Minor or Major Demon?

How can you tell whether it is a minor or major demon? That can be quite difficult. Obviously, a major demon has much more power than a minor one but even the minor demons are capable of some terrifying things. You really need the help of a demonologist to tell the difference between the two. Truthfully, you should not attempt anything on your own anyway. Ridding a home of a demon should be left to those who are specifically trained in that area. You are courting catastrophe if you try it. A demonologist or a well trained experienced, paranormal investigator can tell the difference. I want to make a point here. As I write this, I know what I have to say and I am saying it. However, when you get into devil/demon or minor/major, it is all relative. Does it make a difference if a fire is burning at 500 degrees or 1200 degrees? The answer would be yes. However, it would make no difference to the person trapped inside. He is going to cook and it really does not matter to him what then temperature is. Either way, he is dead and on his way to becoming a ghost. So, in that regard, it probably does not matter what you are dealing with. Odds are though, whichever level you are dealing with, you will need to look for outside help. So, where do you go for help?

Where Do You Get Outside Help?

When you are dealing with a demonic entity, you are going to need the help of trained members of your religious faith. This is usually not easy, depending on your religion and the severity of your problem. For example, having your house blessed should get rid of any negative human spirits. It can sometimes eliminate a minor demon. Usually, a Mass is necessary when dealing with a minor one. When faced with particularly difficult minor demons and all major demons, a solemn exorcism is necessary. That is where the problem comes in.

Any priest or minister can bless a house or say a Mass in one. A member of the clergy who specializes in this must perform an exorcism. While any priest *can* perform an exorcism, a local pastor does not usually do them. However, although any priest can do it, he cannot do it without the approval of his Bishop. If you are a member of a congregation, it is not hard to get a priest or minister to bless your house. Even if you are not a member of the congregation, it might hard to arrange for a blessing, let alone something more. As I said earlier, I heard one story where a priest told someone that the church does not bless houses anymore. It depends on the priest. Where you may run into trouble is explaining why you feel the need to have it done. You do not want to lie and just say that it is something you have always been meaning to do but never got around to it. I do not know how effective a blessing would be if it was done under false pretenses. You would have to be honest and explain your situation if you really hope to end the siege you are experiencing. Beside that, you do not want to subject the priest to any unnecessary danger. There certainly can be danger if it is a demon causing the problem. For his safety, he needs to know why he is there.

The problem is either that many members of the clergy do not believe in spirits or they are afraid to deal with them. That must sound weird. How could a member of the clergy not believe in spirits? You would be surprised. However, even if they do not believe in spirits, they will most likely bless your home. You will find it more difficult trying to have a Mass said. They may not say the Mass for dealing with the haunting but they will most likely do it anyway if they are caring enough about your welfare. You may be fortunate enough to know a member of the clergy who does believe in hauntings and has experience in dealing with it. You are very lucky indeed if that is the case.

The big problem arises when a powerful demon is present. The only way to eliminate that type of demon is through the Rite of Exorcism. When people hear the word exorcism, they automatically assume that a person is possessed. Keep in mind that an exorcism can be performed on a place as well as on a person. In cases of demonic infestation of a location, an exorcism of that location will be necessary to eliminate the demon. A clergyman of the same denomination as you should perform the exorcism. This can get tricky because not all Christian churches *have* a rite of exorcism. If that were the case, you would have to go outside of your denomination for help. This is not to say that an exorcism performed by a Catholic priest will not work if you are not a Catholic. It is just that where possible, you should have it done within your own denomination. Many of the Protestant denominations do what they call "Deliverance." This is actually a form of exorcism although it is regarded to be less powerful than a Catholic solemn exorcism. However, it can be very difficult to get the Catholic Church to perform an exorcism, for out of necessity, they must take precautions. Every time a movie about an exorcism comes on, thousands of phone calls are made to the church by people who believe that they or someone they know is possessed. There are many emotionally disturbed people out there.

Conditions For An Exorcism

The Church's conditions are very strict, which they should be. The Church will only authorize an exorcism after they have done a thorough investigation. Again, that is fine. This is why *you* need to do a thorough and professional investigation. It is especially important how you present your conclusions to the Church authorities. The more professional and sensible you appear, the better your chances are of getting them to listen and if you are lucky, they will believe you and use some of your own evidence. They may use much of your evidence to satisfy some of their conditions. This can save considerable time and time is very important to the family being terrorized. The big problem is getting the Catholic Church to begin an investigation. The obvious first step is to go to your local priest and discuss the situation with him. This priest may already be involved if he was the one who either blessed the home or said a Mass in it, or both. If he did say a Mass in a demonically infested home, there is a good chance that he himself may have experienced some of the phenomena and that can really help your cause. He will most likely be believed before you are. If this particular priest did the blessing but made it obvious that he did not think the problem was supernatural or preternatural, he most likely will not help you in attempting to get an exorcism performed. If your priest is open-minded, he himself may go to the local Bishop and put in a request for an investigation. Even if the local priest does not believe you, have him set up an appointment for you anyway.

Either way, the Bishop will make the decision. If your parish priest will not help you with contacting the Bishop, you or the family will have to do it. This can be a very difficult and frustrating process. A big part of the problem is that people will often think you are insane. There is a good chance that the family has sounded hysterical in their attempts to get help. When you consider the strain they are under, that is not surprising. This is where it helps if the investigators have established a favorable reputation. The Bishop and his staff will then probably take the investigators seriously. For this reason, it is important to develop a favorable relationship with members of the clergy of all denominations.

It may take quite awhile to reach the Bishop himself, if you can at all. You will have to go through his staff and that may be frustrating, at the very least. Where you live will play a pivotal role in getting help from the church. The Catholic Church is known for it unbending rigidity in almost all things. Oddly enough, in matters of the supernatural, there is considerable leeway. The Bishop of the diocese has total control in the matter. If that Bishop does not believe in things supernatural, he alone can prevent an exorcism. On the other hand, if the Bishop of that diocese does believe in demons and the need for exorcisms, you may find the road a little easier to travel. He can then set up an investigation and start the process of having all of the necessary conditions met. Once he is satisfied that the situation is indeed demonic, he will then authorize an exorcism and assign someone to that task.

As paranormal investigators, we need to be aware of those conditions necessary to prove that the problem is diabolical. By knowing this, you can gather evidence and document the phenomena. Hopefully, the priest assigned to do the investigation may well use your evidence, cutting down the work he must do and speeding up the process. These conditions are things we have already covered to some extent. In order to meet the standards of the church, there must be clear-cut evidence of occurrences that are outside the realm of nature. In the case of a home, sightings count to an extent. The movements of heavy objects would count as another. Disembodied voices and desecration of religious objects qualify as conditions. Any outward manifestations are considered as long as they are outside the bounds of nature. One of the problems with infestation of a home is the demon will often remain still while the church investigates. That is more reason why the investigators must do a thorough investigation and have solid proof of their claims. Especially look for things that defy the laws of physics and document those as best you can.

Possession Of A Person

Possession of a person is somewhat different. First, it has to be determined that there is no form of mental illness present. This can be tricky because demons often pick on the mentally ill. They are very vulnerable to begin with and what better place to hide than in a person who no one believes. It is a perfect setting. If mental illness is ruled out, it is necessary to perform medical tests to eliminate any possibility of a medical condition causing the phenomena. This sounds silly but there are cases where medical problems, such as brain tumors cause what seems to be supernatural. One example of this would be voices. Midline brain tumors sometimes result in a person speaking in what sounds like different voices. Diseases such as Parkinson's and Bells palsy can result in pronounced tremors. They can appear to make a bed shake. Someone with Tourette's syndrome may sound possessed. All of that has to be considered.

One of the conditions the church recognizes is speaking in a language that the victim could not know. Speaking backwards is a condition, as well as knowing information that the victim could not possibly know. The information is usually about someone present. In addition, violent reactions to holy water or other sacred objects qualify as a condition. Inhuman or superhuman strength is another condition although that can be hard to determine and even harder to document. What constitutes inhuman and how do you prove it? It would be nice to have a picture of the victim holding a grand piano in one hand but you are not going to get a shot like that. Indisputable evidence almost never comes around, especially when you have a camera in your hand. In many cases of possession, marks may appear on the body of the victim. (This is called *demography.*) These marks may form words or they can appear as a cross or other object. Assaults by unseen forces are another indicator. Knowledge of past events that the victim could not know or knowledge of future events also qualifies. Knowledge of future events would have to be short term. Obviously, there is no way to verify something that is predicted for 20 years from now.

Once enough of the conditions have been met, approval for the exorcism is given. It is important to note that not all of the conditions must be met. Actually, there is no set number of conditions required. The Bishop will study the evidence and make his decision based on the evidence and the opinion of the investigator he assigned to the case. He will then assign an exorcist to the case and he then authorizes the exorcism. The priest selected will likely be an older one. The Roman Ritual recommends a "man of mature years." I always wondered about that. In my mind, I would think that you would want someone young and strong available. Well, you do but you want that person and a few others to be there as assistants. I now understand the reasoning. I have thought a lot about cases I experienced, really bad cases. I then thought about those who I know who really care about doing this work. I do not think I would ask the younger ones to work that kind of a case. You need a wisdom that only age supplies and you have to look at the world in a certain, somewhat cynical way. The actual exorcism may take some time. It is common for the ritual to be repeated several times. In cases involving possession, there is some indicator that the demon has been vanished. However, when you are dealing with a place, you do not always have an indicator. Unfortunately, more than one exorcism may need to be performed. There really is no way to know for sure whether it worked. For that reason, as an investigator you can never really close a case. The problem may abate only to return later. This is sad but true in some instances.

It is common for the smell of roses or other pleasant fragrances to permeate the location where an exorcism has been performed. This is accepted as a sign that the exorcism was successful. This smell may last for some time. It will often go away and return at another time. Unfortunately, it does not guarantee long-term success. Still, for the beleaguered family, this smell is truly a positive sign from Heaven. Any relief is welcomed. However, most exorcisms do work. That is the hope you have to give the family.

One point that should be mentioned while we are on the subject of exorcisms is in regards to "born again" Christians. If you read enough books written by them, they make it sound like deliverance is something that is a simple one, two, three process that just about anyone in their elite club can do. This is not true and it is a dangerous way to think. Exorcism is the most dangerous situation a human can possibly face. Exorcism is a war and that war is being fought against the ultimate evil and it is an evil that is far stronger and wiser than we are. It should be left to the hands of those trained *especially for that purpose.* Again, I am not trying to knock born again Christians; it is just that they make deliverance sound so easy. It is not easy and it is terribly dangerous for all involved.

This should give you an idea about how to obtain outside help. You have to be persistent. The fact of the matter is it can be difficult to get the help that is needed. The key is to keep trying until you get the help that is needed. If you are persistent enough, you will be successful.

One question that arises is what do you do if you are not a Christian? The answer depends on what your religion is. Many other religions have rituals that amount to an exorcism. It may be called something different. Should you have a problem, discuss it with a member of your particular faith. Bare in mind that a Christian exorcism will work whether you are a Christian or not. Suppose you do not belong to any religion? Well, the odds are that you did belong to one at some point in time in your life. If you once were a Catholic, that would be a good starting point. Suppose you do not believe in God? In that case, you have a problem. However, it needs to be mentioned that if you feel you are being attacked by a demon, obviously you must believe in demons. Can you believe in demons and not believe in God? I do not think so, but I could be wrong.

Suppose you know someone who you think is possessed. How do you get them help if they do not want it? In truth, there is not a whole lot you can do if that person is an adult. My suggestion would be to pray for that person and ask God to help him. You can get in touch with paranormal investigators or a demonologist. However, they cannot do anything if the person does not think they need help. How do you reach a demonologist? That can be hard. If you have access to paranormal investigators, they may know one. But, you have to be careful. There are a lot of people out there who call themselves demonologists who do not know squat about demons. The Internet can help you to a point. Again though, you have to be careful. Because someone has a terrific web page does not mean they know what they are talking about.

One idea is to contact church leaders and see if they know how to contact one. There are many universities with parapsychology departments that may be able to help too. There are many reputable organizations such as The American Society For Psychical Research that can help you. At the end of this book, I will list the names, addresses and telephone numbers of reputable places you can turn to. There is help out there.

REMOVING THE HUMAN SPIRIT

Before trying to remove the human spirit, we must presuppose that there is a need to do so. Assuming that is the case, and we will discuss that shortly, the fun begins because folks, it ain't gonna be easy. Before we look at some ways of trying to remove the human spirit, let us bounce back to the first issue. There are different schools of thought as to whether or not we have the right to try to force out a spirit when it has the right to be there. Let me give you an example.

Let's say that my time is up and I bite the big one. Suppose I decide to stick around my trailer because I love it and do not want to leave it yet or maybe I want to stay around because I feel that my wife and animals need me. I am not likely to be too happy about it if some "thinks he knows it all" wise ass (like me) comes in here and tries to throw me out. It is my home and what right does *he* have to tell *me* where to go? It is bad enough that people tell me where to go when I am alive; do I have to put up with that when I am dead too? It is an interesting question, right? It is not an easy one to answer, either.

Paranormal investigators come across this dilemma often since the overwhelming majority of cases they come across, if not all of them, involve human spirits. Before we try to figure out how to get rid of the pesky spirit, we need to figure out first whether we should. There really are no ground rules to work with here. Yes, there are some cases that are clear-cut. When you have a family being terrorized by a spirit, it *needs* to be removed. By intentionally terrorizing its victims, it loses its right to be there. But what if it is not terrorizing them or what if that is not its intent? What do we do there?

I would like to think that when my sentence is up here on earth I would want to move on to whatever lies ahead. However, many spirits choose to stay. There are numerous reasons why they choose to do that and as you will soon see, we will often need to find out what that reason is. Is it better for the spirit to move on? Probably, although we have no way of knowing that for sure. Are we doing them a favor by trying to get them to leave? See the last answer. I do not mean to make too much of it but it can be a dilemma.

A Tricky Situation

Let me tell you about a particular case I worked. In that case, there were four spirits inhabiting a house. Two of those four had a "legal" right to be there. What do I mean by a *legal* right to be there? The two in question were members of the family who were living there. One was the mother of the residents and she had raised her children in that house. That being the case, she had every right in the world to stay there. The problem arose because she would not leave her family alone. One night, I attempted to get her to leave. What we tried to do was sit in a dark room and talk to her. One of us would speak and then we would wait a few minutes before speaking again. We had audiotapes running and I was also using a night-shot camcorder. Well, at one point, I told the spirit that if she would not leave her family alone, I would have to try to remove her. For the record, we had tried many different ways of getting her to either move on or at least leave her family alone. By this point in the investigation, we found that being kind was useless as was asking her nicely to leave. Everyone was frustrated by that point so we tried a shift in strategy. Anyway, on the audio and video recorders, there was a reply to my statement. Clear as day, a voice said: "You bastard!" It is my best EVP captured to date, although it is by far the least flattering one. So what does that tell us?

What it does tell us is that it can be difficult to convince a spirit to move on. It also tells us that spirits still have tempers when they die, at least until they cross over completely. (Maybe not even then.) However, more than anything, I think it tells us where the point is that you have to try to remove a spirit. See if this makes sense to you. I cannot deny that a spirit has the right to stay where it lived. It may be shortchanging itself but it has the right to do that. The dead have the right to stay where they lived, if they so choose. However, the spirits of the dead have no right to affect the lives of the living and that is where you have to draw the line. In the case I mentioned, the spirit frequently touched the family and had its say every time a tape recorder was running. There were also mysterious lights and an occasional audible voice, although it was not the mother's voice. It was driving the spirit's family nuts. They had tried on many, many occasions to convince her to either leave or at least leave them alone. For reasons known only to her, she would not listen to reason. Thus she was crossing the line.

After many months of work and clearing out three of the spirits, a happy medium was reached. The spirit is still there but she rarely bothers anyone. It took a lot of work on the part of many family members to get to that point. Can she ever be made to leave? Probably not. Since she is not evil an exorcism would not be effective. Admonishing a demon to leave "in the name of Christ" is not going to affect her. What it became for those spirits that left was a *spirit rescue.* So, how can you remove a human spirit? We will take a look at some of the things you can do that are effective and we will also look at some ways that while they *can* be effective, they can also be dangerous.

I just got through telling you that you cannot force a human spirit out with an exorcism. While that is true, there is still much that can be accomplished through religious means. What you can accomplish is creating a positive environment that will make the *nasty* human spirit think twice about staying. In addition to that, prayer can be empowering. That is important because we know that fear is the single biggest factor in a haunting. Anything that empowers the victim weakens its oppressor. Having a prayer group in the home can be quite effective. (It is also effective in demonic and diabolical infestations.) It also shows the spirit that it is up against *a lot* of people, not just the residents. That by itself can send a nasty one packing. Having the house blessed helps too as does having a Mass said there. It is not that the spirit is being forced out; it is just creating an environment where the spirit is unlikely to want to stay.

Another way to help a spirit is by praying *for* him. I am not talking about trying to command him to leave using prayer; what I am saying is that we pray for intersession on his behalf. If you know who the spirit is and you know anything about his belief systems, you can also suggest to him that he himself should pray for guidance. That too can be effective. There is tremendous power in prayer and it should be employed. We will now take a look at some things that might work but may not be the safest or most effective way of trying to help a spirit move on.

Using A Psychic

Over the years, there have been many psychics who have had the ability to communicate with spirits. Needless to say, that is a great asset to have when you are investigating a possible haunting. The psychic may be able to make contact quickly and determine who the spirit is and what it wants. Of course, the psychic may also be able to convince the spirit to move on. Even if the psychic cannot do that, she may be able to get information that will help the spirit to move on. That might be the name of a loved one of the spirit or the name of someone living whom the spirit wants to send a message to. It might just want to say goodbye to a loved one.

The problem, of course, is finding a reputable psychic and one that is not going to charge you an arm and a leg. You really need a trance medium, if you can find one. Unfortunately, there are so many horror stories out there of people purporting to be mediums who charge usurious fees and really accomplish nothing except expanding their bank accounts. However, it is still possible to convince a spirit to move on without the aid of a psychic.

Who Is It?

The big question that you have to try to answer before you can find a way to make a spirit leave is *who* are you dealing with. If you can identify the spirit, your chances of getting it to leave are much better than if you are working blind. For example, if you know that it is a relative, you can try to assure him that everything is fine and that you will watch over the spirits loved ones. You can then use the approach that the spirits loved ones *want* him to leave so that he may enjoy the life (if you can call death life) that he deserves and has earned, unless of course, he was a lousy person. He might now want to get what he earned. You can also call on another spirit that is loved by your haunter and maybe get him to come over and ease the spirit through the transition of death.

Sometimes it takes a considerable amount of research to find the identity of the haunting spirit. Record checks can sometimes produce the spirits identity. I worked a case with a tireless assistant who pored over old records and managed to identify some of the spirits that were plaguing a family. Once we knew *who* we were dealing with, we were able to successfully remove them by convincing them that it was time to move on. We did not use a psychic for that spirit rescue. Knowing their identity gave us the means necessary to direct them to move on. What we did was talk to the spirit just like we would have had he been there in the house. Actually, he *was* there. We just could not see him.

Coax It To The Light

One fairly common belief is that when we die, we see a tunnel and that there is a light at the end of that tunnel. The belief is that the light will take us to wherever we ultimately end up. We are supposed to go towards that light. (When I die, there had better be a light or I'm screwed. I won't know what to do.) One belief is that we can direct the spirit to head towards that light. Try to assure them that it is a safe way to go. One problem that we have when we do not have a psychic present is that we are dealing with one-way communication. It is a safe bet that the spirit can hear what we are telling him but it is a safer bet that we cannot hear what *he* is telling *us*. The psychic may get feedback from the spirit. Perhaps the spirit will tell her that he is frightened and does not want to try to go that way. In that case, the psychic can reassure him. You might have a case where the spirit says that there are lights on both sides of him. He may be asking *which* way to go and we keep saying: "Go to the light. It's safe and you will find peace there." The spirit is probably screaming something like: "Which damn light am I supposed to go to?" That makes it harder for us but still not impossible.

We just have to be more patient. We may look like fools too but what can you do?

How To Direct Them

How? Well, you would do that the same way you would direct someone who is living. One very common mistake we make is that we automatically assume that we don't know how to talk to a spirit. Nothing has changed in that regard. They may be dead but they are intellectually the same as they were in life. They may be bright or they may be as impossibly stupid as they were in life. Some people feel that the best way to direct them is by sitting in a dark room, lit only by candlelight. That may be so but I think the reason probably is that sitting in candlelight makes *us* focus better. I doubt it has anything to do with the spirit. One point needs to be made here. You want to avoid holding a séance here. (I will discuss that soon.) The idea here is to focus on sending the spirit to the light; you do not want to attract anyone or anything else.

If you do try to help the spirit cross over, keep in mind the reasons why spirits get stuck on this plane. Since it might not realize it is dead, you may want to mention that when you speak to it. We're not talking something like: "You're history pal so get moving." Just say something like: "It must be hard now that you are no longer on the physical plane but don't be afraid. There is so much more waiting for you when you decide to move forward." What you have done here is tell him that he is dead but that there is nothing to be afraid of. Furthermore, you mentioned something positive that is ahead for him and you worded it in a manner where you are letting him choose the time to go. It is a surprisingly effective way to go. No one likes being told what to do.

Calling For Help

One very successful way to help a spirit cross over is by suggesting to him to think of a relative he was close to who has passed away and call for that relative to come help him. A popular belief today is that another spirit usually does come to help those who die. In some cases it is a spirit guide; in other cases it is a loved one or even a beloved pet. This belief is based on the experiences of many people who have had near death experiences. It would stand to reason that this method would be successful because it can eliminate much of the fear that the spirit is feeling. Remember, we may be afraid of him because he is dead but he may be afraid for himself because he is dead. In fact, he may be more afraid of his situation than we are.

Not A Real Good Idea

One thing that I have found does not work too well at all is threats. If you are dealing with a spirit that more or less has the right to be there, issuing a threat will likely only tick it off and make it all the more determine to stay. That was a lesson I learned with the: "You bastard!" EVP. For the spirit that has a right to be there, you really want to coax it along. Threatening it will not help the situation much at all. Like I said, if anything, it will make it more determined to stay. I know that I would not respond well to a threat. If I have learned how to move objects, I may move one in the general direction of the person who was threatening me. Of course, I would probably miss but that is another matter.

There are some circumstances where threats can be effective. That would be the situation where you have a nasty spirit that *does not* have the right to be there and is causing the victim grief. That spirit needs to leave and if he does not want to, you have every right to try to force him to do so. In that situation, it is fair to tell him that you will try to force him out. You can then tell him that you will pray and ask God to *make* him leave. As with a demon, you do not want to threaten him by means of your own power since in truth, you do not have any. God is the one who can force him out. In many instances, the threat alone will stop the problem. Human spirits really want no part in a fight with God. The key word in that threat (besides God) is *make*. A cantankerous spirit will not want anyone or anything to *make* him do anything. Therefore, if he believes that he will be forced out, he may well go on his own. This way, he feels that *he* made the decision to leave. It is a sort of face-saving situation. The results are the same and that is all that counts.

(Ouija Boards And Séances)

While there is some evidence that Ouija boards and séances can be effective if used properly, I do not recommend them. Let us take a look at the Ouija board first. I have to admit that I do know of some instances where the Ouija board was used for "spirit rescues" (helping a "stuck" spirit to cross over) and I will confess that I have had some success with this method myself but there are risks inherent with it. Just as with using the board for fun, you really have no idea who you are in contact with, if anybody at all. Although there is a tremendous amount of evidence to back up each theory, you cannot be sure whether you are in contact with a spirit, your own subconscious (automatism) or the combined subconscious of everyone using the board. On top of that, there is always the danger of exacerbating the problem if you do contact the spirit causing the haunting and you also run the risk of inviting in a new one.

I do not know what the odds would be of contacting the haunter but I would guess it is fairly low. In addition, even if you do make contact with him, you have no reason to believe that he will "sit down" with you and chat in a meaningful way. Plus, you run the aforementioned risk of exacerbating the situation. For example, let us say that after painstakingly protecting yourself and going through the debris field of the spirit world, you actually make contact with your haunter. Maybe, surprisingly enough, you even start a dialog with him. You ask him why he is haunting you and the answer comes back that he hates you. You may be nice about it and explain to him that he should not hate you because you are a really nice person. His response is to call you a "crack whore," or some other equally unpleasant name. Perhaps he calls your children that. He may even threaten to kill you and your family. For some reason, (intimidation?) nasty spirits *love* to make threats. If I had a dollar for every time a spirit threatened to kill me, I would be having a lot of fun on this plane. Needless to say, you are going to respond to him in kind and the next thing you know, you are arguing with something you cannot see and all you have accomplished is angering him to the point where he will try to haunt you even more.

If you think about it, you cannot expect him to be reasonable because if he were reasonable, he would not be haunting you in the first place. So what is to gain by talking to him? Most likely, all it will do is make the haunting worse because he will probably have said some things that are frightening, such as hurting the children. Even if he can't actually do it, the threat is sure to cause you some fear. Always remember, fear is the main component of a haunting. The more fear generated, the more the haunting affects you.

Now let us say that you contact a spirit who *claims* to be the one haunting you. He may tell you all kinds of stories *plus* he may threaten you too. At the very least, he may have you running around like a lunatic looking for things he says are the key to the haunting. For example, during a session conducted by someone I knew years ago, the spirit they contacted gave them this great story that he was sticking around because he had "unfinished business" to deal with. He told these people that there were papers hidden in their basement that would "clear his name" if they were found. Clear his name of what was never really determined. He gave them some cock and bull story over a long period of time and they fell for it hook, line and sinker. To make a long and somewhat amusing story short, they all but tore the basement apart looking for these "crucial" papers that never existed in the first place. Of course, the haunting continued unabated.

There is also the potential problem of drawing in something else, something that may be far worse than what is already there. People lie so guess what? Spirits lie too. Evil ones are very good at it too. They are not above masquerading as friendly spirits to cause confusion and even worse. They may claim to be relatives or spirit guides or "enlightened" spirits and they may offer suggestions designed to get rid of the troubling spirit and as part of the dupe, the problem may stop. Then, when you contact them again (as they will have told you to do) they will offer to keep the haunting spirit away if you let them stay around. To the person who has been experiencing a frightening haunting, this may sound great. They will, of course, let their new- found friend stay. In fact, they may welcome him with open arms. Guess what, they may have invited a demon in.

Still another problem is the risk of an outward manifestation that can, at the very least frighten everyone half to death, not to mention actually hurting someone. I have seen many outward manifestations during Ouija sessions. One time, at the end of a session that produced nothing, one of the users pushed the card table away in a rather annoyed fashion. He then made some derogatory comment although I do not remember what he said. Anyway, he stood up and began walking away when the planchette went flying past him. At another session, the same thing happened with a shot glass that was being used as a planchette. In that case, the board had been active. The spirit that came through had been rather nasty and threatening. After deciphering one vile message after another, one of the participants told the spirit to do something that is anatomically impossible for a human to do and the result was the shot glass shattered as if it had been filled with an explosive. These manifestations often make the situation worse because of the fear they cause. In some cases, the manifestations that take place during Ouija sessions are worse than the ones that led to the decision to use it in the first place.

If you subscribe to the theory that automatism is the guiding force behind the movements of the planchette, you may also get bogus information created by your (or others) subconscious designed to frighten you. You cannot rely on information from that source either. So, using a Ouija board is a risky situation and a potentially dangerous one as well. There is just no way to be sure what you are contacting. It is a means of blind communication and that is laced with risks. For that reason, I do not recommend using the Ouija board or similar methods to stop a haunting.

Séances

Conducting a séance is another risky endeavor. You run all of the same risks as with the Ouija board. In a séance, the idea again is to try to make contact with the haunting spirit. Since you do not have a board to work with, you can use a "rap" system. For example, rap once for yes, twice for no. The risk you run with a séance is that a spirit may attempt to communicate *through* someone. That can be disastrous, to say the least. Also, as with Ouija sessions, outward manifestations occasionally take place. I have seen tables rise, candles blow out and objects fly across the room during séances. That only serves to frighten everyone unnecessarily. For the miniscule amount of times it may help, it is not worth taking the risk.

Other Methods Of Cleansing A House

For every person you meet who has had a paranormal experience or studied the subject, you will get a different suggestion. Many of these suggestions are similar in nature but are known by different names. Many spiritualists agree that using incense to clear a house is effective. Sage is the fragrance of choice for most of the rituals. The burning sage is usually carried from room to room while the spirits are being addressed. The sage is supposed to force the spirits out. There is some merit to using incense. The Catholic Church has used it for centuries in many of its rituals. Some people refer to this type of cleansing as a "smudging." Another form of this ritual is called "suffimunigation." The origin of this may be found in records of exorcisms where "fumigation with incense" was an integral part of the ritual. The theory behind these rituals are the same.

Beware Of...

Just about every investigator knows of someone who has attempted to have a haunting stopped by hiring an "expert" (a word that makes me cringe) to come in to "cleanse" the house. Some of these people will come in and do elaborate rituals that are anywhere from a voodoo ceremony by a witch doctor to something that were it not so serious, would be pretty funny to watch. These people will often charge ridiculous amounts of money and when the problem continues, they will charge more because after all, it is a *strong* spirit. In the end, the only thing that has left is your money. Whether you are a paranormal investigator or a person suffering through a haunting, beware of the "rip off" artists. There are many around. If during the course of your travels you happen to find a good psychic, keep her name handy because you may need her from time to time. I do the same thing with other research organizations. I try to keep track of the good ones and the bad ones. This way, if a situation arises that I cannot work, I can refer them to the good organizations and steer them away from the bad ones.

(And Then...)

I have heard of some bizarre "cures" for paranormal activity. One of my favorites was told to me by a client. In that case, she had called in some people and their suggestion to her was that she take a bucket and fill it with water, right to the top. I don't know whether you should use hot water or cold water. The pail should then be brought into the bedroom and placed at the bottom of the bed. Great care must be taken to ensure that you do not spill even a tiny drop of the water. (That let's me out. I could not carry a pail half-filled without spilling most of it.) Okay, the pail should be left there for a minimum of 48 hours but not more than 72 hours. (I don't know if closer to 72 is better than 48?) Anyway, take the pail and taking great care to ensure (here we go again) that you do not spill even a tiny drop, bring it to the bathroom and pour it into the toilet. Then flush the toilet. If you have more than one bathroom I am not sure what you should do. I will not even try to figure out how that is supposed to work. I once heard another one about dancing, nude psychics. Over the course of years, I have come across many a "psychic" and I must say that the only way that theory would work is by making the spirit laugh so hard that it hurt. However, there have been a few who I personally would not mind watching while they tried this method. I highly doubt it would work but it would be entertaining.

(In Conclusion)

There are various methods of dealing with human spirits. Some of them work, some of them don't. Some are safe and some are dangerous. Others are silly. The key is to figure out who it is, if possible and then try to help it cross over. There is no easy solution to getting rid of the nasty human spirit. The key is to weaken it by reducing the fear factor. Add a healthy dose of defiance and do your best to live your life as normally as you can under the circumstances. That and your faith are your strongest weapons.

SOME WORDS OF CAUTION

Investigating paranormal phenomena is an exciting field and it has its rewards. Although it is generally safe, there is also no doubt that it can be a risky field and there are some dangers, however rare. You always have to be careful. We learn more and more about psychic phenomena every year. In that sense, there are no experts. You need to continue to learn everything you possibly can. Reading is one way of doing that. Talking to other investigators is another. Never let your ego get in the way. By that, I mean that there is always something to be learned from other investigators, regardless of their training and experience. Never assume that you know it all. Every case is different; therefore you can always learn something. Avoid arrogance; it is the investigator's worst enemy. Also, use common sense. That applies to this field as it does to any other one. However, it is probably needed here more than in other fields. Always keep in mind that you are dealing with something that you cannot see. Well, usually anyway. That can make things hard.

Learn And Grow

Attend classes, if you can. You might try your local high school. Often, they have adult education classes on a wide variety of topics. You might get lucky and find a class or two on the supernatural that way. Also, be on the lookout for lectures being given by experts. Try to learn from the best. If you check out any of the twelve trillion websites that are devoted to the supernatural, you may see a list of lectures they plan to do. It is also a good idea to watch any TV shows that deal with the paranormal. You do not have to agree with everything you see but it is always wise to learn different opinions. Sometimes you will get lucky and catch a talk show that is featuring paranormal phenomena as its theme. Sadly, there are very few talk shows that deal with the subject and many are done in a way that belittles the subject or at least demeans it and those who work in it. These shows usually are poorly researched. These so-called experts have done a lot to discredit the field as well. Ignorance abounds. The point is simply that you need to keep studying the subject. However, always keep an open mind. Just because someone says they are an expert does not mean that they have even the slightest clue as to what they are talking about. Use common sense along with an open mind.

Do Not Over Do It

There is another aspect though that needs to be mentioned. While you do need to keep abreast of the changes in the field, you have to be careful and not let it become an obsession. You cannot "eat, drink and sleep" the subject. It can be a very stressful field at times and burnout is always a possibility, especially if you do case work. There will be times when you need to step back for a while. The key to a successful life is to keep things in balance. Balance = harmony. There is another world out there, away from the paranormal. The thing is that you cannot give up your family or personal life by becoming obsessed with the paranormal. Your family should always be first in your life. To put them on the back burner is not healthy and it is not productive. You need to be sharp on an investigation and you will not be if you do not occasionally divorce yourself from the subject. Sometimes that only takes a few days. I do a tremendous amount of reading on the subject. There are times when my brain just does not want to handle anything paranormal. What I usually do is put the books away and just divorce myself from the subject. In many cases, my desire returns in just a few days. I will often read a book on any other subject just to take my mind off the field.

There is another danger as well. As with anything you do for pleasure, there are times when you cannot get enough of it. Whether you are an adrenaline junkie or an adventurer, there are going to be those times when there is simply nothing going on and the weather may prevent you from finding something to do. When it comes to the paranormal, this is most certainly true. If there are no cases on the horizon, you may need a "fix." Sure, you have the old cemetery shoot to fall back on, whether permitting. If you have the time and the money, you can always go to a famous hotel and do a little ghost hunting there. If you are part of a group, you can get together every so often like a ghost club does. That can be fun. However, there is yet another problem paranormal investigators face and this one is unusual. Speaking from personal experience, when you are used to dealing with the spiritual world, a world few realize exists, it can be hard to find interest in the things of the physical world. Life can be flat out boring. You have to guard against that and that is why it is so important to take care of *all* areas of your life and why you must have interests in the more physical areas of your life. You need to have hobbies and outlets apart from the paranormal world. It makes for a more balanced life and it also makes the slow times easier to deal with.

You also have to be careful about how many investigations you go on. Granted, they do not come up all that often but you may find times when it just does not feel right to do one. Follow your instincts. They may be trying to tell you that you need to skip one. Although rare, there are occasions where you will get one case after another or even find yourself with two at the same time. You cannot conquer the world in one day. You cannot live and die for the field and still be productive. Do not be afraid to do other things that you find relaxing. There is a definite danger in over-extending yourself. Your work should be fun and if you treat it properly, it will be. Treat the field with respect but also make sure that you treat yourself with respect. It is difficult to walk away when someone needs help. Sometimes though, you need a little time for yourself. If you are feeling weary, hand the case over to another investigator. Mistakes happen when you push yourself too hard. This can hurt you and this can hurt the client as well. You can always join the investigation later. If you keep this in mind, you should be fine. You will become a much better investigator for it.

(Relaxing By Doing "Shoots")

From time to time between investigations, you may decide to go around to different places reputed to be haunted just to shoot some pictures and see what you get. Many investigators will do "shoots" in local cemeteries or haunted houses of record for this reason. You can amass an interesting scrapbook doing this and it makes the time between investigations go faster. Investigators tend to get the "itch" when investigations are few and far between.

When you go out on a shoot of any kind, record the date, time, and location. If you do several of them, you will want to keep all the pictures separate. Certain disorganized types of people will sometimes forget to mark the location on the envelope with the pictures thinking, "I'll remember that. (Me!) It is also a good idea to note the weather conditions as well. Note whether it was cloudy, humid, or foggy. This may affect the quality of the photos. It will also give you a good idea of what types of weather conditions give you the best shots. For example, electrical storms will sometimes give you great shots.

Do not put a lot of pressure on yourself in regards to what you expect to find. You may do many shoots and get nothing, and then one day you get some great shots. I usually take at least two rolls of film at a time. Many stories from experienced investigators say that they took 48 shots and got only 1 active picture. They are usually quite happy about that. I have just recently embraced the world of digital cameras. I am looking forward to trying that baby out. Your attitude plays a role too. My theory is that when you press or feel negative about a shoot, you usually do not get anything. The idea here is to have fun while doing your work. The best time to go is after dark although some interesting pictures and recordings have happened on day shoots. The odds are better at night though. The psychic hours are between 9 p.m. and 6 a.m. The peak time of activity is usually between 2 and 4 a.m. with 3:15 a.m. being the most psychic time, in my experience.

Be patient on the shoot. Sometimes there is a tendency to rush through the shoot out of either nervousness or a fear of getting 25 to life when the police show up. In cemeteries, I tend to go quickly out of the fear of disrespecting those buried there. Always say a prayer when you enter a cemetery and tell the residents that you mean them no disrespect and ask God to let them be at peace. Some people believe that you will get better results if you ask the residing spirits for their permission to take pictures. Ditto for EVP work. However, that said, there really is no reason to rush.

As far as being nervous goes, I have never heard of anyone being hurt doing a cemetery shoot ... other than falling over headstones. There really is no reason to be scared. If you take your time, you may start to feel something. That would be an ideal time to shoot. You do not have to use a role of film in five minutes. The idea is to try to have fun while attempting to end the paranormal withdrawal you are feeling due to the lack of any cases to go on.

Good Spirits and Bad Ones

There are haunted places and haunted people. There are good spirits and there are bad spirits. This is true of the human spirits and the inhuman spirits. Angels and elementals are the good inhuman spirits. There is not much in here about them. They do not haunt people and no one needs to be protected from them. If anything, everyone probably wishes he could experience the Angels and elementals more in their lives. We have spent a great deal of time in dealing with the evil or demonic spirit. That was necessary because they do exist and they do cause terrible problems for people. You always have to prepare for the worst. If the worst does not come about, there is no harm done. Benign spirits mean no harm to mankind; if anything, they need our help. However, when you encounter negative forces, and you might, you must know how to protect yourself and how to help the family being afflicted by them. There is great danger whenever you encounter evil or demonic forces. You can get hurt on many different levels if you are not careful. The same is true for the people who are suffering the effects already. The threat is very real.

While hauntings and demonic possession do happen, they are extremely rare. They occur more than most people realize but in truth, they are rare. Most paranormal investigators will tell you that they encounter far more benign spirits than evil or demonic ones. Either many apparent hauntings turn out to be natural occurrences or if spirits are present, they are benign. However, the horrific cases are the ones that stand out. You may do fifty investigations and only come across one or two where there are negative spirits present. But, those one or two will never be forgotten. Never! They may even end your career.

Educating The Oppressed

When people come to paranormal investigators, it is usually because they are frightened. They are experiencing something that they do not understand. It may or may not be the result of spirits. It may also be that they are simply misunderstanding natural phenomena. Once investigators get involved, it gives the concerned person a sense of relief. Once the people involved have been educated, they often find that the problem goes away. Even if there *are* spirits involved, once they know that they are safe, they find that the problem no longer bothers them. There have been many cases on record where the people actually begin to enjoy their ghost.

However, there are those times when the problem is very real and very serious. This is where we come in. It is almost impossible to understand what a haunting is really like unless you have experienced one yourself or know someone close to you who has. You become terrorized in your own home, the one place where you should feel safe. You are always concerned about your loved ones in the home. You do not want to be there but you also do not want to leave a loved one there alone. The same is true for pets. It is a horrible experience and one that is there 24 hours a day, even when there is no activity taking place. You can only imagine the fear, frustration, and anger brought about by a haunting. These people need someone to turn to who can help them through this horror. They need people willing to walk into a war zone, and that is exactly what it is. As you have seen, religious leaders often do little to help them. Somebody has to. There are few people and places where they can go for help.

The Author's Mission

The purpose of this book was to teach you how to investigate paranormal phenomena and how to tell what it is when you find it. Surely, not everyone who reads this book wants to become a paranormal investigator. Many people will read this just because they want to know more about the subject. This is either something you want to do or you don't. If you do, then you must be prepared to enter the world of the paranormal. If you have not experienced a haunting, you must be prepared to see things that will permanently alter your model of the world, often for the better, sometimes for the worse. You will be opening your mind to previously unknown dimensions and you will see things that will change the way you view both life and death.

If I can make a suggestion it is this: read, read, and read. There is always more to learn. As you now know, I have been studying this field for well over a quarter of a century and I have experienced, first hand, what it is like to be haunted. I spent 10 years, from the age of 10 to 20, living in a haunted house. All that aside, I do not for a single minute think that I know it all. No one will ever know it all because knowledge keeps changing. I still attend lectures on the subject, whenever I find them. I am always on the lookout for television programs that deal with the subject and I talk to as many investigators as I can. Furthermore, I will listen to any ghost story anyone wants to tell me.

Most of all, I read. I read everything I can get my hands on. I read the good books and the books. I also read the ones that are self-serving. I read those authors who believe in ghosts and demons. I read books by authors who are skeptical. Some of the stuff is funny; some of it is ridiculously stupid. You can usually tell who are the ones who know what they are talking about and the ones who you know haven't got a clue. You can usually tell when a story is true and when it is a piece of pure fabrication. I try to read it all, even the annoying stuff. I also love a true ghost story. You do not see too many of them around but I am always searching for one. The point is that there is always something to learn. Never stop learning. That may be the best advice I have given you in this book. It will save you a lot of work and frustration. It will also keep your desire strong.

(Beware Of The Mentally Ill)

There is another area that needs to be covered. The world of the paranormal, like anything else attracts a wide variety of individuals. Some of those individuals are mentally ill. If anything, this field attracts more than most. You have to be careful when dealing with them. You have to be on the lookout for them. When you come across them, be careful. They may pose a bigger risk than a demon. The other side of it is that you have to treat them fairly. If you do lectures, there is a good chance that you will eventually come across one. As hard as it may be, always try to treat them with dignity. They may ask the weirdest questions or tell the most bizarre stories. Tap dance around them rather than embarrass them. It is not their fault that they are ill. Most of all, be alert for them. They are out there. Everyone should be treated with dignity, regardless of their position in life.

(Expect Criticism)

By now, I am sure that many of your friends and loved ones know of your interest in the world of the paranormal. One thing I can tell you that you probably already know is that many people will criticize you for your beliefs. Some will make fun of you. It sucks but that is the way it is. Try not to be thin skinned. With some people, if they know they are getting to you, they will lay it on. Once they see that they are not going to get a bite out of you, they will go off and find someone else to bother. The trick is to be able to brush those people off and not let them affect you and the work you do. I believe that I do not have to justify myself and what I do to anyone. If someone wants to think I am nuts, they should go right ahead and think that. Trust me, many do.

People tend not to believe in the things that frighten them so that accounts for some of the problem. Others are just ignorant of the subject. Others still are stupid. Try not to let the loudmouth oafs get to you. I personally avoid arguments on the subject. If you have an open mind and you disagree with my point of view, that is great. We can have many a fruitful discussion on the topic and you will not be expected to agree with me at the end. That is not my goal. There are those who just like to scoff and make fun of everything. I stay away from those types at any cost when I can and I will not argue with them if I can't. It serves no purpose. You are not going to convince them of anything and if you try, you are playing their game. Some people just like to argue. My thinking is that I am too busy working with people who do believe; I do not have the time to worry about the ones who don't and don't want to. Everyone should believe what they want to believe, even if they are way off base. That is what free will is all about and that is a God giving right. And no one should try to take that away from you.

In Conclusion

I hope you had fun reading his book and I hope I was able to clarify some areas of a confusing field. I certainly loved writing it and I hope to write many more in the years to come, God willing. There is nothing like combining your three most favorite pastimes. I am very lucky in that regard. In my case, those three are writing, investigating and studying. There is so much out there to be learned. We need to learn it. I hope you learned some things and I hope that you have enjoyed the journey.

THE LIGHTER SIDE OF HAUNTINGS

Okay, we have taken a look at the frightening stuff. We all know how to set up an investigation, we know all about the demons that are trying to kill us or at least turn us into a "fourth of July" feast. We know all about the planning that goes into an investigation, the collecting of evidence and spending endless hours staring at the TV watching basically nothing in the hopes that something, anything will come out on tape. Never mind capturing a demon on tape, we'll be thrilled just to have an orb or two make an appearance. Even worse than that is listening to endless hours of white noise on audiotape. We know the dangers we face and we have an idea of how to stop a haunting. So, what else is there to talk about? Well, having seen the nasty stuff, let us take a little time to look at the lighter side of hauntings. Yes, there are light sides.

I have been asked many time what I feel is the most frightening part of any investigation. The answer is very easy for me to give, for no real thought needs to go into it. I for one do well at tasks that require no thought. For me, the most frightening part of any investigation is... finding the house! Now if you think I am being facetious, trust me when I tell you that I am not. Anyone who knows me will tell you that I can easily get lost in a shoebox, even with directions. My driveway holds two cars and I can guarantee you that I can get lost in it. Had I been one of the early pioneers, we would all be within a mile of where we started out. Now, you can add to that the following facts:

1) I hate driving.
2) I really hate driving at night because I cannot see worth a dam.
3) I really, really hate driving at night because street signs, when they are there at all are three inches wide.
4) I have absolutely no concept of directions. If you ask me which way I went, the answer will always be: "Forward."
5) I absolutely suck when it comes to taking down directions.
6) I absolutely suck even more when it comes to following directions.
7) I panic the minute I discover that I have no clue as to where I am, even when I'm in my driveway.

Now we can probably add a significant number to the above items but for the sake of giving you a chance of finishing this book in your lifetime, I will refrain from any further examples. I cannot begin to tell you how many times I have driven through some minute town looking for an address. For reasons that only God and a few psychotic engineers know, street signs are always miniscule. On a clear, sunny day, I cannot read those signs. There is no way in hell I can read them in the dark, especially when I have some local driving behind me who wants to drive at 75 mph on some narrow, winding and poorly lit road. Also, the directions people sometimes give are ridiculous at best and I am being as nice here as I possibly can. Let me give you a few examples of directions that have driven me absolutely nuts. Believe it or not, these are real examples.

For the record, my thoughts are in parenthesis. "Okay, do you know how to get to Route 184?" "Yes I do." His response is: "Good, you don't want to get on 184. That will take you to Peachtree Center. You don't want to go there. Now when you pass 184, go for a ah, ah, (more than one ah translates into an uh oh) a mile and a half, maybe two." In my mind I am shouting: "Which is it?" He continues: "From there, (where is there?) jump on the quick way." Me: "Is there a sign for the quick way? Him: "Uh, no. The sign says Route 17." (Then tell me that, for Christ's sake!) He continues: "When you get onto the quick way, follow it until you come to Exit 25, or is it Exit 26?" (Wonderful!) "Once you get off the exit, make a right, no, sorry. Make a left onto county road 99. Now you want to stay on that (do I?) for, oh, about 20 minutes." (At what speed? 20 minutes at 60 mph is a hell of a lot different than 20 minutes at 30 mph.) "Now turn west onto 45 and you want to follow it (do I really?) Northwest for about 2 miles." (Tell me left or right, okay? I don't carry a compass with me.) "You are going to stay on that road for three or four lights." (Which is it since the lights are 20 miles apart on that damn road?) "Finally, you will come to Stretch Drive and we are the second, no wait, the third house on the left." (If *you* don't know where you live, how the hell do you expect *me* to know where you live?) "You can't miss it." (Watch me.) At this point, I ask the person if his house is clearly marked and he again reminds me that I cannot miss it. In other words, it is *not* clearly marked and the house is set back from the road about ½ mile and cannot be seen from the street without night-vision binoculars. (Now you know why I have them.) Once I find the house, 6 hours later than I expected, the guy who gave me the directions usually risks his life by asking me: "So, how were the directions?"

Beware The Family

I have worked many investigations over the years. Some were of the frightening variety and some were of the pleasant variety. I have met some very nice people and I have met more than a few whackados. To some extent, they come with the turf. I have also met people who were far more frightening than the actual haunting. You never know what to expect when you go on a case. I guess that it is best to always expect the unexpected. That way, at least you won't be disappointed.

When I first walk into a house, I always look for several things. The first is an alternate exit. Don't laugh; I only mean that half-jokingly. I once did an investigation where the resident left the house but pad-locked me in. It was a one-night investigation, even though it was amusing. Another thing I look for are books that deal with the occult. People who are being haunted often do buy books on the subject in the hopes of figuring out what is going on and how best to stop it. However, I walked into one house where they had an entire library of books on the occult. They also had pictures of orbs and mist taken in cemeteries proudly displayed on the walls. All that is fine if that is something you like to do but tell me that up front. I hate it when people tell you that they no nothing about the subject but they have been to 103 cemeteries and 14,000 haunted hotels. "Gee, I just can't imagine why these odd things are happening in my house?" "Yeah, right lady. It looks to me like you found what you were looking for." "Seek and ye shall find" or something like that.

Another thing to be wary of are those who want to turn the investigation into a circus. I walked into a house one time and there were 17 people there, of which only 3 actually lived in the house. The whole neighborhood came over to see the "ghost hunters." They all decided to stay overnight too. They did; I didn't. I went to another house where the investigation was actually a party, or at least that was the plan. After a three-hour drive, I entered the house with a team of investigators. After the initial introduction, I looked around the house. The first thing I noticed was a TV set in the living room the size of Arkansas. Needless to say, I did not even bother taking out the gauss meter. Christ, you could almost *feel* the electromagnetic energy in the room. My hair stood on end. The next thing I noticed was that the dining room table was set up for a party. Now many people will lay out snacks for investigators and it is greatly appreciated. In this case, one of the snacks was a tray of cookies. That was a nice gesture because I like to munch when I am sitting vigil in someone's house. However, what got me was that they were cookies in the shape of ghosts and bats and the like. Yep, that was supposed to be a real serious investigation. It lasted about an hour.

Beware The Children

Now I am a believer in having the whole family around for an investigation, providing of course that they all live there. I don't want to see six generations represented but I do like to have all family members who live there present. I believe you get better results that way. In addition, I have nothing against having family members around me during the investigation. Some investigators try to distance themselves from the family. Well, I did a house where every single bit of self-restraint was necessary to keep me from having to do 25 to life in a state penitentiary. In that case, I had a ten-year-old girl decide to follow me around. That was fine with me; she could probably give me a lot of information about the haunting. She volunteered to show me where all of the "terrifying" events took place. First on her list was her bedroom. She took me to a closet near the bed and told me how the door would swing open at night all by itself. When I looked at the door, it was open. I asked her if the door latched right when it was closed. She of course told me that it did. So, I went to the door and pushed it closed. However, it did not latch at all. My next step was to push against it but it still would not stay closed. Finally, I shoved my shoulder against it but still to no avail. That door would not stay closed if you used a hydraulic press to close it. Add to that the fact that there was about 20 pounds of clothing hanging on a hook and it was no surprise that it would swing open. Hell, the surprise would be if it didn't. But wait... there's more!

The next thing the little darling showed me was an area near the bed where the plaster was falling down. Yes, she told me, this was where the *demon* (at least she didn't say *devil*) knocked against the wall. Being the astute, trained observer that I am, I noticed a ball on the bed that just happened to have plaster dust on it. You don't suppose that the demon plays ball, do you? Finally, the little girl showed me her computer. She told me all about how the *poltergeist*, not the demon this time, (she read one too many books, even if it was only one) turned on the computer at night. Now *this* sounded serious. Ugh! Before she went any further, I began to understand why some species eat their young. Okay, I looked at the computer and all of a sudden, the girl began muttering: "Oh my God! Oh my God." With that, she put her left hand over her mouth and pointed her right hand, palm to the side, towards the computer. She continues her "Oh my God" mantra and began slowly backing up. "What is wrong?" I ask the little darling. "The, the, the com, computer just, just turned on by, by, by itself!" I looked at her incredulously and said: "No it didn't." However, the drama queen was not finished. "Don't, don't you see, see? The light, it is, is on." Feeling for the first time in my life that I wanted to commit an act of violence against a child, I told her that the light in question was simply the power indicator signifying that the computer was plugged in. "But, but I never keep, keep it plugged, plugged in!" At this point, the urge to smack the back of her head became almost overwhelming. Showing inhuman restraint, I walked out of the room and went straight to the basement, as far away from the "adorable" darling as possible. There I was greeted by the eight-year-old boy who quickly announced in a most excited tone: "You're gonna be here all night and I am gonna stay with you the whole time!!!" I left the house ten minutes later, wishing that *our* species ate our young.

(Attacked By A 10 Foot Demon)

During one investigation, I spent a lot of time in the basement. The spirit in that house seemed to spend much of its time in the basement and the master bedroom. Obviously, that meant that I spent most of my time in those two locations. (Not at the same time.) I was often touched in that house; the spirit had a thing for pulling my hair. One night as I was sitting in the darkened basement, I heard a noise off to my left so I went to investigate it. I took my trusty flashlight and camera with me, just in case something materialized. Well, I walked to the area where I had heard the noise and took a couple of pictures, blinding myself in the process. As I backed away, I felt something rub up against me. I debated whether to turn on the flashlight or just take a picture. In the process, I dropped the flashlight. Okay, that took care of my decision.

At that point, I decided to spin a 180 and take a picture. I took one step forward and attempted to pivot. As I did that, I stepped on the flashlight and fell right on my butt. However, I did get a shot off. In the instant brilliance of the flash, I saw something *huge* in front of me. In the millisecond it took to think, my first thought was that I had never seen anything quite like it. I fired off a second shot and realized that not only was it huge, it was also *tan.* That was a first. Now, there I was, sprawled on my butt and facing a ten foot tan thing. What to do? Somehow I was not frightened. I guess maybe I was too stupid to be. As I fumbled in the dark for my flashlight, a realization slowly crept in. It was slow in coming but I realized what it was just as I found the flashlight. Turning it on, I came face to face with my ten-foot demon. It was a pair of coveralls hanging on a hanger from one of the rafters. Ugh!

(Pratfalls)

You already read about my infamous cemetery fall. To recap, I was leading a new student into a cemetery for her first shoot. As we walked side by side, I could tell she was nervous. I began to tell her that the only danger in a cemetery was… and as I said that, I tripped on a headstone and fell face first in the mud. Looking up, I finished my sentence: "Falling over headstones."

I was in a famous haunted house one time doing an investigation for a local historical society. It was my first attempt at doing an investigation for "fun." During the course of the night, we all rotated positions to keep the boredom and the cold from finishing us off. When it was my turn to go down the basement, I was eager to try to capture some EVP. I headed towards the basement with my hands full. I had the tape recorder, a night vision scope, a flashlight and a book to read on Ouija boards and related hauntings. Nothing like light reading in a supposedly ghost infested house. Just as I reached the top of the basement stairs, my partner called to me to be careful because there was no light in the basement and the stairs were steep. As I began my descent, I yelled back: "Don't worry I have my night vision…"crash! I did the last four steps on my butt. However, I did not drop any of the equipment.

Then there was another cemetery. This time, we took a class on a field trip to take some photos. There I was, leading my troops through the dark, camera at the ready. I saw a particularly nicely decorated plot so as I walked, I put the camera to my eye and continued forward. For about three steps, that is. That was when I ran out of ground. There happened to be a big drop off. You can picture the rest. There were some hysterical students that night.

(Brain Lock)

I remember the first time I decided to teach a class. I am not one who is particularly comfortable speaking in front of groups of people. Well, not sober anyway. This being my first class, I was more than a little nervous. I wanted everything to be right. Prepared speeches really make me nervous. I speak barely above a whisper as it is so this was a challenge. I managed to survive the prepared segment and we got down to the question and answer part. That is my favorite part of the class. Well, a few questions were thrown out and my partner and I took turns answering them. Then a question was directed at my partner and it had to do with the quality of EVP. Well, he answered the question as best he could while I was shuffling through some papers. He then asked for my opinion. I was completely caught off guard. "Well," I began. "Ah, the poor quality, well it has something to do with the quality of the tape, I guess." Now I began to panic. It is silly in retrospect because it was an easy question to answer but between being nervous and caught off guard, my brain went into lockdown. "I guess the sophistication of the machine is, ah, important and..." (Sweating now.) "I haven't got a clue."

Another time, I was doing a marvelous job answering a question when my partner decided to interject. He went on for a few minutes and his statements drifted into other areas. I listened to him and when he was done, I went back to my answer. The only problem was that I had forgotten what I was going to say and to make matters worse, I had also forgotten the original question. Well, I stared straight ahead for a few seconds, trying to think but it was to no avail; my mind, or what was left of it, went completely blank. The entire room was staring at me waiting for my astute wisdom when I finally looked out and asked: "What the hell was I going to say?" That pretty much broke things up.

(And Then...)

During one investigation, we had a psychic lying in bed next to one of the residents. Our spirit in that house liked to push on the bed. We had even created a crude communication system. Push once for yes; that kind of thing. I was kneeling on the floor next to the bed, closest to the psychic, camera in hand. We were trying to get the spirit to show itself in some way. The psychic explained to the spirit what she wanted him to do and the wait began. Finally, It looked as though something was about to happen. At that point, the psychic told me to look towards the left corner of the room because she thought she saw something move. From where I was kneeling, I had a poor vantage point. To correct this, I leaned over the bed and just about strained my neck trying to see what was happening. "There!" she yelled excitedly. I leaned all the way forward and knelt on a motion detector. Between the pain and the squealing of the machine, I fell forward, my face landing right in the psychic's crotch. Well, it *was* good for me.

In that same house, I came up with the brilliant idea of placing a half filled bowl of water in the center of the bed. I thought it might be easier to see the movement in the water than it was to see a small depression in the bed. We then pointed a camcorder directly over it, hoping to capture the bed's movement. At least that was the plan. It sounded good for three o'clock in the morning. As the woman of the house took up her position on the bed, I laid down next to her. That was good for me too. Gently, I placed the bowl between us. As we asked the first question, the spirit grabbed my left ankle and I bolted up, drowning the bed and the client in one swift motion. That was *not* good for me. It wasn't too good for her either, come to think of it. Yes folks, doing investigations can be a lot of fun.

SECTION 4:

Anatomy Of A Haunting

ANATOMY OF A HAUNTING

Up to this point, we have been looking at the various aspects of a haunting. We have talked about the type of phenomena you are likely to see and we talked about the various things you should be on the look out for and how confusing it can be. We know about the technology available to us to help in the investigation. What I would like to do here is go through a mock haunting to see how it all comes together. This is going to be a condensed version of a haunting based on some of those I have investigated over the years. It is by no means the only way a haunting progresses. For the record, all of the characters are fictitious.

How It Begins

Life was good for the Carter family. Sure, they have their share of problems just like the rest of us. Money was tight at times and there were health issues to be concerned with but all in all, they felt good about their lives. The kids were doing okay in school and work was what it was, a pain but a necessary one. Although the Carter's are Catholics, they rarely went to church. However, they do pray and they tried very hard to live their lives as good people. Overall, they were happy. Then one day, things slowly began to change.

Diane Carter was having a bad day. For one, she was tired. Little Debbie, her 5-year-old kept her up half the night. For the third night in a row, she had had nightmares about something trying to get into bed with her. Of course, the child insisted that it was no nightmare but Diane knew better. After all, nothing tried to climb into her daughter's bed. That was preposterous. When her husband Ted came down for breakfast, they discussed the matter. Ted reminded her that it was "just a phase." He told her to remember back a month or so before when Billy used to claim to see "a dark mist" floating around in his room. Diane laughed about that. It had been a tough couple of weeks with him. Feeling better, she continued with her day.

Later on, something started to bother her. She was sure that she had left her keys on the counter in the kitchen but now they were lost. As she looked around the kitchen, she muttered to herself "everything is disappearing lately." Ted had complained about the same thing. As it was near time for her to go to work, she began to panic a bit. The last thing she needed to do was be late for work again. As it was, she has been late several times in the past few weeks. Something always seemed to go wrong. The kids misplaced something or there was no hot water for the shower. One time the car would not start. Oddly enough, it did start later on when Ted tried it. She did not even remember *half* of the reasons why she had been late. Finally, she said a prayer to St. Anthony asking him to help her find her keys. As always, he came through for her. The only problem was that she could not understand how they had managed to fall into the potted plant on the windowsill in the living room. "It must be the kids," she told herself. Crisis solved, she headed to work where she knew there would be a real crisis' to solve.

After an aggravating day, Diane headed home. She had to pick up the kids at the babysitter's house and then she had to run to the grocery store. After that, she had to feed the kids, help them with their homework and once she got them settled down, she had to work on a report from work that she brought home with her. The pace was sometimes overwhelming for her. After taking care of her errands, she arrived home with the kids. When she put the key in the lock, she found that it was open already. That frightened her a bit. She knew that Ted was at work so who had opened the door? Now she began to worry about a burglar. While she debated what to do, she remembered that she had left out the back door that morning. Maybe when Ted left, he used the front door and had simply forgotten to lock it. That sounded possible.

Just the same, she walked through the house before she lets the kids in. Fortunately, the house was empty.

Once she got inside, she checked the answering machine and heard that Ted was working late again. She was annoyed but she felt bad for Ted. It seems like he had to work late two or three times each week and she knew that it was taking a toll on him. He had been unusually grouchy the past few weeks and she believed it was the long hours at work that were to blame. After the horrors of dinner and homework were history, she settled down on the couch with the report. The kids were playing outside so she knew she would have a little peace. That peace lasted for about 15 minutes. That was when Debbie came running into the house to tell her that there was some woman standing in the window in her room. Annoyed, Diane ran upstairs, knowing full well that she would not find anyone up there. Ordinarily, she would not even had looked but since she did find the door open, she felt that she should check, just to be sure. Of course, no one was there. She called the kids in and when they settled down in front of the TV, she got back to her report. She lit a cigarette, took a puff and puts it in the ashtray on the coffee table in front of her. A few seconds later, the telephone rang. Diane got up to answer the phone in the kitchen and when it turned out to be Ted on the line, they talked for a few minutes. When she hung up the telephone, she went back into the living room. A few seconds later, Billy called her into the kitchen.

"Dad is going to be mad!" Billy told her. "What now?" she asked. Billy didn't say a word; he just pointed to the kitchen counter. On it was her cigarette and it had burned the Formica countertop. "Did one of you do this?" she yelled to the children. Of course, they denied it and that lead to a nasty argument. Finally, she had had enough. She told the kids to get ready for bed and after the usual protests, they finally did as they were told. Only after they fell asleep did Diane work on the report. A short time later, a tired Ted came home. After he finished dinner, the couple went to bed. For the next several weeks, things seem normal in the Carter household.

That normalcy ended when Billy and Debbie get into a big fight. When Diane went to find out what was going on, she found a nearly hysterical Debbie sitting on her bed. "What's wrong, honey?" she asks the sobbing girl. Debbie handed her a doll, her favorite one. The doll no longer had hair. Debbie blamed Billy and Diane did not know what to think. Billy could be a little precocious at times but he had never been destructive before. Diane was starting to wonder what was going on lately. Needless to say, there had been a big battle with Billy over the doll and he was punished for two days. For his part, Billy was furious. He had not touched the doll, or so he swore and he could not believe that he was being punished for something he did not do. "Everybody believes Debbie," he said to himself as he sat in his room.

Strange little things continued to happen in the Carter house. So much so that Diane was beginning to believe that something was not right about it. Although she could not put a finger on it, there had just been too many strange things; too many coincidences taking place. She had mentioned her concerns to Ted but he had been anything but supportive lately. Between his moods, the kids and her job, she was becoming very frustrated. On top of that, Debbie's newest thing was to cry that her bed was shaking every night. Oddly enough, Diane had not yelled at Debbie about it. She was not sure why herself, because God knew, she was feeling more and more frustrated as the days went on. Later that night, she woke up to the sound of Debbie crying. Groggily, she walked into the child's room only to find Debbie asleep. She then walked into Billy's room. He too was asleep but something caught her eye. There was a black, mist-like thing hovering near the bed. Diane panicked and ran toward the bed. The mist disappeared just as she reached it. Then the crying started up again. Diane stayed awake the rest of the night. She was now convinced that something really was wrong with the house. She now began the process of thinking about all of the strange things the children had told her about. She began to feel guilty for all of the times she had yelled at them about it.

The following day, Diane talked to Ted about the situation. As usual, he did not want to hear anything about it. Things continue that way for a while. Then one Thursday night, Ted and Diane were in bed watching TV when Debbie called out. Ted got up and told Diane to relax; he would see what Debbie wanted. A few minutes later, Ted entered the bedroom with Debbie in his arms. Ted looked as pale as a ghost. He sat on the end of the bed and looked at Diane. "What's wrong, honey?" she asked Ted. He looked at her with a strange look in his eyes. "She told me that the bed was shaking," Ted told her quietly. "Oh, that again," Diane said. Ted looked at Diane for a second and then replied: "It was."

Now It Gets Worse

The following morning, Diane found herself in a better mood. Ted was quiet after the incident with the shaking bed but for the first time, he listened as Diane read off the litany of strange occurrences that had taken place in the house. After listening to her talk, he told her: "I have to have time to think about this." Now Diane could not wait until he came down for breakfast so that they could talk about the situation. However, she was surprised when he told her that he may have made too much of the bed shaking incident. He listed several possible causes, none of which made any sense. To Diane, it almost sounded like he was trying to convince *himself*. He then told her to make sure that she didn't scare the kids with any of "those ideas." Diane now felt deflated again and very much alone. She was oddly silent over breakfast. As she got ready for work, she reminded herself that it was Friday. She was tired and needed the weekend off.

After work that night, Ted brought home a pizza and a movie for the family to watch. After they ate, he put the TV on and put the tape into the VCR. The family settled in to watch the movie. About ten minutes into it, the tape ejected by itself and the TV went off. Diane looked at Ted. He got up and muttered something about a power surge and turned the TV back on. Again, they settled down and the movie played. Ted was the first to notice the cold. "Honey, did you turn the heat up when you came in tonight?" She told him that she had. Ted got up and checked the thermostat and was satisfied with the setting. "It must be getting cold out," he announced as he took two blankets out of the closet. "We'll just have to snuggle," he told everyone. The family watched their movie in peace. After it was over, Diane put the kids to bed. Once that was done, she settled onto the couch next to Ted. She wanted to talk to him again about what she felt was a problem in the house but she was afraid to. Instead, she sat quietly next to her husband. Slowly she nodded out, the stress of the week finally hitting her. As she dozed off, she heard a scream. She felt herself being thrown off the couch. As she came awake, she realized that Ted had knocked her off the couch in his haste to run upstairs. Amazingly enough, she reached Billy's room right on Ted's heels.

"What is it?" Ted asked Billy. "In the corner," Billy said as he pointed to the corner by his dresser. "There was something there a minute ago! It was dark and..." Before he could finish, Ted walked over to where Billy had pointed. He picked up a small picture frame that had fallen over. He looked at it and then placed it back down, the picture against the dresser. With that, he told Billy to come down stairs with him. On his way down, he picked up Debbie, who had awakened from Billy's scream. The family was silent as they went downstairs. They settled onto the couch and watched TV in silence. Shortly after eleven, Diane told Ted that she was tired. Since both children were asleep, she suggested that they each take one upstairs. She was surprised when Ted told her that he felt it was best that they let the children sleep downstairs for the night. When she asked him why, he told her that he felt it was best not to wake them. Diane said nothing and went upstairs. After she changed into her nightgown, she walked into Billy's room. She went immediately to the dresser and picked up the picture. Her mouth opened and she let it drop to the floor. The picture, still inside the frame, was shredded.

The Problem Spreads

Ted's parents, Don and Irma came to visit the next day. It had been months since they had been down. They lived about fours away so the family did not get together as often as they liked. Since it was such a long drive, the Carter's would spend the night. The children were thrilled to see their paternal grandparents and they were even happier when they were each given a toy. When they finally went off to play, the adults sat down and talked. Neither Diane nor Ted mentioned any of the strange happenings that had taken place. There was too much else to talk about and while Diane did think about it, she figured there would be plenty of time to discuss it over the next few days. After spending a pleasant day together, the family decided to go out for dinner. Before leaving, Irma went upstairs to use the bathroom. When she came down, she looked pale and shaken. "Oh my God, what's wrong, Ma?" Diane asked her mother-in-law. "I, I just saw something, ah, someone upstairs." Diane immediately called for Ted who had gone down to the basement with his father. Ted and Don came back together. Before Ted could say a word, Diane told him what Irma had told her. Ted and Don both charged up the stairs to see if someone was up there. Ted knew he wouldn't find anyone. When they came back down, they heard Irma describing what she had seen. "She had these dark eyes, almost like they were sunken in." Irma's hands shook as she described the apparition she had witnessed in the bathroom mirror. "Her hair was a dirty blonde," she continued "and it was long and messy." "That is the lady I see in the window all the time," Debbie said. No one had noticed her standing in the doorway. "When do you see her?" Ted asked his daughter. "Once in a while," she answered her father. "Does she ever talk to you?" Don asked. "No, I only see her when I'm outside."

"She talks to me," Billy announced. He had just walked into the kitchen. Diane, her voice trembling, asked Billy what she said to him. "Well, it's kinda like weird stuff, you know, like how this place belongs to her and so do we." "She says what?" Don asked incredulously. "Well, she told me that we were encroaching on her territory and that we belonged to her." Then, seven-year-old Billy looked at his mother and asked her: "Mommy, what does encroaching mean?"

What is happening at the Clark house is typical of the way a haunting often begins. You have a typical family trying to muddle their way through life. They have the usual concerns, jobs, school, and money. However, life begins to change, almost imperceptibly at first. There are usually small annoyances and several examples of coincidences, like misplaced items. Having studied this field for most of my life, I no longer believe in coincidence. Call it what you will but I believe that everything that happens in life has a purpose and that there is an *intelligence* behind everything that happens. (God knows that we rarely use any.) Nothing happens by chance. What is also typical in this case is that the children were the first ones targeted. That could be because they are naturally more psychic than the adults are. That makes it easier for the spirit. On the other hand, they may have been chosen because they were viewed as the weakest links. Which is it?

Also typical is the way that Diane slowly began to realize that something was amiss in the house. Of course, she had her doubts but slowly things piled up and it reached a point where it was hard to deny the problem. Ted's reaction to her attempts to discuss the situation are typical as well. He brushes it off and tells her not to frighten the kids. He sees things and one minute she believes that he realizes that something is wrong but then he waffles. This is hard on her because she is on an emotional roller coaster. This makes her feel isolated. Ted had been grouchy lately. As Diane knew, he was working a lot of overtime. She knew herself that she became short tempered when she was tired and she believed that all Ted needed was an easier schedule and maybe a little extra sleep. Was Ted grouchy because he was tired or was there maybe something else going on? Is it both?

It seems obvious that there are some paranormal events transpiring but how can you be sure which ones really are paranormal? Did Diane inadvertently take her cigarette with her and place it on the counter top where it eventually burned it? What if she didn't do it? Could that be viewed as a malicious act? What about the doll that was found with its hair cut? That one is pretty obvious, or is it? Now, if you agree that this may well be the start of a haunting, what type of spirit are we dealing with? Is it too early to tell?

(Back To The Story)

Ted and Diane were perplexed that Billy hadn't said anything to them about the apparition talking to him. When he was questioned about that, he made a point of telling everyone that no one listened to him when he did tell them things. Both parents felt bad because they knew he was right. During dinner that night, nothing was said about the apparition that Irma saw. No one wanted to frighten the children any more than they already were. Ted and his father did everything they could to make everyone laugh while they ate. Despite the circumstances, everyone had a good time. On the ride back to the house, the mood began to grow somber. Again, Ted and Don did their best to lighten things up. They almost succeeded. When they arrived home, they entered the house tentatively. Irma and Diane went straight to the kitchen. Diane put on a pot of coffee and Irma began putting ice cream in bowls for everyone. The family gathered in the living room and talked. Again, the adults kept the tone lighthearted so as not to frighten the children. Around ten, the children began to get drowsy. Diane was hoping they would be able to sleep. She told the children to kiss their grandparents goodnight and to go up stairs. Billy protested a little; he wanted to stay up with the adults. Debbie was too tired to care. Just as Diane reached the bottom of the stairs, a loud crash sounded from upstairs. Ted flew past Diane and the children and took the stairs two at a time. When he entered the master bedroom, the source of the crash was obvious; a large box of books he had left on the chair had fallen off. Ted had meant to take it off the chair before he left because he knew it was going to fall. However, he had forgotten to do that after the commotion started over the apparition his mother had seen. Ted breathed a sigh of relief when he saw what it was.

Once the children were asleep, the adults talked about the problem. No one really knew what to do. Don and Irma were both believers in the supernatural. They often enjoyed watching shows like "Sightings" and "Haunted History." Talking about it made Diane more nervous. However, Ted took some comfort in it. Other people had hauntings and they all seemed fine. Maybe they were making too much of it, he thought. Finally, everyone decided to go to bed. The rest of the night passed by quietly.

There were no odd occurrences for the next several weeks, so Diane and Ted saw their lives go back to normal. Ted was still working heavy overtime and Diane still brought work home to do. The children got their report cards during that period. Debbie's was good; Billy's was not. Diane began spending more time working with him. His grades had never been a problem in the past and Diane was concerned about it. Ted wrote it off as a case of Billy getting lazy with his studying.

One night, Diane came home from work and entered the kitchen. She was hit with a horribly foul odor. The stench was so bad that it made her gag. She looked all around the kitchen for the source of the odor but she could not find it. She looked in the garbage can under the sink but it was empty. She was about to leave the room when Billy walked in, went to the refrigerator and took out a can of soda. He then sat at the table and began drinking it. Diane was amazed; she was ready to vomit and Billy sat there as if he did not smell a thing. Just then, the telephone rang. Diane answered it and found Ted on the line. He was going to have to work late again. For some reason, this bothered Diane more than usual. She hung up the telephone and walked into the living room. She stopped and turned. In her annoyance at the phone call, she had forgotten about the stench. She entered the kitchen but the odor was gone. She shook her head and went back into the living room.

Two nights later, Diane picked up the dinner dishes and put them in the sink. Ted turned on the coffee pot and offered to do the dishes. Diane was tired and had no problem with that. While she went upstairs, Ted washed the dishes. When she came back down, she found Ted standing in the kitchen. He was holding a broken dinner plate. "Did you drop one, honey?" Diane asked her husband. "It was the weirdest thing," he began. "I washed the dish, stuck it in the drain board and a couple of seconds later, I heard a cracking sound. When I looked to see what it was, the dish had split in two." "It probably had a hairline crack in it, hon. I'm sure that's all it is. These dishes take a beating in this house." Ted smiled at her and agreed that she was right. A short time later, Irma called. Ted answered the phone and stood there listening. Diane was surprised that he was saying nothing. "What is it, Ted?" Ted put his hand up as if to tell Diane to hold on. "Okay, Ma. Calm down. What did Dad say about it?" Ted then listened some more. Diane did not know what to make of it. Then the doorbell rang and Diane went to answer it. At the door was her next-door neighbor. She had just come by to chat.

After she left, Diane asked Ted about the odd call. "Ma said that she saw that ghost again, only this time, it was in her own bathroom mirror." Diane chuckled. "Great, a ghost that lives in mirrors." Ted saw no humor in that. "You didn't think it was funny when it happened here," he told Diane sternly. "I'm sorry, hon," she answered him. He was obviously concerned, she knew but she also knew that he was getting testy again and she was growing tired of it. "What do you think?" she asked him. "I don't know what to think. Ma said that she is going to talk to her priest about it tomorrow." "Do you think that will help,

Ted?" "Maybe, I don't know? Funny thing though," he went on. "When she told me that, there was a loud crashing sound. Dad told me that a picture fell off the wall."

* * * *

There are a number of points here for us to look at. We will see some things that are obvious. We will also see several areas that can best be described as "gray" areas. Those "gray" areas are all too familiar to the experienced investigator and generally result in an over-wracked brain. I have spent many a sleepless night pondering problems such as this. I would be curious to see what you would make of this haunting so far. What are your thoughts? Which way do you see the case heading? These are questions you should be asking yourself as we study this anatomy.

First of all, did you see the effect laughter had. Even if for just a short time, laughing made everyone relax. I will spare you the speech on endorphins and serotonin releases and just say that laughter can be a powerful tool in a haunting. On the other hand, did you notice how talking about the situation made Diane nervous? It stands to reason that it would but that can be a negative tool in a haunting. It can ultimately lead to "spooking" oneself. Still looking at the psychological aspects of the haunting, you can see how knowing that others have lived through hauntings helped the situation. It is a form of coping skill and it is something that the investigator must teach the victims. Unfortunately, you also see the roller coaster the victims ride on a daily basis. You think the problem has ended and you start living your life again in a way that resembles normalcy when, boom, it starts up again. It is a frustrating and common cycle in a haunting. Each time it happens, it takes a greater toll on the victim's nerves. They become hopeful, then everything crashes. It has a nasty cumulative effect and it leads to cynicism. Cynicism is a *bad* element in a haunting. It can greatly increase the power of the spirit. Plus, it leads to a sense of hopelessness and that is a very bad thing in a haunting. Here is another psychological question: Why are Billy's grades starting to suffer? Is it from the pressure of the haunting or is there something more sinister at work? Is it just a normal phase that he is going through? Maybe he is just slacking off on his schoolwork?

Now, let us take a look at some of the phenomena itself. Take a look at the box of books that fell. Was that a natural occurrence or part of the haunting? It could have been a case where the box was put too close to the end of the chair. Ted himself expected the box to fall. It could also be a case where the spirit wanted to make its presence felt. How would you classify that using the "weighing system?" How about the "exploding" plate? Did it have a hairline crack in it or was that another preternatural or supernatural occurrence? Think again of the weighing system. Next on the list is the stench Diane experienced. Why did Billy not smell it? Does that mean that Diane imagined it? Was the odor a form of telepathic impression?

It would appear that the spirit in the Carter house followed Ted's parents to their own home. Can human spirits do that? The last item is the picture that fell of the wall during the phone call. Keeping in mind the weighing system, was that a paranormal occurrence? Also, since it took place while they were discussing the priest, does that appear to have a demonic overtone to it?

(The Story Continues)

Diane did not know what to make of the phone call from Ted's parents. The one thing she knew for sure was that she was frightened again. Very frightened. Ted was also upset by the phone call. Diane could tell that much. However, Ted seemed to turn inward, refusing to talk about it. Diane wondered if the spirit was attempting to possess him. She did not know much about possession but she did know that Ted was growing sullen. She also had the feeling that things were going to turn sour in a hurry. Unfortunately for the Carter family, she was right. Also unfortunately, it did not take long to happen.

It was around three in the morning when she heard Debbie scream. She bolted out of the bed and charged down the hall to her daughter's room. As she entered the room, the door started to close and Diane ran straight into it, cutting her forehead. Temporarily impervious to the pain, Diane went into the room. Flicking on the light, Diane saw Debbie huddled on the floor, sobbing hysterically. "Something grabbed my hand Mommy and it pulled me from the bed." Diane grabbed

Debbie in her arms and tried to calm the hysterical child down. "No, honey. It was just a dream." Debbie continued to sob loudly. "No Mommy, it wasn't a dream. It pulled me from the bed." Diane knew better that to argue with Debbie in the state she was in. Instead, she scooped her up and brought her to her bedroom. She sat Debbie down and knelt in front of her. The first thing she noticed was that Debbie's right hand looked red and swollen. Diane felt a shiver run down her spine.

Despite all of the commotion, Ted never woke up. That surprised Diane. He was not the lightest of sleepers but she was sure that Debbie's scream should have awakened him. Suddenly the room grew ice cold. Diane reached over and shook Ted. She *knew* that something sinister was about to happen. Once again, she was right. She held Debbie tight against her chest, as if shielding her from the horror she knew was coming. Despite being shook by Diane, Ted did not budge; he did not even moan. Shivering more and with panic welling up inside her, Diane screamed at Ted. "Wake up damn it!" she yelled at him. However, Ted continued to lay motionless. Diane could not believe it. She noticed something else. Ted was asleep lying flat on his back. He *never* slept on his back. "Ted, please wake up!" Suddenly the room seemed to fill with a white mist. It was like a fog slowly creeping in and the room grew colder. In the far left corner of the room, a black shape seemed to take form. Diane shook Ted furiously but as before, he would not budge. "Dear God, Ted, wake up!" she screamed. Ted moved slightly. The black shape was darker now and it appeared to be taking on solid form.

Diane's terror increased. Although later on she could not explain it but at that moment she *knew* that there would be serious trouble when the thing in the corner completed taking form. What that trouble would be she couldn't tell you. She just knew that whatever happened would be bad. She squeezed Debbie tighter against her chest. "Please dear God, wake him up!" Ted moaned slightly. The room grew colder still and it began to fill with the same stench Diane had experienced that time in the kitchen. The dark shape was almost solid now; to Diane it resembled a hooded figure. "Please Dear God, please Dear God, wake him up." Diane was frantic now. Suddenly Ted bolted awake. "What the…" He never finished the sentence. Seeing the dark form, Ted bolted from the bed and put himself between it and his family. "You are not going to hurt my family, you son of a…" Before he finished the sentence, there was a loud bang. It sounded as if someone fired a canon in the room. However, with that bang, the black form disappeared and the stench went with it. Gradually the room warmed up.

Diane tried to fill Ted in on what had happened but she could barely talk through her sobbing. Debbie was nearly hysterical as well. When Ted saw the knot on Diane's head, he ran downstairs and got some ice. As Ted tried to comfort his family and hold the ice on Diane's head, the telephone rang. "Christ, what now?" Ted exclaimed. Diane pointed to the telephone. Ted took that to mean that he should answer it. He picked up the telephone and put it to his ear. "Hello," he asked in a flat tone. "Ted, it's Momma. Is everything okay over there? I woke up with this terrible feeling. Dad said I shouldn't call but I was so worried." Irma wasn't giving Ted the chance to answer her. " It's alright, Mom," Ted broke in. "Something happened but I'm not sure what yet." Diane sat and watched Ted as he talked to his mother. She was calmer now and was more concerned with Debbie than herself. "Ted, we have to talk. Dad and I will be over tomorrow night. We'll stay the weekend." "That's good Mom." Diane watched as Ted's brow furrowed. "Ted, I talked to Father…" "What Mom? I can't hear you through the static." Straining, Ted tried to hear his mother. I am going to talk to him…" Again, static filled the phone. After a couple of minutes, the line cleared. Ted hung up the phone and turned toward Diane. She filled him in on the events of the night. Amazingly, Billy was spared the horror. For that night, that is.

What do you think? The plot thickens. Is it becoming clearer or more fuzzy? It is a little of both, I think. Once again, Diane makes mention of Ted's moods. She actually fears possession. What do you think? Are there signs of possession? Mood swings are as normal as breathing, at least in a world such as ours. Still, there *are* some red flags going up. Now, when Diane went into Debbie's room, did the door close on her? In that case, we would have to ask her but it is something that is possible. Does that matter? As you are about to see, it might. The next question concerns Debbie being pulled from the bed. I am not sure that I would readily believe that she *was* pulled but I certainly would not discount it either. My guess would be that she did indeed have her hand grabbed but in pulling away, she may have fallen out of the bed. Does it make a difference? It does; in fact it is an important point.

You see, we now have *possible* evidence of intent. It is one thing for a spirit to *touch* her; it is quite another thing for it to do something that carries with it the possibility of injury. Certainly there is the risk of broken bone or a head injury in a situation like that. This takes us back to the incident with the door Diane "ran" into. If the spirit did close the door, did it do so for the sake of keeping Diane out of the room or did it time it so that she would run into it? That may be a reach but if that is so, we are once again seeing evidence of intent. Does this prove the spirit is negative? In my opinion, yes, it is negative. Whether the idea was to hurt her or not, there was *some* kind of intent. It may have been to keep her out of the room and while that is far different from it trying to cause injury, it still shows *intent.* A benign spirit would not try to stop a mother from coming to the aid of her daughter.

Should we now begin to look closely at the possibility of a demonic haunting? Herein lies the problem. If Debbie *were* pulled from the bed, the answer to those questions would be yes. However, if she *fell* as a result of fright, the answer would be no. Of course, as the investigator on the case, it is quite the quandary. It is our role to protect the family but our potentially best piece of evidence is so shrouded in gray that it is difficult to be sure. We can go on our gut feeling but we would be doing a tremendous disservice to the Carter's if we planted the seed of a demonic haunting, especially if that is not the case. Since hauntings are all about fear, we could inadvertently play right into the hands of the spirit. Even if it *is* a demon, there is nowhere near enough evidence to get an exorcism approved. Hell, there might not even be enough evidence to support a church investigation.

Another point to look at is Ted's inability to wake up. That becomes a telling piece of evidence. It appears to be "psychic paralysis," where a person is kept in a state resembling suspended animation. Can a human spirit do that? Believe it or not, that is a tough one to answer. I would *think* it is a demonic phenomenon but I have experienced it myself from both ends. It is similar to what I call "twilight paralysis," which is when you cannot move but are *conscious* of that fact. In fact, you struggle like hell to break the hold. I view twilight paralysis as a phenomenon that takes place during that brief time between consciousness and sleep. Just as the conscious mind is about to turn things over to the unconscious mind, the person is vulnerable, even if it is just for s very short time. An invading entity may be able to invade just as the process of consciousness is about to change. Now, when that happens, the body is paralyzed, except for the breathing functions while the mind is still awake. It is a frightening phenomenon; especially the first time one experiences it. That has happened to me a number of times and in some of those cases, there was no other evidence of a demonic presence. More gray area.

Did you notice that when Debbie said "God" or "Christ," Ted aroused a bit. Is that a telling sign? It sure *could* be. Why did it leave when Ted jumped up to confront it? Surely it was not afraid of Ted. Perhaps the spirits intent was to focus solely on Diane and when Ted entered the picture, it foiled that strategy. Foiling strategies is an important part of ending a haunting. Lastly, was Diane developing discernment? Indeed she was. Merely being exposed to paranormal phenomena helps discernment to grow. It also appears that Irma Carter is developing it as well. It is no coincidence that the women are developing faster than the men. That is true in most cases.

Escalation

Neither Ted nor Diane slept after the incident. About an hour after things settled down, Debbie did fall asleep. The only positive point Diane could find was that it was Friday. They would just have to crawl through one more day. Ted tried to convince Diane to take the day off. On top of being exhausted, she still had a good-sized lump on her forehead. They discussed the matter while Diane applied makeup to her forehead, hoping to hide most of the damage. The effort was futile. Diane insisted that she had to go to work; as it was, she was going to be bringing some of it home so she could work on it during quiet times over the weekend, if there were any. Finally, Ted gave in, or up as he put it. The one thing Ted was pleased about was that his parents were coming over for the weekend. They had a lot to talk about.

Ted managed to get through his day without too much trouble. For Diane, the day was horrible. It seemed that each minute was an hour long and everyone commented on her damaged forehead. Since she could not tell anyone the truth, she felt paranoid. In her mind, she imagined that everyone assumed that Ted had hit her or something of that nature. Of course, anyone who knew Ted knew that he was not capable of such an act. Just the same, she felt paranoid. When the day finally ended, she picked the children up as usual and went straight home. She had no idea what she would do for dinner but she would worry about that when the time came. They could always order out, she thought.

Billy went straight to his room and Diane sat on the couch with Debbie. She wanted to check to make sure that Debbie had finished her homework at the babysitters. As she looked at some papers, she heard Billy scream. Diane flew off the couch and charged up the stairs to Billy's room. When she entered, she saw that Billy had tears streaming down his face. "What, Billy, what?" Billy stepped to the side and Diane saw what had upset him so much. On top of his bureau were two soccer trophies he had won. Both were badly broken. "Debbie must have broken them. That bitch!" Diane was incredulous. "What did you call her?" she yelled more than asked. "She's a little bitch! She breaks everything I own." Debbie mustered all the patience she possessed and it was not much. "Don't ever let me hear you call her that again. Ever! She did not break those trophies." Billy stormed out of the room. "Then who did?" he said as he bolted down the stairs. Diane was sure that Billy was going to go after Debbie but instead, he sat down in the dining room crying. "Billy, your Dad will fix them when he gets home, I promise." Diane's tone was soft. She realized that Billy was feeling the pressure too. Diane looked up at the ceiling and thought to herself: "You bastard. Show yourself so I can spit in your face." The thought no sooner left her head when she heard three loud bangs.

Everyone jumped at the sound. Oddly enough, no one could tell where there sound had come from. Diane would later tell Don and Irma that the sound "seemed to come from everywhere and nowhere at the same time." Fortunately, all was quiet after that. By the time Ted came home, the household was back to normal, as normal as it could be under the circumstances. Diane discussed dinner plans with Ted and they decided that they would order a bucket of chicken and some sides as soon as Don and Irma arrived. By the time they did, everyone was starving.

Over dinner, Don complained that the usual four-hour drive had turned into closer to a six hour one. Every road they took was lined with traffic. It had been a taxing ride. After dinner was done, Irma took out a cake she had baked and Diane made some coffee. She was exhausted but pleased that her in-laws were there. She really loved the couple. Over dessert, Don told a few corny jokes and being so tired, everyone was in a silly mood. By nine-thirty, both children were fading fast. Once they were tucked in bed, the four adults sat in the living room to discuss the situation. Irma began telling Ted and Diane about the conversation with her priest. She told them that he seemed to genuinely believe what she told him. His suggestion was to have the house blessed. He felt that might do the trick. Of course, since he was four-hours away, Ted and Diane would have to talk to the own parish priest. Diane was anxious about that since they were not regulars at Mass every Sunday. Irma pushed the issue with Diane. "Listen, Dear, Don and I are going to be here on Sunday. We'll go with you to talk to him." "Damn right we will," Don added. As they were talking, they heard children's laughter coming from upstairs along with the sound of running feet. Diane let out a sigh. Before she could say anything, Irma told her to relax. "After all, it is the weekend. Let them have some fun." Diane knew she was right. By eleven, Ted and Diane had just about had it; it had been a long day. Just as they were getting ready to call it a night, they heard footsteps coming down the stairs.

"What are you guys doing up?" Don asked them good-naturedly. "I'm scared, Mommy," Debbie said. Before anyone could say a word, Billy added: "Me too." "Did anything happen?" Diane asked. Both children just shook their heads as if to say: no. Irma smiled. "Why don't you both stretch out on the couch for now." Without saying a word, both children went to the couch. Ted covered them with a small blanket and the adults moved into the kitchen. Oddly enough, they did not discuss the haunting. They were all having fun and none of them wanted to ruin the mood. There had not been too many good moods over the past few weeks. It was just around mid-night when Diane decided to go to bed. She stood up and began clearing off the table when she heard the kids running around again. "Where do they get their energy from?" Diane asked no one in particular. "I don't know?" answered Irma, "but I sure wish I had some of it." Again, they heard laughter coming from the second floor. Ted stood up and stretched. "I'm going up now, I'll put them to bed." Diane just nodded.

Ted was surprised that the children were still awake; they had seemed so tired just a short time ago. He listened to them running around as he headed up the stairs. "Funny thing," he thought to himself, "it sounds like three sets of footsteps up there." He was about halfway up when he glanced at the couch. His children were sound asleep. Ted froze. "What the hell is going on here?" he asked himself. He started back down the stairs just as Don walked into the living room. He saw the children and the look on his son's face. "Good God," he said to Ted. "Is it worth looking around up there?" he asked his son. Ted shook his head. "There won't be anyone up there. There never is."

The adults stayed up for several hours after the running incident. Finally, fatigue got the best of them and they retired for the night. Diane hated putting the children back in their own beds. She felt that they were too far away and she knew that she could not protect them and that made her feel helpless. She stayed awake until the sun began to rise. Things did not seem so frightening to her when it was light out. She was developing an intense dislike for the night and the darkness that went with it. Things lived in the dark, she now believed. Things that had no right to live.

It was after ten when Diane finally got out of bed. She was grateful that her family had let her sleep. The atmosphere was muted for the rest of the morning but it began to change in the afternoon. By late evening, everyone appeared to be in a good mood. Irma decided to cook dinner for everyone. She made Ted's favorite dinner: lasagna. Other than the oven occasionally turning itself off, things in the house were quiet. After dinner, the adults sat in the living room while the children went outside to play with their friends. The mood was light for the most part. Then Diane brought up her nervousness about seeing the priest the following day. As she explained her fears, the glass ashtray on the coffee table suddenly flew into Diane's face, opening up a cut on the bridge of her nose. It began to bleed profusely. Ted raced to his wife while Irma sat frozen in her chair. She kept repeating: "Oh my God, oh my God." It was obvious that Diane needed to go to the emergency room for treatment so Ted took her while Irma and Don watched the children. Ted and Diane came home around ten-thirty. Diane's nose was broken and she received three stitches for the cut. The doctor had given her some medication for the pain and that made Diane drowsy. Shortly after getting home, she went to bed. Ted stayed with her for a while and then went downstairs to talk to his parents. Ted would not sleep at all that night. He began to wonder if he would ever sleep again.

There can no longer be any doubt that we have a bone fide haunting going on here. It is now what I call "a haunting with a purpose." There is no attempt on the spirit's part to hide its presence. If anything, it is getting much bolder. We have gone past the stage where we have to wonder whether the events taking place are normal. We now know that they aren't. Now the problem is that everything is going to be blamed on the haunting. Paranoia reigns supreme now. Also, the spirit is now feeding off of the fear of everyone in the house. This is typical of negative hauntings. Billy was obviously upset about his trophies. Was his reaction normal? I would say so. Calling his sister a "bitch" is fairly mild. Just the same, what you are seeing here is an attempt on the spirits part to drive a wedge between the family members. That is so typical in a haunting. Does that point to the demonic? Not necessarily, although it is a concern.

Did you notice that when Diane thought about spitting in the spirits face that there were three loud knocks? Does the fact that it is three mean that it is demonic? Again, not necessarily but we have a bunch of red flags going up. Did the spirit "read" her mind? It is said that even demons cannot read minds but I can debate that point. I have sure had experiences where it seemed that it could. Perhaps it was able to interpret the energy that Diane put out when she had that thought. There is another theory that might explain this, as is mentioned in Katherine Ramsland's excellent book: "Ghost," published by St. Martin's Paperbacks. In it, she notes that John A. Wheeler, a physicist from Princeton, who believes that memories are not stored in our brains but are "woven into the fabric of the universe." Thus, memories are outside of us and can be accessed by others. What does that have to do with mind reading? Well, if that theory is true, it stands to reason that in order to become memories, the data has to be put there by us. If that theory *is* true, perhaps spirits pick up that information just as we are "depositing" them, unconsciously, of course. That would seem to make some sense. Let us take a look at the fact that it took Don and Irma two hours extra to make the drive to the Carter house. Is that paranormal? Probably not. We have all sat in traffic for hours. Still though, you have to wonder if there is something more involved, especially since one of the main topics to be discussed is the issue of the priest. This is where you have to be careful. You can easily read into the events taking place. Do you see how confusing it can be?

The next incident to look at involves the laughter and the running around that was heard by the family while the children were asleep on the couch. Was the laughter evil? If so, is that a demonic manifestation? The other point to look at is that there appeared to be three sets of feet running. Does that mean that there are three spirits at work? The answer to that is that it could be. Were there actual feet involved or was that a sound that was projected into the adult's heads telepathically? According to years of research, it could be either. There is considerable evidence that sightings and sounds are telepathically projected. However, since we have pictures and tons of audio evidence, we also know that sights and sounds are exactly what they appear to be. In a case like this, what you would have to think about are vibrations. When you hear the running, do you feel a vibration that would occur if solid weight were hitting the floor? Does it matter either way? Not really. For the sake of determining the weight of a haunting, it really does not matter. There have not been enough hauntings investigated to determine whether there is a difference in strength between a spirit that causes "solid" sounds versus the spirit that uses telepathy. Perhaps there is a difference but again, there are not that many hauntings around to really determine anything. Of course, that is a good thing.

You may have noticed how Diane feels that events that are frightening at night are less so in the light of day. I well remember from my haunting how I would lay awake all night and as soon as the sun began to rise, my fear level dropped dramatically. I often chided myself during the day for being so frightened by something that seemed fairly benign during the day. Of course, as soon as it began getting dark out, those fears began to grow again. The last item in this section is the ashtray that struck Diane. It caused her physical injury so that would strongly suggest that there is a demonic spirit operating in the house. If that is the case, the question you would need to answer is whether you have a demonic infestation taking place or do you have a "human" haunting with demonic overtones? What is the difference? Well, a demonic infestation is just that, an infestation. The demon is causing the haunting. However, in the other scenario, you have human spirits doing the haunting but there may be a demonic "puppeteer" at work. The real difference comes when you try to end the haunting. A puppeteer may leave as soon as the attempts to get rid of it heat up. It will probably not want to stick around too long if it believes that an exorcism is forthcoming. That too can happen in an infestation but in those severe cases, the demon will not leave until it is forced out through an exorcism. So it is a big difference.

A Turn For The Worse

On Sunday, the Carter family went to Church. Diane went also even though she was in considerable pain. She felt that her presence would add validity to their story. Right after Mass, Irma cornered Father Michael. He was the youngest priest in the parish and the family thought that they would have a better chance convincing a younger priest of their problem. Father Michael listened patiently to their story and when they were done, he sat quietly for a few moments. It was obvious that Father Michael was uncomfortable. "Well," he began, "I am not sure what to tell you. I mean ghosts and demons are something from the past. These things do not happen in real life." Ted bristled. "Diane's injuries happened in real life Father. Can you explain them?" Ted's statement was more accusatory than questioning. Father Michael shifted nervously in his chair. "I am not questioning her injury, Mr. Carter. No, all I am saying is that there has to be some rational explanation for what happened. I just don't buy into the idea of a ghost doing something like that." He then began to explain some of the possible scientific causes and it became obvious to the Carters that Father Michael really knew nothing about the subject. When Irma pressed him to come to the house and bless it, Father Michael told her that he would have to run it past the Pastor, Father Raymond. The Carters felt deflated. They had purposely chosen Father Michael because they figured he would be their best bet. Father Raymond had the reputation of being grouchy and hardheaded. They felt that he would simply dismiss their claims out of hand. On the positive side, the Carter household was quiet that day. In fact, it would remain quiet for several weeks.

Father Michael was bothered by the Carter's story. He hated to admit it but he was frightened by it. He wanted to talk to Father Raymond about it but he was unsure how his superior would respond to it. Father Michael was new to the parish and he did not want to get on Father Raymond's bad side. Instead, he decided to talk to Father Paul. Father Michael had become friends with Father Paul, even though he was only the weekend assistant. He was a kind and gentle man who was easy to talk to.

After dinner that night, he told Father Paul the story. Before he could finish it, Father Paul waved his hand in a dismissive manner. "It is all nonsense," Father Paul began. "People who believe in that stuff are all sick, if you ask me. I have been a priest for nearly 50 years now and I have never encountered a case of ghosts haunting people. And demons, no less." Father Michael did his best to convince Father Paul of the Carter's sincerity. "Oh, I am not suggesting that they are faking it, son. No, I am just saying that there are no such things as ghosts and demonic hauntings." Father Michael kept the conversation going. "But Father, the Church believes in demonic possession. That is why they have the Rituale Romanum." Father Paul laughed. "Son, that is a prehistoric relic from an era long gone, and rightfully so, I might add." Father Michael knew he could not win the argument so he let the subject drop. However, he would think about it for a long time to come.

It had been over two weeks since anything unusual happened in the Carter home. Although they had not forgotten about it by any means, the family rarely mentioned it. However, one night, Diane began to get the feeling that she was being watched. It was after nine and the children were in bed. Ted was working a double shift so Diane was taking the quiet time to get some work done. Things were easing up at her job and she rarely needed to take work home with her. She hated doing it but she could not work overtime because of the children so she did what she had to do. Just the same, she was glad that things were slowing down at work. It was around ten when Diane began to feel uncomfortable in the living room. She decided to put some water on the stove for some hot chocolate. While the water was heating up, she went upstairs to check on the kids. Both were sound asleep although

Debbie was restless, moaning and tossing around a bit. Diane sat on the edge of the bed and softly rubbed her daughter's head. Debbie let out a sigh and relaxed almost immediately. Feeling better now, Diane went back downstairs to get her hot chocolate. She entered the kitchen only to find that the stove was off. The water was still cold. "Damn," she muttered to herself. "I can forget anything." With that, she turned the stove on again. When she went back into the kitchen a few minutes later, she found the stove off again.

She turned it back on but she could feel panic creeping in. Suddenly, she began to cry. Diane was sure that the nightmare was about to return. When the water was hot, she poured it into a mug and went back to the living room to finish her work. What she saw horrified her: All of the papers she had been working on were shredded. Now the tears came quickly. Diane cried for several minutes. Then, she redid her work. It was nearly midnight when she finally finished. She was putting her papers into her briefcase just as Ted walked through the door. When she saw him, she ran up to him and hugged him. Then she began crying again. Ted did his best to calm her down and the couple went upstairs. After checking on the children, they went to bed.

The conversations over breakfast were muted. Even the children seemed to be depressed. Perhaps they were sensing their parent's mood. After breakfast, Diane straightened the kitchen up and headed off to work. It turned out to be an aggravating day for her. She couldn't wait for it to end. By the time she arrived home, she was at her wits end. Of course, the children picked that night to act up. They argued non-stop, complained about dinner and refused to get ready for bed. Once again, Ted worked late, although he did not do a double shift. When he arrived home around nine, Diane was fit to be tied. It did not take long for the argument to begin. "You are never here when I need you," Diane yelled when Ted asker her what was wrong. "Diane, I don't have a choice, you know that. Did something happen today?" Diane was furious. "No, nothing happened at all. I worked my ass off, picked up the kids, attempted to get them to do their homework and stop fighting with each other and then had to all but wrestle them to get them to put on their pajamas. And the best part is that I get to do this all again tomorrow night and the night after that and the night after that. And you, of course, won't be here for any of it. You never are."

Ted knew that Diane was under pressure but he was so tired and the last thing he needed was to be criticized for working so many hours, especially when it was the last thing he wanted to do. "You don't seem to mind when you get my paycheck. Then it's just fine. Do you think I *like* working all of these hours when I am so goddamn tired all I want to do is crawl into bed and die?" With that, Diane stormed out of the kitchen, crying as she went. As she stormed through the living room, she did not notice the black mist taking shape near the TV. After he finished eating, Ted walked into the living room and turned on the TV. To his surprise, the set did not turn on. He glanced at the entertainment center and saw that there was no power to the VCR or the DVD player. He looked behind the unit and saw that the plug to the power strip was out of the wall. Straining to get behind it, he plugged it back in.

Diane lay in bed, crying softly. She felt that she could not take much more. She knew that she should not be short with Ted. However, her own nerves were frayed, possibly to the breaking point, she feared. Suddenly, there was a loud bang and one of the pictures on the wall went flying. That was followed by another bang. This time, some items on her bureau went flying. Ted was downstairs when he heard the two bangs. He was sure that Diane was throwing a tantrum so he stayed in his chair watching the TV. He did not want to play the role of enabler. Another bang resonated throughout the house. That one was the loudest of the three and it was accompanied by the sound of glass breaking. Ted, furious now, jumped off the chair. He had never felt this angry at his wife. He took the stairs two at a time, steeling for the fight he knew was coming. Just as he reached the bedroom, the door slammed in his face.

Ted pushed against the door but it would not budge. "Open the goddamn door now!" he screamed at Diane. His command was met with another bang. This time, the door was hit and more glass broke. "Son of a bitch!" he screamed. "Open the door now or I'll break the damn thing down!" Ted knew that Diane had lost it completely but he was not going to let her destroy everything they owned. By now, Billy and Debbie were standing in the hallway; both of them were crying. "Why is Mommy doing this?" Billy said, his voice breaking. There was yet another crash against the door and more glass breaking. "Mommy is in danger, Daddy. Help her!" little Debbie pleaded. "Diane, I have had enough! Open the door!" More crashing and glass breaking. "She has done it this time," Ted said to himself. With that, he slammed his body against the door. The door flew open.

Ted could not believe his eyes. The destruction was terrible. He stood still, shocked by what he saw. Suddenly, a book flew towards his head and he had to duck. For the first time, it began to sink in that this was no temper tantrum on Diane's part. He looked for her and saw her crouched down next to the bed, her arms protecting her head, which was covered in broken glass. The children rushed into the room and Ted pushed them out and slammed the door shut. He had no sooner done that when the bureau moved about three feet away from the wall. A hairbrush sailed by Ted, just missing him. He ran towards Diane and leapt on the bed and jumped down to where she was crouching. Just as he reached her, a perfume bottle struck Ted square in the back of his head. Yelling in pain, he put himself over Diane, protecting her from the flying objects. After what seemed like an eternity, the room grew quiet.

Tentatively, Ted stood up, his eyes scanning the room for flying objects. The children were outside the bedroom screaming. Ted half expected the police to arrive shortly. He did not know which way to go. Should he help Diane or get the children? He opted to help Diane. The poor woman was covered in glass and she had several cuts on her face. She was sobbing quietly. As Ted tried to hold her, she pushed him away. "Diane, honey, please let me help you." She slowly stood up, tears streaming down her face. The telephone rang but Ted ignored it. Instead, he put his arms around Diane and led her out of the bedroom. When the door opened, the children ran to their parents. Ted and Diane both gathered their children in their arms and the family headed downstairs.

Once in the kitchen, Ted began cleaning Diane up. She had several small cuts on her face and she said that her ribs hurt. She also had a deep bruise forming on the back of her right hand. It must have successfully blocked something targeted for her head. The children continued to cry hysterically. Diane continued her quiet sobbing. To Ted, his wife appeared to be in a state of shock. Once again, the telephone rang. For the second time, Ted ignored it. He was vaguely aware of the answering machine picking up the call. He thought he heard his father's voice on the phone but at the moment, all he cared about was Diane. He sat her in a chair and went to talk to the children. "Mommy is alright. She's just a little frightened." That did little to assuage the children's fears. "C'mon guys, Mommy is okay. Why don't you put the TV on for a while? Okay?" They went into the living room and Ted heard the TV go on. After a few minutes, the children stopped crying.

Again, the telephone rang. This time, Ted answered it. There was no one on the other end. He set up the coffee maker and sat down next to Diane. He tried to talk to her but it was as if she didn't hear him. Ted was afraid that she was having a nervous breakdown. "Honey, please talk to me," he told her in a soothing tone. It took a good ten minutes before Diane even looked at him. Then she started crying loudly. Ted did not know what to do. He put his arms around Diane and held her tight. "It's gonna be alright, Diane. It's really is." Diane looked up at him and told him that it would never be all right again. "It will honey, I promise you." Ted ran his right hand through his hair and was surprised to find his hair matted. He winced in pain when he touched the area where the perfume bottle had hit. He had a nasty cut to go along with the lump. However, he did not have time for that now.

The couple sat in the kitchen drinking their coffee. Diane sat silently, staring at her coffee mug. For the fourth time, the telephone rang. However, it stopped before Ted could reach it. He glanced at the answering machine and saw that there were two messages. He pushed the button to play them back. "Ted, it's Mom," the first one began. "Answer the phone. I know something is wrong." There was a short pause and his mother told him to call her when he got the chance. The second message then played. It was Ted's dad. This message was more blunt. "Diane, Ted, it's Dad. Pick up the phone." After a short pause: "Ted we're driving down now. We'll be there in a few hours." Ted looked at the time. They would be a good hour into their trip. He hoped his father drove fast, very fast.

Diane stood up and walked slowly into the living room. She wanted to make sure that her children were safe. The two of them sat huddled against each other on one end of the couch. Diane sat next to them and put her arms around them both. No one said a word. Ted decided to go back upstairs and take a look at the damage in the bedroom. He knew that it was severe. He had just taken a few steps towards the stairs when the phone rang again. He answered it right away. "Ted, It's Mom." "Hi Mom," Ted replied. "Ted, I'm calling from the cell phone. We're on our way down. Is everything okay?" "No Mom," Ted answered her. Suddenly, he began to cry. "Please hurry." Irma's heart broke at the sound of her son crying. "We'll be there soon, Ted. Your Dad is flying." "Good, Mom. Please hurry."

After she hung up from her call to Ted, Irma told Don about the state their son was in. That only made Don drive faster but as it was, he was pushing it. He silently prayed that there would be no cops out on the road. For the senior Carter family, the drive seemed to take forever. Once Ted was sure that his family was doing well, as well as they could under the circumstances, he went upstairs to the master bedroom. He was shocked at the amount of damage he saw. He toyed with the idea of fixing the room up but he decided to wait until his parents arrived. He wanted them to see the extent of the damage. Although it was freezing out, Ted knew he would have to open the window. The smell of Diane's perfume permeated the room to the point where it made Ted gag. That too could wait, Ted decided.

Ted went back downstairs and sat in his favorite chair, in the living room. He thought it odd that his living room suddenly seemed alien to him. He had sat in that chair countless times yet now it felt so *foreign* to him. What was once a comfort to him now seemed cold and impersonal. The entity was taking away everything he once found comforting. It added a sense of unreality to his life. He could not wait until his parents arrived. The children were asleep and Diane was slowly nodding off herself. Ted was grateful for that. He had no idea what to say to Diane and he was having problems with his own emotions. After sitting for what seemed like hours, Ted himself began to nod off. Had he looked towards the stairs, he would have seen the black mist. It hovered as if watching the family.

The sound of the doorbell woke Ted up. Groggily, he stood up and walked to the door. When he opened it, no one was there. "Now we're gonna play games, right?" he muttered. A short time later, he heard a car pull up in front of the house. Ted was pleased to see that it was his parents. Once they were in the house, Irma asked her son what was going on. Ted shook his head and told his parents to follow him upstairs. When the entered the master bedroom, Irma let out a gasp. "Oh my

God! What the hell happened in here?" Don asked. Ted filled them in on the night's events. "Don was the first to speak. "You need to pack some things and get out of here tonight. Come stay with us for awhile." Irma nodded her head in agreement. "We can't do that Dad. Diane and I have to work, the kids have school." Irma jumped in. "Ted, you can't live like this." "I know but we can't stop everything and run. Besides, it followed you home that time. It will probably do it again." Don looked around the room. His face was beat red. Irma wasn't sure whether it was anger or high blood pressure but she was concerned. Finally Don spoke: "Then we stay here and fight but we are going to fight this together as a family. I am not leaving here until this thing is over with."

Ted appreciated the gesture but he was concerned for the safety of his parents. Don would hear none of it. "I'm staying. I'll call work and tell them I'm taking a week or two off. Being the boss has *some* privileges. Ted simply shook his head up and down. He knew better than to argue with his father. Don Carter was a tough old dude and he took crap from nobody. Ted thought to add: "Living or dead." Don looked at his son and spoke: "The first thing we had all better do is get some sleep. Then in the morning, we'll fix up this room and find a way to fight this thing." Ted agreed and the three of them went downstairs. Ted went down to the basement and took some sleeping bags from a shelf. He gave those to his parents and he stretched out on his recliner. He dozed off almost immediately.

He woke to the smell of bacon and eggs. Groggily, he climbed from the recliner and walked into the kitchen. Irma was feeding the children and offered him a cup of coffee, which he accepted gratefully. "Mom," he began, "Where is Dad?" "Oh, he's upstairs straightening out the room." Ted smiled. "I should join him." Irma shook her head from side to side. "No Ted, you're going to sit down and have some coffee and some breakfast. You father has already eaten. That was that, end of discussion. Ted sipped his coffee while he waited for his breakfast. As soon as he finished eating, he went up to his bedroom. He was surprised when he entered the room; it did not look all that bad. Don had already done a lot of work. "Dad, you didn't have…" Don waved a hand as if to dismiss what Ted was trying to say. Within a half hour, the room was straightened up. "The only real casualty," Don said, "is the mirror from the dresser and I'm sure that we can get another one. There is also a gouge in the wall across the room but we can spackle that with no problem. With the room finished, the two men went downstairs.

Ted sat at the kitchen table. "Damn, I wish I had thought to take a picture of the room before you fixed it up, Dad." Don smiled and patted his breast pocket. In it was a disposable camera. "I already did that. You know how I always have a camera with me when I see the kids." Ted smiled. "I should have known better," he told his father. Irma walked over to her son and put her arms around him. She looked down at him and touched his head. "Good God, Ted, you have a deep cut on your head. Go upstairs and take a shower. Then we'll have to put something on that cut so it doesn't get infected. Ted did as he was told. While he was in the shower, he realized that he had not seen Diane. When he was finished, he went back downstairs. "Mom, where is Diane?" "Oh, she's in the den working on the computer. She is looking for help on the Internet. Ted stood up and went to the den. When he entered the room, Diane looked up at him and smiled. "Honey, I have been reading up on haunted houses and the people who investigate them. I have the name of three groups that say they help people. I'm going to call them later." Ted was pleased to see that she was doing well. Her silence after the incident had frightened him. Later that day, she made the calls.

She was only able to reach one of the groups. Fortunately for her, they were available and were willing to start the investigation the following day, Friday. The Carter house was quiet on Thursday, for which everyone was grateful. On Friday, Ted and Diane went to work and the children went to school. Around one in the afternoon, the black mist began forming in the living room where Don and Irma were sitting. Don saw it first and he stood up. "You are leaving, you son of a bitch. You are not going to hurt my family anymore." Irma was surprised by her husband's reaction. Apparently the mist was too because it slowly faded away. The rest of the day was quiet. Knowing that the investigators were coming over at six, Ted brought home some pizzas. Everyone ate quickly; they wanted to be done before the investigators arrived.

We have some interesting things going on here. The problem has worsened and that could mean that this will be a very long, severe haunting. It might also be the peak, in which case, the Carter's are through the worst of it. What do you think? The situation with the priests is not surprising. Most of the younger priests today have little or no training in the supernatural. That can make them reluctant to help, even if they *do* believe in it. Unfortunately today, many do not. As you saw with the weekend assistant, even some older priests don't believe in it. It is a crapshoot when you try to get priests to help you today. The degree of difficulty varies from city to city and parish to parish. Then, interestingly enough, the activity stops. You might think that this is a sign of sorts. Let us look at the possibilities. It could mean that at the point where the Carters decided to seek help from the Church, the invading spirit decided to vamoose. It could be that it decided to lay low for a while.

On the other hand, you would think that it would pounce on the "deflated" family. That is consistent with demonic hauntings. Does that lessen the likelihood of a demonic infestation? Truthfully, this is a pattern that is all too common in hauntings. They result in heavy activity and then suddenly stop, only to crank it up again at a later date. In addition, it is next to impossible to predict when it will stop and start. It seems that just when you think it's over, it starts up again and when you expect the activity to be the heaviest, nothing happens. It can drive you insane. I cannot tell you how many times I have expected a haunting to go a particular way and I would bring in extra people for the occasion. Then I would find myself sitting up all night with my thumb up my butt waiting for something to happen, only to have a quiet night.

Again, we see mood shifts with the children. You cannot really read a lot into that scenario. The swings are not terribly pronounced and with children, moods swing a lot. I would all but discount that item. We see Diane having some truly bad days. With hauntings, there are often days when it seems that the whole world is conspiring to get you. Of course, on some days, it might. You might have a tough night in the house due to the spirit. You may get very little sleep and sure enough, Murphy once again demonstrates why he created his law. Of course, that happens to everyone from time to time, haunted or not. When you are down, life decides to kick you in the pants. This may be in part because of the "like attracts like" principal. When you are in a negative mood, you attract negative energy to you. Just the same, you can make book that it will happen more often in a haunting situation.

Did you notice that Diane, in her anger, did not notice the materializing spirit? That will happen from time to time too. It must annoy the hell out of the spirit. It goes through all of that trouble to manifest and no one sees it. One of the best things you can do in a haunting is to not give the spirit or its actions recognition. There are times, certainly, where you cannot help but give recognition but if you can avoid doing that, it can help big time. It can also pump you up a bit. Let's say for example, that Diane *did* see the spirit manifesting. If she acknowledged it, her fear level would have risen dramatically. However, if she kept going anyway, her fear would have been less and she would have felt good about having taken a positive step. So, what you have is a potentially negative situation that due to proper handling, turned into a positive one. It is foiling *its* strategy (to cause fear) by employing *your* strategy. Besides, if it ticks the spirit off, it's a plus. It may do something obvious to make you notice it but it would do that eventually anyway. The more unpleasant you make the environment for the spirit, the quicker it will leave.

It has appeared all along that Diane was the main target of the spirit. Yet during the explosion, Ted was injured by a flying object. Do you think that this reflects a shift in the spirit's strategy or did he simply get hit by something targeted for Diane? It could be either so you would have to make a mental note of it. It *could* be a shift in strategy and if that is the case, than that can be dangerous. So what you have is more gray area to sort through. Personally, I would say that he simply got in the way of an item targeted for Diane. Another interesting thing to note is that during the explosion, Ted and Billy believed that Diane was causing all of the commotion while Debbie told her father that Diane was in trouble and needed his help. Again, we see the female having the stronger discernment. Now we have to wonder why there was a sudden explosion in the house. It could be retaliation for turning to the Church. However, my guess would be that it is just how this particular case is progressing. The retaliation, I would think, would have come right away; it would not have waited for a couple of weeks. Here is another interesting point to ponder. During the explosion, Ted half expected the police to arrive. Fortunately, they didn't. Suppose they had? That would have been interesting, especially if it was still happening and they were able to witness it. For that reason, always ask if there are police reports when you do a case. It makes for one terrific piece of evidence, especially if you need to get the Church involved. Of course, had they shown up *after* the activity had stopped, Ted might have had a big problem on his hands. He could well have been blamed for causing all of the damage and he may even have been charged with assaulting Diane. Officer: "Sure, a ghost did it," he says while slapping on the cuffs.

You may have noticed Diane's reaction. She was not loudly hysterical, instead, she was sobbing quietly. That can be a dangerous sign, especially when it involves someone who is usually loud when upset. This can signify that the pressure is reaching the breaking point. She is internalizing the horror. If she turns too far inward, she may well have a nervous breakdown. Always look for muted emotions; they can be a telling sign. It was obvious that Ted was being badly affected by the haunting. We saw a crack in his armor for the first time when he cried. That had to break his parent's hearts. You can only take but so much and clearly, Ted had taken a lot. The frustration, vulnerability and sense of helplessness can be overwhelming. He is seeing his family being attacked and there appears to be nothing he can do about it. How can you fight what you cannot see? That is the one point that paranormal investigators and especially demonologists make often. How can you fight what you cannot see? There is a feeling of impotence that is horrendous in that situation.

Another point I want to make is about how everything that Ted used to take comfort in suddenly seemed alien and cold. His favorite chair seemed like a stranger to him. That is so common in a haunting. *Nothing* seems as it once did. From a psychological standpoint, this is disassociation. His house is still his house and his chair is still his chair. However, due to the unreality of the situation, he finds himself in a disassociated state. That is so common in a haunting. Nothing seems real anymore. During the commotion and just afterwards, we had a phantom phone call or two. We also had the false alarm with the ringing of the doorbell. That is designed to add fear but more than that, it is like the spirit is sending the message that it is still in charge, lest you forget that with help being on the way. Not that you ever do. Don did a wise thing when he took pictures of the damage in the master bedroom. That is an important piece of evidence. It gives the investigators a good idea of what they are up against because pictures do not exaggerate. It is also good evidence should they have to get the Church involved. Pictures paint a thousand words. Finally, Diane turned to the Internet for help. That can be a tricky situation because you have no idea who you are dealing with. Having a beautiful website does not mean that the group knows what they are doing. We will have to see what happens when the group comes into the picture.

* * * *

The Pre-Investigation Meeting

Ken Tucker hung up the telephone and then he called Tim Leahy, followed by Dawn Hartwick and finally, Dave Sommers. Ken was a paranormal investigator and he had just spoken to a sincere sounding woman by the name of Diane Carter. The story she told was most interesting and somewhat frightening. She needed help and Ken wanted to be the one to provide it. That was why he called his three friends. Tim and Dave had agreed to come over to Ken's house to discuss the new case. Dawn would not be attending; she was a psychic and as such, she needed to avoid learning anything about the case prior to going into the house. Ken had called her to ask about her availability for the following night. He was pleased when he found out she was available. Having a good psychic on an investigation can be of enormous value. Of course, there can be negatives as well.

Tim and Dave arrived at Ken's house at 7:30 pm, as requested. Ken laid out his conversation with Mrs. Carter. "Basically, we have an active house and this thing seems to be powerful," Ken told his friends. "Apparently, it is not shy, either." He then described in detail what Diane had told him about all of the minor events that had occurred and also described the horror of the explosion in the master bedroom. "It's definitely demonic," Tim announced. Dave quickly reminded Tim that there was no evidence to support that theory. "Right now, you are just working off what the lady told Ken. You have no idea how bad it really is yet. When people are scared, things seem larger than life." Ken agreed with Dave. "Even if we think it is, Tim, we cannot say anything to the family until we are 110% sure." Dave agreed with Ken. They did not have much to go on so the meeting was a short one. Unfortunately for

Ken, Dave would be unable to make the Friday night session. He would be available for Saturday night, should Ken decide to go in a second time. Ken was sure that he would. Now, let us meet the investigators.

(Help Is On The Way)

It was just after six when the telephone rang. The call was from the investigators; they were lost. Ted quickly explained where they had gone wrong and hung up. Less than ten minutes later, they arrived. There were three of them. Ken was the group leader. He had been doing investigations for five years and was the senior man. Tim was his assistant. He was new to the paranormal business although he had always been interested in the subject. At 19, he was six years younger than Ken. Dawn was the third member of the group. A strikingly beautiful brunette, Dawn was a psychic who did readings for people in her spare time. She looked much younger than twenty-five, although that was her age. Of the three investigators, Tim looked to be the most nervous.

The family and the investigators settled into the living room. Diane and Irma made coffee for the crew along with some coffee cake that Don had picked up earlier. While the two women were talking, Dawn entered the kitchen. “Mrs. Carter, would you mind if I took a walk through the house to see if I can pick up any impressions?” Diane smiled at the young psychic. “Please, call me Diane. Wouldn’t you like to have some coffee first?” Dawn explained to Diane that she did not want to hear any conversations regarding the problem because she felt that would bias her feelings. Diane readily agreed to let her do her tour. She offered to walk with her if the psychic was nervous but Dawn assured her that she would be okay alone. If anything, she preferred to do the initial tour alone. This way, she picked up only her own senses. There was always the fear that she might pickup impressions from whomever she was with.

While Dawn walked around upstairs, the two male investigators discussed the situation with the Carters. Ken did most of the questioning. Don noted that Tim was looking more and more nervous as the conversation progressed. Ken took a lot of notes while Tim seemed to look around a lot and wring his hands. Meanwhile, Dawn was trying to "read" the house. She sensed very little in Debbie's room but did feel more in Billy's room. She sat down on the bed to get a better "read." After several minutes, whatever she had felt dissipated. Her next stop was the master bedroom. She opened the door and felt overwhelmed. She regretted her decision of doing the walkthrough without her walkie-talkie. Dawn knew that she was not alone but she was not going to run from this thing, whatever it was. At that moment, she was not sure what she was dealing with. All she could tell was that there was a lot of anger associated with that room. Maybe some evil as well but the anger was the stronger of the two. She sat on the bed but she got up after about thirty seconds. That was when *she* began to feel angry herself. She knew better than to let that emotion take over her. She left the room and went downstairs.

Ken was in the process of explaining what he and his team would do that night. Tim had gone out to the car to bring in the equipment. Diane looked at Dawn expectantly but the psychic was far from done. She told Diane that she had to go through the rest of the house. Diane nodded her head. Once she had finished the first floor, Dawn headed for the basement. She hated doing basements and considered asking Ken to go with her. "Nasty things always seem to live in basements," she said to herself. However, she decided against it and made the trip alone. Dawn was pleasantly surprised when she sensed nothing in the basement. Once that was done, she joined the others in the living room.

"Well," she began. "If it is anywhere, it is in the master bedroom." Diane frowned. "What do you mean *if* it's here? I know it is." Before Dawn could reply, Ken jumped in. "Don't get the wrong idea, Diane. What Dawn means is that it may not be in the house at the moment." He went on to explain that haunting spirits do not always remain in the house they are haunting. "They tend to come and go," he told her. "That's especially true of demons," Tim added. Ken and Dawn shot a look at Tim that could best be described as: "keep your mouth shut." Ken tried to save the situation. "Of course, no one is saying that you have a demon here." Dawn also rushed in to try to help. "You see, the only place where I really felt anything was in the master bedroom and the only emotion I felt was anger." Ted looked at Dawn and asked: "I was furious in that room last night. Could that be what you are sensing?" "Yes, it certainly can be that. I'm glad you mentioned that to me." After talking for a short time, Ken and Tim took some of their equipment up to the master bedroom. Dawn stayed downstairs with the family.

Dawn took the time to explain how hauntings work. "Fear is what negative spirits go for. That's what they enjoy." Don laughed. "Well, ours are pretty good at it." Everyone laughed at that point. Irma then put Dawn on the spot: "Tell me dear, do we have a demon or what?" Dawn looked uncomfortable. "Well, it is too early into this for me to give you an answer on that. What I will say is that there seems to be something dark in the house but I didn't feel enough to really tell you anything. Mostly all I felt was anger." "Well, I appreciate your honesty, dear," Irma told her. "But the young boy, Tim, he seems to think it's a demon." That came from Diane. "No, I don't think that was what he meant. Please understand that he is new at this game and he is prone to making some mistakes." Don looked annoyed. "The problem is that this isn't a game." "I know that, sir," Dawn told him. A short time later, Ken joined the group. "Tim is going to stay upstairs for awhile. A little later, we'll set up some closed circuit cameras and that will let us cover most of the house. If anything happens, we will have a good chance of capturing it."

"What if nothing happens?" Irma asked the investigator. "Then we will keep coming back until it does. Sometimes these things will hide from us at first. Please don't be discouraged if that happens. We expect that kind of thing and I promise, *we* won't get discouraged." Diane smiled at the answer. She liked Ken and she liked Dawn. Her first impression of Tim was different; she didn't *dislike* him, she just was not sure what to make of him yet. He seemed to her to be very nervous. Ken went on to explain how some of the equipment worked and he asked whether anyone had any questions before he went about his work. After fielding a few of them, he went upstairs to set up his closed circuit cameras. When he went into the master bedroom, he saw Tim pacing back and forth nervously. "Is everything okay?" he asked the novice investigator. Tim said he was okay but that he had the feeling that something was watching him. Ken tried to make a joke about it to relax Tim. "It's watching us watch it and as soon as the cameras are set up, we're going to watch it watching us watch it." Tim apparently saw no humor in that but he helped Ken set up the cameras. Ken set one up in the master bedroom and he set the other one up in the hall facing the two children's rooms. After that, he ran the wires down the stairs and hooked them up to the monitor he had set up in the living room. Once the system was up, he noticed that the picture from the master bedroom was out of focus. He asked Tim to run up there and adjust the focus. Tim looked at him with an almost pleading look in his eyes but he went up and did as he was instructed.

The family bounced back and forth between the kitchen and the living room. It was only just after eight and things were pretty quiet in the house. Don sat down in the living room with Ken and the two men talked at length about the world of paranormal phenomena. Don liked the young group leader and he was impressed with his knowledge of the field. While they were talking, Dawn walked into the living room. "I am going to take another walk through the house now," she announced to Ken. "Do you want me to come with you?" Ken asked. "No, that's okay." She was about to head up the stairs when Don asked her if he could join her. "Of course, if you'd like to," she replied. "Can't miss the chance to be with a beautiful women, you know," Don joked with her. From the kitchen came Irma's voice: "I heard that, you old codger. Watch out for him, young lady!" Dawn laughed and the two headed up the stairs. They entered Billy's room first and Dawn sat on the bed. Don watched the psychic closely but said nothing. After a minute or so, she stood up and went into Debbie's room.

Dawn stopped short about halfway across the room. "Do you feel something?" Don asked the girl. "Yeah, I do but it's not strong." The she shrugged her shoulders and suggested they try the master bedroom. As soon as they entered the room, Dawn let out a soft moan. That was followed by: "Oh shit." Don looked concerned. "What is it?" Before she could answer, Ken called her over the radio. "Dawn, are you okay up there? I just lost the picture from the master bedroom." "Something is here, Ken." "I'll be right up," Ken told her. That was when it started.

Boom, boom, boom! The pounding was so loud that it actually hurt everyone's ears. Boom, boom, boom! Ken reached the master bedroom just as the second set of three reverberated throughout the house. Boom, boom, boom! Dawn held her hands over her ears. Suddenly, she yelled: "No!" as yet another burst of three was heard. Don immediately grabbed the young psychic and held her tightly. Again the pounding shook the house. Finally, there was silence. Don felt the young psychic shaking. "It's okay, it's stopped." Dawn stepped away. "No, I'm not frightened," she half lied. "It is *so* angry!" "Ken walked over to her. "What is it?" he asked his friend. He instantly regretted asking her that question because she was now on the spot. Dawn shook her head as if to clear it. "It's human, definitely," she told Ken. "Are you sure?" he asked her. "Yes, it's definitely human. Mad but human." Ken then suggested that they all move back downstairs.

Tim was sitting in the living room alone. His face was completely drained of blood. Just as the trio entered, Ted and Diane entered the room as well. "You heard that, right?" implored Diane. "Christ," Don replied. "You could hear that in Mexico!" "First things first," Ken stated. "I think it might be a good idea to bring mattresses down here and have everyone sleep in the same room tonight. Dawn feels that the spirit is very angry and after what happened to you guys the other night, I think it is best that no one be isolated again." Ted and Don agreed with the investigator. "Later on, Tim and I will help you bring them down," Ken offered. "God, I could use a cup of coffee!" Dawn exclaimed. "Then I'll put some on right away," Irma offered. It was now time to talk.

Okay, what do you think of the investigation so far? Right off the top, you saw the way the psychic, Dawn chose to work. She wanted to tour the house first before she heard anything about it. That is what a psychic should do. I have worked with some who wanted a full briefing before going into a house. To me, that makes her (or his) input suspect. If they know that "such and such" happens in a particular room, they are going to go into that room *expecting* to feel something. When she does, I have to wonder if she is only feeling what she is expecting to feel. In Dawn's case, she chose to do the walk through the house alone. It might be so that she can "case" the place looking for the hidden wall safe but in Dawn's case, she wanted to be sure that she was not picking anything up from whoever she was with. While I don't believe that psychics can fully read anyone's mind, it is possible for all of us to occasionally pick up some information when we are with someone. Other psychics I have worked with have asked me to stay with them on the tour. I gladly do that when I am asked. In a case where I fear a demonic force is present, I prefer that I be with them in case they feel overwhelmed by whatever is there. I should point out though that I rarely agree to use a psychic at all if I strongly believe that a demon is present.

So far, at least, I like Ken's approach and although I created him, Tim is getting on my nerves. It is not that he is frightened; that is 100% normal, especially for a young investigator but I do not like what he said regarding demonic hauntings. He did not come out and say that there was a demonic presence in the house but the way he phrased his statement could well have planted a seed and that can be dangerous and possible mentally injurious as well.

In this mock haunting, things are happening fast, probably faster than you would realistically expect in a true haunting. However, since this is a chapter, not a book, I want to keep things moving along. The pounding you read about does not happen in too many cases but when you experience it, it stays with you. Loud, fast pounding used to bother me in my youth. It is much less so these days, possibly signifying that I am losing my hearing with age. It can certainly rattle your cage. Did you notice how Ken asked Diane whether she was sure the spirit was human? That might lead you to think that he is thinking demonic. He may be and based on the anecdotal evidence, I can understand why. However, he is smart enough to keep that feeling to himself, especially in light of the fact that he does not have any concrete evidence to back up his beliefs. He was a little upset with himself when he asked Dawn for her "read" in front of Don. That was an honest enough mistake but you have to be careful with that, especially if you do not know the psychic too well. It appears that Dawn is experienced and educated enough to handle herself and thus, she probably would not blurt out anything about a demon in front of the client. Still, you can never be sure.

After the episode of the pounding, Ken suggested that the family stay together when they sleep. There are two schools of thought on that. One would be that it is an extreme measure and as such, can plant a false sense of danger in the family. However, in this case, Ken was more than justified. Why? Well, he had the anecdotal evidence reported to him regarding the violent acts in the house plus, he had his own experience with the unusual pounding. That to me is enough because there is the real *threat* of danger. Here is an example where if you are going to err, do so on the side of caution. If the only evidence available was the anecdotal report of a ghost sighting, I think it would be a big and counterproductive mistake to take an extreme measure such as having the family camp out together. You have to consider all of the evidence and add in your gut feelings too.

A Long Night

The incident with the pounding shook the Carter family up pretty badly. For the investigators, it was a mixed bag. While they were certainly a little frightened themselves, this was the type of evidence they were hoping to get. After all, that is what they came for. Ken was hoping for the opportunity to speak to his team alone. He wanted to make sure that they were okay. He also wanted to talk to Dawn alone. He did not like the way he was starting to think about the situation in the Carter house.

After having a cup of coffee, Ken decided that he would sit in the master bedroom for a while. Dawn told him that she would be up to see him from time to time and Tim assured him that he would be watching things on the monitor. The cameras were working fine now that a loose cable had been reconnected. As soon as Ken went upstairs, he turned off the light and sat on the bed. He was tempted to lie down but he felt that would make him too vulnerable. It would be a lot faster to vacate the room from a sitting position as opposed to a prone one. He did not like thinking that way but he could not help it; the pounding had rattled him too. A few seconds after he turned the lights off, Tim called him on the radio to tell him that he could not monitor him in the dark. "That's okay, Tim, I want to play it this way." Tim responded quickly: "Ken, this thing isn't too shy. I think it has no problem acting out in the light." "I know," Ken responded, "but I want to use the night vision camcorder and see if I can get a picture of the old boy." "Christ, he wants to sit in the dark with a demon on the loose," Tim stated quietly. The only one who heard that comment was Billy, who had just entered the room. He could not wait to tell his mother what he had just heard.

Dawn sat in the kitchen with the Carters. For the most part, she was entertaining them with stories of other investigations she had worked on. Of course, she was only telling them about the funny things that had happened. She related one story where an investigator she knew had been caught with his pants down, so to speak. Actually, as she told the story, he only had his zipper down, when at a most inopportune time, a ghost decided to let out a "bloody scream," as she described it. Well, the investigator came charging out of the bathroom all right but he had done so having forgotten to return something into the safety of his pants. She told the Carters about how he was running around with his "you know what" flopping around. Everyone got a kick out of that story. And "no," she told them, "it wasn't Ken or Tim."

After what seemed like a long time, Ken got the feeling that he should go into Debbie's room. He radioed his move to Tim since he would now be out of the camera's view. Ken knew that every member of the team should know where every other member is at all times. Investigations can go bad in a hurry and if no one knows where you are, it can be a problem. After a few minutes in Debbie's room, Ken's gauss meter began to sound. "I think I have something," Ken radioed to Tim. "The gauss meter is reading 10 milligauss in here now, up from one. It's also starting to get cold in here. Wait; let me check the temperature. Okay, it's 62 now, that's down almost ten degrees." As soon as Dawn heard this, she excused herself and headed upstairs. Tim told Ken to leave the room and rejoin everyone downstairs. "No way," Ken told him. "Let's see what our friend has." As Dawn reached the landing, she again felt strong anger but off to the side near the master bedroom, she detected movement. She took a few steps in that direction and stopped short. Now she felt something worse than anger: evil. "I'm not liking this," she said to herself as she walked towards Debbie's room.

Ken was standing in the far corner of the room when she entered it. "What's going on?" she asked him. "I just saw the dark mist they have been describing. It was right here. The temp over here is 51 degrees." Before Dawn could say a word, the lamp on the night table toppled over and a baseball that had been on it went flying. It missed Ken's head by an inch. Then the pounding started up again. Boom, boom, boom! Suddenly, the room filled with a horrible stench, so bad that it made the two investigators gag. After less than 30 seconds, they were forced to leave the room. The two of them went downstairs, choking from the stench. Just as they reached the bottom of the stairs, the lights in the house went out. Ken fumbled for his flashlight and found it. The Carters were all gathered in the living room. Mercifully, the pounding stopped after the three bursts. Tim had the presence of mind to turn on his night vision camcorder. What he saw through the screen was amazing. The black mist had followed the investigators down. It now hovered by the stairs. "It's behind you, Dawn." She whirled around but she could not see anything. Ken reached into his pants pocket and pulled out a bottle of holy water. He squirted it behind Dawn. The black mist vanished immediately.

The lights came back on after Ken dowsed the mist with holy water. Ted and Don tried to calm down their wives. The children sat together, huddled on the couch. "We need to talk," Ted announced. Ken sat on the floor and Dawn joined him. "What are we going to do about this?" Don asked. Ken looked weary. "Listen, you said that you spoke to a priest, right?" Diane nodded her head up and down. Ken continued: "We need to speak to him again." "So you are saying that it is a demon then," Ted told the investigator. Ken thought carefully before he said anything. "No, I am not saying that but whatever is in this house is nasty. Whether it's human or not, you need protection. The holy water made the mist go away so we know we have a weapon. Irma spoke next. "We don't have any in the house. I knew I should have brought some with me. On Sunday, I'll pick some up." "I have enough for tonight," Ken began, but we'll need to pick some up tomorrow. You have to keep some around here at all times." He then looked at Dawn and asked her what she thought. "What I felt earlier was definitely human and it is angry. However, I also felt something evil upstairs too. I don't think you have a demonic haunting here but there is something dark pulling the human's strings."

Tim stood up and stretched. "I've got pictures of this thing. Maybe we can set up a meeting with that priest you talked to?" Irma told him that she would call Father Michael in the morning. "Good idea," Ken responded. "We'll talk to him ourselves, if you want." Tim asked anyone if they wanted anything from the kitchen but no one did. He went towards it to get himself a soda. Just as he entered the room, he stopped and began backing up. "It's, it's in here." Ken and Dawn bolted up, as did Ted and Don.

When they entered the kitchen, the saw the black form hovering near the refrigerator. Tim stood still while Ken fumbled through his pockets looking for his holy water. He did not find it. The figure appeared to be growing solid for a few seconds but then it faded away. Ken needed to talk to Dawn but he knew he would have to be careful. He did not want to do anything that might make the Carters nervous. He feared that would happen if he called her aside so he decided to bide his time. He had some serious concerns and he hoped that he could hide that from the Carters. It was around eleven that night when Irma and Diane put the children to bed. They had waited outside the bathroom while each child took a shower. No one wanted to be alone under any circumstances. Debbie was the first to take a shower. She insisted that Diane keep the door open. Billy, on the other hand hated the idea that the two women waited outside the door. He insisted that he was not frightened but Diane would not budge on the issue.

While the family was preparing for bed, Ken went down to the basement. He hoped that Dawn would follow him and he was sad when she didn't. Don and Ted sat in the living room talking to Tim. Both men were impressed with his knowledge of the paranormal. Ted would later comment to Diane that he was very intelligent and very frightened as well. Dawn decided to take a walk through the house again. Her first stop was the basement. She chose to start at the bottom of the house because she sensed that Ken needed to talk to her. When she reached the bottom of the stairs, Ken smiled. "I was hoping you would come down here," he told his friend. "I had a feeling that you wanted to talk to me but I wanted to wait until the family was distracted so that they wouldn't notice that we were missing." Ken smiled. "On the ball as always," he told her. "What's wrong, Ken?" The young team leader sighed. "There are two things I'm worried about, my dear. For one, are you *sure* that this thing is human?" Dawn wasted no time answering him. "I am, Ken. It is human." Ken shook his head in disbelief. "Dawn, I've known you for a long time and I know that you are good but that thing in the kitchen was not human. Some of the shit happening here can't be done by a human spirit." Dawn smiled at Ken. "I know what you're thinking but the only spirit I am sensing is human." Ken stood up and sighed. "I don't know what to think." "What's the other thing that is bothering you?" she asked. Ken sighed again. "I think I've bitten off more than I can chew. We're out of our league here." Dawn took Ken's hand and led him to a chair. She sat down next to him. "Listen Ken, we don't know what we've got here so don't panic yet. Dave can be here tomorrow if we come back. He's been at this a lot longer than we have."

Once the children were finished, they sat in the living room. The Carters decided to use the den for the investigators. Ted and Tim moved the camera equipment into that room. By the time that was done, Ken and Dawn had returned from the basement. Ken went into the kitchen to have a cup of coffee and Dawn decided to walk around upstairs. She was pleased when she felt nothing up there. When she was done, she returned to the living room. She talked with the children for a few minutes and then she joined Ken in the kitchen. Diane entered the room a few seconds later. The three sat and talked for a few minutes. Diane was feeling better. Just having the investigators in the house made her feel more secure. The fact that something had actually happened while they were there was the icing on the cake for her. After talking for a while, the three went into the den. They wanted to see what the tape of the dark mist showed. Tim rewound the tape and once he found the spot, he played it back.

Since it was filmed in night vision, the images were in black and white. However, the dark form was clearly visible on the tape. It looked like a cloud following Ken and Dawn downstairs. They were surprised to see how it faded away when Ken sprayed the holy water Dawn had given him. "I think we found a weapon," Diane announced happily. "You sure did," Dawn replied, equally as cheerily. "We'll pick up some more tomorrow," Ken told Diane. Diane laughed. "You're a doll," she told Ken.

The house was quiet for several hours. By two am, Ted was nodding out in his chair. Don and Ted had brought the children's mattresses down as well as the one from the master bedroom. Don and Irma would sleep on the couch and there were also sleeping bags in the room should the investigators decide to sleep. Irma hoped that they would. She felt bad for them. In addition to being investigators, they had regular jobs just like everyone else. Tim was slumped over the desk in the den. Had he been awake, he would have seen bright lights appearing in the master bedroom. Dawn was talking to Diane in the kitchen when Ken came in. "I'm gonna hang out upstairs for a bit," he announced. With that, he left. As soon as he entered the master bedroom, he saw the light show. "I've got something up here," he called into his radio. That woke Tim up and it sent Dawn upstairs. Diane decided to go into the den to see what was going on. She was amazed when she saw the light show on the monitor. "My God, look at that," she gasped. Tim said nothing but he could not take his eyes of the screen.

Dawn and Ken watched the lights flash around the room. Ken picked up his digital camera and took several shots. The lights continued appearing for about two minutes, then it stopped. "What is that smell?" Dawn asked Ken. "It's ozone," Ken answered. "Oh great, tell me we are going to have a thunderstorm in here," Dawn quipped. The two investigators waited for close to a half hour but nothing else happened. Finally, they went downstairs. Ken went to the den to check up on Tim and Dawn settled down in the living room. The rest of the night was uneventful in the Carter house.

Ken started packing up around 6am, Saturday. Ted helped him with his task. "Will you be coming back tonight?" Ted asked the tired team leader. "Absolutely, if you want us," he answered. After seeing how much better Diane seemed, he told Ken that he was welcome to move in completely. Ken laughed but he appreciated Ted's words. Ken told Ted that they would all be back around nine that night. He also told them that they would be bringing Dave with them as well. Ted assured him that Dave was welcome to join them. A short time later, the three investigators left the Carter house.

Everyone was tired from the long night and fatigue changes the way you think. No one knew what to make of the investigators. They all agreed that they were intelligent and sincere but what, if anything was accomplished by them, remained to be seen. Don was unsure whether they could really help them. "All the gizmos and gadgets look great but how does that help us get rid of this thing?" he asked. Diane was the first to offer an answer. "Well, Ken told me that the first thing they needed to do was be sure they knew what they were dealing with. Once they knew that, they could look for ways of stopping it. He did say that it would take time." "How long is the question?" Don asked. Ted spoke next: "Well, they know we have something so that's a start. I think we have to give them a chance to prove whether they stop this thing or not. Let's give them some time." "I agree," Irma added. "Me too," Diane agreed. Don let out a sigh. "Well, Dawn sure isn't hard to look at, that's for sure. We'll give them some time." Ted laughed at his father. "You are just an old pervert, Dad." "Here, here," Irma said.

When Ken got home, he went straight to bed. He planned on getting up around ten. At that time, he would call Dave. He fell asleep quickly. Then he had a dream. He was in the Carter house, alone on the second floor. He could hear Dawn and Tim talking downstairs. For some reason, he walked into Billy's room, or what was supposed to be Billy's room. In the dream, it was set up differently than it actually was. He sat down on the bed and found himself growing tired, so he stretched out on the bed. Suddenly, the black mist appeared in the doorway. It began to darken and as it did, it moved slowly towards him. As soon as it had cleared the doorway, the door slammed shut. Oddly enough, he could still hear Dawn and Tim talking. Apparently, they had not heard the door slam.

The thing was definitely taking on form. Ken tried to get off the bed but he could barely move; it was as if something was holding him down. The black mist was growing darker, more solid and Ken could see that it was now in the shape of a man. He tried to move but he was still stuck. He could now make out the shape of a hood on the figure. Within seconds, it was almost solid. It was definitely a hooded figure. Ken tried to scream, hoping Tim or Dawn would hear him but he was unable to do even that much. Downstairs, Tim and Dawn laughed. "She is a psychic," Ken told himself. "Why doesn't she know that I'm in trouble?" The figure started to move towards Ken. He could now see eyes, bright red ones. He could feel cold overtake him and the room began to smell horrible. The creature reached the side of the bed and Ken tried frantically to move. Finally, the creature was within inches of Ken's face. He was hit with a stench that was unimaginable. Panic welled up within him and the hooded specter let out a terrifying laugh. With that, Ken woke up.

He sat up and swung his legs over the side of the bed. His heart was pounding and he was drenched in sweat. He sat there, his hands over his face. "It was just a dream," he told himself. "That's all it was, just a dream." He dropped his hands and glanced at the clock. It was nearly ten so he turned off his alarm and went to his kitchen and turned on the coffee maker. Once the coffee was ready, he poured himself a cup and went into his living room. He took a couple of sips and picked up his phone. He dialed Dave's number and waited. Dave answered the phone on the fourth ring. "Hi Dave, it's me." "Hey, Ken, how goes it?" Ken began telling Dave what had transpired but static kept interrupting them. Dave suggested that they hang up and he would call Ken back, hoping to get a better connection. When he called back, the connection was clear. "Okay, you were saying something about pounding in the walls," Dave said. "Yeah, it was wild." Before he could say anything else, the static returned. After a few seconds, the line cleared. "Look, something is going on here," Ken told Dave. "If you are still interested in coming with us tonight, maybe we can get together here around six or so?" Dave sounded excited. "Hell yes, I'm still interested. I'll see you at six at your place." Ken felt relieved. "Great, I'll see you then."

Back at the Carter's house, things were quiet. Diane and Irma had gone out shopping. They wanted to pick up some things for themselves and the investigators as well. Diane had felt bad that she had not had much to offer them when they were there. After doing the shopping, they stopped at the Church to pick up some holy water. Irma had brought along two plastic bottles. Once they were filled, the two women went back to their car. They had no sooner started the car when they were nearly overcome by the foul stench. Irma gagged and Diane threw open her door. "My God, this is horrible," she yelled. Irma fought back the need to vomit. Without saying a word, she opened one of the bottles and sprinkled some holy water into the back of the car. Within seconds, the stench faded away. "Take that!" she yelled. Diane smiled and got back into the car. The rest of the ride home was uneventful.

When the women got home, they found Don sleeping on the couch. Ted and the children were outside tossing a small football around. When he saw the car pull up, Ted went to the front to help bring the packages in. Once that was done, Diane could not wait to tell Ted what had happened in the car. He listened, amazed. "Wow, the holy water really does work." "It sure does," Irma told her son. "You know," Diane began. "Just knowing that we have a defense and can stop some of the crap makes things a lot easier to take. You see, the investigators have already paid a dividend." "I'll say," Ted added. For the first time since the haunting began, the Carter family felt empowered. They were on their way but they still had a long road ahead of them.

The investigation is moving along fairly quickly. It is rare when you have a lot happening on the first night. So far, it is being handled pretty well. Aside from Tim's errant comment, everything seems to be getting done properly. The conversation that Dawn had with the family about the investigator with his "you know what" hanging out is a good one. To me, an essential part of any case is a good rapport with the client. It makes life easier for them and it does so for the investigators as well. Nobody ever wants to dread going on an investigation. As serious as they are, there is still the need and plenty of room for some fun. Laughter is a powerful tool and you can bet that the silly story Dawn told took a lot of pressure off of everyone. She did not behave like a buffoon or the class clown but she made everyone laugh and that is priceless.

Did you notice the smell of ozone? That is very common where there are about to be manifestations of some kind. They do not have to be negative manifestations and they do not only occur in haunting situations. I have heard of ozone odors during all kinds of investigations. An interesting item is Ken's dream. Is it paranormal in nature? That is one that you cannot be sure about. Certainly, in a haunting, you might expect a dream like that. It is believed that spirits communicate with us best while we are sleeping. On the other hand, a dream of that nature can be caused simply by stress alone. This is an example of the gray area investigators face. There really is no way to be sure.

We saw the black mist make another appearance. There were two things to note about that. The first and most important is that the holy water stopped it. Did you see the sense of empowerment that having a weapon created? That is a biggie because that sense of empowerment gives them strength and that alone can weaken the entity's grip. Always remember: anything that makes the victim stronger weakens the entity. Of course, the reverse is also true. I must point out that empowerment of this nature can be fleeting, as you will soon see. The second is that they were able to capture it on film. The latter item is rare but the former is common. Does that conclusively *prove* that the entity is demonic? Not really, although it is a strong piece of evidence in that favor. Sometimes human manifestations can be stopped with holy water, especially if there is an evil intent involved. However, the fact that it is appearing as a mist is also telling. However, you should not pronounce the case demonic just yet and you will see why when we get back to the story.

(The Second Night)

Dave went over to Ken's apartment at six. He arrived armed with two pizzas. Ken filled him in on the events of the previous night, this time without the static interfering. Ken wanted to pick Dave's brain. In his mid-forties, Dave had worked many cases in his time. Two of them were bad ones. After the second one, he dropped out of the field for over two years. It was only once he met Ken and Dawn that he decided to go back into the field. Ken had a great deal of respect for Dave and he valued his opinions and he trusted his judgment. Ken felt that they were facing a demonic haunting. In his mind, there was no doubt. What he could not understand was why Dawn felt that it was human. "You are asking her to tell you what she is feeling and she is saying that what she feels is human. That is fine." Ken put down his pizza and then began talking. "Dave, this thing appears as a *mist*! It can't be human." "It might not be, I agree," Dave responded. "Well then," Ken started, "why isn't she feeling it?" Dave took his second slice of pizza. "Here's the thing," he began. "It is possible that she is having trouble reading the house." Ken cut him off before he could finish his sentence. "A psychic should always be able to tell what is going on in a haunting. How can she misread a demon?" Dave smiled at his younger friend.

"First of all, the psychics would have you believe that they can read any house but in my experience, it just ain't so. I have worked with quite a few psychics before I met Dawn and most of them were quite good, well, some of them. Anyway, I have had them totally disagree with each other on a given case. It is not as cut and dry as they would like you to believe. They have problems in their lives too and times when they have things on their minds and that has to color their perception to some degree. So yes, she could be misreading the house." Ken nodded at him. "The other thing, Ken, is that there may be so much anger on the part of the human that is so strong that it is overriding her senses. Also, and give this one some thought, you may have a human haunting with demonic overtones." Ken looked puzzled. "I'm not sure that I get you?" "What I mean is that you may have one nasty human ghost on your hands and that human negativity may have caught the attention of something demonic. It swoops in and starts to use the ghost as a puppet. It may be in effect hiding behind the human anger so that Dawn isn't able to sense it." Ken looked perplexed. "What's the difference, I mean either way it's a demon?" "There is a huge difference, my friend," Dave told him. "If it is a demonic haunting, the only way to end this would be through a Church sanctioned exorcism. However, if it is an opportunistic demon, once things start getting rough for it, it will probably move on. If that *is* the case, a blessing or a Mass is all we will need." Ken was beginning to understand. "But, I have a question. Couldn't it be a demon masquerading as a human spirit?" "Sure," Dave replied. "That is why we need to spend some time there. It is one of the things we have to figure out. It's not always easy, is it?" Ken laughed. "No it isn't." A few seconds later, the doorbell rang; Tim had arrived. Dawn arrived about ten minutes after Tim. They joined Ken and Dave in devouring the pizza.

Diane was tired and she wanted to take a nap before the crew of investigators arrived. It had been a busy day for her but as she grew more fatigued, her enthusiasm began to wane. The fact that darkness had fallen did not help any either. She took off her clothes and put on her robe. She went into the bathroom to take some aspirin. After taking them, she glanced in the mirror. To her, she felt that she looked old. "God, I'm the oldest 35 I've ever seen," she muttered to herself. She leaned closer to the mirror to examine the creases in her face. She frowned when she saw them. Suddenly, another face showed up in the mirror. It was the face of an old woman and she had a piece of wood in her hand. Diane watched in horror as the woman swung the stick at her. She let out a horrified scream.

Dave talked to Dawn about her feelings. She agreed with everything he had told Ken. She admitted that it *was* possible that she was misreading the house but she was convinced that there was a human spirit there. She also admitted that there might also be a demon there and that it was just off her radar screen. She said that she would try to focus on that possibility when they went over to the Carter's house. That presented something of a quandary for Ken and Dave. Since she would be looking for a demonic presence, how trustworthy would her feelings be when she found one, if she found one, that is? It would be a wait and see type of thing for them. Something began bothering Dave and he wanted to talk to Ken alone. In fact, he kicked himself for not thinking of it sooner. If there was a demonic spirit in the house, Dawn really should not be allowed back in there. Dave believed that keeping her involved in the case could be dangerous. He would have to think about that one.

When Diane screamed, everyone charged up the stairs to help her. However, when they reached the bathroom, Diane was alone. Ted took her into the master bedroom and sat her on the bed. Irma sat next to her, holding her hand. Don stood in the doorway while Ted knelt in front of her. "What was it Di, what happened?" Ken asked his terrified wife. Through her tears, Diane told him what had happened. Don's face turned red when he heard her story. You could see the rage building up inside of him. In his mind, he kept thinking over and over that there had to be some way to stop this thing. Once Diane was calmer, Ted went downstairs with Don. Irma stayed with Diane. "Take a nap, Dear," Irma told Diane in a soothing voice. "I'll stay with you the whole time." Diane felt like a baby but Irma would hear none of it. "This has nothing to do with being a baby, dear. We are all scared out of our wits but you need to get some sleep." Diane promised that she would try.

The pizza devoured, the crew of investigators prepared to leave. Dawn went into the bathroom and closed the door. However, when she went to leave, the door would not open. "Ken," she yelled, "I'm stuck in the bathroom." Ken walked over and tried to open the door but it would not budge. "Dave, can you give me a hand?" Dave came over and he tried to open it. Again, it would not budge. "Tim, get me some holy water, please." Tim did as asked and Dave sprinkled some water on the door but it still would not budge." "Has this ever happened before?" Dave asked Ken. "No, never," was Ken's answer. Then the door slowly opened. An ashen face Dawn walked into the hall. Behind her the door slammed shut. They all jumped a bit when they heard the door slam; it seemed unusually loud to them. "You've got yourself a demon," Dawn told the group. "This time, I felt it." Dave was not sure what to think. Dawn's physiology backed up her assertion; her hands were shaking badly.

The investigators decided to take two cars to the Carter house. The fewer cars taken, the less risk of an accident. One car would have been better but Dave knew that cars sometimes mysteriously die on investigations and they did not want to take the chance of being stranded somewhere. When they arrived, they found the Carter household nervous. Don quickly told the group what had happened and Ken related their story. It looked like it would be an active night. Tim wasted no time in setting up the equipment. Dawn volunteered to assist him. Diane was asleep when the two went upstairs to set up the cameras. They worked silently in Diane's room and then they set up the hall camera. Once that was done, they went back downstairs.

Don, Ted, Ken and Dave were discussing the haunting in the living room. Don put the investigators on the spot. "Tell me the truth, are we dealing with a demon?" Ken shifted uncomfortably in his chair. Seeing that, Dave chose to answer the question. "Honestly, we are not sure yet but I would not rule it out. On the other hand, the last thing I want to do is scare you needlessly." Ted jumped in at that point. "We are already scared as hell. How much worse could it get?" Dave laughed. "Never ask that question. It can get a *lot* worse. But..." he added with emphasis, "we're not going to let it get that bad." "How do you propose to stop it?" Don asked. "Well, if it is a demonic haunting, we can do some things ourselves but most likely, we'll need an exorcism done. If it is a demon hiding behind a human spirit, then we might be able to chase it out by ourselves. It can be tricky but it can be done. We may know more after tonight, if our "friend" here cooperates."

Ted was concerned with what happened to Diane. "Could that ghost have hurt Diane with that stick she was swinging?" "No," Dave began. "Neither the spirit nor the stick were real or solid. That was an attempt to scare her." "It did that, all right," Don added. Dawn decided to take a tour of the house. She had it in mind to "feel" for a demon. She started her walk in the basement and moved upward. She felt nothing in the basement and nothing on the ground floor. However, as she made her way upstairs, he senses began to tingle. By the top of the landing, she knew that a presence was near. She walked towards the master bedroom and looked in. Diane, having just awakened, waved to Dawn. After returning the wave, she walked to the other end of the floor and entered Billy's room. There was nothing strong in there. Her last stop was Debbie's room. As soon as she entered it, she felt a strong presence. There was no mistaking the feeling; she was not alone. "What do you want?" she asked the spirit, sounding braver than she felt. She knew that she should call Ken but she was hoping to get some answers first, if she could. She waited for about thirty seconds but she felt nothing more.

Diane felt better after her nap. She was still frightened but it was not that overwhelming sense of fear that had engulfed her when she saw the spirit in the mirror. Together, she and Irma left the room and went downstairs to join the others. Irma greeted everyone and then went to the kitchen to make some coffee. Diane was introduced to Dave. In her present state of mind, she wished that there were more investigators. She took a seat next to Ken and told everyone her story. When Dawn entered the room, all eyes went towards her. Ken spoke quickly: "Did you feel anything?" Dawn nodded her head up and down. "Yes, in Debbie's room, there was a strong sense of a presence. It was angry but it is human. I'm sure of that." Ken frowned although Dave took the news well. "That's what I wanted to hear."

The house was quiet that night until around eleven. However, before that time, the investigators had split up, each taking an area. It did not take long for boredom to set in. After spending an hour alone, Ken told everyone to meet in the living room. He wanted to give everyone a break from the boredom. Once everyone was there, Diane and Irma served coffee. Dave began telling stories from some of his past investigations. Everyone got a good laugh from them. Irma especially enjoyed the session. "Dawn told us one story last night about one poor investigators problem while he was in the bathroom." "Oh no," Dave said, "she told you that one?" Oh, so now we know who the culprit was!" Diane said excitedly. Dave turned red. "Yep, it was yours truly," he told her. They all got a good laugh out of that one. However, the laughter did not last long. Everyone was still in the living room when there was a crash in the kitchen. Ted, Dave, Don and Ken all bolted from their seats. Ted reached the kitchen first. "Oh my God," was all he said. The door to the china cabinet was open and a pile of broken dishes was on the floor. When Diane saw them, she started to cry. Those dishes had belonged to her late mother. Ted was furious. "Show yourself to me, you son of a bitch!" he screamed. "Let's see how tough you really are." Dave grabbed Ted and tried to calm him down. "Ted, don't challenge it," he told him sternly but Ted was not finished. "Challenge it, I want the piece of shit to stop playing hit and run games. You want to be tough, show yourself and take me on now." He had no sooner said those words when a coffee cup in the sink rose up and flew across the room, striking Diane on the side of her head. Instinctively, Ken ran over to Diane and grabbed her, pulling her into him. More items began flying around the room, all of them targeted for Diane. Since he was acting as a human shield, Ken took the brunt of the hits.

Finally, things calmed down. Ken looked at Diane's head and saw small lump but no cut where she was hit. He himself had a few lumps on his head. Dawn walked up to Diane and took her into the living room. Diane was hysterical and all Dawn wanted to do was keep her out of harms way. Irma relieved Dawn, who then went into the kitchen to survey the damage. She helped Ted and Don clean up the mess. Ted was shaking. "Why did it go after her?" Dave looked at him and tried to explain what had just happened. "These things are cowards, plain and simple. It knows that throwing something at you won't mean that much to you. However, it will mean a lot to you if it hurts your wife. You can never challenge a spirit, especially a negative one and this one is definitely as negative as you can get. "How do we stop this thing?" Ted asked. "Well," Dave began, "what we have to try to do is figure out why it is here and that may tell us how to get rid of it.

Once everything was cleaned up, Dave asked that the adults join him in the living room. Diane sent the children into the den to watch TV while the adults discussed the situation in the house. Dave began by asking many of the same questions that Ken had asked previously. What he was looking for was anything that might have drawn a spirit into the house. Both Ted and Diane admitted having used Ouija boards but both agreed they had never done that while they were living in their present house. Irma admitted to having seen a psychic on a few occasions but that too was in the past. After talking about possible causes for a good half-hour, Ken and Dave were at a loss to explain why the family was being terrorized. They next started asking questions about the house. Ted and Diane had been living there for over two years. They had done some remodeling since they had moved in but nothing major until the added what was now the den. Dave explained to the Carters that major changes in a house sometimes awaken dormant spirits. It was an idea worth looking into.

While they were talking, they heard a scream come from the den. Ted was the first to arrive and he saw the black figure hovering near the TV. After a few seconds, the apparition began to fade away. Dawn went upstairs to the master bedroom and decided to sit on the bed. After a couple of minutes, she saw the black figure. Immediately, she radioed for help. Ken was the first to enter the room. As before, the spirit began to fade. However, as it did so, a sardonic laugh echoed through the house; it was the same laughter from Ken's dream. The young investigator's face went ashen when he heard it. He looked at Dawn and told her about his dream. Dave looked at his friend. He was concerned about him because of the way he reacted to the disembodied laughter. He wanted to get Ken to leave the house but he would not hear of it. For that matter, Dave wanted Dawn to leave as well. The next few hours were quiet in the Carter house.

That peacefulness was shattered when the pounding started. The burst lasted a good two minutes. When it was finally over, objects began flying around the room. Everyone was shaken but the most frightened appeared to be Tim. When he was able to get Dave alone, he told him that he wanted to leave the house. At that point, he was fairly sure that he wanted out of the business altogether. Dave understood that and told Tim that he could leave. Tim wasted no time in doing so. Don was surprised when he found out that Tim had left. "You guys are supposed to be helping us and you are too frightened to stick around. How is my family supposed to feel?" Dave understood Don's point but he reminded Don that Tim was young and that this was a particularly difficult case. That did little to appease the older man. "If you can't stand the heat," Before Don finished the statement, Dave interjected: "Mr. Carter, this is a heat that no one can stand. Tim is a good man but he needs grooming and he needs time. I don't know how many people you will find that would willingly take on this kind of heat for nothing in return." Ken, who was behind Don wanted to applaud but he chose not to. Don, although still annoyed, mumbled something about understanding and he walked back into the living room.

When everyone was gathered in the living room, Dave suggested that they set up a meeting with Father Michael. "There is more here than meets the eye and I think it might be a good idea to get the house blessed, if nothing else. The Carters agreed. Irma felt bad because she had meant to call the rectory that day but she had forgotten. She felt even worse considering that she had been at the Church earlier in the day for the holy water. The family slept together in the living room that night. Dave and Ken decided to stay up. However, by three in the morning, both men were nodding out. That left Dawn as the only person awake in the house. She walked into the kitchen to get a glass of soda. When she entered the room, she was surprised at how cold it was in there. She immediately backed out of the room and tried to wake up Ken and Dave. Ken was out cold but Dave woke right up. He followed Dawn into the kitchen. The room was indeed extremely cold. "I was afraid that you wouldn't wake up when I called you," she told Dave. "Not to worry, my dear," he assured her. "I'm an incredibly light sleeper." The two investigators stood still. Both of them knew that something was going to happen; it was just a matter of time.

After waiting several minutes, the room began to warm up. Just as they were about to leave, Dawn saw a figure. It was clearly a woman and she was standing near the refrigerator. She touched Dave's arm and he turned to look. "Look at her," he said, astonished. The two investigators watched the female apparition for a few seconds. Finally, she faded away. Dave looked at Dawn. "Is that what you have been feeling?" he asked the psychic. "Yes, she is." Dave asked another question. "Is she still angry?" "Furious," Dawn replied. "Then she needs to be dealt with," Dave told her.

Later, Dave woke up Ken and talked about the possibility of blessing the house himself. "If only I could be sure that it is not a demonic haunting, I would do it in a second," he told Ken. "Well, Dave, we know what Dawn said back at my house; it is a demon." Dave frowned. "Yes, but is it a demonic haunting?" he asked Ken. The younger investigator shrugged his shoulders. There was no further conversation between the two. As much as he wanted to do something, Dave decided against taking any chances. He simply did not have enough to go on to warrant taking any action on his own. He knew that he could stir up a hornet's nest if he was wrong about the demon. Instead, he went into the den to monitor the cameras. In the living room, the children were asleep on their mattresses while Don and Irma sat on the couch, talking quietly among themselves. They had awakened just after the spirit manifested in the kitchen. Diane woke up as well. Ted was dozing in his recliner and Dawn sat in one corner of the room, watching everyone. Her senses were quiet; she felt that the likelihood was that the activity was finished for the night. She was wrong.

Diane sat in the kitchen talking to Ken. She really liked the young investigator. In truth, she found herself attracted to him but she knew that was not a good thing. She asked him if he had ever worked a case as bad as this one. He told her that in all honesty, he had not. He did explain to her that Dave had worked a couple of cases similar to this one but somewhat more horrific. Diane shuddered at the thought. "I can't believe that anything could be more horrific than this," she told him incredulously. "Ah, sweet Diane, you would be surprised. I have heard of much worse." Diane looked at her lap for a few seconds. "Ken, be honest with me, okay? Can this case become worse?" Ken sighed. "It's possible but that is why we are here, to make sure that it doesn't get any worse." Diane smiled at Ken. "Can you guarantee that?" she asked him. "No, I can't." Both were silent for a few minutes. Finally, Diane began asking Ken personal questions. She did not want to talk about the haunting anymore.

Dawn found herself nodding out. She was tempted to open up one of the sleeping bags and stretch out but she decided against it. To stay awake, she stood up and stretched. "I'm gonna take a run upstairs," she said more to herself than anyone. Don heard the comment and nodded at her. Dave was having trouble staying awake also. Staring at the monitors was making him drowsy. He watched as Dawn went into the master bedroom and sat on the floor. With the mattresses gone, she had little choice. On the other monitor, Dave saw a shadow. He assumed it was probably Ken but he wanted to be sure. He saw the shadow again and realized that it was a woman. The only problem was he could not make out a face because the camera was showing a fuzzy picture. Then he saw the black mist move past the camera. It was either coming downstairs or going into the master bedroom. He grabbed his radio and yelled to Dawn to come down. Ken heard the call over the radio and he ran into the den. Diane was right on his tail. Suddenly, they heard a loud bang followed by a scream.

Dawn was still sitting on the floor when a shadow stood in the doorway. She looked up to see who it was and saw the silhouette of a woman. "Hi," she said, thinking it was either Diane or Irma. Suddenly her senses turned on, flooding her with the familiar anger and fear engulfed her. The door slammed shut and the figure moved towards her. She tried to stand up but tripped and fell on her hands and knees.

The figure was on her then and she felt it grab her hair and pull. She screamed in a combination of fear and pain. She flung her arms wildly, trying to dislodge the hand that had her hair. However, even though she could feel the pain, there was no hand to swat away. Dave and Ken tore from the den and raced up the stairs. Ted and Don followed. As soon as they reached the top of the stairs, all of the lights in the house went out. Dave was the first to reach the bedroom where Dawn continued screaming. He turned the knob and slammed his shoulder against it but the door opened just a little and then he was pushed back. Again, he slammed his shoulder against it but the results were the same. Repeated attempts produced the same results.

Diane could hear Dawn screaming from upstairs. The children were now awake as well and they were hysterical. Diane found the lamp near the couch but nothing happened when she turned the switch. She could hear the men upstairs yelling and she kept hearing a thumping noise. She knew that they were trying to open a door. Irma was still in the living room. Diane could hear her talking softly. "Dear God, please stop this, please stop this, Dear God." Diane held her children tightly against her, shielding them from whatever might be in the room. Suddenly, there was a cold breeze and Diane knew that something was in the room with them. Were she not holding her terrified children in her arms, she was sure she would have fainted.

The four men continued to slam against the door with no results. Inside the room, Dawn continued to scream. Finally, Ted hit the door and they all heard a splintering sound; the frame had finally given way. Dawn was in the far corner of the room. In the little light that came in from the window, the men could see her hair standing up as if someone was pulling it. However, they saw no one. Dave raced over to Dawn and tried to pick her up. However, when he did so, Dawn let out another scream. Finally, Ken reached into his back pocket and pulled out some holy water. He poured it over Dawn and after a few seconds, she stopped screaming. Dave pulled her up and led her quickly out of the room. They were heading down the stairs when Diane let out a scream. "My God, what now?" Dave asked as he went down the stairs and entered the darkened living room.

There was pandemonium in the Carter house, the lights were still off, Dawn was nearly hysterical and now there was a problem in the living room. Ted was the first to enter the room. Unfortunately, he tripped on something and went down. Don then tripped over him and went down also. Had it not been so serious, it would have been comical. Dave managed to reach Diane and as soon as he grabbed her, he felt an icy hand grab his wrist. He felt a burning sensation but he barely registered the pain. As soon as he got his arms around Diane, the lights went back on. The living room was a shambles. Pictures were no longer on the walls, a table lamp lay broken near the sofa and there were coffee cups scattered about. Diane was in tears. She was holding her children tightly against her and she would not let go. Irma sat on the couch, her hands shaking. She was barely able to speak. Dave looked around for his team members. Ken was sitting on the floor holding a still hysterical Dawn. Seeing that everyone was apparently safe, he picked up a bottle of holy water and charged upstairs. His first stop was the master bedroom. He entered the room and looked around. There was a clump of hair on the floor. It had obviously been Dawns. He opened the bottle and began pouring it in the room. "In the name of Jesus Christ, I command you to leave." He repeated that line over and over. "I bless this room in the name of the Father, the Son and the Holy Spirit." He then went down the hall and repeated the same procedure in the two children's rooms. That done, he made his way downstairs. He went room to room on that level too. Everyone was paired with someone else and no one seemed to pay much attention to Dave. Once he was finished on that level, he went down to the basement and did the same ritual. Whether it was the blessing or a case where the spirit had simply burned itself out, the house would remain calm for the rest of the night.

It took several hours before some sense of normalcy returned that night. Eventually the children fell asleep although the adults stayed awake. No one knew what to do but no one was going to chance falling asleep. There was a lot of pacing going on in the dining room. Dawn and Diane, although quiet now, had been terribly affected by the night's events. Dave had what appeared to be a burn in the shape of a hand on his wrist. He was sure that was from the icy hand he had felt during the explosion. As the sun started to rise, Ken and Dave packed up their equipment. Irma offered to make breakfast for everyone but one by one, everyone refused. Ken left with Dawn around seven. Dave stayed behind because he wanted to meet with Father Michael. Once

Ken left, he had no ride home but Don assured him that he would take him home. Only Don, Irma and Dave went to Mass that morning. The Mass was being said by Father Paul but after the Mass, Don asked to priest to contact Father Michael.

"Father Michael won't be back until later tonight," the older priest told Don affably. "Perhaps I can help you with something?" he offered. "Well Father," Don began, "we have already talked to Father Michael about our problem. We were hoping to be able to follow up with him." "Can you tell me what this is about?" the Priest asked. Dave spoke up: "It is about a haunting, Father. These people need help and they need it right away." The old priest smiled. "Oh, I see. Yes, you must be the family that he told me about." Irma's eyes brightened. Perhaps Father Paul would be able to help them. Dave continued talking. "We need to have the house blessed and the Church is going to have to investigate this situation." Once again, the priest smiled a kindly smile. "Son, I'll tell you what I told Father Michael. There is no such nonsense as haunted houses and demons and gremlins and all of that stuff." Don's face turned red. "Listen pal, you haven't been in our house so don't give me the sanctimonious bullshit." The priest stepped back. "No one talks to me that way. I'll ask you to leave now." Dave grabbed Don's arm and pulled him back. He was afraid of what Don might do. That was a wise move because Don was fit to be tied.

Dave stepped between the two to diffuse what he feared might take place. "Just give Father Michael the message. In the mean time, we'll go see the pastor." Dave led the couple away. As they left, they heard Father Paul yell to them: "Good luck." It sounded far more sarcastic than wishful. "Idiot," Dave muttered as they went to the rectory. Unfortunately, the pastor, Father Raymond, was away until later that afternoon. However, his housekeeper told them that she would give him the message. As the three tired people walked away, you could feel the sense of dejection that overpowered them. They walked silently, with slumped shoulders, their spirits having just taken a direct hit.

When they arrived home, Ted had the place cleaned up. Diane was asleep on the couch and the children were playing outside the house. Ted saw the dejection on the faces of his parents and Dave. After hearing their story, he commented that he was not surprised in the least. "Nothing would surprise me at this point," he added. Dave looked exhausted and Don offered to drive him home. However, he wanted to stay until they heard from one of the priests. However, he did concede when it was suggested to him that he try to get some sleep. He took one of the children's mattresses upstairs and he placed it in Debbie's room. He tried to think of other things he could try if the Church would not help them. However, he was so tired that he could barely think. He closed his eyes and was asleep within minutes.

The day passed by slowly. Every time the telephone rang, Ted or Don jumped up to answer it. However, they were disappointed every time when it was always someone other than one of the priests. Around five-thirty that evening, Father Michael called. He listened patiently to Ted's story and he decided to come to the house. That excited the Carters. Don went upstairs to wake Dave up. Although it only took twenty minutes, the wait for the priest seemed like hours. When he finally arrived, the family jumped up to greet him. The young priest seemed nervous. "I am going to bless the house for you. After that, I honestly don't know what else to do. After having some coffee and cake, the young priest went from room to room and did the blessing. He was getting ready to leave when three loud bangs reverberated throughout the house. The priest's face lost all of its color when he heard the bangs. "That is what we are talking about Father," Don told the priest. "We are going to need help," the priest replied.

We are nearing the end of the story. A lot has happened in a short period of time. You may never see this in real life. If you do, then you have a horrific case on your hands. We just met an experienced investigator, Dave. He has been through some horrific cases. He almost left the field completely after a particularly serious haunting. His experience will be valuable to the investigation. Although he obviously knows far more than Ken, he chooses to be a worker as opposed to a leader. This is not uncommon when you are dealing with someone who has had a lot of bad experiences. At the meeting at Ken's house, we saw Dawn get locked in the bathroom. To me, that sounds like the spirit was sending a message. When Diane emerged, she felt that there was a demon involved. She is probably right but it is tough when a psychic tries to analyze a traumatic event that happened to her. Her own fear had to play a role in her assessment. Dave was wise to believe that it may not be a demonic haunting per se; he believes that the demon is hiding in the shadows. However, the events taking place are crossing the line so now it is fair to think that it might be a demonic haunting. What can also be happening is that the demon knows that his time is short so he is getting as many licks in as he can.

Earlier, we saw how empowering it was to have the holy water as a weapon. Unfortunately, that kind of empowerment can be fleeting. When things started to get out of hand, the holy water was all but forgotten. The investigators should be reinforcing that with the Carter family but they too get caught up in the activity themselves. It is human nature so you cannot be too critical of them. It is very easy to sit back after the fact and say what everyone should have done. Another interesting thing is Diane's stick wielding apparition. No, she was not in real physical danger; the stick in question was not real. However, try convincing Diane of that. For the victims, it is hard for them to believe that they are safe. Physically safe, anyway. That can take a lot of work on the part of the investigators.

You may have noticed that two cars were used for the trip to the Carter house. This is a wise idea. Cars often fail to start when the destination is a haunted house. In addition, having two cars instead of four cuts down the risk of an accident. There are some who believe that demons can cause car accidents. I do not doubt the possibility although events like that are extremely rare, if they happen at all. I have heard of steering wheels being pulled from the driver although my belief is that the most likely way they will cause an accident is by frightening the driver. If you glance in your rear view mirror and see something horrible in it, I am sure that you would have a problem on your hands. We saw the destruction of precious plates. That kind of thing is common in a negative haunting. I often recommend that valuable items, figurines, etc, should be wrapped up and put somewhere safe until the haunting is over. However, plates in a kitchen cabinet should be safe. Unfortunately, in this case, they were not. Sadly, long after the haunting stops, Diane will feel the loss of something she considered precious.

We saw Tim leave the investigation. You cannot be too critical about that. The big thing is that he is young and talking about cases is surely fun but when it comes to *working* them, it is a horse of a different color. He may or may not continue his career in the field. I have seen cases like his go both ways. Dave considered blessing the house but he was initially against the idea. His fear was that he might open up Pandora's box or cause a firestorm if the haunting is demonic. However, once things exploded, there was really no harm in doing the blessing. The entity was already on the attack so there was not much to fear as far as retaliation goes. The spirit was already retaliating so this becomes a reactive action as opposed to a proactive one. What is wrong with being proactive? If you know how to stop a firestorm, there is nothing wrong with it. However, most people do not know how to stop a major problem unless they have been trained in how to do so and are experienced enough to be comfortable with doing it. We saw Dawn being locked in the master bedroom while being attacked. Physical attacks are rare. I put that in there merely to show you what *can* happen. That would appear to be a demonic attack. I highly doubt that a human spirit, acting alone could perform such a feat.

When Dave decided to do the blessing in the house, he did everything in the name of Christ. That is extremely important. You should never issue a command to a negative spirit on your own authority. We have very little and no spirit is going to be intimidated by a human's power. Always add God's name to a command. It is far more effective and far safer than trying to command a spirit on your own. Lastly, we once again saw Father Paul's reaction. Sadly, that is not uncommon. Dealing with a priest is a giant crapshoot. You just never know what you will get. Father Michael did agree to bless the house. That was good. You will notice that the entity made sure that the priest knew he was there. Often, the exact opposite will happen. You could have a case where a priest sat vigil for hours with nothing happening. That makes it extremely difficult because the Church is skeptical to begin with and having no activity only makes things worse.

Nearing The End

Father Michael stayed at the Carter house for close to two hours. He apologized profusely for not getting more involved with them earlier. He admitted that he knew very little about the supernatural world. Every so often, the spirit haunting the Carters would do something like move a glass across a counter or shake the table in the dining room where everyone was sitting. Dave told the priest that it was the spirits way of letting him know that he was still there. Towards the end of his visit, Father Michael made a decision. He was going to talk to Father Raymond about the situation when he got back to the rectory. He admitted that he was fearful of the meeting but he felt that he would have to risk the wrath of the old pastor. The alternative was to let the Carters suffer. Diane could not thank him enough for blessing the house and she hoped that Father Raymond would be reasonable about the situation. So too did Father Michael.

On the short ride back to the rectory, Father Michael tried to rehearse his approach with Father Raymond. No matter how hard he tried, he could not think of a good way to bring the subject up. He decided that he would just say what came to him, good, bad or indifferent. As soon as he was back in the rectory, he went straight to Father Raymond's study. Knocking lightly, he asked the older priest if he could discuss something with him. Father Raymond motioned him in. "What can I do for you son?" the pastor asked. "Father, I don't know how to start this conversation. I mean, it is a strange situation and I'm not quite sure what to say." The older priest said nothing, which only made Father Michael more uncomfortable. "Okay Father, here goes. A few weeks ago, a family approached me after Mass and asked for my help." The young priest was quite nervous and it showed. However, Father Raymond was not about to let him off the hook too easily. "You see, Father, they believe that they are being haunted by *something* although they don't know what." Father Raymond frowned. "Tell me Michael, why do they think they are being haunted?" The young priest took a deep breath. "They say that objects fly around the house of their own volition, something pulls hair, stinks up the house and they see dark shapes." The older priest frowned again. "Do these people sound sincere?" "Very much so," Father Michael answered.

Father Michael then told the pastor about his visit to the house. The older priest's face reddened. "Why didn't you come to me first, Michael?" The young priest was taken aback by the harshness of his tone. "Well," he stammered, "to be honest, I was afraid about how you would react." The older priest was clearly angry. "That is not an excuse. You have had no training on that subject. I would have expected you to confide in me first, as a courtesy, if for no other reason." Father Michael was very uncomfortable now. He tried to explain to his superior how he had talked to Father Paul first to see how he would react and how he was put down by him. Father Raymond's face reddened some more. "He is nothing but an old idiot with an emphasis on the word "idiot." Fine, I understand now why you chose to keep this from me. In the future, Father Michael, come to me with unusual problems." The young priest agreed that he would.

Father Raymond thought for a few seconds and then spoke: "Tell me again everything that happened while you were there," Father Raymond instructed Father Michael. When the young priest was finished, Father Raymond sat silently. Finally, he spoke. "Now, Michael, the question is what do we do with this?" The young priest looked excited. "You mean you believe me?" he asked. "Of course I believe you. Why wouldn't I?" The young priest said nothing for a few seconds. "I suppose we could go to the chancery with this," he offered. Father Raymond shook his head from side to side. "No, it is too early for that yet. First, we must see what we can do. The blessing appears to have had little effect so I would suggest a Mass being said in the house. Then if necessary, we can call the chancery." The older priest sat quietly for a few moments. "I will want to meet with the family myself. I also want to meet with anyone from outside the house who has experienced anything out of the ordinary." At that point, Father Michael told his pastor about the team of investigators involved in the case. Father Raymond looked concerned. "That can be a problem. For all we know, these people are looking for publicity or fame or something. Yes, that can be a real problem." The young priest tried to convince his superior that they seemed earnest, based on his conversation with Dave. "Then I will want to talk to him before I go over there," Father Raymond told Father Michael. "Father, he is there now, I believe. Would you like me to call him?" The older priest nodded "yes."

Diane answered the phone on the second ring. "Hello Diane, this is Father Michael." "Father, yes, how are you?" Diane sounded upbeat, despite the situation. "Diane, I need to talk to Dave, if I may. Is he still there?" "Yes, he is, Father. I'll go get him." When Dave picked up the phone, Father Michael explained that Father Raymond wanted to talk to him. When Father Raymond took the phone, he began questioning Dave on his motives for the investigation. Dave explained why they were involved and he assured the concerned priest that this would be handled in an extremely confidential manner. He then explained how he had worked with the Church on two other occasions. That seemed to please Father Raymond. He explained to the investigator the dangers of publicity in a situation like the one he was now facing. Once he was satisfied that the case would be treated confidentially, he agreed to help. He then asked the investigator for a run down on everything that had happened. Their conversation lasted for over an hour. When it was done, an appointment had been set up. Father Raymond and Father Michael would be over to the Carter house at six the following evening. When Dave relayed that information to Diane, she announced that she would make dinner for them. The priest smiled. "Tell the young lady that she may never get rid of me if she does that." Dave relayed the comment to Diane.

When he hung up the phone, Father Raymond went to a small cabinet near his desk and took out a bottle of bourbon. He looked at his young colleague: "Care to join me for a drink, Michael. We have lots to talk about." Father Michael gladly accepted the offer. He spent the next two hours learning about the supernatural. As it turned out, Father Raymond had been involved in several paranormal cases over the years. Father Michael was surprised to see that Father Raymond cared deeply about the Carter family. He thought to himself how odd it was that Father Paul could be so dismissive while Father Raymond was eager to help. He also thought how ironic it was that the priest he feared talking to was helpful while the one he guessed would be helpful turned out to be the disappointment. He had just learned a lesson in judging a book y it's cover. During their conversation, Father Raymond asked Father Michael for the address of the house. When he was told, he was silent for a second. "Is something wrong, Father?" the young priest asked. "I'm thinking. That address sounds familiar to me." With that, he stood up and walked over to one of his filing cabinets and unlocked it. He then started shuffling through some files and finally removed one. He took the file over to his desk and refilled the two glasses with a generous amount of bourbon.

"My God," he began. "Yes, I've been to that house before. That was almost ten years ago, before I was even assigned to this parish." Father Michael watched the older priest go through the file. "It is coming back to me now. A very disturbed woman once resided there. She was mentally ill and she had a penchant for the occult. She committed suicide in that house. A year or so after that, a young couple moved in and apparently they had some problems there. I was asked to bless the house by the former pastor." Father Michael smiled. "What happened then?" he asked Father Raymond. Evidently, things calmed down somewhat but a few years later, the family moved out. That was the end of it as far as I knew. I guess I knew wrong."

Father Michael asked a few questions and was surprised at the amount of knowledge Father Raymond had. "Did the investigators find anything occult-like in the house?" Father Raymond asked. "Not that I know of," replied the young priest. "Well, I think a Mass is in order. My question is why the old woman stuck around?" Of course, Father Michael had no answer to that question. "Father Raymond, do you think there is a demon involved?" The older priest did not hesitate for a second. "Absolutely, no question about that. However, I don't think an exorcism is necessary. The foul spirit will leave when the woman does and I think that will be tomorrow." Father Michael hoped he was right.

Back in the Carter house, the atmosphere was upbeat. Diane really believed that the end of the haunting was in sight. How she wanted to live a normal life again. Perhaps she would but that normal life was not about to start then and there. She had put the children to bed in the living room and she went upstairs to get something. She was in her bedroom for less than a minute when the door slammed shut and the lights went out. Then she heard growling. She immediately screamed for help. The growling began to grow louder. Whatever was in the room with her was moving closer to her. Then she felt an icy hand grab the back of her neck. Diane fainted on the spot.

Amazingly, no one heard her scream. It was almost twenty minutes later that Ted realized that Diane was missing. After asking his parents where she was, he walked up the stairs. He had a feeling that Diane was in their bedroom so he went there. Sure enough, he found her on the floor. He called down to his parents and picked her up. Slowly, she woke up. Then she started to cry. Don and Irma tried to calm their daughter-in-law down. It took a good twenty minutes to do so. Ted wished that Dave had stayed the night. Unfortunately, he had to go to work in the morning so Don had driven him home. Ted knew that it would be a sleepless night.

Aside from that one incident, the house was quiet that night and everyone got at least a little sleep. In the morning, Diane got the children off to school and then she went to work herself. She could not wait until the evening. The phone in the Carter house rang around eleven that morning. The call was from Father Michael, who wanted to see how things were going. He also asked Don a few questions concerning the haunting. Once he was satisfied, he told the Carters that he and Father Raymond would be there by six. Don thanked the priest and hung up. Don and Irma sat talking about what they hoped would happen when the priests came over that night. The house seemed so peaceful that day. Diane called twice to see how things were going. She seemed to be in a good mood. The question was whether she would be able to stay in that mood. Only time would tell.

At five thirty that evening Ken, Dawn and Dave showed up. The Carters were surprised to see Dawn. After what had happened to her, they assumed that she would never be back. "I'm okay," Dawn told Diane. "That was the worst thing I've experienced yet but I guess it will make things easier the next time something bad happens. I guess I'm being desensitized." Diane laughed. "Well, I am just glad that you are here and that you are okay." At just before six, the doorbell rang. Irma opened it and greeted the two priests. Irma had spent the day making dinner for everyone and as Irma talked with the priests, Diane set the table. Ted arrived home from work just as Diane was finishing setting the table.

Over dinner, the conversation was light. With the children present, the priests were reluctant to discuss the haunting. Dawn felt a sense of apprehension. She later described the atmosphere in the house as "tense." Once dinner was done, Diane served dessert and coffee. After that, the children went outside to play. Diane found that she liked Father Raymond. He may have looked grouchy but he was a pleasant man with a good sense of humor. She later told Ted that she had just learned a lesson about judging books by their covers. Unbeknownst to her, that was two people in two days. With the children outside, Father Raymond explained that he would walk around the house to see what kind of reaction, if any, there would be on the part of the entity. He started in the basement and then he walked through the ground floor. Finally, he headed upstairs.

He did not sense anything until he walked into the master bedroom. In there, he felt a presence and he did not like it one bit. He stayed in the room for several minutes but he did nothing. He wanted to see what the spirit would do. When he was about to leave, he blessed himself and announced: "By the power of Christ, you are going to leave tonight, you vile, corrupt coward. With that, he left. Once in the living room, he asked the investigators if they had been able to find a reason for the haunting. They told him that they hadn't. "There has to be a reason why this thing is here," he told everyone. "It wants something." Diane looked at the priest. "Maybe it just wants us out?" "Could be," the priest told her. "It could be something else too." Before anyone could ask him what he though the reason was, he turned to Ted. "When you moved into the house, did you find anything unusual in it?" Ted shook his head from side to side. "It was pretty well cleaned out when we came to see it. Why do you ask, Father?"

"At one time, a old woman lived here. She was a little on the wacky side but what is more significant is that she used to be big on the occult. I am just wondering if that is the reason why all of this is happening." "How do you know that, Father?" Irma asked him. He then told her how he was once involved with the house. That surprised everyone. He had another surprise for them. "I am not going to say the Mass tonight," he told the family. Everyone was shocked and Diane looked crushed. "But Father," she began but the priest raised his hand. "Diane, I have every intention of getting rid of this thing. I just want to make sure I do it right. I will do the Mass on Saturday, I promise. Tonight, I want to spend some time here and get a feel for whatever this thing is. He then asked the investigators if they would let him read any notes they had as well as see any pictures they had taken that showed anomalies. They were more than happy to share their information with the priest.

Father Raymond looked at Ted. "Son, is the attic above your bedroom?" "Well Father, it is actually little more than a crawlspace. That's the one thing this house lacks. But yes, it is above the bedroom." The priest thought for a second before he spoke. "Can we take a look at it?" he asked Ted. "Of course, Father. There are some boxes that we stuffed in there but I can move them." The priest then asked Ken whether he had been up there. "No Father, actually we haven't." Dave rolled his eyes when he heard that. "What do you think is up there, Father?" Don asked. "Oh, probably nothing. I just get the feeling that the spirit stays up there." "Why is that?" Dave asked. Father Michael shifted in his seat. For some reason, he was beginning to feel uncomfortable. Father Raymond then answered the question. "From what you have all told me and what I felt myself when I was up there, the master bedroom seems to be the focal point in this house. I am just wondering why. If the attic is above it, maybe that is why that room is singled out."

Father Raymond stood up and announced that he wanted to sit in the master bedroom for a few minutes. Suddenly, three loud bangs reverberated throughout the house. Shortly after the first burst, a second began. "You have made your point, idiot. Now stop this nonsense in the name of God!" Father Raymond said in a booming voice. There was no third burst. Since our friend here decided to tip his hand, I am going to go upstairs now and begin blessing the house. Father Michael joined him and the two holy men went upstairs. Father Raymond went straight to the master bedroom. "In the name of Jesus Christ, Almighty, I bless this room and demand in the Savior's name that you leave this house." He then sprinkled holy water around the room. He then went into Debbie's room and repeated the procedure. After that, he went into each room. When he was finished, he declined a cup of coffee. He asked Ted to take a look around in the attic sometime during the week, if he had time. "It's just a hunch." A few minutes later, the two priests left the Carter house with the instruction that they were to call either him or Father Michael if anything happened. They took with them the reports and tapes from the investigators.

We see right away that Father Raymond is not the old grump that everyone thought he was. As it turns out, not only does he believe in the supernatural but he also was quite well versed on the subject. That makes him a rare priest in these days. Why do you think he decided to put off saying the Mass in the house? Is it because he felt something? And what about his hunch regarding the attic? He was wise to take the investigators reports with him. He obviously wants to make sure he knows what he is dealing with before he does anything in the house. How much stock he will put into those reports is anybody's guess but at least he wants to see them.

He made an interesting point when he asked whether the investigators knew why the haunting was taking place. Knowing that can make a huge difference when it comes time to cleanse the house. The investigators made one serious error; they had never gone into the attic crawlspace. They may not have found anything but it was an area of the house that was ignored. If something *was* up there, they may have found it. If the spirit was up there, they could have blessed that space as well. However, you may have noticed that Father Raymond did not bless it either. In his case, he had a reason. You saw where Dave rolled his eyes when he heard that no one had gone up there. In all fairness to Ken and his crew, Dave never asked them about an attic. Being an experienced investigator, he should have at least asked whether anyone had been up there. Mistakes are going to be made in an investigation. No one is perfect. I have made a fair share of mistakes myself. That is why it is good to have meetings with the team. Things like the attic could have come up earlier. I am sure that over the course of time, it would have been caught but since this is an accelerated haunting, there was not much time for meetings. Let us see how this continues.

("The Tribe Has Spoken")

On the ride back to the rectory, Father Michael asked his superior why he had chosen not to say the Mass. "I want to make sure that we are not dealing with a full fledged demonic haunting. I don't think we are but I want to be sure." Father Michael looked at the older priest. "Father, why don't we just do an exorcism and be done with it?" Father Raymond wasted no time answering the question. "You see, Michael, an exorcism can only be performed with the approval of our Bishop. That requires a long investigation. However, I don't believe it is necessary." Father Michael was confused. "Why not? I mean, even if it is not demonic, why not just say an exorcism and throw the kitchen sink at this thing?" "An exorcism is a powerful ritual, Michael, and not one to take lightly. Performing an exorcism where it is not needed can draw the attention of something that will swoop in and cause a bigger problem. I do think there is a demon there but I do not think it is doing the haunting. A solemn Mass with a few specific prayers should do the trick. If it doesn't, then one more condition has been met and I will have a case to present to the diocese."

Back at the Carter house, everyone was hopeful. Since nothing would happen until the weekend, Don decided to make the long drive home so that he could go to work for a few days. Although he trusted his employees, he did not want to take a chance on letting them run it for too long. You cannot help being a little paranoid when you own your own business. Irma stayed with her son and his family. The next few days were quiet in the Carter house. However, at the rectory, doors were opening and closing by themselves from time to time. Father Raymond found it amusing while Father Michael found it frightening.

On Thursday night, Ted decided to look around in the attic. He moved everything out, all the while complaining of all the junk they had accumulated. Once the area was cleared, he took a look around. He had to admit that the space felt "creepy" but he attributed that to his imagination. He searched the area for a half-hour but he found nothing. "Your hunch was wrong, Father," he mumbled to himself as he was about to leave the crawlspace. Just near the entrance to it, he felt a loose floorboard. "Hum, what have we here?" he asked as he tried to lift it. He was surprised when it came up easily, along with several others as well. Peeking in with the flashlight, he saw a box about the size of an average shoebox. It was made of wood and it was black. It also had a pentagram carved into it. He started to take it out when the pounding started. Ted dropped the box and covered his ears. The pounding was coming from his left and as he tried to crawl out and on to the ladder, he slipped and fell. Ted crashed to the floor hard, hurting his wrist in the process. The pounding stopped as he fell.

Diane was frightened by the pounding but she was more concerned with Ted. His wrist was really painful and Diane feared that he might have broken it in the fall. Despite his protests to the contrary, Diane took him to the hospital. He wrist was indeed broken. After a cast was placed on it, Ted and Diane went home. Irma was upset when she saw the cast on her son's wrist and hand. Ted tried to downplay it but his mother remained upset. "Mom, it's gonna be fine. Besides, now I can have a little vacation." "Some vacation," his mother replied. Before going to bed that night, Ted had one thing he wanted to do. He went up the ladder again and removed the wooden box. Once he accomplished that task, he brought the box downstairs. The box was locked but Diane and Irma were able to force it open. Inside was a half burned black candle and an old book on casting spells. "Good God," Diane said, "Father Raymond was right." Although it was late, Irma called the rectory.

Father Michael answered the phone and he was excited about the find. Father Raymond had left on a sick call, he told Irma. However, he promised to tell him about it when he came in. Irma never mentioned her son's broken wrist. As soon as Father Raymond arrived back at the rectory, the young priest told him about the box and its contents. "They must throw out the candle and burn the book," he told Father Michael. I would like to see it first. "Perhaps tomorrow, we can go over there and take a look at it." The young priest agreed.

After having breakfast the next morning, Father Raymond called the Carter house. Irma was home alone and she was glad to hear from the priest. She told him that she had felt uneasy since Ted discovered the box. She explained the whole story to him. The priest felt bad for Ted and he promised to mention him at his next Mass. He told her that he would stop by sometime that evening to look at the book. Then they would need to dispose of it. After she hung up the phone, Irma's unease seemed to grow stronger. Being alone in the house during the day had bothered her all week but on this day, it was worse. She wanted to look at the book but it frightened her. She felt it was best not to go near it. Around eleven, she began to feel cold. She shuddered and looked at the thermostat. It was reading sixty-five but it seemed colder to her. She put on a sweater and looked out the kitchen window. Snow was falling lightly outside. She went into the living room and turned the TV on. She switched to the Weather Channel and waited for the local forecast. When it came on, she read that they were expecting 1 to 2 inches. "That's not so bad," she said to herself.

A short time later, she decided to make herself a cup of tea. When she entered the kitchen, she saw a woman standing next to the refrigerator. Her heart pounded but she stood frozen. "What do you want?" she asked the apparition. Of course, there was no answer. "Get out of here!" she yelled at it but if it heard her, it gave no sign of it. Irma wished she had the holy water handy. Slowly, the apparition faded away. Suddenly, the kitchen filled with a horrible stench. Irma gagged and backed into the living room. She wanted to leave the house but she had nowhere to go. Don had taken the car home with him; Diane and Ted were at work. She had expected Ted to come home early since he would not be able to work but he had called and told her that he was put into a supervisory capacity and he would be able to work even with the broken wrist.

The stench now drifted in from the kitchen. Irma was sure she was going to be sick. She thought about going upstairs until she saw the black mist hovering in the middle of them. "Dear God, help me," she begged. Slowly, the odor went away and the mist floated upstairs. Irma went back into the kitchen and made her tea. She did so with hands shaking from fear. As the water heated up, she glanced out the window. The snow was coming down hard now and it looked like it was accumulating as well. When her tea was ready, she put the TV on again and waited for the forecast; it had not changed from before. Now Irma began to worry about Don. He would have to drive in the storm and a four-hour drive now figured to last a lot longer, not to mention the danger involved. Irma was worrying herself into a terrible state.

Once the children were home, Irma began to relax. Of course, they wanted to play outside in the snow and Irma saw no reason to stop them. By then, well over five inches had fallen. Once again, Irma turned on the TV. This time, the forecast had changed and it said that they could expect up to four inches across the region. "Well, they are getting closer," Irma said to herself. Needless to say, the children were having a ball outside. Irma stood by the window watching them play. How she wished she were young again. While she was daydreaming, the black mist was hovering at the bottom of the stairs.

When Diane got home, Irma told her about the day. Diane hoped and prayed that the night would not be active. She also hoped and prayed that the Mass would not be cancelled. She did not know how much more she could take. She was relieved when Ted pulled up in front of the house. "Christ, is this some storm or what?" he asked. "I'm going to have to get the snow blower going," he told his wife. "Honey, you can't do that with your wrist." "Hmmm, I can try." Ted went outside and a few minutes later Diane heard the snow blower. While Ted was outside clearing away the snow and dodging snowballs, a car pulled up in front of the house. Out stepped Dave, Dawn, Ken and Tim. Ted was surprised that they would come over in such a storm but he was grateful. He was even more grateful when Tim relieved him of the snow blower.

Just as the team walked into the house, the telephone rang. Don was on the other end when Diane picked it up. He had left work early and was just outside of town. He asked Diane if she wanted him to pick up some pizza or anything else. That made her happy; he was safe and on top of that, she would not have to cook. Less than an hour later, Don arrived. A few minutes later, the two priests arrived as well.

Everybody had some pizza and the conversation centered around the nasty snowstorm. Irma complained about the weather predictions. "They say snow up to four inches when there are already seven on the ground. "Father Michael laughed. "I always trust the Weather Channel, you know, weather you can count on." Everybody laughed and as a goof, Ted turned it on. With almost a foot of snow on the ground, they channel was announcing a winter weather advisory. "Oh well, at least they're not predicting sunny and seventy," Ted joked. When the supper was finished, everyone went into the living room except for the children and Father Michael; they went outside for a snowball fight. Diane was amazed that everyone had come over in such bad weather. To those present, it was no big deal. There was a party atmosphere in the house that night and that was a good thing. Father Raymond asked to see the spell book and the candle so Ted went upstairs to get them. When he reached into the closet where he had stuck them, the door slammed shut, hitting him in the back. He winced and spun around, half expecting to see the black mist. He was relieved to see nothing.

The priest looked at the book silently. After several minutes, he tossed it on the coffee table. "That book is very old and judging by the shape of it, well read. However, I don't see anything in there about conjuring demons, so that is a plus. She highlighted some spells designed to bring money. It is a safe bet they didn't work. I suggest you burn the book." "Consider it done," Ted said. "What about the candle?" Dave asked. The priest thought for a minute. "That one I am not so sure about. We could burn it but since it was used in some sort of occult ritual, I wouldn't want to do that." "Could that cause a problem?" Diane asked. "I don't know, to be honest about it," the priest answered. He looked at Dave to see if he had any suggestions. "Well, I think you're right about not burning it. Maybe I can chop it up and then just throw it into the garbage." Everyone agreed that it would be a good idea. Ted told Dave that he had a hand axe in the basement he could use. The two men went down the basement and a few seconds later, banging was heard. "It sounds like the candle is history," Don said. "I doubt it," the priest replied. "The candle is still here."

A few minutes later, Ted and Dave came up from the basement. "Diane looked at Ted and asked what had caused the banging. "A disgruntled ghost," Dave answered. Oddly enough, everyone laughed. Dave took the candle downstairs and the next set of bangs was caused by his destruction of the candle. Don stood up and started to set up a fire in the fireplace. Once the fire was burning well, Father Raymond picked up the book and threw it into the flames. At first, it did not burn. "You have got to be kidding me," Irma exclaimed. However, the book finally caught on fire and within a few minutes, it was engulfed in flames. "Throw the box in too," he added. "When you clean that out in the morning, sprinkle this blessed salt on it before you dispose of the ashes." With that, he placed a plastic bottle on the table. He continued: "Then put a little holy water in the fireplace. Put some salt and holy water in the bag with the remains of the candle too."

A short time later, a snow covered Father Michael entered the house followed by the children. "They won the snow ball fight," he announced to everyone. "Well Michael, I think we had better brave the snow and head back to the rectory. We have some preparing to do." Although he dreaded driving in the snow, he knew that Father Raymond was right. As the two men approached the door, they saw the black mist blocking their way. Father Michael opened a small vial of holy water and tossed it on at the mist. "The tribe has spoken," he said. "Time for you to go." Everyone laughed at that, especially Father Raymond and the mist disappeared. On the way home, Father Raymond told Father Michael what he had done with the book, the box and the candle.

We are at the end now but there are still a few surprises in store. Finding the occult paraphernalia was important because that alone could be what was keeping the human spirit in the house. What you may have overlooked but is very significant is the fact that the book in question was a spell book and not a conjuring book. That is significant because if it was a conjuring book, the possibility existed that the demon had been brought in by the old lady and then you would have had a full demonic infestation to deal with. That would have required a solemn exorcism to cleanse the house. Since it was a spell book, the chances are that the demonic presence was there simply to puppeteer the human spirit. Of course, you cannot be 100% certain of that.

Think about the situation involving Ted's accident and the broken wrist. Physical injuries as a direct result of a negative spirit, be it human or demonic, are rare. However, *indirect* injuries certainly can occur in any haunting. Here, Ted fell as a result of the spirit's actions but the spirit did not *directly* cause the injury. It may appear to be a small difference but it is not. That is why it is important to be careful on an investigation. Most physical injuries occur as a result of how the injured responded to a given phenomenon. That is an important lesson to learn.

It is important to note that the mood in the house was jovial. That is so important in a situation like this. Instead of everyone being afraid of the activity, they found something to be amused about. Already the invading spirit was losing its grip on the family. Of course, it is easy to feel safe when you have a room full of people there. Still, you cannot underestimate the value of having everyone feeling good. It is such a powerful tool in a haunting. For Father Michael, a major step was taken when he stood up to the spirit and even went so far as to make a joke of it. That showed that he had listened to what Father Raymond told him about the supernatural. It is a sign that his personal fears were leaving. Are you surprised that Tim is back? Everyone is but you will understand his motives shortly. It is all about growing up.

* * * *

(Goodbye, So Long, Farewell)

The Carter family hoped it would be a quiet night and for the most part it was. The old woman spirit showed up a couple of times but her visits were brief. There was no pounding that night, nor did the black mist show up. There was an air of expectancy however. Ted and Diane found it hard to sleep that night. That was okay because with the investigators there, a lot of laughing took place. Diane spoke to Tim alone for a while. She was surprised he came back and she wanted to thank him for coming. Tim apologized for his leaving that night. He told Diane that he truly felt overwhelmed. He had no idea that things could be so bad. Nothing in his limited experience had prepared him for what he encountered in the Carter house. He explained to Diane how he read about such cases but he never believed that things like that actually took place. He had assumed that most of what he had read was embellished greatly or were flat out lies. He needed time to digest what had happened. When he took a few days to reflect on it, he realized that he had made a terrible mistake in leaving. Now he wanted to redeem himself.

Diane told him how unnecessary his apology was. No one, she figured could experience the events in that house and not find themselves frightened half to death. Tim told her that he felt like a coward and a traitor. Diane worked hard to convince him that he had no reason to feel either way. He was brave for having come on the case in the first place. It took a while but Tim did feel much better after their talk. Even prior to their conversation, Tim could not be helpful enough around the house. He spent a great deal of time outside shoveling snow and clearing off the cars. By eleven that night, thirteen inches of snow had fallen and it was still snowing out.

Don spent a lot time talking to Dave and Ken. He could not understand why they wanted to be in their line of work. Dave explained to him that the most honest answer he could give was that he himself was not sure why he did it. He said all of the usual stuff: the desire to help people, the excitement, the chance to learn some of the secrets to life and that it was almost a calling. It was just something he felt compelled to do. Ken agreed with that assessment. Dawn spent a lot of time talking with Ted and Irma. They loved hearing her stories of readings she had done for people. Irma wanted her to do a reading for her but Dawn declined. She told Irma she would be happy to give her a reading but not until the haunting was over and not in that house. She believed that it was too dangerous.

Back at the rectory, Father Raymond was working with Father Michael on the homily he wanted to say at the Mass and they also discussed prayers that they would say. Father Raymond had set it up for three priests. That confused Father Michael but he did not argue the point. He figured they would "wing" it once they got to the house. While they were talking, the room grew cold. "Oh no you're not," Father Raymond said as he picked up a bottle of holy water and sprinkled it in his office. Father Michael shuddered. However, after a few seconds, the room grew warm again. The two priests said goodnight and went to their respective rooms. After reading their breviaries, both priests said extra prayers. Father Raymond fell asleep quickly but Father Michael had trouble falling asleep. His mind was racing and he kept thinking about the upcoming Mass at the Carter house. Eventually, he fell asleep, although is was a restless one. When he woke up in the morning, he was surprised to see that the parish car was not in the driveway. He hoped there had not been any trouble at the Carter house.

Once everyone was awake, Ted and Don took all of the mattresses back to their rooms. Diane and Irma made up the beds. They were hoping that everyone would be sleeping in their own rooms again. The camping out in the living room was okay at first; everyone felt safer and there was some novelty value as well but it quickly grew annoying. Outside, the snow had stopped falling. All told, they had gotten sixteen inches of the white stuff. Diane hoped the priests would still be able to come over. At eleven-thirty, they did, all three of them. When Diane opened the door, Father Raymond led the way. He was carrying a large duffel bag. Behind him was an old priest whom she did not recognize. Father Michael brought up the rear. He had a mischievous smile on his face when Father Raymond introduced Father Paul to Diane. She could not wait to ask Father Michael what that was all about. She greeted the old priest warmly. "Thank you for coming, Father," she said as she shook his hand. Then she turned to Father Raymond. "Bringing in reinforcements, huh?" Father Raymond laughed. "You can never have too many priests around in a haunted house," he told her. Father Paul merely rolled his eyes.

As Diane would later find out from Father Michael, Father Raymond had called Father Paul and asked him to join them for the Mass. Of course, the old priest put up an argument, saying that there are no such things as ghosts. However, the pastor convinced him to go with an open mind. "You don't have to believe in ghosts, Father, but you do believe in the Mass so join us. After a long debate, the priest agreed, although he made it clear that he did not believe in ghosts and still would not after the day was done. Father Raymond accepted that. As soon as Don and Irma saw father Paul, they recognized him immediately. However, both chose to say nothing. Diane made coffee for everyone. After that, the priests began setting up a makeshift alter in the living room.

As the final preparations were being set up, Father Paul excused himself and went into the bathroom. With Father Raymond's permission, Ken and Dave set up camcorders to film the Mass. They were hoping to record something paranormal, should anything happen. When Father Paul emerged from the bathroom, his face was drained of all of its color. "Father, are you alright?" Dawn asked the priest. He sat down and looked at his shaking hands. "My God, I just saw a woman in the bathroom mirror. I must be going crazy." "You are not going crazy, Father," Dawn told him. "You just saw a ghost," Father Raymond told him. The old priest nodded his head up and down. "Good God, I don't know what is going on here but it cannot be natural," he told the pastor. "That is why we are here," Father Raymond told him.

Once Father Paul calmed down, the Mass began. Father Raymond had brought a tape of religious hymns with him and he chose the song: "Be Not Afraid" as the opening hymn. The house was quiet through the opening prayers and the two readings. However, when Father Raymond read the Gospel, the almost deafening pounding started up. Despite the racket, the priest continued reading the gospel. Just as he finished reading it, the pounding stopped. He then began his homily. "God's words cannot be silenced as the spirits in this house now know. God has offered them life; He has offered them His kingdom. They chose to refuse those offers and now, as a result of their folly, they are abominations. They shall not be allowed to stay in a house belonging to the children of God." A strong vibration shook the house as the priest continued. "Parlor tricks will do no good; in the eyes of God, this is the same as a child throwing a temper tantrum. They deserve no more recognition from us. Jesus died for our sins, *all* of our sins. That includes those spirits that have chosen the path of darkness. They have rejected that sacrifice, the sacrifice that offered them eternal happiness. On the day of Jesus death, Satan rejoiced. After all, he had the ultimate triumph. He had killed the Son of God! It was his greatest day, his greatest victory. Or so he thought. He must have celebrated wildly. One can only imagine the depth of his joy. However, on the third day, that joy turned to horror for he had not defeated the Son of God; what he had done was raise him on his throne, at the right side of His Father. Indeed, Satan soon realized that he had suffered his greatest defeat."

The house was amazingly silent as Father Raymond spoke. "Satan is still reeling from that defeat and will for all eternity. So in a bogus attempt at revenge, he assaults God's children, thinking that he is getting even with God. In actuality, he is setting himself up for another fall. God does not abandon his children. Not now, not ever. Satan knows that too but he tries to get his shots in so that he can attempt to hide his shame in the face of his demons. He was and is humiliated and his minions know that too. They laugh at him as well. In this house, we have restless spirits. One appears to have been human once. Perhaps she is a pawn of Satan. Perhaps her own negativity and sins attracted something far more sinister. I will not pass judgment on her for that is not my place. God is merciful and He will do with her what He chooses. I am willing to bet that He will wrap her in His arms and forgive her sins."

Suddenly, a book shot off a shelf and nearly hit Father Raymond. If it was an attempt to stop the priest, it failed for the spirit had underestimated his strength and resolve. "Perhaps God will forgive even the demons. That would also not surprise me." With that, the pounding started up again. Father Raymond simply spoke louder. "This house is going to be filled with the Holy Spirit. It is going to be filled with God's loving light. There is no room here for darkness. God the Father in Heaven commands all evil spirits to leave, be they human or otherwise. God the Son commands it and God the Holy Spirit commands it."

The priest began using incense in the living room. When he was finished with that, he sprinkled holy water throughout the room and he sprinkled it on everyone in the room. Then he began blessing the gifts. As he consecrated the gifts, the vibrations in the house started again but it did not last long. As Father Raymond passed out the wafer, the "Ave Maria" played loudly. There was an almost instantaneous calm in the house at that point. Almost everyone had tears in their eyes. Just as he was finishing up the Mass, one loud bang was heard and the Carter family knew they had their house back.

When the Mass was over, the three priests went into every room with the incense and holy water. They even blessed the crawlspace. Finally, they were done. They sat around for a while talking and having coffee and cake. It was around four when they left. The investigators left a short time later, promising they would keep in touch with the family. Father Raymond told the Carters that they could always call him if they needed to. He left them a few tapes of religious music and encouraged them to play them often. They took his advice. Finally, their haunting was over.

The Mass is a very powerful tool. There are some who consider it to be even more effective than the ritual of exorcism. There were a couple of surprises here. The first was Tim trying to redeem himself. That took a lot of courage, not just because of the haunting but also because of the embarrassment he must surely have felt. The other surprise was the addition of Father Paul for the Mass. This may sound a little too easy and you probably expected to have it end with something like: "And they lived happily ever after." Hey, that line has worked for centuries. Could the haunting start up again? Possibly but I would doubt it. Getting rid of the occult paraphernalia was important. It may have been the key to it all. Having stuff like that in the home could keep the spirits there.

You may have found this little section corny. What I wanted to do was present a case with the idea of letting you see what you may face in a real haunting situation. They are rarely as clear-cut as this one was but you had the chance to see how confusing it can be determining what is going on in a haunting. You had the early stages where oddities were overlooked, then you had the family splitting and that was followed by the spirit going all out, regardless of who was present. Hopefully you got an idea of what investigators face. It is not always easy to tell what is going on in a house. I asked you many questions but I did not answer all of them. I did this for two reasons. For one, I wanted you to think of the various possibilities. The other reason is that in many hauntings, many questions go unanswered. I have walked away from cases that had been successfully completed but I was not always 100% sure of all the answers. In some cases, the events that took place were so borderline that it was impossible to tell for certain whether the spirit was human or inhuman. However, as long as it was successfully stopped, those answers were not critical. Truthfully, there probably were no answers. We like to believe that there are always answers to our questions but in truth, there often aren't. Our world is not so clear and tidy. As I have said, (probably a hundred times) this was an accelerated case. In a real haunting, it might have been years between the early occurrences and the truly frightening stuff. Also, the investigation itself might have taken months as opposed to weeks. You just never know.

It is doubtful that you would be able to get the Church to help so quickly. Again though, it depends on the individual priest. In this case, it was fairly easy because the parish priest happened to believe in the supernatural and he also had some experience in dealing with it. That is a rare commodity today. I hope you enjoyed this mock case and more so, I hope you learned something from it. Again, it was simplistic and fast moving but as you work cases yourself, you will come across a lot of the things you saw here. All of the events that transpired here, apparitions, hair pulling, etc. are all things that I have experienced over the years. None were made up. They were just items taken from many different cases. If nothing else, this should give you some idea of what to expect when taking on a case. Good luck in your own work.

SECTION 5:

Client Information

CLIENT INFORMATION

The purpose of this section is to give you a good idea of why we are here and what we may be able to do for you. You have every right to know exactly what we can and cannot do. You should be informed of the process we undergo during an investigation. There are certain things that we would like you to do and certain things we do not want you to do, like inviting half the neighborhood over for the investigation. It is important that everyone is on the same page and in agreement with each other before beginning an investigation. Nothing is allowed that may pose a risk to an investigator. Nothing is allowed that may pose a risk to you unless there is something that may be effective but is also risky. In that event, once you know the risks and weigh them against the possible results, you can then make the decision on how to proceed. Going over this with you before hand makes the investigation process much easier, more productive and more enjoyable for all parties involved.

Confusion can create havoc on an investigation. For that reason alone, it is a good idea to explain, in as much detail as possible, the step-by-step process involved in the investigation. It has the benefit of reducing some of the confusion and it helps you in two ways:

1) You know what to expect.
2) You feel a part of the investigation right from the start.

This is important because it shows our professionalism and that directly affects your confidence in us. Confidence, in turn, makes the group feel more hopeful. The group's state of mind can have a direct effect on the haunting itself. Demons, if they are involved, feed off the negative energy of the clients and investigators and whoever else is around. If they are feeling down, there is something the demon can feast on. If they feel confident and hopeful, it cuts down on the feast. There is no way to promise an outcome. You should be told what we hope the outcome will be but we cannot guarantee that we will stop the haunting. However, if we cannot, we will work with you to find someone who can.

There is so much that we can do for you and that is what we will emphasize. You will be learning coping skills and defenses, designed to ease the problems and make it easier for you to deal with the problem. In that regard, the situation will improve immediately. You will be able to receive plenty of support when you need it. This can have quite an impact on your situation. In addition, we can offer information. This, in itself, can make the dark days seem a little brighter, the night a little less long. You are no longer alone in this battle. Every little bit helps when you are in this type of situation.

Momentum is a big factor in a haunting. As you begin to feel more positive about your situation, you not only become stronger, it becomes harder for the negative forces to hurt you Momentum, however, can swing the other way, as well. If you begin to feel more hopeless about your situation, you become a bigger target to the negative forces around you. Try to emphasize the positive. You have been under siege for a while. That is why you contacted us in the first place. You will need support and guidance to maintain a positive attitude. Always be ready to receive it.

The first step in ending haunting phenomena is to ascertain what is happening and what is causing the problem. To some extent, it is similar to detective work. You have to look for clues to the haunting. As you get more information, you can begin to draw a picture. Eventually, you may be able to solve the puzzle based on what information has been gathered. What I need to do is determine the anatomy of the haunting. I do that by looking for the following four items.

We Look For Four Things

1) Determine *if* something is there.
2) Determine *what* it is.
3) Determine *why* it is there.
4) If it is human, *who* is it?

Determining If Something Is There

People will sometimes get upset when they hear the part about determining *if* something is there. Please understand that no one doubts what you are reporting. It may seem silly to you, who have watched your furniture rearrange itself, to hear an investigator say they need to determine *if* something is there. You probably want to scream something like: "What do you mean *if*? I wake up in the morning and find myself and the bed in the backyard and then you tell me *if*!" Believe me, we would not mind if you did feel that way. In fact, we do believe you, if we did not, we would not be here, on site. We just have to be very careful. Sometimes there are very natural types of phenomena that seem to be supernatural in origin. Believe me, we have all been burned at some point by attaching a supernatural label to a natural occurrence. We would be doing you a disservice if we did not take a careful approach. For the record, this is the easiest of the four to prove. I only have to get by one self-propelled table lamp to convince me that something is there.

Determining What Is There

Once we have determined *if* something is there and that is the easy part, we now try to focus on *what* it is. That one can be tricky. There are different types of spirits, human ones, inhuman ones, and then different levels of each category. There are times when it may appear that you have a ghost present. Upon investigating, we may find that you are not dealing with a ghost at all. You may protest and tell us that you actually saw it. This is where we tend to duck, lest we are hit with the frying pan hurled at us by the client, not the ghost. We may then explain to you that what you are seeing is an energy imprint or psychic recording, as it is sometimes called, not a real ghost. Yes, you are seeing a person but it is just a motion picture of a past event, so to speak, not the actual person. On the other hand, if there is a spirit present, we have to determine what kind it is. The type of spirit you have determines how to get rid of it, assuming you do want to get rid of it. Do not laugh, when people discover they have a friendly spirit, in some cases they decide that they want to keep it. This is not all that uncommon. It may or may not be a good idea though. There are those who believe that where there is one spirit, more may follow. However, we can usually tell fairly quickly what we are dealing with. There are certain things that only inhuman spirits can do. Sometimes they do something so overt they almost make our job easy. Therefore, what they are doing can tell us what type of spirit they are.

Determining Why It Is There

The next big question becomes *why* it is there? This can be the toughest one to solve. In many cases, there are obvious reasons why someone is haunted. It could be because of something they have done, devil worship, for example. It could be a result of innocent use of an Ouija board. It may be because there is a history of a haunting in the building you are living in. The ghost may be part of the house. Sometimes, certain people are haunted wherever they go. However, there are times when you cannot come up with a good reason to explain a haunting. Some people are just chosen, for whatever reason. I wish I could say we have all the answers but I don't.

Once we have the answers to the preceding questions, we can begin working on a way to end the problems you are experiencing. One note, even if we do not know *why* you are being haunted, we still proceed with trying to end the problem. It is just much easier if we can ascertain why it is there. It may be something as simple as stopping a certain activity that may be causing the problem. One example would be using an Ouija board. In some cases, if you stop using the board, your problems stop as well. One of the keys is to get as much evidence as we possibly can.

Should we have to go to an outside organization for help, they will require proof of our claims. This is especially true in circumstances where the Church must get involved. You can never have enough evidence to convince them. Traditionally, the Catholic Church is slow in acting. Admittedly, they have to be careful but sometimes they just plain do not want to listen. For that reason, we need to get as much evidence as we possibly can. But, if the problem can be ended before I even load a camera, I will consider it a job well done. That is the ultimate goal. While I am not an exorcist, I will do my best to help you through this situation. I will teach you some ways of defending yourselves. I will also teach you some coping skills as well. I cannot guarantee that I will end your problem but I will work with you until someone does. (For example, the Church.) I will do so in a manner that is respectful to you and your property.

Determining Who It Is

If it turns out that the spirit is human, it is important to find out *who* it is. That can make the job of moving the spirit out of the house much easier to do. In some cases, knowing who the spirit is takes away the fear of it and that by itself can stop a haunting. Let's say that the spirit is that of someone who died there one hundred years ago. What had been happening has been frightening since you had no idea what was going on. However, once it is determined that the spirit happens to be great-grandfather Joe, the fear of him is gone. *Fear is the biggest and most destructive part of a haunting.* Of course, there is always the chance that you will not be able to determine who that spirit is. In that event, it can be harder to remove it but certainly not impossible.

Investigations Can Take Time

There is no way to predict how long an investigation will take. In some cases, the mere fact that investigators are involved is enough to end the activity. In many cases though, spirits will try to hide from the investigators. Do not be discouraged if nothing happens when the investigators are present. It is sort of like the way your car stops making that funny noise as soon as you pull into the repair shop. I expect this. Also, things are not always what they appear. There have been numerous investigations where it seemed as though nothing had happened. However, when the film from the photographs taken was developed, I was surprised to find some anomalies in the pictures. So, you just never know. All that time you thought noting was there. There are times when the activity will intensify after the start of the investigation, almost as if to punish you.

There are occasions where the entity doing the haunting will attempt to retaliate after you call someone in for help. Please do not be put off by that. This is truer of demons but nasty human spirits may try as well. You cannot give in to them. The human spirit can only do so much and it can really only do things designed to frighten you. In the event of the demonic haunting, they can do more but I always point out that they are not capable of compassion. They are not going to give you a break because you are tired and they are not going to cut you some slack because your idiot boss made you day miserable. If anything, they will pounce on that. They are not going to hold anything back. They are going to do what they intended to do all along. All the investigation will do is speed up the process. It will not make it do something it wasn't already planning to do. Of course, if you are already being terrorized, the investigation is well worth the risk. The problem is not going to go away on its own. So, going ahead with the investigation is something that you must decide on after you have received all of the facts and weighed the possible effects. Either way, no one will criticize you.

Throughout the course of the investigation, I will make a number of suggestions to you. I will explain in detail why I am suggesting certain things and how I feel it will help you. The final decision will always rest with you. I will do my best to accommodate all of your requests. If however, something arises that may put an investigator unnecessarily in harms way, I will advise you of that. An example would be if it was determined that someone using spells from a book on witchcraft caused the problem, I would advise you that the practice must stop immediately. If that person decided they would not stop, then I am being put in a position where a) the investigators are being put in a potentially harmful, unnecessary situation and b) I cannot correct the problem you are experiencing because of that. At that point, I would stop the investigation. That rarely happens. It is just that there have been cases where clients created unnecessary risks to the investigators.

Enclosed you will find some "Generic Ghost Advice." This may help you a bit. I have also enclosed some simple dos and don'ts. They are just common sense items. It is important that you realize that the fact I am giving you this advice does not presuppose that you have a ghost or worse yet, a demon present. If there is nothing there, no harm can come from the advice I am giving you. Please read the material and do not be afraid to ask any questions. There really are no stupid questions. Knowledge can be your best ally. I will do my very best to answer any questions you may have and I will gladly explain everything I do, every step of the way. Also, if an investigator is doing something that you want stopped, do not be afraid to tell him. Let the group leader know if you are having problems with a particular investigator. If they cannot respect your wishes, they should not be here. It is that simple.

Conducting The Investigation

What I would like to do now is give you an idea about how we will go about conducting the actual investigation. The fact you are reading this means that I have most likely met or you have talked to someone connected with me. That being the case, I likely know the problem, to some degree. However, in some cases, this information is given to a relative or friend of the person experiencing the problem. I sometimes do this so they have an idea who I am, what I do, and what they need to do for us to help them. Thus, they are able to get started before actually meeting me or anyone working with me.

The way I like to start an investigation is by meeting the clients away from the home, if possible. I like to do this so that we can discuss the situation away from the influence of the home. It is easier to be objective when you are not sitting in a room where there has been frightening activity. These meetings can take place in a diner or even in my own home, providing you live locally. I would never ask anyone to travel any distance for this. However, none of this is carved in stone. Our initial discussion can take place on the telephone although it would be preferable if you were not calling from the home in question. More than anything, this is suggested because telephones have a way of going on the fritz in a house experiencing paranormal problems. All I may hear is static but that is certainly not always the case. I can also have this meeting in the home, if necessary. Sometimes, due to location and time, this is necessary, so it certainly can be done. Where possible, I just prefer to do it away from the home.

Interviewing The Family

Once we have met and determined that the situation warrants an investigation, (they usually do) I will set up an appointment to do formal interviews. These can be done in the home. If our first discussion took place in the home, we can go ahead and do the formal interviews right then and there. The formal interviews are used as a diagnostic tool. From them, I may be able to determine what the problem is and in some cases, why it is there also. There are two parts to this interview. The first part is strictly about the phenomenon that is occurring. The second part has to do with belief systems, the environment, and the family dynamics. As a rule, I like to do the interviews on videotape or at least audiotape. This is helpful to me in that I can go back over the tapes from time to time to see if I have missed anything that may be important. I do work off a written questionnaire but even with that, there are times when the interviewer may miss something because he is concentrating on the questions he is asking and not necessarily thinking of other questions to ask.

People will often say something that is overlooked if it is not directly in line with the question being asked. There will be some personal questions asked. Before I ask them, I will tell you why I am asking them and how I want you to answer them. For example, I may ask a personal question concerning certain stressors that may be affecting your marriage. It is not necessary to know what those stressors are; especially if I feel detailed answers will have no bearing on the case. I may just need to know *if* something is wrong but not necessarily, *what* is wrong. The reason being that if there is a problem there, you may need to work on it to cut down on the fuel for the forces that are afflicting you. So, in that instance, I may just want a yes or no answer. If you have a concern about any questions, feel free to ask them. You have the right to refuse to answer a question if it offends you or you feel it is too personal. Again, I will tell you why I am asking it but it is up to you whether you want to answer it or not. It is important that certain questions get asked. For that reason, I do encourage you to answer them.

You can also ask that I shut off any recording devices before answering certain questions. I will certainly do my best to accommodate you. (For the record, when I ask personal questions, I usually turn off the recorders. It is important to record questions involving activity and possible causes but when it comes to personal information, there is usually no need to have a recording of those answers.) The one thing I must insist on is that you answer the questions honestly. Giving a wrong answer may change how I look at a situation. No one is going to judge you. No one will blame you. Let us say we feel the problem was caused by someone using a Ouija board. The last thing I am going to do is rant and rave and scream: "This is your fault!" I just need to know what may have contributed to the problem or even caused it. What it is and why it is there can go a long way towards finding the way to ending the problem. It would be better if you do not answer a question at all then to provide an incorrect one. Again, how the questions are answered often point us in a particular direction. A lot of time can be wasted if I am led in the wrong direction and time is a huge factor in a haunting. The quicker it ends, the quicker you can go back to having a normal life.

Interviews are done privately. For example, I would not interview a husband in front of his wife or vise versa. This can affect the answers given. If we are discussing phenomena, you may have something in mind you want to tell us. However, if you are sitting in the room while your spouse is being interviewed, your spouse may touch on something that you wish to expound on when you are interviewed. Then, during your interview, you discuss that item and forget the one you wanted to tell us. Thus, I miss something that may later prove to be important. During the personal section, there may be things you are hesitant to mention in front of your spouse. These interviews are strictly confidential. We need them to determine what may be going on. That is the *only* reason why I do them. If your spouse wanted to know how you answered a personal question, I will not give him/her the answer.

(Group Discussion and Walk Through)

During the interview stage, I would like to talk to everyone we can who have experienced some of the occurrences. I need to get as much information as I possibly can about the situation. People who are not living in the house are not given the full interview. I am only concerned in getting information about sightings and other occurrences.

After everyone has been interviewed, I will sometimes gather everyone involved and have a group discussion. Here is where everyone can discuss the activity and that can jar memories. This discussion is only about the phenomena that are taking place. We will not discuss anything of a private nature. During that session, you can ask as many questions as you can think of and I will do my best to answer them. I will give my suggestions and kick around some ideas on what I want to do and how to go about doing that. I also want your input on the matter. You are living it so there are certainly things you would like to see addressed. Your input can be very valuable.

On the first trip to your home, one or more of us will do a walk through of your home with you. The purpose of this is to get an idea of the layout of the home and so you can show us what has gone on and where. We will also take pictures to see if something shows up on film. We will want to make a diagram of the house. The diagram helps us to plan where we want to place investigators and any fixed equipment we decide to use. If you reported that activity breaks out in the basement at 3 a.m. you can bet that at 3 a.m., there will be investigators in the basement, sitting in the dark waiting. If I have someone with strong discernment powers available to me, I will have that person go through the house as well. The psychic should not be told anything about any activity or it's location. I want to make sure we get an objective assessment from her or him.

Once the investigation begins, I will have as many investigators come in as is reasonable, depending on schedules and of course, space. It would be silly to have twelve investigators involved in a possible haunting of a studio apartment. For the most part, in the average size house, three or four investigators would probably be the most involved at any given time.

How You Can Help Us

There is something you can do that will be helpful to the investigation. This will have been discussed with you but by listing it here, we can save time and get a more accurate picture of what is going on. I always ask clients to buy a notebook. In it, I want you to list anything at all that you think may have been a paranormal incident. Even if it is probably normal in nature, list it anyway. Write as much detail as possible. It is fine to say that something happened "around three months ago." Note when it happened, if you remember. Also, list who was there at the time, if possible. At some point, we will sit down and look at that information and decide what seems to be paranormal. You might have listed fifty items and only three may turn out to be paranormal. However, those three may be important.

Going forward, list everything new that happens. Be as detailed as possible. List the day, date, location, witnesses and anything else you can think of. What I do is try to find any patterns to the activity that is taking place. That can help determine what is causing the problem and possibly why it is happening. Perhaps we will find that there are always problems on Thursday nights. That is helpful information. At the very least, it tells me that I need to be there on Thursday nights and it will tell me where it may be best to set up equipment. Also, solving hauntings can be detective work as much as anything and patterns can tell us a lot.

Keeping a detailed journal can also tell us if one or more people are being targeted. There are also cases where one person triggers phenomena. Knowing that can be very helpful as well. Any information we can get about the problem makes it that much easier to determine the mechanics of the haunting. It can help us to know where to set up and what to look for. All of that information is used to help end the problem. Everyone involved in the activity taking place should keep a similar journal. The more information we gather, the better the picture we can draw.

(The Night Investigation)

I always try to begin the investigation on a weekend, usually a Saturday night. Ideally, I like to do at least one overnight session. This is, of course, subject to your approval. Activity is most likely to break out during the night and wee hours of the morning. I will bring in a variety of equipment such as cameras, (lots of them) camcorders, thermometers, electromagnetic field detectors and motion detectors, just to name a few. Once again, I will do a walk through the home, this time with equipment so that I can detect any activity that may be going on and to establish baseline readings if there is no activity at the time. I will try to gather as much documentation as possible of any activity that may occur.

On the night of the investigation, you will have the choice of whether to stay up with the investigators or not. Personally, I feel that it can be very helpful to have at least one family member around. I prefer to have all resident family members home since activity is most likely to occur if you are all there. It creates a more natural atmosphere, or as natural as it can be when you have investigators running around. It also gives us a chance to interact with the family and thus to teach the family some concepts that may help. However, it is not a good idea to have friends and family members not living in the home come by to check things out. It can create a circus atmosphere and hinders the investigation. Investigations have been done when half of the neighborhood was present. Needless to say, nothing happened that night. Having all the residents of the home around is okay; it can even be helpful. If you have a particular friend or relative who has been with you throughout the problem and you really want that person there, that is fine. I would have no objections to that. However, I will advise you what I need to do to make sure I can conduct a proper and worthwhile investigation.

Somewhere along the line, we will teach you ways of defending yourself against whatever forces that may be present in your home. In the early stages, we will try to teach you some coping skills that should make things a little easier for you to deal with. We will tell you what to do and what not to do. Once we are sure about what is going on and what is causing it, we will teach you concepts designed specifically for the type of problem you are experiencing. We will make a number of suggestions based on what evidence has been found. If I feel that I have an idea of what has caused it, I will tell you that. If something that someone is doing is causing or exacerbating the problem, I will identify that and tell you that it must be stopped. If the situation warrants religious intervention, I will work with you to get that type of help. If we can do something ourselves, we will do it.

Investigations take time. Often, in the beginning of an investigation, the spirit causing the problem, assuming there is one, will hide from investigators. We know this and we do take that into account. I am not discouraged when nothing happens and you should not be either. We will devote as much time as we possibly can to you. Once things start happening, we will begin documenting the phenomena as well as we can. This becomes necessary if outside help is necessary. Plus it helps us to learn more about hauntings and it is a great teaching tool for new investigators. If the situation is one where you can take steps yourself to stop the phenomena from occurring, i.e. blessing the house, I will do that for you if you would like and I will teach you how to do it as well. If the problem requires stronger action, I will advise you what steps need to be taken and equally importantly, what steps to avoid. I will give you some prayers that are particularly helpful in these types of situations. This, of course, depends on your religious beliefs.

Remember that we are here to help you. Please feel free to ask any questions you want. If you are considering any drastic steps, such as calling in the press or enlisting the aid of a psychic, please tell me beforehand. There are many things you can do that can actually make the situation worse. That may seem impossible if the activity is bad but trust me, it can get worse. Calling in the press is never a good idea. They can cause problems for you that will make the haunting seem easy by comparison, if you can imagine that. They can destroy your privacy. In addition, the last thing you need is 200 sightseers camped out on your front lawn or to have your children harassed at school. The best thing to do is check with me beforehand.

While I cannot guarantee results, I will do everything humanly possible to help you, even if that means calling in others who I feel can help you. My ego aside, helping you is the only objective here. I do not forget that. If it seems that I do, let me know right away. As I mentioned earlier, your input is both needed and wanted. This is your home and you have every right to make suggestions. I am not all-powerful and all knowing, although I have known some who thought they were. The point is that we are human, therefore there may be things we miss or there may be ideas on your part that may be worth trying. Do not be afraid to make suggestions or to comment on anything I may do. There might be a good reason why I do something. You certainly have the right to know what it is. You will find that we will meet often to discuss what has been found and what ideas I am kicking around. Communication is important in solving the mysteries of a haunting. No one has all of the answers so ideas are often thrown back and forth. All ideas are important because in discussing them, even more ideas may pop up. One of those ideas could hold the key to ending the haunting.

You may reach the point where you get sick and tired of investigators being in your home so much. You have to tell us when you feel that way. We may be so busy trying to get to collect evidence that we do not realize we have become a problem. Also, there may be times when the investigator's themselves need to get away for a bit. Please try to understand that, if it happens. The success of the investigation lies in good teamwork, both within the group of investigators and with the investigators and the family. It is my belief that your problem can be alleviated and towards that end, I will do everything possible to attain that goal. Working together, I believe we can accomplish a positive outcome. Good luck to you.

ADVICE TO THE FAMILY

While surveys show that the majority of people believe in ghosts, they are often surprised when the see evidence of them. Consequently, when odd things begin happening in their own lives, they are filled with a sense of fear and confusion. It is the old thing about believing that: "Something like that can't happen to me." So, when it happens to them, they find themselves in a state of shock and denial. One of the best ways to overcome those problems is to know as much as possible about them. We usually fear the unknown more than anything else. Once something becomes *known* to us, much of the power is taken from it. The biggest hurdle that I have noticed in dealing with many hauntings is that people have a hard time with the unreality of the problem. They almost disassociate from their normal lives, much like we do when we face a tragedy or terrible loss. After a while, *nothing* seems normal. The most routine things in your life suddenly seems alien to you.

This is quite a natural phenomenon but it is one that has to be worked through when you find yourself dealing with things that appear to be of a paranormal nature. In a somewhat disassociated state such as shock, we do not make clear decisions. To some extent, we become almost like driftwood floating on the ocean, heading to parts known only to God, the wind and the current. If you are dealing with a haunting type of situation, this state of mind has to be changed. It is only when seen through a clear mind that people are able to deal with a haunting. Being driftwood in a haunting is frightening and dangerous. It is also unnecessary, providing you know how to stop it.

The presence of what appears to be a spirit is not necessarily anything to fear, in and of itself. However, fear is the most natural reaction to a sighting. Again, knowledge and familiarity are key components to counteracting that fear. Not all apparitions constitute a ghost and not all ghosts constitute a haunting. Not all hauntings constitute evil and not all evil is demonic. Good old humans are quite capable of committing evil acts. I doubt I will get an argument from anyone on that point. Many times the apparition seen is a recording of sorts, a recording of events that occurred in the past, sometimes the long ago past. In other cases, the apparition may be real but it most likely means no harm to anyone. In fact, many are there for good purposes. Others are just as confused as we are. We should let actions dictate intent, not mere presence.

When it comes to actions, you have to avoid jumping to conclusions. Seeing an object fall from a shelf is not necessarily and act of evil, even if the object broke as a result of the fall. Seeing a coffee mug fly through your television set would constitute an evil intent. I guess what I am so poorly trying to say is that you should avoid jumping to conclusions when paranormal activity takes place. That can save you untold grief. In the majority of hauntings I have encountered, very few were malevolent in nature. More times than not, the spirit present meant no harm to anyone. It was just there for one reason or another. Once it was no longer feared, life returned to normal for everyone. However, although they are rare, there are serious hauntings too.

If you find yourself in a haunting, there are things you can do that can be very helpful. One he other hand, there are also things that you can do that will make the problem worse. It is important to know the difference. I am not presupposing that you have an evil spirit at work. In about 95% of hauntings, there are human culprits and the vast majority of them mean no harm. However, this information is good to know and even if there are no demonic spirits at work, these things certainly will not cause any harm. If I am going to err, I will do so on the side of caution. If you can handle a worst-case scenario, the lesser haunting may seem easy. Maybe easy is the right word but bearable at least. Some of the things I will discuss here are going to elicit responses such as: "Yeah right, ignore it! You try ignoring something that pulls you out of bed." Try not to be frightened. This is written out for you so that I am not around you when you get the urge to throw an ashtray or some other deadly object at me for saying something that sounds so absurd. However, the thing is that how victims think and act can determine how severe the haunting becomes. You really do have *some* control over what happens, how often it happens and how it affects everyone when it does happen.

Having said that, what I want to do is give you some advice before hand. These things can be done right away, before investigators show up at your door carrying 72 cameras each. In the early stages of a haunting, things can progress slowly. It is not uncommon for investigators to show up only to have nothing happen. As I said before, I think it follows the same principle as when you take your car to the mechanic because it keeps making a horrible squealing sound. By some as of yet unknown law of nature, the car never makes that noise when you are at the mechanics. That being the case, sometimes the only real help we can offer is in the form of lending support and teaching defenses and coping skills. That can make the haunting easier to deal with and that alone can ease the degree of the haunting. Some of these things are listed in the general do's and don'ts but they bear further discussion. Let us discuss the things not to do first.

Point number one is to give the spirit and the phenomena it causes as little recognition as you possibly can. Naturally this is a tall and to a certain extent, impossible order. You just cannot train yourself to completely ignore what is taking place around you. Emotions cannot be easily turned on and off. However, what you must not do is dwell on and become obsessed with everything that happens. Some of the stuff that happens is minor and should be treated as such. We usually regard minor activity as "parlor tricks." By and large, that is all it is. Do not fall into the trap of making something bigger than it actually is. The more you obsess on the haunting, the worse it will be. Try not to discuss the haunting while you are in the house. The spirit wants to be noticed. Be a little defiant. Ignore it as much as possible. Don't give it the stage it wants. This is hard but you will be surprised by the results. It can make a huge difference. How you react to phenomena is up to you to some degree. It is helpful to change the way you interpret whatever activity occurs. Remember the old adage: "Don't sweat the small stuff." Trust me, enough will happen that will be frightening and demand your attention. Treat the minor stuff as minor. Do not give it any more power than it already has. Slowly begin to take back your life.

Point number two and I drill this into my investigator's heads, is do not challenge whatever force is operating there. You cannot be sure what it is but if it is something evil, however doubtful that may be, challenging it may well lead to disaster in a hurry. Part of that means keeping control of your temper. As frightened as you may be, you want to protect your loved ones. That is the most natural of all responses. When you see them suffering, you want to protect them at all cost. However, this is where you can get into trouble. In your anger, you may say something like "I can beat you, you SOB" or "I'll take you on." That can have disastrous consequences. If there is something evil there, it will most likely accept your challenge and you cannot beat it unless you have been trained in how to do so. Even the most seasoned investigator should not challenge whatever is there. The experienced investigator knows this. In your attempt to protect your loved ones, you may actually be putting them at a greater risk than already exists.

One of the most important things to know is that evil spirits have a game plan, a strategy. They want you to be afraid and they want you to be angry, frustrated, and most of all, beaten. This is the type of thing they feed off. Negative energy is what gives them power, so the better you do at controlling negative emotions, the better the situation will be. They have a strategy. Let me explain what I mean. If a spirit wants to scare you, it will do something designed to create that fear. Once you experience that fear, it grows stronger. Being stronger, it can then do something more frightening. That in turns adds to your fear. Thus, it gets stronger. Soon, it becomes a case of the spring being wound tighter and tighter. They do not waste any actions. Everything they do is cold and calculated. It is important to know that. You are going to be afraid, that is a fact. The thing is to control that fear as much as you can. Cut down on the evil spirit's food supply, so to speak, whenever you can speak. Doing this weakens its grip on you. You can actually unwind the spring. The less fear you have, the weaker it gets. The weaker it gets, the less it can do that will cause you fear. Around and around it goes, only this time it is in your favor. That makes it much easier to beat it. Hauntings are all about fear. Initially, it may try to turn up the heat if it is not getting what it wants but you have to continue to try to control yourself. The harder it tries, the more you must resist. Know that it is not all-powerful.

Evil spirits create chaos. They also try to split families. Be aware of this. If they can drive a wedge between family members, they are then free to work on the one they perceive to be the weakest. It is literally playing "divide and conquer." You need a united front if you are going to survive intact. For that reason, do your best not to argue with each other, especially at home. Again, this creates the negative energy that they find so tasty. Cuttings down on the negativity helps by itself but do not stop there. Create as much *positive* energy as you can. Turn the energy game around. Instead of just fending off the negative, go on the offensive and create positive energy. "Stab the devil with his own pitchfork," as I once heard Ed Warren say. Make him swim in his own swamp, so to speak. How do you create positive energy? Love is something that evil forces hate. Love is positive energy. Express your love for one another. Be kind to each other and help each other. Try to keep as positive an outlook as you can. This is difficult but it is worth it. It will pay off for you. Like attracts like. If you try to be positive, positive things will be drawn to you. Unfortunately, the reverse is also true.

Activities That Can Cause A Haunting

There are certain activities that can cause a haunting by themselves or make a bad one worse. Conducting seances, using a Ouija board, reading spell books or conjuring books can be extremely dangerous. Practicing any form of witchcraft or magic can lead to trouble. So can automatic writing, tarot cards, and pendulum swinging. These are all forms of divination; ways of contacting spirits. If you do not know what these things are, so much the better. My best advice would be to keep it that way too. Be attentive to the music your children are listening to. Anything paying homage to the devil must be stopped. Songs about suicide must also be stopped. Any form of contacting spirits of any kind is dangerous, even if you are only trying to contact a deceased loved one. You cannot be sure what will enter if you open the door. Avoid going to see psychics to have a reading done. If any of these activities are taking place, stop them immediately! Be careful with fantasy games. While they are for the most part harmless, it is easy for some to become obsessed with it. It is that obsession that might attract something unwanted into your life.

Make sure you know what your children are up to. Are they involved in any kind of cult or occult activity? You need to find that out. Are they secretly doing any of the things listed in the paragraph above? If so, stress the necessity of stopping that immediately. Talk to your children and make them aware of the dangers. Do not judge them; simply explain the seriousness of the situation. A mistake that people who feel they are being haunted sometimes make is trying to contact the entity causing all the trouble. Do not try to make contact with it using any of the means mentioned in the above paragraph. If it is evil, you will not be able to reason with it and you may well bring something else into the home in the process. Trust me, you have to be careful if you try to communicate with it.

Be careful in regards to alcohol consumption. I am not saying that you cannot have a glass of wine with dinner but excessive consumption can open you up to further problems. If there is alcoholism involved, that person must get help right away. Alcoholism and drug use create negative energy. In addition, negative forces will attack you at your weakest link. If drinking is a problem, they will try to get you to drink more. They also create an environment that negative forces find inviting. If someone in the household is suffering from depression, get help for that too. Depression creates a negative environment as well. In addition, depression can be caused by the entity. It is fair to say that anyone being haunted will at some point, become depressed. That is only logical. However, it is important to determine whether you are suffering from a situational depression or a clinical one. Be wary of excessive feelings of guilt or shame. A little of both are necessary otherwise we would all be sociopaths. However, negative forces will take normal guilt and make it into something unnatural. They want you to think you are worthless.

Also, if you meditate regularly, be careful. Avoid it if you can unless you are meditating on something *very* positive. There is nothing wrong with meditation. The reason I mention this is because you want to avoid doing anything that displaces your consciousness. You do not want to leave yourself open to a spirit's influence. The same is true of self-hypnosis, which is much like meditation. You always want to remain on your guard and in control of yourself. I am certainly not saying that you will become possessed; it is just better not to open yourself up to whatever is operating there. It may fill your head with all kinds of garbage.

This next item you may find surprising. It is always a good idea to pray but do not take a cross and start blessing the house. While this may seem like the right thing to do, it can actually make things worse. By doing this, you may do what we call "*religious provocation*." The fact that you are reading this means that we will be coming in to investigate the problem soon. Please wait until we get there. Provoking the entity can be very dangerous. Even having the house blessed by a priest can be dangerous if the priest does not know what is going on. If he does know what the problem is and has had experience in dealing with that type of thing, then it is fine for him to do that. If it is a lower form of spirit, the blessing may drive it out. If however, it is demonic in nature, it may well retaliate. Talk to the priest beforehand so that he fully understands the situation. He may turn out to be very helpful in your battle. Ultimately, the Church may have to get involved to stop the problem. They may be the only ones who can solve it. Having a priest familiar with the situation can save you a lot of time. Plus, there is the chance that he may have experienced some of the phenomena and will make getting outside help that much easier.

Let me make something clear. Many people have their house or apartment blessed when they move in. There is never anything wrong with that and you should feel free to do that under normal circumstances. However, if you are experiencing haunting phenomena, having the house blessed by a priest who is unaware of the problem can be dangerous, as stated above. There is a difference between blessing a house as a matter of routine and blessing it as a form of attack against a potentially evil spirit. It is a judgment call. What you have to do is look at what is happening in the home. If you are experiencing minor activity such as the movement of small objects or seeing what looks like a human spirit, a blessing may be in order. However, if you have large objects moving or are seeing bizarre apparitions, things that do not look human, you may have a bigger problem than you realize. It really all depends on what is transpiring in the home. Again though, having a house blessed as a matter of routine is fine. Can doing that wake up a dormant spirit? I would have to say that it could but I would be inclined to doubt it. The type of spirit that would react negatively to a religious blessing, it would, in all likelihood, not be dormant. I would have to believe that a general blessing might help keep something dormant as opposed to waking it up.

Should you find yourself in a situation where something calls out your name or tells you to do something like go down to the basement, do not do it. Let us say that you are alone in the house. Your spouse is working late and is not expected home for several hours. All of a sudden, you hear him/her call you. You get up and realize that the voice is coming from the basement. The first thing that comes to your mind is that it cannot be your spouse. Before you go down there, check your driveway. If your spouse's car is not there, do not go down in the basement. Demons have the ability to mimic anyone. If it really is your spouse, he will come upstairs if he really wants to talk to you.

Another example might be that you are home alone. Again, you hear what sounds like a child crying and begging for help. The sound seems to be coming from the attic. It may be a heartbreaking cry. Before you go rushing up there, ask yourself this: "Is there any way a child could have gotten into the attic?" If the answer is no, which it obviously is, then do not go up there, no matter how much your emotions tell you to. You never know what could happen to you if you respond to a disembodied voice. You might find yourself locked in the attic. These things will do anything in their power to trick you and they are very good at it. I cannot stress that enough. The one exception would be if someone you know is in the room. The same would be true for a pet that may be in there.

There are a number of things that will help you here. Prayer is very powerful. You need to pray for protection. Praying the Rosary is the most powerful form of defense. Even the worst of demons fear these special prayers. Another thing is to visualize yourself in a white light. (This is often referred to as a Christ light or a God light depending on your religious beliefs.) Use this practice whenever you are afraid. Praying is not the same thing as provoking a spirit. Religious provocation is *proactive*. Praying because something is frightening you is *reactive*. That is okay. In fact, it is a good idea.

This next item will seem impossible to do but do your best to give this thing as little recognition as possible. Try to live your life as normally as you can. Usually, when I tell people this one, I have to duck very fast to avoid the aforementioned ashtray, usually propelled by a human entity, that being the person I just told this to. Try though; it helps. Try to go out to those places you enjoy, even if it is just for dinner. See a movie once in awhile, if that is what you like to do. You need pleasure in your life to enable you to become stronger. You have to resist the negative influences and doing something positive helps. The worst thing you can do is to stay in the house all of the time. This will burn you out in a hurry. If you like to take walks in the evening, take them. If you have children, treat them to the things they enjoy. You and your family need an outlet. These things make you stronger and give you more energy to fight with. You will need all of that you can get.

Keep holy water handy. Always have it in the house. Should activity flare up, take the holy water and sprinkle it and demand, not ask, the entity to stop what its doing "In the name of God." Do not be meek. The meek may inherit the earth but they will not stop a negative spirit from its rampage. Yell at the cursed thing; demand that it stop immediately in the name of God. You may have to say it many times but it will work. How is this any different from getting the house blessed? With this, you are taking action to stop what *it* has started; you are not provoking it. That is an important difference.

Whatever you do, do not lose hope! That is so important. Once you become apathetic, this thing will pounce on you. If it is inhuman, it is not capable of showing mercy. It abhors goodness and everything that goes with it. Even when you think that you cannot handle any more, keep fighting. Sadly, a haunting can take some time to end. There is no sure cure for it. In fact, there is no cure, only defenses. This is not comforting but it is true. However, those defenses are very effective. Believe that God will stop the problem when the time is right. Pray for strength and He will give it to you. Never, never, never lose hope. It is one of the strongest weapons you have in your arsenal. Hope, faith, and love are the things that evil spirits hate the most. Give them a good dose of it. Keep in mind that they are bullies of the worst order. The will do all the things bullies like to do. Do not give in to them. Never show them respect. They are contemptible creatures and deserve to be treated as such. Believe me, a little defiance will go a long way.

When things really start to get bad, try to remember that it will eventually end. There are cases where the activity suddenly just stops. That is especially true when dealing with poltergeist explosions. We do not know why this is, but it does happen. Try to remind yourself that it will stop and that life will go back to being normal. That is not always easy to believe, especially during times of increased activity. However, you must keep believe that. I have never yet come across a haunting that did not end, either on its own or as a result of some form of intervention. Remember too, your faith does play a major role. Positive visualization has been found to be helpful. We do not know how our minds work but we do know that how we think affects what happens around us. What we truly believe often becomes fact. Confident people tend to get the things they want. Believe confidently that God will end the problem and it will happen.

Make your home into a place where negative spirits will not want to live in. Religious music, parties and a generally happy environment is not a good thing to a negative spirit. It wants to be around misery. Don't give it what it wants. I would also suggest that if there is a lot of activity and it looks like the situation is turning destructive, I would recommend that you take items that are fragile and put them away until the situation ends. You do not want cherished items destroyed. Unfortunately, that often happens in negative hauntings and poltergeist explosions.

This will give you an idea about what to do and what not to do. You will have been advised that you can talk to the investigators should you have any questions. This is for you to use, as you need to. Do not be afraid to call them if you feel you need to. Do not be afraid to ask questions. We are here to help in any way we can, even if it is just to talk to you, reassure you, or lend some support. Our ultimate goal is to see the problem end. Towards that end, we will do everything in our power. If you find an investigator who does not want to be "bothered," find another investigator. Most investigators will put their heart and soul into trying to solve a haunting but there are jerks in this field as there are in every field. Now consider this general list of do's and don'ts.

(Some Do's and Don'ts)

1) Everyone involved should keep a specific journal of happenings.
2) If you sense a presence, do not give it recognition or talk about it in the house. They want attention and sometimes, if you ignore them, they will go away.
3) If some activity on your part has been identified as the cause, you must stop it.
4) If the above is true, you must renounce what you did.
5) Again, if the above is true, do not beat yourself up because of it. That just adds fuel to the fire.
6) Try to make your house as nice and comfortable as possible. Buy flowers, redecorate or whatever helps cheer up the atmosphere.
7) Laugh a lot. It annoys the hell out of them, no pun intended.
8) Be a little defiant. It is *your* home.
9) Avoid negative conversations in the home. If your boss is an idiot, avoid discussing him in the home. Nasty spirits love negativity, wherever and whomever it is directed at.
10) Keep negative people out of the house as much as possible.
11) Try not to read negative literature in the house.
12) Avoid watching negative shows on TV.
13) Avoid reading about frightening hauntings.
14) Avoid watching frightening movies in the house.
15) Beware of scam artists who claim they can solve your problem for a fee.
16) Avoid excessive alcohol consumption and drug use.
17) Avoid deep meditation or hypnosis.
18) Try your best to keep your faith. This and love are your best defenses.
19) Try to maintain as positive an outlook as you can. Remember that they feed off of your emotions.
20) Never challenge an entity. Whatever you do must be done in God's name.
21) Mentally protect yourself constantly. Remember the "Christ" light.
22) Try not to panic. That is what it wants you to do.

23) As bad as things may seem, do not lose hope. That is super-critical.
24) Avoid arguments with your family, especially in the house. They want to split you up. It is part of their "divide and conquer" strategy.
25) Pray, pray, pray! They hate that.
26) Play religious music. They hate that too.
27) They may intensify activity in retaliation. Do not give in or give up.
28) Love really does conquer all, even a haunting.
29) Try to live your life as normal as possible. Plan fun events. It may be something as simple as buying a pizza and having a "Blockbuster" night.
30) Take it a step further and throw a party.
31) Create an environment that is repulsive to the spirit.
32) Keep religious items handy, especially holy water. Keep a good supply on hand. I have a friend who brings a five-gallon bottle of water to his church and has it blessed.
33) Visualize an end to the haunting and believe in it.
34) Never lose sight of the fact that these things *do* happen and they *do* end.
35) Never respond to a disembodied voice unless you are directed to a room that you know is occupied. (This holds true in your home. If you are out in public and do not know *who* is in a room, I would not go into it.)
36) If there is major activity taking place, it is a good idea to wrap up items that are precious to you to protect them until the situation ends.

STEPS TO PREVENT BEING HAUNTED

Okay, you are not being haunted. That is a good thing; believe me. Now the trick is to stay that way. We have discussed some of the ways in which people can become haunted. It would make sense, therefore, that you would simply have to do the opposite of those things in order to prevent a haunting. There is a little more to it than that, however. Not doing those specific things that can result in a haunting would be considered a defensive approach, reactive so to speak. However, proactive or offensive tact will help you to live a life free from negative forces. That is what I would like to discuss here.

We know about the theory that "like attracts like." We know that negativity attracts negativity. Therefore, we should make every attempt to become positive people. You might be thinking that if I am not being negative, then I am obviously being positive. It is not quite as simple as that. As with everything else in life, where black meets white, we have some gray area to deal with. Let me give you an example. Suppose you have a coworker or a friend who has the ability to irritate you. (I have more than I can handle myself.) You think about how aggravated you sometimes get and decide that you need to stop being so negative about this person. With that thought in mind, you make a conscious effort to be more patient or tolerant with him. Okay, that is good; you are making progress. For one, you will be treating him better and you will help yourself by not becoming so agitated about him. Therefore, by default, you are treating yourself better and that is a good thing.

What you have done is stopping yourself from experiencing those negative thoughts about him. That is fine but let us take it a step further. As hard as it might be, suppose you really made an effort to see the good in this person. I am sure there is something there, although you may need an electron microscope to find it. Suppose you decided to act positively towards him. If you do that, you will have gone from not feeling negative to becoming positive. They are very different animals. We all have quirks that annoy others. Once you accept that, you might be surprised to find that you actually become better friends to each other. Do you see the difference? It is not just a question of stopping negativity; it is the start of positiveness. This is very effective, as you will see, if you do it. It can be a little difficult at first but it can be done. We know that evil spirits feed off negativity, so cutting off their "food supply" is a good thing. Being positive does even more. By doing this, you are creating an atmosphere that evil spirits find intolerable.

Another effective thing you can do that is preventive is to work to create harmony in your home. This will not be discussed at length here because this is discussed in detail in the section "Love, Laughter & Other Things." The idea again, is to create an atmosphere that is inhospitable to dark forces. Prayer is another wise thing to do. I am not suggesting that you have to go to Church everyday or even weekly. It most certainly does not hurt to go to church occasionally. Besides the comfort you receive, you can make some good friends there. It can do a lot to lift your spirits and that is always a good thing. But again, I am not trying to preach to you. You have to follow your heart on such matters. I am also not suggesting that there is any one church you should go to. I personally do not believe that there is any one religion that is *the* religion. Whatever your faith, be it Christian or non-Christian, acknowledge God's love and thank Him for it. When you pray, ask God for His help and protection and thank Him for all He has done. If you stop and think about it, there is a lot to be thankful for.

Try to live your life in the light. Create an environment that is positive. I was not born yesterday, (it was a huge amount of yesterdays ago) so I am not saying that you must always walk around with a huge smile on your face. To suggest that would be absurd. God knows that I would fail miserably in the first hour alone. We all face innumerable pressures in life and they are going to affect you. That is cut and dried.

Evil spirits are not going to overtake your life because you have been having some bad days. The trick is to prevent yourself from letting the problems in life wear you down to the point where you begin to feel apathetic. Apathy is what may well cause a spirit to try to get into your life. It is not a few bad days. If that were the case, we would all probably be possessed by a legion of negative entities, starting with me. For that matter, we would have to find a spirit willing to work on crowd control. Just try your best to remain positive. This is not to say that the negativity is going to attract a demon. However, if there is a miserable old spirit floating around, he may look at the excessive negativity and decide he finally found a place where people think like he does.

Make an effort to be charitable. If you see someone in distress, try to help him. If you see someone who is down and out, say a prayer for him. Putting out positive energy towards others comes back to us many times over. The same is true of putting out negative energy towards another. One of the problems is we do not always see the good things that come our way. They do come, though. Avoid messing around with the occult. The word *occult* means *hidden*. There is a reason why it is hidden and it should probably stay that way. There are limitless books out on spell conjuring and witchcraft. As for conjuring, I have never known anyone who was happy in life because of things they obtained by using spells. If these spells did work, there would be millions of billionaires running around. Life just does not work that way. Why is it that psychics never win the lottery? Do you get my point? The witchcraft issue is a little different. True witchcraft is a benign religion. It is what is known as an "earth" religion. True witches do not run around trying to cast evil spells and slaughter animals left and right. Unfortunately, people equate every slain, gutted animal to be a product of witchcraft. This is simply not so. There are many cults out there and there is a lot of Satanism out there as well. Many of these cults are self-styled versions being practiced by teenagers. They slaughter the animals. Sometimes, they kill people as well. They call themselves witches and warlocks. They are not. Give the real witches a break.

The press has a lot to do with the myth. They will use sensational headlines every time there is a killing that appears to be ritualistic in nature. To them, it is automatically witchcraft. They rarely ever follow up on these stories and you almost never see objective articles done on true witches. The few articles you do see are often done in a tongue in cheek manner. The point is that we can get into trouble by taking a book on witchcraft spells and trying to use them for our personal gain. We should not be dabbling with something we know nothing about. Many of these spell books are about everything but witchcraft. Some of the incantations are directed to Satan and his demons. Witches do not pray to Satan. Neither should we. The old line that says: "we should be careful what we wish for because we might get it" is far truer than we realize. If you start saying incantations to the devil, he may just answer you. Then you are in big trouble, with no easy way out.

Other things to avoid are forms of divination. (Learning information from the dead.) Ouija boards, tarot cards and the like *can* be dangerous. No, I am not saying that using the Ouija will get you haunted, just like that. It probably won't. To some extent, it has gotten a bad rap. What I am saying though is that in many cases of severe hauntings, Ouija boards have been the means through which the door to another world was opened. It is not so difficult to open doors but it can be very hard to close them. You need to be aware of that. Although I would advise you to stay away from it completely, you have to make your own choices in life. If you are going to use the Ouija board, try to make sure you know who you are communicating with. There is no way to be sure so you have to go by the message you are getting. If it appears malicious in nature, discontinue the session. Remember too that spirits lie. If you ask something like "are there any spirits out there who would like to talk to us..." you could get into big trouble. You would have to make sure you use the words "positive or good" spirits. Also, always pray to God for protection and make sure everyone covers himself or herself with the "white light." It is probably better to stay away from it altogether. If you need protection, then you know it is dangerous. Why put yourself in needless danger? Trust me when I tell you that nothing good will come from it.

If you have children in the home, especially teenagers, pay attention to what kind of music they listen to. Since the dawn of time parents have always hated the music their children listen to. Just be aware that there are many heavy metal groups that preach Satan worship and suicide. If your child loves a particular song that is directed at Satan and he loves to sing those lyrics, eventually, he just may contact him or at least be oppressed by him. Just be alert to what they are doing. Also, look for signs that your children may be dabbling in the occult. Look for things like black candles, satanic drawings, pentagrams and books about conjuring. Is your child obsessed with fantasy games? That is something else to look for. Merely playing these games is not a problem in itself. Millions of children play these games safely. There is nothing wrong with fantasy. However, you have to look for signs of obsession. Does the child want to play the game constantly? In the beginning, that may be normal. There is always the novelty factor but if it should continue for a long period of time, you have to start looking into it. Does the child stay in the fantasy character all of the time? That would be a huge red flag. Fantasy has to stop at some point. You just have to be aware of what is going on in your children's lives. If you are not in control of them, something or someone out there will be.

If your house is a battleground on a daily basis, you must work to stop this. Constant battling give off extremely strong, negative vibrations. Guess who loves to feed on those? Whether it is parent/parent battles, parent/children battles, or children/children battles, do what you can to prevent them. Children will fight with each other from time to time. That is a fact of life. However, if it is a constant thing, you have to act. The same is true if there is any form of abuse going on in the home. Whether it is verbal, physical, or sexual, it must be stopped immediately. Not only will it destroy your family, it is an easy way to attract a spirit and even possibly get haunted in the process. Remember too that not all hauntings are of the "furniture flying" variety. Many are very subtle and can go virtually unnoticed. The more horrible the crime, the more negative spirits are attracted. You must try to create an atmosphere of good. Do not just stop the negative energy, create positive energy. You have to work on that, especially in this day and age of constant negativity. If the problem is parent/parent, do not just stop the fighting, treat each other nicely. This is so important. It also makes your environment much more pleasant to live in and will help your children's development. They learn from their environment and if they are raised in negativity, they will suffer from it all of their lives. They will then pass it on to their own children.

Do not bring items of a negative nature into your home. Sometimes when people travel, they buy neat little statues that represent the country they visited. Depending on the country, you may bring back an icon that is used in voodoo, for example. You do not know what may be attached to it. Before you buy it, ask the clerk what it means, assuming the clerk speaks your language. Instead, bring back things that are positive in nature. If you are a Christian, bring back a statue of the Blessed Mother. Again, you are not just negating the negative, you are producing the positive.

Do not harbor ill will against anyone. If you cannot think of anything positive about a person, and there are some in everyone's lives, try not to think about him at all. Be very careful when it comes to excessive drug or alcohol use. These things will attract negative spirits, if you abuse them. Try to live a good life. People who routinely break the law sometimes have problems with malevolent spirits. This is especially true where they commit crimes against others. I am not saying that they are possessed but I can assure you that they are being tempted on a regular basis. As I just said, not all hauntings have physical manifestations. Sometimes hauntings occur on an emotional level. You are doing the devil's work if you engage in these practices. Also, as much as someone may have hurt you, do not harbor revenge. It will not help the matter; all it will do is eat away at you. Moreover, it makes a tasty morsel for something negative.

Obviously, as humans, we are going to experience negative emotions. Nothing is going to stop that. It is normal to feel negative emotions; just do not let them eat away at you. Don't let them consume you. That is an easy trap to fall into. Problems build up over time and they have a cumulative effect on you. It is so easy to lose your perspective in life. If you suffer from depression, try to get help for it. Evil spirits will do whatever they can to hurt you. If depression is an area in which you are vulnerable, they will attack it. If you ever think about suicide, please see someone immediately. The demonic loves it when someone kills himself or herself. To them, it is a victory over God. If you are thinking about it, they will do everything they can to push you over the edge. They will fill your head with all kinds of negative emotions, self- doubt, worthlessness, and so on. If you have poor self-esteem, you have given them a target to focus on. They can be like vultures swooping down on their prey. They can be brutally effective. Don't give them ammunition they can use against you.

This brings us to the last item. If you do not already do so, learn to love yourself. People who do not possess self-love become easy victims for the evil in this world. There is plenty of it out there too. A person who loves himself and is able to forgive himself for his mistakes becomes a difficult target for the demonic. They like to prey on the vulnerable. To them, it is easy work and they love easy work. Those who do not love themselves are essentially inviting negative forces into their lives. There are plenty of forces out there that will take great pleasure in making you hate yourself even more. So, if you do not love yourself, try to learn how. God loves you and so do other people. You should learn to love yourself too. Work on it. The dividends it pays are great and often come quickly. You will surely find that it helps you in many areas of your life.

You can take these steps right away. They require no miracles. They are within your power to control, although they may not be easy. Work on it; fight for it. Take action. Make a conscious effort to help yourself. Push away the negative and embrace the positive. Not only will it stop you from being haunted, it will improve the quality of you life. It really is simple. Take victories where you can get them. Be proud of your accomplishments. Do something positive every day and when you go to bed at night, acknowledge what you accomplished, however small. Make sure that you are doing your thinking. Don't let something alien do it for you.

LOVE, LAUGHTER AND OTHER THINGS

You have read quite a bit about protecting yourself using prayer and the God light. There is no questioning the power of prayer. When faced with evil, only God can defeat it. We may be the vehicles He uses but it is God who does all the work. However, there are other concepts worth mentioning that you will find helpful. The beauty of them is that they are so simple. In this complicated, hi-tech world, we often miss the simple things in life. In many cases, they are the most important things.

We know that evil spirits feed off us, so to speak. They take the negative energy we put out and feed off it. They enjoy the terror they inflict and they use the energy that results to inflict even more terror. They enjoy the negativity that results from their actions and they become stronger and more powerful because of it. Knowing this, it makes sense to create an atmosphere that they will find unpleasant. That alone may make them leave and even if it does not, it will weaken them. If you can create a positive environment, it will greatly increase your chances of getting rid of whatever is there. In addition, always remembering the "like attracts like" principle, you may actually attract positive spirits. That can be a great help to you as they may guide you and give you more strength with which to fight. So, now the question is how do you create a positive environment when that environment has a negative force present?

(Creating A Positive Environment)

Well ... prayer, belief, faith, and trust in God are a great start. In fact, that has to be the first step as it is the most important one. If you are a Christian, pray to the Holy Spirit to help you. If you are not a Christian, pray to God in your traditional way. Whatever method is employed, God is the one who will end the siege. However, emotions can be an effective weapon as well.

Since we know that negative emotion strengthens them, it stands to reason that positive emotions weaken them. When you think of a positive emotion, love is usually the first thought that comes to mind. Love is an incredibly positive and powerful emotion, probably the best. Let me change that, love is by far the most powerful emotion. It can even beat hate. If you can fill your heart with love, you always have a fighting chance. You need to love yourself because one of the things demons or other nasty spirits like to do is mess with people's heads and they are very good at it.

They will do their best to make you hate yourself because they can feed off that. With some people, it takes a lot to make them hate themselves. For others, it takes very little because they are halfway there before the haunting became a factor. Trust me, no matter how much work it takes, they will try to find a way. They will plant thoughts in your head of everything you feel sorry for in your life. If you are grappling with some sin of yours, they will pounce on it. If your self-esteem is low, (and whose isn't) expect to get hit hard there. They do not fight fair, as you know by now. Do you have a bad temper? They know that. Do you suffer from depression? They know that too. Do you have a substance abuse problem? And on and on it goes. Fight back. Try to clear away all of the baggage you have remorse about. If you feel guilty about something, understand that God has forgiven it and you should do likewise. Self-directed guilt is both powerful and dangerous.

For that matter, they will try to get everyone in the home to turn against each other. They really love an environment where there is turmoil, chaos, and negativity. How do they go about doing that? Well, they start to wear you down. When you are being haunted, you quickly learn to dread the night and the darkness it brings. Sleep becomes a big issue. If there is, or has been, a lot of activity, you are going to find it next to impossible to get any sleep at all. Even when there is no activity taking place, you find yourself sleeping with one eye open, waiting for the activity that you know is going to start sooner or later. Obviously, when you are tired your patience is short. In addition, all negative events become magnified. You may have a son who often leaves his bike at the end of the driveway. This annoys you because you have to get out of your car and move it so you can pull in. Consequently, you have asked him repeatedly not to leave it there. It is really no big deal, most of the time. However, when you are bone tired and you come home feeling beaten and you have to get out and move the bike, it becomes something far worse than it actually is. In your anger, you may feel like running over the bike, just to teach him a lesson. That is a bit extreme (and expensive) but it can happen. Maybe you move it but when you get inside, you punish him. Your actions will be out of proportion to the offense. The coworker who tends to be an annoying pain in the butt now becomes someone you loathe to be around. Every time you see him, you lament that there are no public executions anymore, no such thing as retroactive abortions. Maybe it is your annoying neighbor, the one that makes you wonder why humans are a species that don't eat their young. The point is that he has not changed; he is the same idiot he always is only now you see him in a different light. Ditto for a boss or a teacher or anyone else who you have to deal with on a regular basis.

So, what happened here is the problem became magnified by your exhaustion and tension. Now you have a situation that is very negative on your hands. Your son is not talking to you and maybe your spouse is not either. On top of that, you don't even want to talk to yourself. Not only that, you are probably going to feel guilty about your actions later on and that alone will keep you from getting a good nights sleep even if the negative spirit takes the night off. You may even start to hate yourself a bit. In whose best interest is that? In short, you are putting out a lot of negative energy. Negative spirits: "time for dinner!" Okay, so now we have a negative situation. This in turn gives the negative spirit more power, which it will turn around and use to create even more negativity and around and around we go. Like attracts like. Negativity attracts negativity. Remember that there is always a strategy behind their actions. You must first realize this fact and then you must develop your own strategy to combat theirs. Although it may not be easy, believe me, it can be done.

The Best Strategy Is Love

The best strategy in the world is love. You have to cut yourself some slack and try to love yourself. You also must show love for one another. When you come home and find that bike in the driveway, think about your response. Is it appropriate for the situation? If you allow yourself to react in anger, aren't you playing right into the negative spirit's hands? You have to ask yourself these questions. If you do not do this and you allow yourself to react, you will almost assuredly do something you will regret later. Guilt tastes good to negative spirits too.

Fill your heart with love, love for yourself and love for your loved ones. This can be so difficult when everything is going wrong but it is a must. Nasty, negative and demonic spirits hate love. It actually hurts them, if you can believe that. You should. The more they try to make you hate, the more you must try to love. This is not something you want to do with just your loved ones. You have to try to do this with everyone. Certainly there are those around you who if you saw them drowning, you would throw them a box of rocks. When it comes to them, and hopefully there aren't too many of them, just try not to think about them at all. Better to not think about them than to think bad things about them. What goes around, comes around. That is one lesson I have learned in life. What you put out comes back to you, be it good or bad. Like attracts like.

In addition, it is important that you do not allow your negative feeling to come out in your home. For example, maybe your boss is a royal pain in the butt. Maybe he likes to make your life miserable. Maybe he is very good at it too. Your anger towards him may be more than justified. However, when you come home from work, try not to dwell on it and try not to discuss it beyond mentioning it to your spouse. It is fine to get things off your chest and you need to unless you want to mentally implode but just do not make it bigger than it is. Don't dwell on it. However warranted, anger and hate are negative emotions. At the very least, it is unhealthy for you. The negative spirits do not care who you hate. They do not care whether you are angry with your spouse, your boss, or Joe Blow down the street, the one who always has music blasting at all hours. Hate is hate and anger is anger. Wherever it is directed, it still amounts to the same thing: soups on for the negative spirit!

Negative spirits will pounce on any weakness they can find. They know what scares you and they know your weaknesses and what your vulnerabilities are. They will focus on those weaknesses, whether it is hatred towards your boss or your own self-esteem problems. Whatever it is, they will zero in on it. Try not to give them fuel for their fire. If you do not have anything good to say about someone, then do not say anything. If you find yourself thinking bad things, consciously try to change your thinking. Once they get inside your head, they will magnify every negative feeling you have. They will also try to suppress all of your positive feelings. They will try to convince you to do destructive things either to yourself or to others. Do not fall into that trap. Fill your heart with love and try hard not to think negatively.

Family Unity Is Important

Stick together. Those are two simple words but they are critically important. Let your love for one another bond you together. Negative spirits like to use the divide and conquer strategy. They want to split your family into pieces. That is why they often begin their haunting by picking on only one person. The woman of the house may see things or things may happen to her and no one else. Thus, the rest of the family begins to think she is nuts. Then they can work on everyone separately. If you stick together and love one another, the demon will have a hard time driving that wedge between you. Everyone has heard the phrase "love conquers all." There is a lot of truth to that. You have to persevere and you have to work on this constantly. Space and time do not bind evil spirits. What seems like a long and trying week to you is a millisecond to them. After several days of trying to love others, your patience may be tested. However, they continue to persevere in trying to make you hate. You have to persevere as well. Just as they are trying to wear you down, you can do the same to them. They are not invincible. You must know that and you must never forget it. They can be beaten.

(Laughter, Singing, And Socializing)

Something you do not hear too much of in haunted houses is laughter. There is nothing funny about a haunting. However, laughter is something that negative spirits find intolerable. As with prayer and love, it hurts them. If you are laughing about something, your negative spirit, be he human or inhuman will not want to hang around you. However difficult it may be to find anything to laugh about, you must try. If something amusing happened to you at work, tell the story over dinner. If you heard a good joke, however crude it may be, tell it. Rent a comedy at your local video store. Find something to laugh about. Tell about a funny experience from your past. If you have children, regale them with humorous stories from your own childhood. That always works. It also brings them closer to you. However you do it, laugh and laugh often. It really is effective.

The trick is to create as much positive energy as you possibly can. If you like to sing when you are doing work around the house, then sing. This will help create a good atmosphere. Remember, what is a good atmosphere for us in a lousy one for them. Have a party every now and again. If you still have any friends left at this point, invite them over every once in awhile, even if it is just for coffee and cake. These are simple little things but they are the types of things the negative spirits try to take away from you. Do not let them. The battle is waged on many levels and different fronts. Live your life as fully as is possible under the circumstances. Realize that part of their strategy is to make you as miserable as they can. They will do everything they can to make you not want to do the things you have always enjoyed doing. For that reason, force yourself to go out and do the things you like to do.

Speaking about going out, they have a strategy there too. If they can get away with it, they will try to oppress you to the point where you do not want to leave the home at all. They do not want you to go out and give yourself a chance to recharge your cells, so to speak. They want to force you to stay where they can keep you under assault. That is part of the wearing down process. In these instances, the victim simply feels like "I am not in the mood" to do such and such. It is not necessarily a case where there is something overt happening. Often, it is quite subtle. If you were you to ask the family about going out, they would tell you that it has nothing to do with the haunting, they just do not feel like going out that day. After a short time, a pattern begins to develop. This pattern is dangerous and you must do everything you can to prevent it. That is a trap they are setting for you. Don't fall into it.

There are other little tricks negative spirits like to play to keep you under their influence. You may find that you feel physically ill when you decide to go out. Worse yet, they may follow you when you go out. You may notice them in the car or they may do something at the location you are going to. That can be quite a problem. The game plan is to keep you in the house and that is an effective way of doing that. Hopefully that won't happen. If you get into the habit of praying before you go out, that will be a big help. You will find that sprinkling holy water in your car will cut down on this problem and may even prevent it completely. All of this is easy to say but not so easy to do. These suggestions do work. What it all amounts to is you have to be as positive as you can. You are not going to be happy about being haunted but if you can laugh for just 10 minutes out of a day, it is a start. If nothing else, at least you are happy for 10 minutes. You can build on that. Every single positive thing you do is a start. Take it one step at a time. It may be five minutes one day, maybe fifteen the next. Slowly regain your turf. It has no right to take it away from you but that is exactly what it is trying to do. Resist it any way you can. It is your birthright to be happy. Exercise that right, anyway you can.

You may find that this becomes easier as you go along. It is as if you are gaining momentum. Sometimes just knowing that you have a strategy and that you are fighting back helps. You may not feel so helpless anymore. Ride that wave. Yes, there will still be pitfalls but remember, as you become stronger, your oppressor becomes weaker. Use this to your advantage. You will be quite surprised how effective this can be. Baby steps are all that is needed. Little by little, reclaim your home and your life. It can be done as long as you do not give up the fight. Love and laughter ... these are powerful weapons in you are arsenal. Do not be afraid to use them.

When you are home, play happy music. As you are going about your day, if something starts to happen like a chair moving, try to ignore it. Send a message to the demon that you are going to go about your business regardless of his attempts to stop you. Do not give him recognition. If something happens that you cannot ignore, toss some holy water around and say a prayer asking God to make him stop bothering you. Then, tell him where to go and do so forcefully. This is no time for meekness. Believe; truly believe that God is on your side even if it doesn't look that way at the moment. Take comfort from that. Allow yourself to become confident that you can fight this terrible thing.

Husbands, bring home flowers for your wife. It will cheer her up and it will add beauty and life to the home. Guess who does not like to witness these happenings? If you have kids, surprise them with a toy. Make family plans to go out to dinner and a movie on the weekend. That will be fun of course but it will also give you something to look forward to throughout the week. Anything that makes life more bearable is a plus.

The Haunting Will End

You must realize that this has happened to many others. They have gone through the same thing and they came out of it in one piece. Yes, they may have changed a little but they are living normal lives now. Eventually, the problem was resolved. Know that ultimately, it will be resolved in your situation as well. This is a fact. Take comfort from that. It always begins and it always ends, as well. Avoid feeling sorry for yourself as easy as that is to do. That is such a dangerous and even deadly trap. You may not know why this has happened to you but there must be a reason. Nothing happens by chance. I have been asked many times why God allows this to happen to His children. I do not have an answer to that question. I know that nothing in this world can happen without God allowing it. I cannot understand why some people have to suffer through a haunting any more than I can understand why God allows children to be hurt, abused, and killed. Truly, there is a reason for those happenings although I cannot begin to comprehend what it may be. God knows what He is doing. I do believe that. I also believe that He will not tell us. I base that on the fact that if he would not answer Job's questions, He will not likely answer ours either. Maybe someday, you will serve as an inspiration to someone else suffering through the same type of haunting. Your courage and strength in dealing with this scourge may give courage and strength to others. As a child and even as a young adult, I could not understand why I had to endure a terrible haunting. Now, I realize that I would not be doing this work had it not happened. It has driven me to do work that is fulfilling beyond my wildest dreams. Again, nothing happens by chance.

The single most important thing to remember is that God does indeed love you! The second biggest thing to remember is that the haunting can and will end. There is no way to predict how or when but it will happen. Hauntings are completely unpredictable. They can start out of nowhere and they can end just as quickly as they started. Accept that fact and you are well on your way to freedom. Create a positive environment, one that makes the nasty spirit uncomfortable. Look for patterns. Does it seem to leave you alone when you invite certain friends over? If so, invite them a lot, assuming you can stand them. Lastly, remember love, laughter, and other things.

COMMONLY ASKED QUESTIONS

Can spirits or demons physically hurt or kill someone? It is believed that inhuman spirits can hurt and even kill in extreme instances. However, it is incredibly rare for a demon or devil to kill someone as that will result in their destruction by God. They are capable of hurting people and animals. In most cases, injuries result not so much from the demons as much as from people fleeing from them. I have heard of a few cases where the demon itself caused an injury but again, that is the rarest of the rare. The fear they cause however could certainly cause problems with someone who has a heart condition or other health problems. The stress and fear of living in a demonically infested house will surely take a toll as well. That cannot be discounted. I will say that there are many cases on record where priests performing exorcisms have been severely injured by the person possessed. Of course, they are in direct battle with the demon, thus they are susceptible to attack. Most attacks, however, are mental.

What is the difference between a parapsychologist, a demonologist or a paranormal researcher? Parapsychology by my definition is the scientific study of a field that cannot be studied scientifically. Truthfully, a parapsychologist is someone who studies psychic phenomena with the belief that it is al human generated. It is a broad answer but it is a scientific approach to understanding paranormal events. Parapsychologists believe that most paranormal phenomena are the result of something that the human mind creates. For example, the movement of objects is believed to be the result of mind over matter. There is considerable validity to the theories of parapsychology. However, it does not explain *all* paranormal phenomena. A demonologist is one who studies demons and their actions. Almost all demonologists are clergymen. A paranormal researcher or investigator covers anyone who deals with paranormal phenomena. Be wary of labels though, they can be dangerous. People can pretty much call themselves whatever they want. Pay more attention to the person than they label they may have given themselves.

If you feel cold when a spirit manifests itself, does that mean it is evil? No, whenever a spirits manifests, it does so by drawing energy from the environment or from a person, which produces the cold. In and of itself, the cold means little. The popular conception is that cold denotes evil but that is not true.

Should I be afraid of a ghost? No. As I have said many times, the overwhelming majority of ghostly encounters are benign and even benevolent. It is natural to fear something that you do not understand but when you think about it, ghosts are pretty much natural and common. Once you accept that fact, you will find your fear fading away.

If you move out of a haunted house, will you be safe? That depends on a number of things. The most important factor is *what* was doing the haunting? Spirits have the ability to move around. However, in most cases, a human spirit will likely stay at one location although there appears to be no rule that it must. If the spirit was demonic, it certainly has the ability to follow you. The next big question is *why* the haunting occurred in the first place. If the spirit was indigenous to the location, it may well stay there. In fact, it almost always will. If however, the haunting occurred because of some action on your part, such as a conjuring spell, the spirit you summoned will follow you wherever you go. The only way to stop this type of spirit would be through an exorcism. Spirits sometimes attach themselves to an object. It may be a piece of furniture or it may be something like jewelry. In that case, the spirit will go wherever the object it has attached itself goes.

Are there such things as haunted people? Yes, there are. There are people who find themselves haunted wherever they go. In some cases, this may be due to something they did as mentioned above. (Spells, etc.) Sometimes you cannot pinpoint a reason why a person is haunted. There are a number of theories, such as curses or spells. In some cases, it seems that good people are singled out by the demonic because they *are* such good people. What better way to hurt God than to go after good people? In some cases, people are haunted because of the fact that they can be. This sounds absurd but in truth, it really isn't. You see, some people just have the ability to see spirits more so than others. It may have to do with their overall sensitivity. It may be that their brains are simply more in tune with the spirit world than most. If you picture the brain as something of a receiver, their brain may just be better at picking up signals. Aren't they lucky! Since spirits know they can get through to that person, they will try.

Can a haunting just stop on its own? In some instances, yes. Some hauntings stop as suddenly and inexplicably as they start. This is often the case with poltergeist manifestations. They seem to come out of nowhere and then, one day, it stops. As always, it depends on *what* is doing the haunting and *why* it is doing it.

Can anyone develop discernment? Yes, please review the chapter on this subject. It is believed that everyone has some of this ability, although not everyone realizes it. It would stand to reason that if one were to use this skill, it would become sharper. Most people ignore their "sixth" sense because it is drowned out by the other five senses. Others lack a developed sixth sense because they try too hard to use it. It is something that must come naturally. However, meditation can strengthen it to some degree.

Can the existence of ghosts be proven? From a purely scientific point of view, the answer is no. In order to prove anything scientifically, it must be studied in a controlled setting and it must be able to be duplicated at will. This cannot happen since spirits will not allow themselves to be studied in a lab. Still, there are mountains of evidence that points to the probability of ghosts existing. There are simply too many examples to ignore. Ask anyone who has seen one.

Are there different types of equipment you can use to prove their existence? There are many different pieces of equipment available that are commonly used by paranormal investigators. For example, there are devices that measure electromagnetic energy fields. When spirits manifest, they draw energy from either the environment or a person. It is believed that in undergoing this process, an electromagnetic field is created. Through research and experience, we have come to learn that this is so. Therefore, when an EMF detector goes off, it may be due to a spirit manifestation and it has happened enough times that you can equate the two. However, from a scientific point of view, all we can prove is that there is an electromagnetic field forming. We cannot prove what is causing it. There are other pieces of equipment that are used to produce evidence. Camcorders, cameras, various types of thermometers, along with other things help build a case.

What about pictures, aren't they proof? Again, from a scientific point of view, no. You will often see pictures that show an amorphous, mist like energy field. This fog like substance is rarely seen by the naked eye. To any paranormal investigator, these energy fields are consistent with spirit manifestations. However, to a scientist, they are pictures are of an energy field or mist and that is all. They may not be able to explain why it is there but since it cannot be duplicated under controlled conditions, they cannot state that these fields are spirit related. Today we have great technology that has allowed people to get some amazing photographs. The problem is that we have great technology that has allowed people to "create" amazing photographs. There has never been better equipment and there has never been better fraud.

If I play with a Ouija board, will I become haunted? This is an interesting question. The odds are that you would not be haunted but let me explain this. Many of the more difficult hauntings have happened to people who have played with the board. It has proven to be the only common denominator when cases have been studied. In theory, you are contacting spirits and inviting them into your home. If you come across one that does not want to leave, you have a problem on your hands. However, millions of people regularly use Ouija boards. Certainly, there are not millions of people who are haunted. Based on that premise, your chances of being haunted because of the Ouija board are pretty small. I should point out that almost everyone I have talked to who have used the board a few times had an interesting story or two to tell about their experiences. The vast majority are benign in nature. Obviously, there may be something else going on with the people who do get haunted from using it. In theory, if you ask only to deal with positive spirits from the light and you pray for protection, you should be okay. You just have to realize that using it puts you at a higher risk level than people who do not use it. The more you use it, the better the chance that you will experience some form of paranormal phenomena.

Are there such things as ghost animals? Yes, indeed. Many people who have lost a cherished pet report seeing or feeling their pet with them when they go to bed. It seems that the pet is doing its best to comfort its grieving owner. Many will call this wishful thinking but there is tremendous anecdotal evidence to support this belief. I have personally had experiences with deceased animals. So too has my wife. Unfortunately, it is rare. I wish it would happen more.

Is it possible to contact a deceased loved one? According to many psychics, yes. Personally, I have had no experience with this but there are credible psychics who claim to communicate with deceased spirits. I would love to find someone who can. There are many loved ones whom I would like to contact. It must be pointed out that there are many, many "psychics" out there who will gladly take your money and tell you extremely obvious things. Most of those people have about as much of a chance of contacting your deceased loved ones as the average doorknob.

Can I contact a deceased loved one by using a Ouija board? Theoretically, you probably can. However, I would never advise it. The chances are slim that you will contact who you are looking for. In addition, you have no idea who or what you have contacted, if you contact anyone at all. Probably more importantly, you run the risk of hurting yourself emotionally. Imagine what would happen if you could not contact the one you are trying to reach. That would hurt. Even worse would be if you contacted someone who *claimed* to be your loved one and they began spelling out terribly hurtful things. There is no easy answer to grief. When you lose a loved one, you are going to hurt for as long as you hurt. There is no anesthetic for that. Even making the attempt to contact a deceased loved one points to an obsession on your part. Unfortunately, you have to go on. Besides, your loved one may well visit you in some manner when the time is right, most likely in a dream state.

I sometimes smell perfume that my mother used to use. Is it possible that she is visiting? Yes, it is possible. In fact, it is a fairly common phenomenon. Many people report smelling a scent associated with a deceased loved during times of great stress or joy.

I sometimes experience unusual phenomena in my house but it is never things like tables flying around the room or gook chasing me down the stairs. My troubles are more like the TV's turning on and off or water faucets opening. Is it possible that my house is haunted? Yes, it is possible although without knowing more information and actually investigating it, I cannot say for sure. What you have described does fit the pattern of a haunting but again, I cannot be sure without more data. This question brings up a good point. All hauntings are not full blown activity all day long. A haunting can be very subtle, a thing or two happens here, something else happens there. You do not need to have tons of phenomena occurring on a daily basis to be haunted. Bear in mind too that all cases of a spirit being around is not necessarily a haunting.

If I am experiencing phenomena in my home, is it a good idea for me to bless it? That depends on *what* is causing the activity. If you were dealing with an evil, *human* spirit, the blessing would be a good idea. If, however, an *inhuman* spirit is causing the problem, the blessing may provoke the entity and it may retaliate. Therefore, what you have here is a tricky situation. You really need to know *what* you are dealing with. My advice to you would be to contact one of the paranormal organizations in your area and have the situation investigated. There are many to choose from, if you are on the Internet. Most organizations do not charge for their services except for travel and lodging, so try to find one that is local. Also, if you feel that a blessing is needed, you might want to have it done by a priest or minister. That makes the blessing stronger. Still though, the entity may retaliate. Keep something in mind though, the mere presence of a spirit does not mean that you are being haunted in a negative way. Most spirit encounters are benign. The movement of objects by itself does not constitute a negative haunting. Running around yelling prayers is not necessary in a benign haunting and it really will not have much of an effect. However, there is nothing wrong with blessing your house or having a priest do it. You just have to be careful if you think there may be something demonic going on.

Let us say that my house is haunted. How long would it take to end the haunting? There is no easy answer to this question. How quickly you end it depends on several factors. For openers, it depends on *what* it is and *why* it is there. Expelling a human spirit is much easier then expelling an inhuman one in the sense of safety. However, human hauntings can take a long time to unravel. Another part of the equation is how you respond to the situation. Is your faith strong or is it weak? If the haunting is the result of some action on the part of a family member, has this precipitating factor been stopped? There is also the question of your personal strength. I know this is not telling you much but these factors play a huge role in ending the attack. There have been many cases where the activity just suddenly stopped on its own or stopped when investigators arrived. Unfortunately, a haunting can last for years. It really is something that has to be taken on a case-to-case basis.

Are all hauntings bad? That all depends on how you classify a haunting. To me, a haunting is a situation where you have a negative spirit at work, be it human or inhuman. In my mind, the presence of a benign human spirit does not constitute a haunting. Therefore by my definition, a haunting is bad. However, many people consider a haunting to be a situation where any spirit is present and some even call the presence of a psychic recording a haunting. By their definition, all hauntings are not bad.

My son, Johnny, who is twelve, has been acting very weird lately. Could he be possessed? Well, the first question that come to mind is what exactly do you feel is "weird?" He is at the age where he is entering puberty and that causes massive hormonal changes, which can affect behavior. Another question that arises is whether he may be taking some form of drug. That too, will affect behavior. Is he hanging out with a bad crowd? In addition, is your son exhibiting behavior that should be looked at by a counselor? Could there be medical problems? These are all things that should be looked at before you even consider something like possession. Demonic possession is extremely rare and should be the last thing looked at since it is by far the most unlikely cause.

If my home is infested by a demon, can I beat it on my own? Anything is possible but I would have to say that you would need the help of either a demonologist or a clergyman. I would not suggest you that you try to do it on your own. The first issue here is determining that you have a demon in the first place. Unless you have completely bizarre things happening, it can be difficult to be sure just what you are dealing with. However, if you are sure that the problem is demonic, my advice is to find someone who is experienced in dealing with that type of haunting.

If I am haunted, do I have to believe in God? Since I consider a haunting to be negative in nature, (I do not consider the presence of a benign spirit a haunting.) I would have to say yes, if are dealing with a negative spirit. Demons are creations of God and I believe the only way to get rid of them is through belief in God and through His help. It does not necessarily matter what you faith is, it only matters that you do believe in God.

Do voodoo, curses, and the like really happen? This is a tough one for me to answer because I believe that these things work only if the victim believes they do. You will hear some very different answers from other people but I feel that it is most likely the power of suggestion that makes them work. I must point out that I have seen voodoo do some terrible things to someone I knew. To make a long story short, this woman put a spell on my friend and myself. This friend of mine was terribly worried about this spell and it took a severe toll on her. I did not believe in it for one second and consequently, nothing bad happened to me. Did I just get lucky?

Do spells work? Again, it is a tough question. There is evidence that spells work but I am skeptical about that. However, I could be wrong.

Are conjuring books dangerous? Yes, they are. When you dabble with those things, you have no idea what forces are at work, if any. Certainly nothing good will come from it. It is like playing with fire. There is a good chance that you will be burned.

Can you really conjure a demon? Probably. There are some credible stories out there. However, what makes people dangerous is that they *believe* they can and will thus do whatever they feel it takes to achieve their goal. That can involve sacrifices and the like. I will say this much, demons do not do our bidding for us. If they offer anything, there is a horrible price to be paid.

Can anyone see a ghost? Probably. What is interesting is the fact that four people can be sitting in a room and two will see a ghost and two will not see it. This can cause some serious confusion when one spouse is trying to convince the other that a haunting is taking place. There are people who are more sensitive to the spirit world and they will most often see a spirit. For that reason, women see spirits more so than men. However, I have heard many stories of even the most skeptical of men finding themselves confronted by a spirit. One thing to consider is that many times, people will see a spirit but not know it since in some cases, spirits will look as solid as we do.

What are the chances of me seeing a ghost? Probably very strong. However, the thing is you may not know that the person who just smiled at you as they passed by is a ghost.

Is there anything wrong with going to haunted locations, like on ghost tours? Absolutely not. Going on ghost tours is becoming very popular today. The same is true for people deciding to go on their own to famous haunted places. You are in no danger if you do this. The only thing I tell people is that if you go to enough places, you may well encounter a spirit. Of course, that is why you went there, after all. It is perfectly safe.

If I feel my house is being haunted and I go to my priest, will he help me? That depends on the priest. The sad fact of the matter is that he may not. The clergy are often the last people who will believe that something supernatural is going on. You do find one or two precious priests who will believe what you tell him and do his best to help you. In many cases, priests do not know how to handle haunting phenomena.

Is it a good idea to go to the press if I think my house is haunted? No, actually it is a bad idea. Going to the press creates a bigger problem that the one you already have. Newspapers want headlines, not necessarily truth. If they smell a big story, they will be relentless with you. They are not going to seriously look into the problem, they are going to write what they think will attract readers. You will be besieged by reporters looking for an interview. The second big problem is that people will be knocking on your door and camping out on your lawn and will besiege you wherever you go. Your children will be harassed going to and from school, your telephone will ring constantly and every wackadoo in the area will try to get in touch with you or your ghosts. The living human problem becomes larger than the dead human/inhuman one. I do not like to go anywhere near a case when I know the press is involved. Nothing good ever comes of it.

Are there things I can do to prevent being haunted? There are things you can do to prevent a haunting from occurring. Please see the chapter in this book for details. One thing to note, if you move into a haunted house, you may have a problem no matter what you do. However, there are things you can do to prevent one from happening where you already are. Obviously the biggest thing is to not dabble in the occult. Also, you want to create an environment in your home that will repel negative forces.

If someone who is being haunted comes to stay with me for a while, can this thing come into my home? Spirits are capable of moving around, so unfortunately, it can indeed follow your friend to your home. This most often occurs in hauntings involving strong, negative spirits. Usually the spirit will leave with the person who is being besieged.

If a haunting stops, can it start up again? In some cases, yes it can. There are times when an exorcism is performed and the problem abates for a while. Sadly, it may start up again. You are never quite sure what the outcome will be. In addition, some hauntings are subtle. Activity will come and go from time to time. We really do not have a handle on why this happens.

Can you help an earthbound spirit cross over? Yes, you can. A psychic will have an easier time doing this than you might but it can be done. In many cases, earthbound spirits do not know they are dead. With gentle coaxing, you can sometimes convince a spirit to cross over. Sometimes a spirit is afraid to move on. Again, gentle coaxing can help. One way that has been successful for me is to ask the spirit to call a deceased loved one to come and help them.

What is deliverance? Deliverance is similar to exorcism. It is the process of eliminating spirits or demons from a place or a person by binding and casting it out in the name of God. However, Deliverance will not be effective if a person is severely demonically possessed. In that case, a solemn exorcism would be required to free the person. Deliverance is good for oppression of a person, as opposed to possession.

Can anyone do Deliverance or does it have to be done by a priest? In truth, anyone can do deliverance although you must be well trained. In doing Deliverance, you are attacking the evil entity and you are therefore taking a major risk. If you do not know how to deal with demons, you can get yourself in big trouble by trying to do this. However, according to the Bible, anyone who is baptized and believes in Him (Jesus) has this ability. In Mark 16:17, Jesus states this about those who believe in Him. "All these signs will follow those who believe: In My name they will cast out demons: they will speak in new tongues. However, it is always wise to leave this to the people who are trained to do this. Demons are cunning and they are crafty. The person performing a Deliverance service is at risk for psychic attacks. Solemn Exorcisms should only be performed by a qualified Priest who has the approval of his Bishop. You can open yourself to a world of hurt if you try to perform an exorcism on your own.

If I am working on a case and nothing is happening, should I try religious provocation? Under *no* circumstances should you use religious provocation at any time. If there were to be a demonic spirit present, you can create a firestorm that that you cannot control. Doing so puts everyone involved in danger. Only trained, experienced people should attempt provocation and that is only done in the worst of cases. In addition, provocation will not make a human spirit show itself. If nothing is happening, you have no idea what may be there. It is extremely dangerous to use provocation.

What is the difference between demons and devils? Basically, it is a matter of power and title. Devils are stronger than demons, and are smarter as well. As for the title, you have to look at angels; they are listed as archangels and angels. Demons and devils are technically angels. The devils would be the archangels.

I thought there was only one devil? Again, devil is merely a title. The figure always listed as the devil is Satan. He is the leader of the pack as he is strongest.

Do you think some mentally ill people are possessed and vice-versa? I believe that there are probably many cases where this is true. However, there is no way to know how often this is the case. One problem is the many of the symptoms are the same for both. In this day and age where people do not want to believe in anything spiritual, it is easy to label people as being mentally ill. What can decide the two are outward manifestations. (Items flying around by themselves.) If you think about it, if a person who has been diagnosed as being schizophrenic sees his doctor and tells him how his furniture moved around by itself the night before, I can almost guarantee you that the doctor will adjust his medication. Another thought: the mentally ill are the best targets for possession because no one will believe them anyway.

What is the difference between demonic and diabolical? Demonic pertains to demons while diabolical pertains to devils.

Are the psychics who channel spirits for real? I hate that question. I would like to say that there are probably some out there who are legit. What bothers me is that when you see these things on TV, the information given is so general that it can fit most people. It's kind of like one size fits all. In some cases, it seems like the "psychic" is fishing for information. Many bring questions on their own heads because of the outrageous rates they charge for readings. There is a long history of fraud in this field. There have been too many cases of people profiteering off the suffering of others. I am personally skeptical of those who say they can channel at will, especially for a large fee.

What do you think about the "pet psychic" shows? This will probably get me in trouble but my answer is: not much. I have trouble believing the "human" psychics on TV. Although they seem to "fish" for answers, there is some way of verifying what they are telling the person being read. I cannot believe it when a pet psychic says that Fido hates the neighbor's cat because she meows too much or gives him dirty looks when he is watering the fire hydrant.

If someone kills me, can I come back and haunt them? There is evidence that this sometimes happens but whether it is something any spirit can do is another question. Perhaps it is so rare because the deceased passes over quickly. I really cannot answer that question with any degree of certainty.

APPENDIX

GLOSSARY OF TERMS

Abnormal Phenomena- See Paranormal phenomena.

Amorphous- Having no definite form or shape. Spirits often appear in mist-like forms.

Angels- A spiritual being created by God to serve as a messenger to man. Angels can be good or bad. Demons still carry the title of Angels.

Anti-Christ- Satan. The opposite of Christ. Many feel that the Anti-Christ will be seen as a man whose appearance will mark the end of the world. Some believe that the Anti-Christ is already among us.

Apparition- The appearance of a spirit that can be recognized as such.

Apport- Arrival of objects, either animate or inanimate during a seance or a haunting. Apports are sometimes made of teeth, hair, feces or vomit of either an animal or human. Any object that appears out of nowhere can be an apport.

Arcane- Anything hidden or secret. Used often to describe secret rites or societies.

Archangel- Higher order of Angels. St. Michael and St. Gabriel are two of the Angels that battled Lucifer and his legions. Lucifer still carries the title of Archangel.

Asport- Disappearance of objects that fail to turn up again.

Astral Body- An invisible spirit that is an exact replica of the human body, which enters the astral plane.

Astral Plane- The level through which spirits must pass after death. People can sometimes reach this level while alive through astral projection.

Astral Projection- When the spirit travels outside of the body either to the astral plane or another location on this plane. Also known as *out of body experience.* (See remote viewing.)

Astral World- The next sphere after the death of the body through which we pass on our way to the light.

Astrology- The study professing to foretell the future as a result of interpreting the heavenly bodies, stars, moons and planets.

Aura- An emanation of energy that surrounds all living things. Many with psychic abilities are able to see and interpret this energy. The energy can be viewed using Kirlian photography. It is felt that our physical health is reflected in our auras.

Automatic Writing- Phenomena in which people write without conscious thought. Many feel that it is spirits writing through the body of a living person. Parapsychologists feel that the phenomenon is due to automatism.

Automatism- The theory in which the subconscious communicates with the conscious by means of a vehicle such as a Ouija board, automatic writing, or pendulum swinging.

Autoscope- Any mechanical means whereby communication from the unknown may reach us. Examples would be a seance or the planchette of a Ouija board.

Baptism- Christian sacrament of initiation into the church. This is done to absolve the person being baptized from original sin

Benign Spirit- A spirit that is not evil or harmful to man. Angels and spirit guides fall into this category as would spirits of loved ones that come back to tell us something. Elementals are benign spirits.

Bilocation- When an object is seen in two locations at the same time. Padre Pio was said to exhibit bilocation.

Black Magic- Magic used for evil often with the intent of injuring or killing someone. It may also be done for the personal gain of the practitioner.

Black Mass- Performed by Satanists; this is a mock of the Catholic Mass. Black candles are used instead of white ones. Also, many Christian prayers are read backwards and blood is usually drunk at these ceremonies.

Botanica- Store that sells paraphernalia for use with Santeria.

Bruja- Spanish for witch.

Brujeria- Combination of Aztec pagan religion and Catholicism. Can be used for good or bad.

Changelings- In Scottish lore, the substitution of a little old manikin of the elf race for a young child.

Cherubim- Order of Angel, celestial being usually depicted as a beautiful, winged child. Occasionally depicted as being half human and half animal. They are rated second in the hierarchy of Angels.

Circumambulation- Ceremonially surrounding an object or living thing for the purpose of protection.

Clairaudient- Psychic ability to hear sounds or voices inaudible to the normal ear.

Clairsentient- Psychic ability to feel things not normally felt by most people.

Clairvoyant- Psychic ability to see persons or events that are distant. (Can be past events or future ones.) Children are naturally clairvoyant up to the age of 12.

Conjuring- Any attempt to call upon spirits to help the living, usually for the purpose of hurting or killing someone or for personal gain.

Coven- A group of occult practitioners. Covens usually consist of 13 people.

Craft- Short for witchcraft.

Crystal Gazing- modes of divination using crystals, water, or mirrors. (See Scrying.)

Cults- Any group gathering as a religious or pseudo-scientific organization that use ceremonies as a form of worship.

Curse- To speak a wish of evil against someone or call down forces to hurt someone.

Deep Trance Medium- A psychic who allows a spirit to enter his/her body so that the spirit may communicate with the living. I offer refer to them as "trancers."

Deliverance- Christian ritual designed to rid a person of negative forces or influence. This is a lesser form of Exorcism.

Dematerialization- The sudden disappearance of an item. An asport.

Demon- An evil, inhuman spirit bent on the destruction of man. Demons are said to be the fallen Angels banished by God and thrown out of Heaven by St. Michael.

Demonic- Any activity or manifestation caused by demons.

Demonologist- One who studies demons and their actions.

Demonology- The study of demons and devils.

Devil- Lucifer or Satan, the leader of the fallen angels banished from Heaven. Although there are different opinions, many feel there are multiple devils with Satan being the leader. Devils are more powerful than demons. It is much like an angel and an archangel.

Diabolical- Any action caused by the devil. Extremely atrocious or inhuman.

Discarnate- Spirit existing without a physical body.

Discernment- To perceive or feel using the mind or senses.

Disembodied- Spirit functioning without a body.

Disembodied Voice- A voice heard that comes from no physical body.

Divination- Obtaining knowledge of the unknown or the future by contacting forces outside of nature. This usually relies on spirits of the dead.

Doppelganger- An opposite double of a person or a spirit of a person outside of the body.

Ectoplasm- A substance which emanates from them body of a medium during a trance. This is often seen in pictures as a mist like substance.

Elementals- Spirits of the earth. Elementals are benign, almost angelic spirits who watch over the four elements, air-sylphs, earth-gnomes, fire-salamanders, and water nymphs. Also, lesser spirits of nature are called *undines.*

Electromagnetic Field- A field propagated by a combination of electric and magnetic energy that radiates from radio and light waves to gamma and cosmic rays. It is believed that when spirits manifest, they create an electromagnetic field.

EMF Detector- An instrument that measures electromagnetic energy. Also known as a Gauss Meter or galvanometer.

Energy- The driving force behind all forms of life.

ESP- Extra Sensory Perception. A parapsychological term to denote awareness apparently received through channels other than the natural senses. Telekinesis and psychokinesis are forms of ESP.

Evil- Malignant, malicious. The act of doing something designed to hurt others or God Himself.

Evil Spirits- Spirits whose intents are to hurt or destroy all that is good. They make every attempt to hurt man or cause chaos. Evil spirits can be human or inhuman.

E.V.P.- Electronic voice phenomena. This is where voices are recorded where no one is present. It is felt by many that these voices are from spirits attempting to communicate with living people. They usually record very grainy, although that is not always the case. This is a form of equipmental transcommunication.

Exorcism- Ritual designed to free someone from the possession of a demon or devil. An exorcism can also be performed on an inanimate object, such as a dwelling. Deliverance and Suffimunigation are lesser forms of exorcism.

Exorcist- One who performs exorcisms. In almost all cases, exorcists are ordained ministers of their particular religion.

Fairies- Supernatural beings said to be most beautiful. Benign spirits who are occasionally inclined towards mischief.

Fairy Lights- Small lights given off by fairies who want to be seen. Fairy lights usually look like Christmas tree lights in that they flicker on and off in different locations. Most commonly seen near woods.

Familiar- A spirit who aids a witch, usually in the form of an animal. Cats are favorite familiars for witches.

Gauss Meter- An instrument that measures electromagnetic fields. Also call EMF detectors.

Ghost- Generic term to describe a deceased person or image appearing to the living. Animals can also be ghosts.

Ghost Lights- Lights that sometimes appear in haunted houses or in some cases, woods. Not necessarily evil, these lights are often photographed.

Ghoul- An evil spirit who preys on corpses. One who takes pleasure in revolting things.

Globule- A tiny sphere of electromagnetic energy. Spirits often appear on film as globules. Also known as *orbs*. These are not always perfect circles.

Gnomes- The elemental spirit of *earth*.

Grave- Final resting-place for the physical body after the spirit has left.

Grave Yard- Cemetery.

Grimoire- A book of spells and rituals designed to conjure spirits.

Guardian Angels- These are Angels who are assigned to protect all living creatures. People are said to have their own Guardian Angel.

Haunted- A person or place to which negative spirits are attached. These spirits can be human or inhuman in nature.

Haunting- The act of being haunted. Only the presence of a negative spirit would constitute a true haunting. Where a benign spirit present, it is not really a haunting.

Hell- The place where God sent all devils, demons and evil spirits for punishment. It is believed that evil people are also sent to hell.

Holy Water- Water that has been blessed by a member of the clergy. Holy water is said to have the ability negate negative forces. Through years of experience, I must say that is true.

Human Sacrifice- The act of killing a person during a satanic ritual. Animals are often sacrificed as well.

Human Spirit- the spirit of a person who has lived in the physical plane. These spirits can be earthbound for a number of reasons.

Imp- An evil spirit or small or minor demon. Some texts consider imps to be benign, playful spirits.

Incarnate- Embodied in flesh, to exist on the physical plane.

Incubus- A demon that has sex with a women. Demons do not have a gender so the same demon can also be a *succubus.*

Infestation- Condition that occurs when evil spirits inhabit a location. Infestation in a person is called *possession.*

Inhuman Spirit- The spirit of a creature that has never lived on the physical plane. Good spirits are Angels; evil ones are demons and devils.

Kirlian Photography- Taking of pictures of the human aura. Two Russian scientists, Semyon and Valentina Kirlian founded this process.

Kill Crop- Half human, half demon. They usually look like humans.

Law Of Attraction- The idea that a spirit will come into a person's life because it is attracted by something that person is doing. Like attracts like.

Law Of Indigeny- A spirit that is indigenous to a location.

Law Of Invitation- Calling a spirit into your life, intentionally or unintentionally. Use of a Ouija board falls under this category.

Law Of Opportunity- A spirit that is looking for an opportunity to get into someone's life and look around for the chance.

Levitation- The rising of an object or person by no visible means. This is in defiance of the laws of physics. It is one of the conditions in the Roman Ritual that supports the idea of a demonic or diabolical presence.

Light Trance Medium- A person whom spirits can communicate through. In contrast to deep trance mediums, the spirit wishing to communicate through them does not enter light trance mediums.

Lucifer- Satan. Name literally means the "lightbearer." Satan is the leader of the Angels banished from Heaven by the Archangel Michael after they revolted against God.

Lycanthropy- The condition where a person becomes or believes he becomes a werewolf. While someone suffering from this affliction may display some minor physical changes, they do not actually turn into wolves.

Malevolent- Wishing evil or harm towards others. A malevolent spirit is one that wishes to hurt man.

Malicious- A spirit that is evil or spiteful. These spirits will destroy things of personal or financial value for the sake of causing misery.

Malignant- Having an evil disposition towards others.

Manifestation- The appearance or taking form of an entity. Can also mean the outbreak of activity.

Materialization- A formation by a spirit of a temporary physical organization, visible and palpable, which can touch material objects.

Meditation- To reach a state of deep relaxation designed to clear the mind stress or tension. Opening oneself to ambient energy. Meditation is also a form of self-hypnosis or autohypnosis.

Medium- A psychic through whom spirits can communicate. There are two types of mediums, light and deep trance.

Metaphysics- Derived from the Latin word "meta" which means "beyond," metaphysics would literally mean that which is beyond the laws of physics. In short, it is the study of psychical research.

Miracles- Occurrence of something good that could not have come about without the help of the Divine.

Necromancy- A way of conjuring power from dead spirits sometimes using bones, burned ash or any other part of a corpse.

Necronomicon- The book of the dead.

Necrophilia- Having sexual relations with a corpse. Many necrophiliacs become possessed.

Nymphs- Name of the elemental spirit of *water.*

Obsession- The second stage of a haunting where the invading entity begins to exert its power over its victim.

Occult- A body of knowledge that is hidden or secret in the areas of the paranormal, preternatural or supernatural.

Opportunistic Spirit- A spirit, usually an evil one that will ride the coat tails or piggy back its way into a haunting with another spirit. In this case, you may have a human spirit operating in a house and a demon, seeing a situation it likes will join in. This can explain why some people are haunted after using some form of divination while others aren't. They just happened to use the divination method while an opportunistic spirit was flying around.

Oppression- The first stage of a haunting where the invading entity attempt to gain access to the location or person victimized.

Orb- A tiny sphere of electromagnetic energy given off by spirits. Also called a *globule.*

Orishas- Santeria gods, syncretized with Catholic Saints.

Ouija Board- Game board made by Parker Brothers used to communicate with spirits. Many feel this communication is actually with the collective unconscious of the participants. (Automatism.)

Out Of Body Experience- State in which the spirit of a person travels to the astral plane. It is said that people can in some instances travel to other locations on the physical plane. Also known as *OBE, OOBE, astral projection* or *remote viewing.*

Outward Manifestation- Any event of paranormal activity, i.e.: disembodied voices, movement of objects, horrible smells, manipulation with temperatures, etc.

Pact With The Devil- Selling your soul to Satan for personal gain in this life.

Pagan- Someone who worships the natural gods. The name literally means *people of the earth.*

Parakinesis- Movement of objects with contact that is insufficient to explain it. Spoon bending, where there is very little contact involved is an example of this.

Paranormal- Events that take place which are outside the natural order of things. This can involve ghosts, UFO's, ESP, and any other things not easily explained by nature but in the realm of the natural.

Parapsychology- Derived from the Latin word "para," which means "beyond." Parapsychology literally means "beyond" psychology. However, it is most known as the scientific study of paranormal phenomena. This includes everything from ESP to haunting phenomena although it deals mostly with areas that are open to being studied under controlled, laboratory conditions and are believed to be the result of a human's mind. (Mind over matter.)

Parapsychologist- One who studies parapsychology. Parapsychologists usually study psychic phenomena such as ESP. However, they will sometimes study hauntings.

Pendulum Swinging- A form of divination in which an object tied to a string is held over a board with numbers and letters and in some cases, words. In theory, the pendulum is moved by a spirit and can answer questions. Parapsychologists believe it is a form of *automatism.*

Pentacle- A pentagram within a circle.

Pentagram- A five- pointed star depicting the four elements surrounded by the spirit. In black magic or Satanism, the pentagram is turned upside down. When this is done, the symbol appears as a devil. It is also inverted to negate any positive nature.

Phantom- Something that exists only in appearance, such as an apparition or a specter.

Phantomania- Paralysis occurring when someone is under attack by preternatural or supernatural forces.

Physical Medium- A psychic who can manifest living or other physical things.

Planchette- The pointer device used with a Ouija board. It is almost triangular and has a clear plastic circle with a pin through it.

Poltergeist- Destructive spirit which has the ability to manipulate the environment by the use of electromagnetic energy fields that results in the movement of objects and teleportation. The word poltergeist comes from the German words meaning noisy ghost.

Possession- Having a spirit enter the physical body of someone. There are different types of possession. Mediums will often "allow" a spirit to enter them for the sake of communication. In demonic possession, the invading entity will not remove itself. There is partial possession where the host remains in the body. In full or perfect possession, the spirit of the host is dislodged from the physical body. Only an exorcism can dislodge a possessing entity.

Precognition- Supernormal knowledge of pending or future events.

Premonition- Feeling or warning about a future event. This may be a vague feeling or it can be quite specific.

Preternatural- Diverging from or exceeding the common order of nature but not outside the natural order as distinguished from the supernatural. Human spirits would be preternatural, inhuman spirits would be supernatural.

Provocation- Any effort to provoke or draw out a spirit. See religious provocation.

Pseudo-death- Deep trance state that simulates death. Similar to near death experience.

Psychic- A person with the ability to see, hear, and feel by use of senses other than the natural senses. Also a classification of unusual happenings. It has become something of an all-encompassing term and thus, has reached the point of ambiguity.

Psychic Attack- Being attacked either physically or mentally by a spirit. This spirit may be visible or invisible during the attack. It is believed that in some cases, living people are capable of psychically attacking others.

Psychic Cold- This is a situation where one feels *unnaturally* cold. There are two types of psychic cold. In one case, a spirit attempting to materialize will draw its energy from the environment. This will result in a lowering of the actual room temperature. In the second instance, the materializing spirit will draw its energy from the people in the room. Here, the people will feel quite cold but the thermometer will not register a lowering of the ambient temperature. However, it should be pointed out that situations of great stress could result in this same type of cold without a drop in the actual temperature. Serious fatigue can do this as well.

Psychic Imprint- An energy field that takes on the appearance of a person. This usually occurs due to severe emotional energy, which is imprinted in the environment. While someone may think they are seeing a ghost, it is actually a projected image, not an actual spirit. Also known as psychic *recording* or *projection*.

Psychic Paralysis- A condition in which a person is fully awake but is unable to move. I refer to this as *twilight paralysis.*

Psychic Photograph- A picture that shows any paranormal phenomena such as a spirit orb or an apparition. Many psychic pictures depict a mist like form and in some cases, you will actually see the face of a spirit.

Psychic Photographer- One who takes psychic photos.

Psychic Projection- See psychic imprint.

Psychic Recording- See psychic imprint.

Psychic Research- The broad study of paranormal phenomena, which includes ESP, PK, RSPK, OBE'S, hauntings etc.

Psychic Sleep- Deep, trance like sleep from which a person cannot be aroused. This is caused by an inhuman spirit usually occurring when another person is under attack.

Psychic Wounds- These are wounds caused by a spirit. They may appear as scratches or bites. Bruising and burns can also occur from the encounter.

Psychokinesis- This is the movement of objects by use of the mind either consciously or unconsciously as in poltergiest like manifestations. Also known as PK or RSPK. (Recurrent Spontaneous Psycho Kinesis.)

Psychomancy- Divination by use of spirits or the art of evoking the dead.

Psychomanteum- A large box or small room that is draped in black and lit only by a candle placed behind someone sitting looking at a mirror. The person can then see spirits or visions in the mirror.

Psychometry- The ability to "read" objects being held or touched. This is often used successfully in police work involving missing persons.

Rapping- This can vary from a light knocking sound to a heavy pounding. It often emanates from the walls but sounds as if it is coming from everywhere. Spirits will sometimes communicate through rapping.

Reincarnate- To cause to undergo reincarnation.

Reincarnation- A rebirth of a soul into a new body.

Relic- The body or part of the body of a Saint or any sacred momento. Relics are sometimes pieces of cloth worn by the Saint or in some cases, a Holy person.

Religious Provocation- An attempt to draw out an evil spirit through invoking the name of God or Christ. Religious provocation can be extremely dangerous and should not be attempted by anyone inexperienced in this.

Remote Viewing- A form of out of body experience in which one can see things in a different location.

Retrocognition- The ability to see something or know something from the past.

Ritual- A prescribed form or method for the performance of a religious, solemn ceremony. Rituals can be used for good or bad.

Ritual Abuse- The abuse, physical or sexual done as part of a satanic ceremony.

RSPK- Recurrent spontaneous psychokinesis. This is the repeated action of objects moving through the power of the mind.

Salamander- The elemental spirit of *fire.*

Santeria- Afro-Caribbean religion, which is a combination of Catholicism and voodoo. There are seven powers or gods in Santeria and they are syncretized with Catholic Saints.

Satan- Chief of the fallen Angels who opposed God and was banished from Heaven. Also known as Lucifer.

Satanic- Having anything to do with Satan, as in worshipping him.

Satanic Bible- A "how to" book on Satanism written by Anton Szandor LaVey, who founded the *Church Of Satan.*

Scrying- A form of divination using a mirror. This can be done using a mirror, crystals or water.

Scrying Mirror- Mirror used for divination.

Sensitive- A person with psychic abilities.

Seraphim- The Angels of love, light and fire. They are the highest order of the hierarchy of choirs.

Shadow Ghost- A black, mist like spirit that has no discernable features. In my experience, a shadow ghost is exactly that, a *shadow* or *silhouette* of spirit.

Solidification Of Air- One possible theory to explain the movement of objects by spirits. Electromagnetic energy fields are another theory, one that holds more credence.

Specter- Something that exists only in appearance. Same as *phantom.*

Spirit- Any being that exists without a physical body. This can range from humans to demons or animals.

Spontaneous Combustion- Fire that starts suddenly and with no apparent cause. This can happen to animate or inanimate objects.

Spook- Slang term for ghost. Scaring yourself by thinking, talking or reading about spirits or frightening stories.

Stigmata- Phenomena where a person will bleed from the same areas as the wounds of Jesus. Padre Pio was a stigmatist. There are said to be five wounds. The wrists, feet, back, (scourging) head (Crown of thorns) and side.

Subnatural- Anything that happens which seems to be unnatural by still falls within the realm of the natural as opposed to the preternatural or the supernatural.

Suffimunigation- A religious cleansing ritual that involves the use of prayers, incense, holy water, and beeswax candles. Suffimunigation is used to clear spirits from a dwelling. This can be considered part one of the exorcism trilogy with Deliverance being the second level and solemn Exorcism the highest level. Term may have originated from the fumigation with incense during exorcism.

Supernatural- Events that happen which have no natural explanation. Usually refers to the divine but can also be caused by negative forces. An inhuman spirit would be supernatural; a human spirit would be preternatural.

Succubus- A demon that has sex with men. Demons do not have a gender so the same demon can be an *incubus* also.

Sylphs- The elemental spirits of the *air.*

Talisman- Powerful object, usually an amulet believed to bring about good luck or protection.

Tarot Cards- Picture cards that are used to predict future events. This is one form of divination.

Telekinesis- Although often confused with psychokinesis, telekinesis is the projection of perceived movements into ones mind. An example would be of a wall that appears to be moving. The wall is not actually moving but it is projected into the mind making that person believe it is. An argument can be made that it is the same as psychokinesis.

Telepathy- Communication of one's mind with another by means other than the normal senses.

Teleportation- The movement of objects or people from one place to another by supernatural means.

Trancer- My term used for a person who can channel spirits while in a trance state.

Transfiguration- The changing of features or other characteristics without a natural cause.

Transmigration- Reincarnation as a different species.

Twilight Paralysis- Term I have created to describe what is often referred to as *psychic paralysis.* It is my belief that at the point where the conscious mind is about to turn the body over to the subconscious mind, as in the moments between wakefulness and sleep, a spirit can somehow invade during that small window of vulnerability and cause the body to freeze, (minus the respiratory system and usually the eyes) while the mind is still conscious. For those who experience it, this can be terribly frightening. During one case I worked, I suffered this for over ninety minutes. The session was being taped (as it had happened to me one time prior in that same house) and during the event, all that could be heard on the tape was a whimper as I tried to call for help.

Undines- Lesser spirits of nature.

Vodoun- Anthropologist's term for voodoo, literally means "*protective spirit.*"

Voodoo- African religion that believes in seven gods and uses spells and conjuring for personal gain or to hurt others.

Voodoo Doll- Doll used during voodoo rituals. It is often used to bring about harm to others. It is believed that the person intended to be hurt must know about the attempt for it to be successful. This would indicate that it works through the power of suggestion or self-fulfilling prophecy.

Warlock- Term used for male witch. Many witches dispute this term and say that all practitioners of witchcraft are witches regardless of their gender.

Werewolf- A person who is or believed to be possessed by the spirit of a wolf.

White Witch- Term used to describe people who practice benign or good magic.

Wicca- Literally means "wise one." Used to describe one who practices witchcraft.

Witch- One who practices witchcraft.

Witchcraft- One of the oldest known religions, witchcraft is the worship of nature gods. Contrary to popular belief, true witchcraft is not evil and is not satanic. Unfortunately, many equate demons, curses and sacrifices, both human and animal to be the results of witchcraft.

PRAYERS

There are many prayers that can be used when dealing with paranormal phenomena. There are specific prayers that can be used which are very effective but any will do in a pinch. Prayers do not have to be formal. Talking to God in your own words is fine. In a situation where you are dealing with a haunting, you want to say prayers designed to protect you. Always imagine your prayers as tangible things, things that have power. Visualize your prayers going to God and visualize the "white" light of God surrounding you much as a force field would. In fact, the powers of your prayers and the God light *are* a force field, the strongest kind imaginable. They *will* protect you. There are certain prayers that are very effective in particular situation. It is always a good idea to learn them. The prayer to St. Michael the Archangel is a *must* for the paranormal investigator to know. Praying the Holy Rosary is a must in a dangerous situation. There is no more powerful prayer known to man. Even the worst demonic forces want no part of the Blessed Mother.

Never panic in a haunting situation. If you feel something, be confident in the fact that your prayers will protect you. Your confidence alone makes you less of a target. If there is activity going on, you can also use prayers to command the entity to stop immediately. Say a simple prayer to yourself asking God to give you the power to stop the activity and expel the cause. Then, confidently and forcefully *command* the entity to leave. Do not be meek about it. Be forceful. Remember too, always have Holy Water available in a potentially dangerous situation. In fact, it is a good thing to have around you whenever you are doing *anything* that involves evil, whether that entails talking about it or reading about it, etc. It gives you another very strong weapon against dark forces.

If you are going to be discussing cases or just discussing the subject of ghosts and demons, always say a prayer to protect yourself before you start. Discussing the subject can in itself attract a spirit to you. You want to make sure it does not stick around. One way to think of the attracting power of discussing hauntings is to think of seagulls on the beach. They fly around minding their own business looking for food. If you decide to throw bread towards one of them, watch all the others swoop down. The food attracted them and they come in to have a look. If you don't feed them, they go away. Discussing the paranormal is like that. There are spirits all around us. When they spot the energy released by your discussion, they fly in to have a look. When they see that you protected yourself, they know they are not going to be fed so they fly away. That may be an oversimplification, but it is fairly accurate.

The same goes when it comes to reading books of this nature or reading case notes or any other things related to a case. Just say a simple prayer of protection. If you are going on a case or just doing a "shoot", (taking pictures in a cemetery, for example) say a prayer before going in and another leaving. I always recommend a prayer in your house, car and on site. Bless your home and your pets. You have heard this often in this text. Say simple prayers. Believe me, you don't have to walk around mumbling to yourself all day. It would not look too good anyway. Most people know the major prayers, like The Hail Mary or the Lords Prayer. (Our Father.) If not, you can pick up prayer books in any religious store. I will now list some prayers you might not know but they are pretty good ones to learn.

ST. MICHAEL THE ARCHANGEL

St. Michael the Archangel, defend us in battle. Be our protection against the wickedness and the snares of the devil. May God rebuke him, we humbly pray, and do thou o Prince of the Heavenly Host, by the divine power of God, cast into hell Satan and all evil spirits who wander now throughout the world seeking the ruin of souls. Amen. 1

PRAYER OF CONFINEMENT

In the name of Jesus Christ, I command all human spirits to be bound to the confines of this cemetery. I command all inhuman spirits to go where Jesus Christ tells you to go, for it is He who commands you. 2

A CLEANSING PRAYER

Heavenly Father, I ask that your blessing be upon this house and all its occupants. Protect all who dwell here and deliver them from any and all evil influences. Bind and remove any unclean spirits that may be here and protect this family from further attacks. I ask this in the name of Your Son, Jesus Christ, Our Lord. I Bless this room (Making the Sign Of the Cross) **In the name of the Father, the Son and the Holy Spirit. Amen.** 3

PRAYER FOR PROTECTION

Lord Jesus, I ask you to protect my family and friends (NAME) **from sickness, from all harm and from accidents. If any of us have been subjected to any curses, hexes or spells, I declare these curses, hexes or spells null and void in the name of Jesus Christ.**

If any evil spirits have been sent against us, I decommission you in the name of Jesus Christ and I send you to Jesus to deal with as He will. Then Lord, I ask you to send Your Holy Angels to guard and protect all of us. Amen. 4

PRAYER FOR DELIVERANCE

In the name of Jesus Christ, I command you to depart without doing harm to (NAME) **or anyone else in this house, or in their family and without making any noise or disturbance and I command you to go straight to Jesus Christ to dispose of as He will. Furthermore, I command you never again to return.** 5

EXAMPLES OF FORMS

Note: These are general forms. You may find some questions inappropriate or you may wish to add other questions. This is only a general guide.

NAME ______________________________ *DATE* __________

ADDRESS ______________________________ *CASE ID #* ________

____

PHONE # ______________________________

GENERAL BACKGROUND

1) List names & ages of all occupants: ______________________________

____

2) Are you employed? __________ Occupation: __________________

3) How long at this address? ______________________________

4) Circle major stressors: *financial, health, relationship, other* __________

5) Did you attend public or private school? ______________________

6) Do you have pets? ___________ Do they react to phenomena? ____

7) Are you very suggestible? _______ emotional? __________________ scared easily? __________________

8) Are you on any type of medication? _____ Type: _______________

9) Do you consider yourself a positive or negative person? ____________

10) Do you have a bad temper or ever feel rage for no apparent reason? __ ______________________________

11) Do you ever throw or break things when angry? __________________

12) Have you or family ever been treated for a mental illness? _________ List: ______________________

13) Are you prone towards depression or anxiety attacks? _____________

14) List any hobbies: ______________________________

15) List any memberships: ______________________________

16) Do you drink excessively? _____ Use any drugs? _______________

17) Do you meditate _____chant _____ practice eastern teachings? ____

18) Do you ever feel excessively (circle) ashamed _____ guilty? _______

19) Do you know anything about the previous occupants of the house? __
____

20) If yes, please explain. ______________________________

21) Do you know anything about the history of the house? ___________

22) If yes, please explain. ______________________________

BELIEF SYSTEMS

1) Do you believe in God or a higher power? ___________________
Heaven & hell? _____________

2) What is your religion? _______________ Do you practice it? ______

3) Have you been baptized? ___________ Do you pray _____________
receive sacraments? ________________

4) Do you believe in (circle) the devil, demons, ghosts, hauntings or exorcism?

5) Have you or anyone close to you ever use or do: (circle) *Ouija board, seance, automatic writing, visited a psychic, attempted to contact a deceased loved one, attended a black mass, witchcraft, Satanism, Afro-Caribbean religions, cults, voodoo, try to cast a spell either for personal gain or to hurt someone, sacrifice an animal, play fantasy games such as D&D.*

6) Have you ever intentionally hurt someone? ___________________

7) Do you believe that you are psychic? ______________________
Have you ever been hypnotized? __________________________

8) Do you believe in an afterlife? _________ Reincarnation? _________

9) Have you ever tried *astral projection or remote viewing*? ___________

10) Have you ever experienced something you believe to have been *supernatural*? ______________________________

11) Have you ever experienced a *haunting* before? ______________

12) Has anyone you know ever experienced a *haunting*? __________

13) Are you sick of answering these questions? ________________

Notes: ____

____

____

____

____

____

____

case id ___________

PHENOMENA

1) Has any of the following happened to you?

    a) Seen an apparition? ______ Have others seen them? _________

    b) Did it appear that they responded to you? __________________

    c) Seen objects levitate? _____ furniture move? _______________

    d) Experienced foul smells that had no apparent source? _________

    e) Been touched by an unseen entity? ________________________

    f) See objects thrown around? _____________________________

    g) Had things disappear before your eyes? ___________________

    h) Found objects from no apparent source? __________________

    i) Have scratch marks or bite marks appear on your body? _______

    j) Have electronic items turn themselves on or off? _____________

    k) Heard unidentified scratching noises? _____________________
    Pounding in walls? _______

    l) Have doors or drawers open and close by themselves? _________

    m) Felt unnatural cold? ______________ Heat? ______________

    n) Sensed a presence? ________________________________
    Evil or benign? ____________________________________

    o) Felt paralyzed or unable to wake up? ______________________

    p) See religious objects be destroyed or inverted? _______________

    q) Have you experienced any other unusual or unexplained phenomena? ____

    r) If yes, explain. ____________________________________

2) When did you first notice unusual phenomena? _______________

3) How long has it been going on? ____________________________

4) Has there been a noticeable pattern? ______________________

5) Does the phenomena seem to center around one person? _________

6) How do you sleep in general? ______________________________
Have there been any changes? ______________________________

7) Do you find that you wake up at the same time during the night?
____

8) If yes, what time? ___________________________________

9) Does the phenomena usually start at a particular time? _________
End? ________________

10) Do the problems increase or decrease around religious holidays?
____

11) Do you ever get the feeling you are not alone? ______________
watched? ______________

12) Have you tried blessing the house using Prayers, Holy Water or a Cross? ____

13) Did that help or make it worse? ___________________________

14) Are there any police reports about any occurrences? ___________

15) Have any members of the clergy been involved? _____________

16) Have they Blessed the house or said a Mass there? ___________

17) Did that help or make it worse? ___________________________

18) What was the longest period of time *without* activity? _________

19) Has anyone been physically hurt? __________________________

20) Is the phenomena increasing or decreasing or staying the same? ____

21) Have you noticed any personality changes in family? __________

22) If yes, who & how? ________________________________

23) Have you noticed any physical changes in family? ____________

24) If yes, who & how? ________________________________

25) What do you want as an outcome? ______________________________

26) How did you hear about us? ___________________________________

27) Comments: ____

Notes: ____

About The Author

Thomas Cooney has been studying the fields of parapsychology and demonology for over thirty years. He has worked successfully on many cases during that time, which helped him hone his craft. His interest in the field began when he was ten years old and found himself living in a haunted house, a house that had an evil side to it. In addition, he has taught numerous classes on the supernatural.